The Wild Blue Yonder AND *Beyond*

Related Potomac Titles

Untold Valor: Forgotten Stories of American Bomber Crews over Europe in World War II—Rob Morris

B-17s Over Berlin: Personal Stories from the 95th Bomb Group (H)—Ian Hawkins, ed.

ROB MORRIS with IAN HAWKINS

The Wild Blue Yonder and *Beyond*

The 95th Bomb Group in War and Peace

Potomac Books
Washington, D.C.

Published in the United States by Potomac Books, Inc. All rights reserved.
No part of this book may be reproduced in any manner whatsoever without
written permission from the publisher, except in the case of brief quotations
embodied in critical articles and reviews.

Library of Congress Cataloging-in-Publication Data
Morris, Rob, 1959–
  The wild blue yonder and beyond : the 95th Bomb Group in war and peace /
Rob Morris with Ian Hawkins.
      p. cm.
  Includes bibliographical references and index.
  ISBN 978-1-59797-712-8 (hbk. : alk. paper)
  ISBN 978-1-59797-717-3 (electronic)
 1. United States. Army Air Forces. Bomb Group (H), 95th.—History.
2. World War, 1939–1945—Aerial operations, American. 3. World War,
1939–1945—Regimental histories—United States. 4. World War,
1939–1945—Campaigns—Western Front. I. Hawkins, Ian. II. Title.
  D790.25395th .M65 2012
  940.54'4973–dc23
                              2012016070

Printed in the United States of America on acid-free paper that meets
the American National Standards Institute Z39-48 Standard.

Potomac Books
22841 Quicksilver Drive
Dulles, Virginia 20166

First Edition

10 9 8 7 6 5 4 3 2

To the men and women of the 95th Bomb Group
and especially to

William E. "Ed" Charles, Leonard Herman,
Ellis Scripture, and William "Dub" Vandegriff

Contents

Preface

Puddles in the old runway reflect a leaden sky with small patches of blue. I am on the former air base of the 95th Bomb Group, Heavy, a group that once comprised thousands of men and hundreds of aircraft. Between 1943 and 1945, the 95th's B-17 Flying Fortresses and their crews thundered down this runway in rural Suffolk, England, destined for targets hundreds of miles away. These crews, and the thousands of ground-bound men who lived and worked in the small city that sprawled over hundreds of acres of fields and woods, now watch me from amber wheat fields and stands of leafy green trees. Some have their flight gear on—layers of clothing to protect them from bullets, flak, and the cold. The eyes in drawn and weary faces have circles under them. Others watch me in greasy coveralls, their ball caps tipped back on their heads. They grip a tool or a half-packed parachute. Cooks in aprons and clerks lean against trees, as if simply taking a short break from baking or typing. At the spot where the control tower once stood, the group leaders stand, binoculars raised to their eyes, watching me, watching the sky.

Down at the end, where the narrow country road cuts across the runway, I see the English residents of Horham, young children waiting for gum or ice cream, old men and women with canes. It's as if they are waiting to watch the planes take off, so that they can wave at the young American airmen who are on their way to bomb Hitler's Europe and wish them luck and a safe return. They know these young men, these Yanks, and have come to love them. And the Yanks love them back. The English residents of the small town of Horham and the American residents of the air base have become one community.

The stillness is eerie and disconcerting. Rain has turned the June countryside lush and green, and bright red poppies dance on a salty breeze blowing from the nearby North Sea. As I stand on the runway, I see older men walking slowly through the fields, some with canes and many donning worn A-2 leather flight jackets. Some have their wives at their sides and their middle-aged children. And finally, breaking the stillness, hundreds of grandchildren and great-grandchildren dash through the tall fields, laughing and playing.

Why have all these people come to meet me on this lonely runway in England thousands of miles from the United States? What are they doing here? I know why I have come—to write the history of the 95th Bomb Group. But what about them? As if on cue, everyone stops and stands in a large ragged circle around me. Slowly, from out near the woods, I see a lone figure approaching. He's young, no more than nineteen or twenty, and he's decked out in a leather flight suit. He walks slowly and heavily in his over-sized fleece-lined flight boots, hauling his parachute pack. His oxygen mask hangs to one side, snapped to his leather flight helmet. He looks tired—very tired—and as he gets closer I can see the deep lines in his face caused by the stress of flying missions and facing death.

He walks right up to me and drops his parachute pack down on the runway. He takes a moment to scan the thousands of people who now stand around us in the lonely field, and I follow his gaze. He looks back at me, focusing on me with eyes that have seen more than mine ever will. He raises his hand and places it gently but firmly on my shoulder.

"Tell our story," he says. "Please get it right."

Then he turns and walks away, followed by the other young men, by the old men, by the women and children and grandchildren. Soon, I am standing alone on the tarmac with only the wind as my companion. The immense weight of my undertaking crushes down upon me.

I must let the group tell the story through me. To do so, I have relied on hundreds, possibly over a thousand, individuals who in one way or another are part of the story—the men of the 95th, their wives, their children, the English who lived on and near the base. I have interviewed many personally, and others left me their contributions in the form of diaries, letters, taped interviews, and self-published memoirs. With these, I have relied on the work of those who came before me, not only each man and woman who kept a diary or a letter or a crinkled photograph, but also those who began, early on, compiling the history of the group and kept it alive and intact.

The 95th Bomb Group is a representative B-17 bomb group. If you read its history, you will get a good idea of the history of many American bomber groups stationed in East Anglia during World War II. For that reason, I hope anyone who wants to recapture and truly understand the entire bomb group experience reads this book. It is primarily a story of people. It is also a sad story at times, with instant death, years of captivity, and great mental and physical hardship as recurring themes. No interview hit me harder than talking with the widow of 95th pilot Fred Delbern, lost in the North Sea in 1943. If one could personify a broken heart and a lifetime of loss, Geri Delburn did that for me. It is a story of combat. It is a story of humor and funny situations. And it is a continuing story. The group still meets every year, both in the States and at Horham, though the number of original veterans is rapidly dwindling and soon no one will be left. Their children, grandchildren, and great-grandchildren have taken up the challenge of preserving history. This book is part of the group's goal of telling the story to those generations to come that will have no eyewitnesses to talk to. As you read its pages, listen carefully to what its characters tell you. For as you turn the pages, they will all come alive, and you will see them, as I did.

Rarely does a day go by that I do not see the face of the young airman who walked up to me on the runway. I take his charge seriously. His charge to me is sacred. "Tell our story. Get it right." I hope I have done that.

Acknowledgments

Much as each bomber mission flown by the 95th Bomb Group required teamwork from air crews, ground crews, intelligence officers, maintenance men, and other support personnel, so this book has been a team effort.

Leading the effort was the 95th Bomb Group (H) Memorial Foundation and its Unit History Committee chaired by Mike Darter and Nancy McKnight Smith. The 95th had the foresight to commission this comprehensive work before there were no men and women left to interview, and at some considerable expense it flew me to England; to reunions in Tucson, Dallas, and Washington, D.C.; and to other places in the United States for research and interviews.

William E. "Ed" Charles, former 95th navigator, and Leonard Herman, former 95th bombardier, laid the research groundwork. Along with former 95th navigator Ellis Scripture, in 1997 they spearheaded the 95th Bomb Group's Oral History Project, which generated more than 150 interviews (subsequently donated to the Library of Congress's Oral History Project) with veterans and their spouses and also led to the publication of the group's seminal oral history, *B-17s Over Berlin*. Many accolades also go to William "Dub" Vandegriff, former 95th radio operator, who spent hundreds of hours putting together the book *Contrails II* along with his wife, Mary, and his son David; to Ian Hawkins, who as a young historian edited the 95th's oral history *B-17s Over Berlin* and who is my coauthor on this project; to the incredibly dedicated research crew of Rod Hupp, Russ Askey, Helynn Shufletowski, and Bob "Peeps" Pieper, who spent thousands of volunteer hours tracking down, scanning, and preserving the group's history; to James Mutton and the 95th Heritage Association and all the men and women "on the other side of the pond" who so faithfully kept the 95th's flame kindled through their work with the 95th Red Feather Club Museum in Horham, Suffolk; to Tony Albrow, who at great personal expense has rebuilt the 95th Bomb Group's hospital at Horham; and to the many, many veterans, both living and passed, who shared so freely with me over the years beginning in 2000. A comprehensive list of those men can be found in the bibliography, as can the names of the dozens of wives and descendants of the 95th's men, English villagers, and others who have worked so tirelessly to make this book a reality. In the interest of reducing endnotes, all quotes I obtained in interviews are not endnoted, but an extensive interview list in the bibliography includes all interviewees and the dates of the interviews.

My thanks go to four dedicated 95th veterans who proofread and vetted the final manuscript: Gale House, a pilot from the original cadre; Robert Capen, ball turret gunner; Art Watson, ground crew member who spent the entire war at Horham; and John Walter, pilot.

My close friend Leonard Herman gave me many, many hours of information and conversation about the group. I also drew extensively on the memories of Robert Cozens, Pat Cozens, Irv Rothman, John Chaffin, Eldon Broman, Geri Delbern Marshall, Bettylou Capen, Franklyn Coleman, William Owen, Adam Hinojos, Keith Murray, Carl Voss, Ed Charles, and Maurice Rockett. I stayed in Horham for a week in 2008 and visited extensively with Alan Johnson, James Mutton, Frank Sherman, and many villagers. I have also spent hours talking to Mike Darter about his brother Eugene Darter and those who went missing in action. Special thanks to Gerald Grove and his father, Ronald Grove, for their help with the chapter on Swiss internment, as well as my longtime friend Dan Culler. Thanks also to James Fournier for sharing his experiences about Swedish internees.

My thanks to my friend Paul Dillon, son of ace ball turret gunner and prisoner of war, Red Dillon, for his incredible line drawings that begin each chapter and to my talented cover artist, Englishman James Baldwin, for perfectly capturing the idea for the cover that came to me one night.

Thanks again to my coauthor, Ian Hawkins, who has been my mentor and my friend for longer than a decade. Though Ian is in less-than-perfect health, he meticulously went through every line of this manuscript in early 2010 and vetted it. In my mind, there is no greater English aviation historian than Ian.

Thanks to my family for putting up with my long nights and summers spent at my computer rather than with them. Thanks to my students at Clair E. Gale Junior High in Idaho Falls for their support as their teacher juggled two full-time jobs—writing and teaching. And to my principal at Gale, Robin Busch, who always supported me and found a way for me to balance both jobs.

Finally, thanks to my publisher Potomac Books for believing in this book, especially my friends and editors Sam Dorrance and Elizabeth Demers. Also, a world of thanks to Potomac's developmental editor Don McKeon, who took a surgeon's scalpel to the manuscript and made it better. Thanks also to Potomac's Vicki Chamlee for her razor-sharp copyediting.

Any errors contained in this book are mine alone. It has been a two-year journey and an extremely challenging one. This book ran to more than 230,000 words. I had to cut 100,000 of them. I still tried very hard to include everyone who participated in this huge project.

1 The Creation of an Air Force

In the summer of 1941, young men across America were growing up, their lives focused on finishing high school or college, playing sports, working on farms or in factories, falling in love, and planning for the future. They were part of a more serious generation. Raised as children during the Great Depression, many were accustomed to hardship and attuned to the need to work hard and take nothing for granted. Even in mid-1941, the rumblings of war from across the seas seemed far away, confined to newsreels and newspapers. These young men, most only in their teens, worked and played with the common belief of the young that life would go on forever, extended into a distant future, with wives, careers, children, and grandchildren. Despite the worries and concerns of the Depression, most were filled with youthful optimism that was only slightly tempered by the concerns of an unstable world that seemed distant and unrelated to their daily lives.

But through chance or fate, thousands of these young men from across the wide expanses of the United States—many of whom had never heard of a B-17 Flying Fortress or even ridden in an airplane—would form the heart and soul of a heavy B-17 bombardment group. The men would live in a foreign land they'd only studied in textbooks and fly or support deadly missions over Adolf Hitler's Fortress Europe.

None would return from the war unchanged. They would never forget the bonds forged in those intense years. Men whom chance had thrown together came to love each other as brothers. Sixty years later, these boys, old and gray, would meet again each year, sharing a camaraderie that no outsider would ever be able to understand and taking a moment to notice additional empty chairs as time claimed them, one by one.

When the Americans joined the war, it had been a mere thirty years since Lt. Philip O. Parmalee, piloting a Wright C, and Lt. M. S. Crissy had been the first to drop a bomb from an airplane. Airplanes had barely passed out of their infancy and most Americans had never flown in one when the first Boeing B-17 took to the air in 1935. Many of the pilots who would be entrusted with flying a B-17 in a few short years were still learning to drive the family car.

In the late thirties, the B-17 was as fast as most fighters of the day, armed with modern equipment. The invention of a liquid pressurized oxygen system in 1928 allowed flight crews to fly at altitudes that previously would have quickly killed them by anoxia. C. L. Norden designed an instrument that gave bombardiers incredible precision. Superchargers forced thin, high-altitude air into engines that before would have sputtered and died, and the many .50-caliber machine guns jutting from the B-17's fuselage gave rise to the conception of its impregnability and its nickname, the Flying Fortress.

The entire B-17 program was nearly scrapped when an auditor at Wright Field, Ohio, objected to the high cost of the new plane, $205,000. Boeing Aircraft was forced to slash the price by $8,000, and only after Lt. Col. Carl A. "Tooey" Spaatz of the U.S. Army Air Corps (USAAC) cut some of the standard equipment on the plane was Boeing able to produce it without losing money. The original contract called for a mere thirty-eight B-17s.

In 1941, twenty B-17s were given to the Royal Air Force (RAF) as part of the American Lend-Lease program. This early model, tagged the B-17C, proved inadequate to the task, and British crews quickly dubbed it the Flying Target. With a combat radius of only seven hundred miles and a meager bomb load of twenty-four hundred pounds, the plane was also underarmed. The German air force (hereafter called the Luftwaffe) cut it to ribbons. The Brits proclaimed the plane "dull" and insisted it could never be an effective daylight bomber.[1]

Boeing improved the model, resulting in the B-17E. The new model had the B-17's now-famous swooping dorsal fin (which gave rise to its nickname, the Big-Assed Bird), a thousand-mile range, and a bomb load of eight thousand pounds. The E also bristled with nine heavy machine guns, including eight .50-caliber guns, and first saw combat with American crews in the European theater of operations (ETO) on August 17, 1942.

Engineers at Boeing continued refining the design to reflect the needs of crews in combat. In 1943 the first B-17Fs entered the fray, with extra fuel cells that fed its four thirsty engines up to twenty-six hundred gallons of fuel and with up to thirteen .50-caliber machine guns. By September, a redesign resulted in the Boeing B-17G, instantly recognizable by the Bendix chin turret mounted under the nose to protect against head-on fighter attacks.

Each variation of the B-17 was heavier and slower. In fact, the B-17G weighed nine thousand pounds more than the B-17C did. Newer models were delivered without the original green camouflage paint scheme; instead, they were bright, gleaming aluminum. Skipping the paint job made the plane a little lighter and a little faster.

Seeing a B-17 in a book or movie, one would imagine it to be a large aircraft; however, looks are deceptive. The first thing most people comment on while going through a B-17 today is its incredibly cramped interior, replete with tiny hatchways, claustrophobic compartments, and sharp edges. One comes away with a greater appreciation for how tough it must have been to get around in it, especially for wartime crews dressed in layers of bulky cold-weather gear, hooked up to oxygen, and fighting off enemy fighters five miles in the sky and in temperatures of fifty degrees below zero.

A B-17 bomber required a crew of ten. The pilot and copilot sat on the raised flight deck. A bombardier and navigator were positioned in the nose, below and slightly in front of the pilots. Like the pilot and copilot, the bombardier and navigator were commissioned officers. The remaining crewmen were noncommissioned officers (NCOs). The flight engineer, who was responsible for maintaining all things mechanical in flight, joined the flight crew in the cockpit as needed and also manned the top turret directly behind the cockpit. On the other side of the bomb bay from the flight deck, the radio operator received and transmitted messages. Two waist gunners manned .50-caliber machine guns on either side of the aircraft. The ball turret gunner defended the bottom of the aircraft from his station in the cramped Sperry ball turret, while in the tail, the tail gunner defended the aircraft's rear.

These young men had no inkling that they would grow to love this piece of machinery, to name it, to baby it, to become a functioning part of it, to depend on it for their very survival. Some would bleed in it and some would die in it, but the B-17 would also bring many of them home when logic dictated otherwise—with parts of wings, tails, and ailerons missing, and with engines feathered or burning.

Despite the grumblings of critics who discredited the very idea that airplanes would serve any meaningful role in combat, President Franklin D. Roosevelt realized the importance of having an air corps. On June 20, 1941, the U.S. Army Air Corps was born as a functioning element of the U.S. Army.[2]

Americans watched as Europe crumbled under the fierce German blitzkrieg, but the tiny island nation of Great Britain remained free. The British had already suffered through two years of war. They had narrowly held off the German Luftwaffe in the Battle of Britain, during which their cities had been bombed. In the quiet green fields of East Anglia, not far from the North Sea, British farmers occasionally stopped in their fields and squinted at low-flying German aircraft. Within a year, their isolated piece of England would become a massive aerodrome, with huge air bases carved out of tilled fields, the narrow lanes and centuries-old pubs would ring with the strange accents of American boys, and the sky would reverberate with the droning of hundreds of aircraft departing for or returning from missions over occupied Europe. By D-Day, June 6, 1944, East Anglia would average one air base every eight miles.[3]

The Japanese attack on the United States on December 7, 1941, changed everything. Suddenly, the war was not a distant action. The United States was a part of it now. Many young men—driven by patriotism, a sense of adventure, a desire to avenge Pearl Harbor, or any of a hundred different reasons—volunteered to serve in the months directly after the attack. One of the choices for the new recruits was the U.S. Army Air Corps.

Flight remained a relatively new and exotic option, reinforced by the exploits of the early U.S. Air Mail pilots and the barnstormers. Glamorized in Hollywood movies and the pulp fiction that was a staple in many young boys' lives, the airmen of World War I were extolled as dashing modern-day knights of the air, resplendent in leather helmets and silk scarves. Young men across America took the opportunity to join this elite brotherhood.

In January 1942, only a month after Pearl Harbor and America's declaration of war, the Eighth Bomber Command, commonly called the Eighth Air Force, was born when its headquarters was activated in Savannah, Georgia. Its mission was to form the main attack force for the army air force out of Great Britain. On February 20, seven American officers in civilian clothing arrived at RAF Headquarters at High Wycombe, Buckinghamshire. Led by Brig. Gen. Ira Eaker, they had been charged with forming an American daylight bombing force to complement the Royal Air Force's nighttime bombing strategy. Plans called for the Eighth Air Force to create sixty combat groups in the United Kingdom, and it was hoped that the Eighth could muster thirty-five hundred aircraft by April 1943.

The logistics for this endeavor were mind boggling. Seventy-five airfields would eventually be built to accommodate these groups. Meanwhile, early arriving American bomb groups would fly out of preexisting British air bases as construction of additional bases began at a frantic pace.

Constructing a typical bomber base was a monumental undertaking. After clearing eight miles of hedgerows, "1,500 trees had to be felled. 400,000 cubic yards of topsoil had to be moved. Ten miles of road had to be laid down, as well as twenty miles of drains, ten miles of conduit, six miles of water mains, and four miles of sewers. The runways required a staggering 175,000 cubic yards of concrete, and the perimeter areas another 32,000 cubic yards. The base buildings used four and a half million bricks."[4]

Near the future permanent base of the 95th Bomb Group (BG), life in the small village of Horham, Suffolk, in East Anglia had gone on largely unchanged for hundreds of years. The ancient Church of St. Mary stood where a Christian church had existed since the 1200s. Some houses in town were seven hundred years old, and many still had traditional thatched roofs. The people of this bucolic farming village could not have imagined in their wildest dreams that their hamlet would become the home of the 95th Bomb Group in 1943.

The sudden appearance that year of massive heavy equipment and the men who operated them fascinated six-year-old Alan Johnson, whose father served as the Horham postmaster. "There was lots of traffic," Alan told me in 2008, as we sat at the kitchen table of Ancient House, his seven-hundred-year-old stone and timber home a block from the Church of St. Mary and the lush village green. Even today, the roads are merely country lanes lined with hedges in this rural section of England. "Lorries came through all day long, carting sand and stone and cement to make the runways. Some of the drivers would check in with their loads, get credit, and then circle around with their loads still in the truck and get credited twice."

Working two ten-hour shifts, British workers labored from first light until late in the evening. Trucks loaded with gravel, sand, cement, and bomb rubble from England's cities hauled the loads to the building site. These loads then went onto other trucks, which in turn dumped their loads into huge paving machines. A good crew could lay as much as a half mile of runway a day.

As the base was built, it expanded to the edges of backyards of cottages in the village, and a few homes even ended up on the base. British authorities approached the local farmers to requisition land for the base. Gerald Cooper's family lived at the large White House Farm near Horham. The British Air Ministry requisitioned much of the farm for £25 an acre, and the Coopers moved to the nearby town of Stradbroke. The Coopers occasionally watched as construction crews erected petrol tanks and dispersal points on their farmland.

By October 1942 twenty-seven American bomber and fighter groups were stationed in England. The first combat sortie by an American Air Force crew took place June 29, 1942. The first group assigned to the base at Horham was from the Royal Canadian Air Force (RCAF). The first Eighth Air Force planes to be stationed at Horham were A-20 Havocs, which were later replaced by B-26 Marauders.

By December 1942 thirty thousand American airmen were stationed in England. But the vast majority of the men of the Eighth Air Force, including those who would become the 95th Bomb Group (Heavy), was still in training and had yet to arrive.

When the 95th was formed on June 15, 1942, at Barksdale Field, Louisiana, it existed mainly on paper. Special Order 295 transferred the group, initially composed of 45 officers and 208 enlisted men, to Ephrata, Washington, on October 31, 1942. Under the command of Col. Alfred A. Kessler, Jr., the group had four squadrons: the 334th, commanded by Capt. Al Wilder; the 335th by Capt. David "Dave" McKnight; the 336th by Capt. Edgar B. Cole; and the 412th by Capt. Harry "Grif" Mumford.[5]

During the prewar years, winning a coveted commission as an army pilot was extremely rigorous. South Dakota State College junior Gale House joined the U.S. Army Air Corps in October 1939 after taking a pilot physical. Of the 150 applicants, House recalls that he was among only 8 who passed the physical. House went to the Santa Maria USAAC Training Base in California in June 1940. Only half of the 300-plus students enrolled there passed the program. Those who did were sent to Basic Flight Training at Randolph Field, San Antonio, Texas.

At Randolph Field, House remembers, "of the 500 students, perhaps 200 were washed out and finally, most of those remaining 290 pilots were commissioned and received their wings at the Advanced Training Base, Kelly Field, Texas. The attrition was enormous in these early stages whereas in later years, you could almost pass the physical and flight test by someone just counting your eyes!"

At Spokane's Geiger Field, First Lieutenant House flew as a check pilot, certifying the proficiency of pilots who were fresh out of flying school, first in B-24s and then in B-17s. The pilots rotating through Spokane were then farmed out to various stations. "I think it was in October word came around that a new group was being formed here, and we were tired of instructing and wanted to get overseas where the action was," remembers House.

House and some of the other pilots at Geiger noticed a short, jug-eared man scrutinizing the flying abilities of the pilots at the field. Quietly and astutely, Colonel Kessler was beginning to build his future bomb group—and he wanted only the best. At his side was longtime pilot Lt. Col. John H. "Jack" Gibson, his air executive.

Kessler and Gibson are widely considered the fathers of the 95th Bomb Group. Kessler was a West Point graduate and World War I veteran. Gibson was an army pilot who had racked up more than ten thousand hours and helped found American Airlines.

Pilot Harry Conley remembers that Colonel Kessler scouted out the crews at Geiger Field, cherry-picking the best for his fledgling group. Conley firmly believes that the 95th's record in combat was a result of Kessler's selectivity.

Pilot Mumford also enlisted before Pearl Harbor, completing his flight training in 1942. Shortly thereafter, he was assigned to the 95th Bomb Group as the 412th Squadron's commander.

The 334th Squadron commander Al Wilder recruited pilots Conley and Robert "Bob" Cozens into the 95th. Wilder told the duo: "If you fellows would like to go to Europe with me, we'll go fight some Nazis. If you go with me, I can make both of you flight commanders with an immediate promotion to first lieutenant."[6]

Most of the airmen in the new group were still short on flying experience. "The average navigator and bombardier assigned to the 95th had about thirty-five total flying hours," recalled group navigator Ellis "Scrip" Scripture. "New first pilots had logged a total of about 150 hours through flight schools and multiengine transition; copilots, even less."

One of the more experienced pilots in the 95th was the diminutive David McKnight, the 335th Squadron's commander. McKnight had originally joined the Royal Canadian Air Force before the United States entered the war. He subsequently left the RCAF and joined the U.S. Army Air Forces (USAAF), ending up in the 95th.

Bombardier Keith Murray remembers McKnight flying many more than the required twenty-five missions. "He erased his name [after flying missions] so he wouldn't get credit," claims Murray. "As near as I could figure, he was supposed to be home after twenty-five missions. As near as I could figure, he had seventy-two." Murray also remembers the time that McKnight, known as a red-hot pilot, looped a B-17 over the field. "They weren't supposed to loop a B-17, but he did."

Conley remembers McKnight flying upside down in a fighter above two B-17s between cloud layers and trying to convince the pilots they were upside down. "McKnight also buzzed the Eiffel Tower after the liberation of Paris, resulting in General 'Ike' Eisenhower issuing an order barring all Allied military personnel from buzzing it," Conley wrote.[7]

Marvin Casaday remembers that McKnight flew to Scotland on occasion and picked up vast quantities of liquor from a friend of his who owned a distillery. He would often squeeze in a little golf on these mercy missions to supply the Officers' Club with good booze.

Another early addition to the group was Bombardier Marshall Thixton, who lived his early life at the State Orphan's Home in Corsicana, Texas. Upon his graduation in 1941, Thixton left the home with all his worldly possessions slung in a bag over his shoulder and six dollars and fifty cents in his pocket. He entered Bombardier Preflight Training in May 1942, stuffing himself full of bananas to satisfy the 130-pound minimum weight, and was commissioned a second lieutenant on April 1, 1943.

After training at dozens of bases around the United States in their crew specialty, individuals arrived in Salt Lake City, Utah, for their crew assignments. They were now considered ready to be part of a flight crew and from then on would train as a crew, live as a crew, fight as a crew, and in some cases, die as a crew. Most pilots remember that they had little or no say in how their crew was put together. In most cases, the assignments appeared to be random.

The 95th Bomb Group crews then returned to Geiger Field for crew training. In this phase, the pilots were restricted to base twenty-four hours a day, six days a week. Their wives stayed together in local hotels. On the pilot's sole day off, he and his wife would have the use of the hotel bedroom.

A handful of devoted wives followed their officer husbands from base to base while the husbands trained. Unlike their spouses, whose days were packed with training, wives often had little to do but wait for their husband's one day off a week. Cozens remembers that his wife, Patsy Ann (Pat), spent a great deal of time waiting around for him and traveling after him on cars, buses, and trains. "I have great respect for her for that," he says.

In addition to the flying personnel, the group had a strong cadre of ground support personnel. Originally trained separately in their respective fields, they were eventually assigned to the 95th.

Orders issued on October 29, 1942, transferred the group to Ephrata, Washington, about 150 miles west of Spokane. The men arrived at 1 p.m. on October 31, 1942. They found the base spartan and unsuitable, with only tents for barracks, no fuel for the stoves, bad food, and a shortage of hangars.

Gale House describes the base as "a forsaken, sagebrush-lined runway about 4,000 feet in length and ending up against a mountain if you should overshoot. The quarters were barren, [with] coal-fired stoves that belched soot, speckling the pillowcases and clogging nasal passages. Jackrabbits and sagebrush were the only living things around."

Ellis Scripture remembers that "the [Geiger and Ephrata] bases in Washington were plagued with rain, fog, and snow to the point where the group was falling far behind in scheduled training flights." The foul weather convinced the powers that be to move the 95th Bomb Group to Rapid City, South Dakota, to continue training, and it arrived at that base on November 24. The base, called Rapid City Air Force Base at the time, is now known as Ellsworth Air Force Base.

By the end of November 1942, the 95th had grown to 191 officers, 2 warrant officers, and 944 enlisted men. By year's end, the number would swell to 221 officers, 2 warrant officers, and 1,386 enlisted men.

Before the group moved to Rapid City, Colonel Kessler strongly advised the married men not to bring their wives with them. The 95th then boarded a train for the journey to Rapid City, a town in the western part of the state nestled between the Black Hills and the Badlands. Bob Cozens obediently sent Pat home to California, only to discover that other men had brought their wives to Rapid City anyway.

Most of the crews found Rapid City to be little, if any, better than Ephrata was. Scripture describes it by saying, "It should have been the training center for the Arctic sled forces. It was so cold that the thermometer fluid formed icicles!" He conceded, "The cold weather had some advantages. It gave the married men additional time to spend with their wives in Rapid City, where we learned that buffalo steaks weren't on the ration coupon list, and the Alex Johnson Hotel had the best bar in town."[8] Scripture also remembers an officer-hating, beer-drinking dog named Sergeant Bismarck that drank with the noncoms at the NCO Club and barked at the officers when he saw them.

"The Alex Johnson Hotel was the center of festivities although the wives mostly stayed in motels nearby. Wives had plenty of time on their hands. They could only see their husbands from Saturday noon until Sunday at six p.m.

"The air base at Rapid was great, the weather cold, sometimes reaching 25 below zero, and yet we flew," continues Scripture. Many days, the aircraft engines refused to turn over. The weather stayed clear into January, but the severe cold convinced Colonel Kessler to rotate the group, one squadron at a time, to Pueblo, Colorado. "This made it possible by the end of January to complete [the] 2nd phase [of] training with averages of over 80 hours per Combat Crew for the month of January 1943, when the temperature plunged to well below zero," Scripture said. "Various training missions were made to Cheyenne, Wyoming, and Pueblo, Colorado. Our Squadron honed up its formation skills." However, Bob Cozens remembers that most of the group's formation training was learned the hard way—in combat over Europe.

The first accident to mar the group's training happened in January near Pierre, South Dakota. Three of the crew bailed out of the plane, but those left on board brought the ship back with considerable damage. In another close call, Dave McKnight's plane was forced to make an emergency landing at Sheridan, Wyoming, using the headlights from police cars lined up along the runway. The worst accident involved a B-17 piloted by 2nd Lt. E. E. Woodward, who became lost in the blinding snowstorm and flew into the side of a mountain near Ordway, Colorado, killing everyone on board.

After this crash, the Johnny Johnson crew was assigned to the 95th Bomb Group. Johnson's bombardier Leonard Herman, a man of diminutive size, had to be carried over some of the larger snowdrifts to get around the base.

Meanwhile, Bob Cozens took note that Colonel Kessler had taken no punitive action against the men who had brought their wives to Rapid City. He phoned Pat and told her to join him.

While in Rapid City the group received the brand-new B-17Fs to replace the B-17Es that the group had been flying. The extensive training gave each crew time to learn how to work as a team. The members learned vital skills that would help them survive once in combat.

Of the B-17's ten-man combat crew, four were officers: the pilot, copilot, navigator, and bombardier. The other six—a flight engineer, radio operator, ball turret gunner, two waist gunners, and a tail gunner—were NCOs and almost all sergeants. Though many crews were randomly thrown together, most bonded quickly out of necessity. Their very lives depended on functioning as a unit.

For pilots, many of whom were barely out of their teens, there came the tremendous burden of leadership and the responsibility for the rest of the crew. Pilot Cozens felt that responsibility keenly: "The first and fore-most demand is the pilot's moral and physical responsibility for the safety of the other nine members of his crew."

95th pilot John Walter later wrote:

> The crew of a heavy bomber was, in fact, a team of trained specialists led by the Pilot. The Pilot, or Aircraft Commander, had the primary responsibility of flying the aircraft. He directed and monitored the training and in-flight activities of the eight or nine other members of the crew. A major element in developing the crew into a cohesive unit was the training of the Co-pilot so he was as capable as the Pilot to fly the B-17.
>
> Because of the length and strenuous nature of the combat mission, the Pilot and the Co-pilot shared time at the flight con-trols. The B-17 was a forgiving aircraft, but required great physical strength to man the controls. Working in their cramped cockpit, sometimes flying blind and often under attack by fighters and flak, a Pilot and Co-pilot could be drenched in sweat even though the temperature dipped to sixty below zero.

The extreme cold and the lack of oxygen at altitude were two addi-tional enemies of bomber crewmen. Walter continued,

> The cockpit and nose sections of the B-17 were equipped with heat-ers. However, I don't recall ever flying an airplane with a heater that actually worked. Because of this, it was necessary for us to dress so we could sit in that deep freeze for five or more hours and not turn into an icicle.
>
> To prepare myself for these sessions in the "cooler" . . . I first put on my regular olive drab boxer shorts and T-shirt. Then on top of that went two piece (shirt and drawers) long "johns," then a wool khaki Class B shirt and pants, followed by a two piece electrically heated flying suit and topped off with a gabardine flying suit and an A-2 leather jacket. . . . For the feet two pairs of socks, G.I. high top shoes, electrically heated and fleece-lined flying boots. The hands

were covered by silk gloves and topped with electrically heated fleece-lined leather gloves. The purpose of the silk gloves was to prevent your fingers sticking to any cold metal surfaces should it be necessary to remove the bulky heated gloves to perform an adjustment.

By each crew station there was an electrical outlet with a rheostat control knob. The upper portion of the heated suit had a cord with a plug on the end of it, just like a toaster. The lower portion of the suit connected electrically to the upper part with snap connections somewhat similar to 9V battery connectors. Connections for the gloves and boots were provided at the end of the suit sleeves and legs, respectively. When all these connections were made we were really wired.

Protection for the face and head was provided by the oxygen mask, headset, sunglasses and flak helmet or Officer's cap. The latter was worn only when not being shot at. While being shot at—the steel helmet.

On top of the A-2 jacket was the parachute harness . . . and the Mae West life jacket. When we were over enemy territory, the flak jacket became the icing on the cake. . . . Some air crew members used extra flak vests to armor the bottom of the seats (to protect vital equipment) and other adjacent surfaces. The parachute could not be worn comfortably while flying the plane, and most pilots stored it near their seat. If the plane was hit, the pilot could clip the chute quickly to his harness.[9]

"In the up-front greenhouse," remembers 95th bombardier Maurice Rockett, "bombardiers sit suspended in near-outer-space." Anyone who has been inside of a B-17 knows how vulnerable the bombardier position is to attack. Meanwhile, the bombardier had the responsibility of ensuring each trip through dangerous enemy territory was not wasted by a poor bomb drop.

"Each bomb had a front and rear fuse," remembers one early bombardier, "secured by arming wires; when the bomb was released the arming wire would leave the fuses and the bomb would be live. That could only happen when the bombardier had removed the safety pins. This required the bombardier to leave his position in the nose, strap on a portable oxygen tank, and crawl back to the bomb bay." The bomb bay was divided by a nine-inch-wide catwalk above the bombs, and bombardiers had to inch out onto the catwalk and remove the pins with a pair of pliers. The area was so snug that often bombardiers ventured out onto the catwalk sans parachutes.[10]

The Norden bombsight was a top secret piece of equipment. Early in the war, remembers bombardier Leonard Herman, "we carried a .45-caliber pistol with us at all times [on missions]. If we got shot down, we were supposed to put a bullet through the lens. We carried the Norden bombsight to and from the plane in a case to keep it hidden."

Despite its top secret rating, Rockett comments that "the $10,000 Norden bombsight was quite familiar to Germany, who'd known about it since 1937. They built one."

Rockett also doubts the accuracy of the Norden, publicized as being able to drop a bomb into a pickle barrel. "Even in training, under ideal conditions rarely encountered in combat, to make such an accurate hit would be remarkable. Let's be realistic on bombing results. Precision bombing, which we seldom did, could not be done with a large group of planes. Add to this the bouncing aircraft from heavy turbulence caused by flak and other possibilities like prop wash, and there would not be a needed level platform for the lead bombardier. Secondly, should the gyros in the sight topple, all accuracy is lost. Tumbled gyros were an ever-existent peril to lead crews. And you can add to this the loss of accuracy due to loose formations."

During the bomb run, the bombardier used the Norden to line up the target. Exposed in his Plexiglas bubble, he had to put his fears aside and keep his eye in the sight until he heard, "Bombs away!" "Through a small telescope, we faced exploding 20mm, 30mm, 88mm, and 105mm shells. What a way to possibly meet one's maker, as many bombardiers did," remembers Rockett, who nearly did himself.

Squinting through the rubber eyepiece of the Norden also gave bombardiers a black circle around one eye. People could always identify the bombardier after a mission, recalls Leonard Herman.

Many bombardiers had some rudimentary navigation skills, in case the navigator was wounded or killed. The bombardier also manned the nearly useless cheek guns on the F model B-17 and was responsible for calling out oxygen checks on all crewmen and taking immediate action if someone on the crew did not respond. Bombardiers liked to joke with their pilots that the bombardier was the most important man on the ship and that the pilot was simply his driver who got him where he needed to be to drop his bombs.

The navigator was responsible for getting the plane to and from the target. He sat directly behind the bombardier and had his own small wooden table, a window, and even a bubble-shaped astrodome to make fixes using the stars. This job required a special kind of individual who was good with calculations and able to work fast under extreme pressure. The navigator kept the aircraft on course. This skill was less important in a bomber stream, perhaps, but became vital when a ship became separated and had to go it alone. Also, many early crews flew their ships from the United States to Europe, and often the planes traveled alone. It was up to the navigator to get the crew safely across the Atlantic using dead reckoning and celestial navigation. Like the bombardier, he would also be called upon to fire the guns in the nose of the plane during combat with fighters.

The top turret gunner usually also served as the flight engineer. This man was selected for his mechanical aptitude and was thoroughly knowledgeable about the aircraft, capable of doing in-flight troubleshooting as necessary, and provided important information and advice to the pilots.

The radio operator monitored all incoming and outgoing signals on his radio set and had his own compartment in the midsection of the ship. Early on, he had a gun mounted in the ceiling, but the manufacturer later removed this weapon.

The gunner in the Sperry ball turret curled up in it like a ball, sometimes for hours at a time, and protected the aircraft from attacks from below. With a .50-caliber gun inches from either side of his head, the ball turret gunner could rotate the ball through 360 degrees of horizontal motion and 90 degrees of vertical motion.[11] The 95th ball turret gunner Robert "Bob" Capen remembers the predominant sounds he heard in the ball were the droning of the four huge engines outside, while the ball smelled of 100-octane fuel, ozone, hydraulic fluid, and oil. "All I could see were the two wheels hanging down, the engine nacelles, and the ship's radio antenna."[12]

Two waist gunners manned .50-caliber guns in the rear half of the ship. In later G models, they were staggered slightly so as to stay out of each other's way. The waist gunner was responsible for protecting the ship from fighter attacks from his side of the aircraft. Early in the war, the waist position was open to the elements, and the waist could get exceptionally cold. These men dressed in many layers of protective gear.

The tail gunner was responsible for protecting the aircraft from attacks from the rear. He had a lonely, cramped position in the stinger-like tail of the aircraft. He rode into battle facing aft and sitting on a bicycle seat.

In addition to the flying personnel, a huge cadre of ground support personnel had been trained specifically for the many roles it took to run a large air base on foreign soil. Unlike almost all the flying personnel, who could go home when they finished between twenty-five and thirty-five missions, the ground echelon would remain overseas on the base until the end of the war.

Adam Hinojos ended up in the 95th's 457th Sub Depot. The Sub Depot's training began at Hammer Field in Fresno, California, with 7 officers, 2 warrant officers, and 245 enlisted men. From Fresno, the group went to Walla Walla Air Base, Washington State, where additional personnel—including Hinojos—joined the group. At Walla Walla, they were assigned to the new 95th Bomb Group. After traveling on three troop trains to Sioux City, Iowa, for extensive training before going overseas, the group was divided into four main mobile repair units. Hinojos writes: "Each one of these consisted of the following: a medical section, administration, machine shop, electrical shop, paint and fabric shop, instrument shop, sheet metal shop, welding shop, cabinet shop, parachute shop, prop shop, warehouse supply shop, and transportation shop. Each of the mobile repair units were set up in buildings on base."[13]

Once overseas, the 457th would be responsible for all the heavy repairs on the B-17s and all the heavy transportation equipment. The crew chiefs of each aircraft did the minor repairs, but the Sub Depot did the main repairs on the planes, such as armory, gunnery, radio, engine replacement, bombsights, painting, parachutes, and so forth. It also kept track of all fuel and parts, and it supplied the individual crew chiefs with the parts they needed.

Some of the ground personnel were older. Art Watson remembers a man named Fucan who joined the group in Spokane and ended up in the 335th Squadron in the armor section. "He was in his middle 40s and we called him 'Pop.' He was a veteran of World War I and the only man in the outfit that I knew that wore a World War I Victory Medal, except for some of our officers. He was from the mountains and, being a mountain man, trapped and hunted for his living. He also told me that he found a gold mine, but that it would cost him too much to get a road back to it.

"Pop was in the barracks with the armorers and was pretty private as to his life before the service. While in Rapid City, they were reassigning the men that they thought would not be able to hold up under the workloads assigned or were misfits for our Group. Pop was on the reassignment list for replacement. Dr. Imes, the medical doctor for the 335th, had placed Pop on that list. Pop was heartbroken and tried to get off the reassignment list, but Doc felt he was too old for the rigors of war.

"While at Rapid City, and before the reassignment was put into effect, the group had an opportunity to visit Mount Rushmore. Pop went along and when the bus got to the monument, Pop was off the bus and ran all the way up the steps to the top of the carvings. Most of the men took a rest about halfway up, but not Pop. Dr. Imes was impressed with Pop's stamina and took him off of the list. Pop Fucan went to England with us."

Watson also ended up in the 457th Sub Depot, but his journey to the 95th was anything but routine. "When I went to basic [training]," he told me, "they gave us four tests. Then you got to choose what you wanted to do. I passed all four. I wanted to be an armorer.

"So then, I waited. For one and a half months, I was the company bugler and was there pretty much all by myself. I couldn't understand why. 'I can't blow a bugle,' I told them. 'I don't know the songs.' But I was forced to do it. The company bugler that was leaving taught me a little bit. I walked around the base with my mouthpiece, practicing, to strengthen my lips.

"It turned out the reason that I had to stay there and be the bugler was that they were running a security background check on me." The air corps had plans to put Watson in charge of some of its top secret equipment, including the Norden bombsight.

One evening around midnight in early March, the 95th Bomb Group was informed that it was to be deployed overseas in the near future. "By two o'clock," remembers Bob Cozens, "we piled into a car and drove thirty-six hours from Rapid City back to California and dropped off our wives." His wife, Pat, recalls, "I was six months pregnant at the time. It wasn't a pleasant trip." Bob and Pat arrived at Pat's father's house in Vallejos, where Bob met his father-in-law for the first time. "All I had time to say was, 'Hi, Dad, glad to meet you,'" chuckles Bob. "'Take good care of my wife—I'm going to fight the war.' And then I was gone."

The time for Stateside training was over. On March 8, 1943, in preparation to move overseas, the group received orders for a permanent change of station. Four days later, Special Order Number 41 was issued, which among other items, finalized the assignment of airmen and aircraft. The group moved to Kearney, Nebraska, where they were outfitted for war overseas, and they finally found out where they would be headed, the ETO.

The ground echelon stayed in Rapid City and spent the rest of March creating and processing requisitions for supplies and personnel. By the end of March, the 95th had 224 officers, 1 warrant officer, and 1,312 enlisted men.

The flight crews began their journey overseas here, and on April 17 the officers and men of the 95th's ground echelon followed. The echelon took up four trains, arriving at Camp Kilmer, New Jersey, on April 21. As the original flyboys of the 95th prepared to travel to the war zone, they knew that for some it would be a one-way trip. Of the 399 original members of the 95th Bomb Group's 334th, 335th, 336th, and 412th Squadrons, some of whom did not fly, only eighteen men would complete their twenty-five-mission tour of duty. Of the forty original flight crews of the 95th, four crews would be lost completely, and the majority would lose at least one man.

2   Across Oceans and Continents

On March 30, 1943, after months of preparation, the 95th Bomb Group was on its way to England and combat. En route, the aircrews would see four continents. Most would fly alone over vast expanses of jungle and ocean, landing at primitive airstrips, sightseeing in exotic locales, and interacting with people the likes of which they had only seen in *National Geographic*. The ground personnel faced a longer journey by train and ship. Few of the 95th personnel would ever forget the adventure of simply getting to England for combat.

So as not to alert the Germans that a new bomb group was heading to England, the 95th's planes would leave Morrison Field, West Palm Beach, Florida, individually, depending on the skill of the navigators to guide them. The idea that they would be flying across the Atlantic filled many of the young men with wonder and excitement. They'd grown up reading and hearing about the daring exploits of Charles "Lucky Lindy" Lindbergh, who only fifteen years before had thrilled millions by soaring alone over the same vast and lonely expanse.

The Atlantic crossing was fraught with peril. First and foremost was the danger of getting lost. Each aircraft was flying an unfamiliar route, and the stress on the young navigators was immense. The average 95th navigator at that time had only thirty-five hours of flight time.

Each plane was under strict orders to maintain absolute radio silence, necessitated by "the tendency at that time for the Krauts to get on your wavelength and order you back to your last base," says Leonard Herman, with the hope that the American bombers would run out of gas and crash in the South Atlantic.[1]

Mechanical problems quickly became life threatening over so much open water. And early B-17 models had many design flaws. In fact, thirteen of the original thirty-nine B-17s in the 95th had to be replaced.[2] Though crews could contact ships and submarines along the route, rescue could take many hours or even days.

The 95th would take the southern route to Europe owing to the poor weather on the northern route that time of year. The 95th's flight plan called for stops in Borinquen, Puerto Rico; Atkinson Field, British Guiana; Belém, Brazil; Natal, Brazil; Dakar, Senegal; Marrakech, Morocco; and finally St. Eval, England, en route to their first base of operations at Alconbury, East Anglia.

Crews took with them all the things they thought they might need in England. The list included the occasional record player, sets of golf clubs, books, and cameras, but Gale House remembers that for the most part his flight crew took only the basics with them. "Taking all our 'stuff' on the flight was easy. None of the crew members had very much to take. Spare uniforms, underwear, some jackets, and two pairs of shoes were about it. A few of the crews filled the ball turret with beer and rum from Puerto Rico."

Bob Cozens has similar recollections: "The crew members had all of their personal belongings on board. It is possible that there may have been a few bottles of bourbon on board."

March 30, 1943, would be a day David McKnight would never forget. He led nine airplanes of the 95th's B-17s to Borinquen Field, Puerto Rico, on a flight of six hours. Mechanical problems delayed a number of ships.

Once in the air, each plane's pilot, copilot, and navigator were all kept busy. The rest of the crews had nothing at all to do. Some men sacked out on their duffel bags. Others looked out the windows at the steaming green jungles and the shimmering expanse of water below. Bob Cozens's crew played poker.

Pilot Bill "Catfish" Lindley remembers taking off in his B-17, nicknamed *Zoot Suiters*. The crew soon found that their navigator was either drunk or hung over and had dozed off for several hours. They were way off course. Bill Lindley's decision to fly straight to South America was nearly his last.

"With red warning lights lit on the gas tank gauges," Lindley remembers, "we finally spotted a small town with a very short gravel runway. I put her down on one end and almost immediately ran off the other end. The right wing clipped two thatched huts and scattered several irate natives . . . I turned the B-17 around, hit another thatched hut with the same wing, and bent the number 4 propeller. The plane eventually finished up back on the airfield. All of us expected hell to break loose about then.

"Some military-looking men approached in an ancient car as did several curious natives on cows and on foot. It turned out we had landed near Caracas, Venezuela. We asked the location to the nearest bar and were transported into town to a reasonable looking hotel. No one had raised any kind of protest. With hospitality like this the only thing to do was have a drink and talk the situation over. All we needed to get to England was a new propeller for number 4 and sufficient fuel.

"A telephone call to Trinidad got us a new propeller that was flown in via a C-47 transport. Technical Sergeant Barnett and crew changed the prop; the local government supplied the gasoline and a bulldozer to extend the ends of the runway. All the crew except Barnett and me went back to Trinidad in the C-47. The next day with a most favorable headwind we got the B-17 airborne and headed back to Trinidad to collect the crew. To this day I have no idea who paid for the hotel rooms, the bar bill, the phone call, or the gasoline."[3]

Jungle flying presented dangers of its own. "Over South America we flew over dense jungle, and a forced landing there would have been almost impossible—nor would survival have been likely," says Gale House.

Bob Cozens remembers that "we were asked to look for any signs of a medium bomber which apparently went down a day or two before. An interesting sidelight—the lost pilot was Tommy Harmon, a well-known All-American football player of that era. We were later advised that he had survived."

"One of the interesting aspects concerning the South American portion of the trip was the weather we encountered," remembers Dave McKnight. "The weather people at our stops on our way had warned us of the extremely heavy rain storms we would encounter occasionally. I recall approaching Belém when we hit the granddaddy of them all! About fifteen miles from the field we had to go under one of these things. It was a solid sheet of rain with a very large black cloud on top, and it was so dark as we went through it that we had to switch on the cockpit lights to see our instrumentation. But, as they had predicted, we emerged after about five minutes and the base came into sight."

The lush, green, steamy jungles of Brazil were an awe-inspiring sight to the men, many of whom had never been out of the United States. The locals offered up many exotic items to the men, and more than a few crews bought animals. McKnight marveled at the strange Brazilian butter, formulated not to melt in extreme temperatures, that he compared to axle grease. Another fast-moving souvenir item was the especially well-made boots that the South American cowboys wore. By the time Stateside training had ended, cowboy boots were already becoming something of a fad in the 95th, much to the chagrin of Col. Alfred Kessler, who felt that they detracted from the group's professionalism.

Dave McKnight wrote many years later: "When we were training in the States, Colonel Kessler used to tell the four Squadron Commanders that he was rather disgusted with all the boys wearing cowboy boots stomping around and speaking 'western' talk when half of them were from the Bronx. Also he thought their stomping around the barracks at two o'clock in the morning singing 'The Yellow Rose of Texas' was a little off balance because very few of them were from Texas."

From Brazil, the crews began the most dangerous leg of the oceanic crossing, the flight to Dakar. If one looks at a map, one can see that the stretch from Brazil to Senegal is the shortest way across the South Atlantic. But it was still a long way across open water for single crews, under radio silence and with fairly new navigators, to travel.

"On midnight of 4 April we took off with full fuel tanks from Natal for Dakar, West Africa," remembers Dave McKnight. "Taking off into the middle of the South Atlantic on a pitch-black night is the ultimate trip into nothingness."

Before each aircraft took off, its crew was reminded to maintain strict radio silence. Once out over the Atlantic Ocean, Dave McKnight received a radio call. Shortly thereafter, while he flew along the top of an undercast, a very bright light appeared through the clouds and tracked his aircraft.

"I never did know what it was but the Intelligence people at Dakar told us that it probably was a German submarine with a high-intensity light and an unpleasant piece of machinery on board with which to shoot at us."[4]

The pilots kept themselves alert on the eleven-hour flight with coffee and cigarettes. Gale House remembers thinking how alone each plane was, so far from any possible rescue should something go wrong. And he recalls a strange event. "About four hours into the flight over the Atlantic we ran into a huge thunderstorm [while] flying at our assigned altitude of 9,000 feet. The lightning was so bright and filled the sky constantly so we turned on the interior lights of the cockpit so as not to be blinded. The air was supercharged with electricity, and St. Elmo's fire had produced a brilliant band of blue corona around each propeller, off the propeller hubs, wing tips, and all promontories. Small lightning streaks were flying around on every one of the gauges on the instrument panel. The air was so supercharged with electricity, and you could feel it.

"Sgt. Matheson brought a small spider monkey up to the cockpit. He had traded a flashlight for it in South America. The normally slim body [of] about two inches in diameter was now so expanded it looked like a small dog! It also was intrigued with all the lightning streaks on the instrument panel and had a funny look on its face because of all this strange light and was the center of all our attention in the cockpit. The eerie blue light all around us magnified the situation.

"Then, all of a sudden, we felt a tremendous lift in our seats and watched the rate of climb indicator show we were gaining altitude at the rate of 500 feet per minute. I made no attempt to poke the nose down to hold our original altitude at 9,000 feet because I was certain we would hit the opposite side of this updraft and be faced with a serious downdraft. Accordingly I held this attitude, and all of a sudden we were popped out on top of the thunderstorm in clear skies at 13,000 feet and never had to face the downdraft I had expected to occur! Wow, what a deal!"

Hours passed, and each lone plane churned onward. All eyes were peeled for the first sight of the African coast. "As the trip wore on, I continued to ask my navigator how we were doing and received an 'on course, on time' response," says Bob Cozens, perhaps thousands of miles away from Gale House's plane at the time. "As we approached some eleven hours of flight time I again asked the same question, and received the same response, to which I responded, 'Africa is pretty big. How come I can't see it?'

"It turned out that the haze factor was such that looking horizontally you could not see much, but looking straight down you could see well. My navigator earned my respect as we made landfall within five miles of our intended landfall."

After hours of looking down at the flashing waters of the Atlantic Ocean, the coast of Africa was a welcome sight to the men of the 95th. Dave McKnight remembers: "As we were taxiing, the control tower called and said we had to go out again and search for one of our planes. That shook us a bit but it turned out to be good news/bad news. One of our airplanes was down, ditched in the sea, due to engine trouble. Its pilot, Raymond Abbott, must have done a beautiful job because everyone got out and into the life rafts. They were picked up safely the next day."[5]

Edgar B. Cole, now a major and commander of the 336th Squadron, ditched his B-17 about two hundred miles short of Dakar after an engine failed. British Air-Sea Rescue retrieved all the crew members.

Bill Lindley's first attempt at a crossing was scrubbed halfway across the Atlantic because of fuel concerns. On the second try, both he and his copilot became violently ill from a box of cookies they had eaten immediately after departure. The third time was a charm for Lindley and his *Zoot Suiters*. After landing in Dakar, Lindley admitted: "With all the bad luck that we had been experiencing, it seemed that a lucky mascot was in order. While we were in Dakar the crew picked out a big green parrot with a mean and spiteful disposition."[6]

Leonard Herman remembers that at one of the stops en route to Africa, the Johnny Johnson crew went to the base mess for some lunch. "We got our trays, came back to our table, and there was this smelly . . . cigar at the table where we had put our stuff. Little old Leonard opened his big mouth and said, 'Who the hell does this stinking cigar belong to!?'

"Just then a full Colonel came over to say, 'Sorry if I'm in your way, boys,' and stuck the cigar in his mouth and walked away. It was Colonel Curtis LeMay. He never smoked 'em, just chewed 'em. His cigars always looked like big, soggy turds."[7]

Leave it to Leonard Herman to insult the future leader of the Eighth Air Force!

From Dakar, the planes flew to Marrakech, Morocco. Dave McKnight flew into the base in a blinding dust storm. "I recalled a briefing about the Atlas Mountains being on our route, so I asked my navigator as we broke out and could see forward again, 'Where are those mountains?' He said, 'Look over your shoulder.' And there were the mountains with the peaks rising above us, on either side. He had brought us safely through the middle of the lowest area."[8]

Herman writes that "Marrakech had a pretty decent airport. The French ran it. The quarters were not all that bad. When we landed the French were in command and the landing crew called our pilot Johnny Johnson 'Le Chauffeur.' I liked that. I often kidded him that's all he was—he flew me to and from targets so that I could drop the bombs."[9]

The meticulous Bob Cozens recorded the length of each hop in his log. From Morrison Field to Waller Field in Trinidad was 10.45 hours. Flying to Belém took 7.20 hours, and the hop to Natal took another 7. The Atlantic crossing from Natal to Dakar took 11.45 hours. The flight to Marrakech was another 7.45 hours.

"When we eventually arrived in Marrakesh," remembers Lindley, "we were billeted in what was probably the largest open bay barracks in the world. It was as long as a football field with a very high ceiling. Bunks were packed into every available space, two deep. Every row of bunks had poker, dice, and blackjack games in progress with people standing around, waiting to get in. That was the only action available since we were warned not to go into Marrakech, particularly at night."

The second night, Lindley decided "to heck with the warning," and along with several others, he "found a smelly Arab with a dilapidated buggy to take us to a night club. I was to protect us from marauders with the .45 if necessary. We were looking for and anticipating something like the night club featured in Humphrey Bogart's *Casablanca*." Instead, they ended up in a basement club that Lindley describes as dirtier than a chicken coop and with drinks reminiscent of paint thinner. "Not one of the locals in the joint said a word after we arrived. Every one of them looked mean enough to take my .45 away and feed it to me in pieces. I wanted to stay, but the crew voted to depart in a hurry. They won and I beat them to the door. To hell with Bogart." The Lindley crew did not return to Marrakech.[10]

The Johnny Johnson crew was delayed in Marrakech while pilot Johnson recovered from dysentery. "While we were waiting for Johnny to recover," says Herman. "We got to know the natives. The natives would kill you for your shoes." Herman and his friends got around town in an old Ford chassis drawn by two horses. Prostitutes were a common sight. A huge man with a sword guarded one cathouse.

The final leg of the 95th flight crews' journey was from Marrakech to St. Eval, England. Bob Cozens recorded the trip at 8.4 hours upon his arrival on April 17, 1943. Dave McKnight remembers flying the last leg at night, "well out into the Bay of Biscay in order to avoid the German fighters who were patrolling the bay with their night fighters."[11]

From St. Eval, the crews flew to the replacement depot at Bovingdon. "Bovingdon apparently did not expect us as part of a completely new bombardment group, and we were told to unload our airplanes and get all our baggage off," remembers Lindley. "It sounded as if something was wrong with the deal because I knew we shouldn't be giving up our airplanes at that point. I told them I was working for a pretty tough boss and that if I gave the airplanes up and lost the crews, he'd have my you-know-what. Although they weren't too impressed, they called the Eighth Air Force headquarters and told them. As a result we were instructed to fly to Alconbury, near Huntingdon, that same afternoon. At Alconbury we joined the 92nd Bomb Group, which at that time was 'a training group for combat' and some of their personnel flew with us on several of our first missions."[12]

To his men's surprise, Colonel Kessler showed up at Alconbury "wearing the finest pair of gaucho boots that you ever saw," remembers McKnight. Apparently, after his harangues against the 95th's drugstore cowboys, "Uncle Ugh" had broken down and become one himself!

It took Bill Lindley's *Zoot Suiters* another ten days to finally make it to Alconbury. Lindley's lucky parrot had been unceremoniously dumped from the plane over the ocean at about twelve thousand feet after it "crapped all over the steering wheel," in the words of Bill Lindley. When the *Zoot Suiters* finally arrived, they were in time to see the 95th Bomb Group's B-17s returning from their second mission. Despite its inauspicious beginnings, the Lindley crew became one of the top crews in the 95th.

The original flight cadre had arrived. Postwar records of the 95th Bomb Group "would reveal that 77 percent of the combat crewmen who made up the original group would not complete a full tour of twenty-five missions."[13]

In comparison to the relatively quick trip that the flight crews made from the United States to England, the ground echelon faced a longer, slower exodus. Among them was Joseph Florian, who was well into a successful career in the design and engineering fields when he was tapped for the army air force. "I was suddenly thrust into an entirely new and bewildering life that was completely different from anything I'd known previously," he writes. Upon entering the force, Florian was assigned to the 95th Bomb Group's S-2 (intelligence) section.

> Troop trains took the 95th Group's ground personnel from Rapid City to Camp Kilmer and from there to Hoboken pier, New York. We boarded the *Queen Elizabeth*, a British 83,000-ton luxury liner in the Hudson River on 2 May, 1943, for the five-day, zig-zag crossing of the U-Boat-infested Atlantic Ocean. We bade farewell to the magnificent skyline of New York City to the blasting horns of every ship in the harbor. Little did the 16,000 troops, who were packed like sardines onto a ship designed for 3,000 passengers and crew, realize that it would be exactly two years, almost to the day, when they would see the same sight and from the same ship, on their return journey.[14]

At the time, the Battle of the Atlantic was raging. German U-boats operated with near impunity, and their goal was to starve Great Britain into submission by blockading men and matériel, most of it from the United States, from reaching the island. The elite force, led by Adm. Karl Dönitz, in 1942 had begun hunting in "wolf packs" and sank more than a thousand Allied ships in the North Atlantic that year alone.

Some time during the early morning hours after they boarded, the men of the 95th were taken to a room below deck crammed with tiered bunks stacked so tightly that a man had to lie down flat and then slide or roll in to his spot. They also had to sleep in two shifts. From noon until noon the following day one shift had the bunk, and from then until the next noon the second shift took over, leaving the other to sleep on deck. The men on deck soon found their own nooks or cubbyholes in which to spend the night.

The *Queen Elizabeth* relied on its great speed to travel the Mid-Atlantic unescorted through the submarine-infested waters, relying on escorts only at the eastern and western parts of the voyage. As a result, the ship traveled at speed and arrived in the British Isles in only six days safely through the submarine-infested waters. In contrast, some convoys took nearly a month to reach the British Isles.

The first few days at sea, the men could see planes flying overhead and blimps hovering over the water while searching for subs. But after two days, the ship was alone on a vast ocean. Once in a while the men saw a school of porpoises playing alongside the ship and once sighted a large convoy, but as submarines were likely to follow convoys, the *Queen Elizabeth* turned sharply away.

The chow lines wound snakelike through the ship, along halls, and up and down the stairs. The first day some of the men waited two and a half hours to eat, and in their eagerness some men got into the line that was going out of the mess hall and never ate at all.[15]

"The chow lines were so long, that after the second day, I never went to chow," remembers Art Watson. "I saw a stack of boxes against the bulkhead of one of the rooms, so I stole one and took it to my bunk." To Watson's delight, it was filled with Baby Ruth candy bars! "I made a deal with the other guys that whoever brought me a sandwich or something edible from the mess hall, I would give them a candy bar. I never had to stand in line again."

Art Watson remembers that "the latrines on the Promenade Deck were temporary, long gutter-like receptacles that were always full and running over. Many of the troops had to sleep on this deck. When the *Queen Elizabeth* would roll due to rough water, the gutters would overflow and run down the deck, and if a man wasn't quick enough, his sleeping sack would get soaked."

Many gambled to pass the time. Florian remembers one officer counting $4,000 in winnings, all in small denomination bills. GIs formed a band and played several dances, which were made more pleasant with the presence of the nurses, Red Cross girls, and members of the Women's Auxiliary

Corps (WAC) on board. Given the prevalence of shipboard romances, it quickly became a rule that no women were allowed on the sun deck after blackout hours. Further, the officers could enjoy whiskey in their club, but the enlisted men had to make do with Coke.[16]

On the morning of the sixth day, passengers awoke to find that the *Queen Elizabeth* was moving slowly up a loch lined on each side by emerald-green hills dotted with gray stone cottages with red-tiled roofs. The ship docked at Greenrock, Scotland. The voyage was over. From Greenrock, the ground echelon boarded a train for the twenty-hour, four-hundred-mile journey to Wickham Market, Suffolk, in East Anglia. In Wickham Market, they boarded a convoy of trucks, and the 200 officers and 1,000 enlisted men arrived at their new base outside Framlingham, Suffolk, on May 12.

3 Alconbury and Early Missions

After processing at the receiving base at Bovington, the 95th Bomb Group's first stop was the former Royal Air Force base at Alconbury. The Air Ministry originally acquired the 150-acre base, near the village of Little Stukely, in the spring of 1938. The RAF continued to use the field primarily for Wellington heavy bombers through August 1942, when the base was turned over to the United States. Crews lengthened the runway to more than thirteen hundred yards for the B-17s' use.

The first American bomb group to occupy Alconbury was the 93rd Bomb Group, a B-24 Liberator outfit that later transferred to North Africa. The 92nd Bomb Group, a B-17 outfit, followed and moved in during January 1943. It was fitted with the older B-17E aircraft and assigned to train new combat crews as they arrived in England. On April 8, 1943, the 95th Bomb Group officially arrived in England and was originally assigned to the Fourth Combat Wing. On April 15, the group arrived at Alconbury for operational training and to await the completion of its new base at Horham, RAF Station 119.[1]

An understanding of the administrative hierarchy of the U.S. Army Air Forces is necessary at this point. Each area of operations had a distinct air force that was roughly equal in status to a ground field army. The 95th became part of the Eighth Air Force, one of many U.S. Army Air Forces existing at the time, and it had the vital role of carrying out aerial operations from England. Each air force was further broken down into combat wings, usually comprising three bomb groups whose bases were in close proximity. The group also would fly missions together. A combat wing was comparable to a ground army's division, and each of the wing's three combat groups was roughly equal to an army regiment. Each bomb group flew from its own base and was further broken down into four squadrons of twelve planes, with each squadron equivalent to an army battalion. Each of the 95th Bomb Group's four squadrons—the 334th, 335th, 336th, and 412th—was further divided into elements of two planes. Later in the war, when the Eighth Bomber Command simply had too many combat wings to handle effectively, three bombardment division headquarters were inserted between the top command and combat wing level. Each of these new bombardment division headquarters oversaw three to five combat wings.[2]

While the 95th Bomb Group's flight crews trained with the 92nd in Alconbury, the ground crews were sent straight to the base at Framlingham, where the 95th would be moving after training. The first night the ground echelon was at Framlingham, the Germans bombed the base, convincing Art Watson and the others that they needed to take defensive precautions seriously.

At Alconbury, the 95th's flight crews began learning the intricacies of flying in a totally different environment from that in which the group had trained in the States. East Anglia was fast becoming a large, crowded air base. Copilot John Chaffin on Eldon Broman's crew writes: "There were so many B-17 bases in addition to B-26 and B-25 and Fighter bases in East Anglia that it was a popular joke that just a few more and that part of England was going to break off and either sink or float away. With the airfields so close together, take-off and landing patterns almost overlapped. There was an ever-present fear of mid-air collisions."[3] As each plane was packed with four thousand pounds of bombs and thousands of rounds of .50-caliber ammunition, hundreds of planes circling in a small area that was often shrouded in dense clouds or fog left little room for human error. With one false move, two or more airplanes and their crews were instantly destroyed.

Chaffin and command pilot Broman practiced mightily to hone their skills before entering combat. So did fellow pilot Harry Conley, who writes:

Uncle Ugh (Col. Kessler) wasted no time in getting all of us in the air practicing the skills we would need in actual combat. He was a stickler for flying close formations, reminding us again and again that a B-17 alone was no match for a squadron of Me-109s [Messerschmitt fighter planes] or FW-190s [Focke-Wulf fighter planes], but that a flight of three or four B-17s flying in a close formation could defend themselves by their concentrations of firepower. A squadron of three or four flights would be even more defensible. We also had to practice our timing in everything we had to do; preparing for takeoff, taking off and assembling into a group formation, changing direction in a group, preparing to bomb, and so on.[4]

Morale and expectations were high in the 95th. "The newcomers came in a war-winning, perhaps overconfident mood," writes British Eighth Air Force historian Roger Freeman. "Although the enemy's caliber was never underrated during Stateside training, personnel were apt to be influenced by sources, such as the US press, which presented a somewhat inflated picture of Eighth Air Force successes . . . the arrival of new groups also coincided with a stiffening of Luftwaffe opposition. . . . There was no longer a period of kindergarten missions for the new groups, including the 95th."[5]

At the time the 95th arrived in England, the Eighth Air Force had developed a bombing strategy in conjunction with the Royal Air Force. By late spring of 1943, the Eighth had finally reached what Allied planners considered to be the target strength to put daylight precision bombing to the test. Brig. Gen. Ira Eaker had written to Lt. Gen. Carl Spaatz in late 1942 that his senior officers were convinced that three hundred bombers flying in formation could provide enough defensive firepower to fly to and from their targets without fighter escort. Not that there was any alternative. At the time, the only fighter capable of escorting the heavies, the RAF Spitfire, had a range of only 175 miles.

The USAAF and the RAF followed a defined target priority list, which the Combined Bomber Offensive Plan had established. It divided objectives into three groups. At the top of the list was the elimination of German fighter strength, seen as the main obstacle to precision daylight bombing. Second-tier objectives were the German submarine yards and bases, the remainder of the German aircraft industry, ball bearing factories, and oil facilities. Following were factories that produced synthetic rubber, tires, and military transport vehicles.

The British would bomb at night while the Eighth would carry out unescorted precision bombing by day. This strategy gave rise to the term "round-the-clock-bombing." Leadership was confident that given the larger numbers of B-17s available for missions, the bombers would get through without heavy losses and would finally begin to function as planned.[6]

The 95th arrived exactly as the precision bombing theory was about to be put to the test. Unbeknownst to the men, they were about to become guinea pigs in a high-stakes experiment, and the results would not be good.

On May 13, 1943, the Fourth Combat Wing flew its first combat mission. The three groups in the wing—the 94th, 95th, and 96th—launched seventy-two B-17s on a mission to bomb the Luftwaffe airfield at St. Omer, France. Leonard Herman remembers the mission as "short and simple. There was very little flak. There were no fighters at all. After that trip, when we got back, our attitude was, 'Let us at 'em!' We said, 'We'll knock their pants off! We'll be going home in a month or two!' What a lot of nonsense. I think the Germans purposely did that so you would get a little indoctrination, a little confidence, and then they would jump all over your ass and shoot you down!"[7]

Mission number one for the 95th Bomb Group lasted four hours and fifteen minutes, according to the official records. The 95th crews participating were: G. A. Tyler flying B-17 23171; H. M. Conley, 229780; J. L. Nunes, 229679; W. K. Thomas, 229803; C. U. Watson, 229685; G. W. House, 229808; L. D. Clark, 229702; A. V. Stone, 229675; N. S. Rothschild, 229703; R. P. Bender, 229704; R. E. Robinson, 229737; D. M. Eastling, 229740; J. W. Johnson, 23111; H. A. Stirwalt, 229827; M. B. MacKinnon, 229693; and J. A. Storie, 229680.

"The second mission was the next day," remembers Herman. "We went to Antwerp. Now, at that time, Belgium was one of our allies, so we had to bomb carefully. The mission was short, only about four hours. On this mission, we lost our first crew." The J. E. McKinley crew, flying B-17 23115, was one of twenty-four 95th Bomb Group aircraft to take off for the mission. Fighters jumped the crew, flying its first mission, around 12:20 p.m. over the Dutch island of Zuid. The Fortress spun out of formation and crashed on the island of Noord-Beveland. Pilot McKinley, copilot J. L. White, navigator J. M. Smith, bombardier J. A. Payne, top turret C. G. Trent, radio operator F. A. Skwiat, ball turret gunner J. R. Hilliard, left waist gunner A. R. Pasco, right waist gunner R. B. Redding, and tail gunner J. A. Conlin were all killed in the crash and became the 95th Bomb Group's first combat casualties of the war. Two returning crewmen were injured—radio operator W. A. Rogers on R. C. Mason's crew and J. G. Schatz of Gale House's crew.[8]

May 14 was also a historic day for the Eighth Air Force for three reasons. The Eighth had dispatched more than two hundred bombers for the first time. Next, the B-26 Marauder made its combat debut with the Eighth Air Force. And finally, the 303rd Bomb Group's B-17 *Hell's Angels* became the first of the Eighth Air Force's B-17s to complete twenty-five missions successfully.[9]

The stress of combat, however, began to take its toll almost from the outset. Herman remembers that around the time of the second mission, "we lost our co-pilot. He never flew combat after that. He claimed he had back trouble and was sent to the hospital. They couldn't find anything wrong with him. He was reclassified and sent off base to some training command in Northern Ireland."[10]

The 95th's third mission, to Emden, Germany, on May 15, saw no losses and only one man wounded. But mission 4, to Lorient, France, resulted in the loss of the second 95th BG aircraft, that of pilot R. P. Bender, when it crashed on landing.

On mission 6, May 21, the 95th lost another aircraft. Pilot D. C. Schnebly, copilot G. E. Miller, and top turret gunner P. H. Auld were killed while the rest of the crew became prisoners of war (POWs). The empty beds after each mission served as constant reminders to the men of the 95th that they were in a shooting war and that each day was precious.

However, it was a disaster on the ground that shook the group to the core a few days later. On May 27, at about 8:30 p.m., ground crews were going about their usual business in preparation for the next day's mission and loading planes with five-hundred-pound bombs.

Without warning the bomb load on ship No. 229685 exploded with a horrifying blast. The plane, as such, literally disappeared, taking its ground crew with it. The sky rained debris from the blast. The shock waves travelled hundreds of feet in every direction. Nineteen men were killed, twenty seriously injured and the grim caprice of the concussion took an erratic toll. GIs picked up an ordnance officer some distance away. He was dead, unmarked by so much as a piece of flying metal. An engineer, standing among other men at a point on the field dropped to the ground, apparently in a faint. Men ran to aid him. He was gone. Others, a few feet away from him were untouched.[11]

Pilot Gale House remembered the "numbing tragedy" of the blast well. "At this time bombs were being loaded the night before the mission and were fused before loading. My crew was sitting on blankets and the gunners were cleaning their guns. I and Lt. Frank Metzger, navigator, were sitting on a separate blanket. I was leaning over close to the ground, blowing into the ear of a small Chihuahua dog my radio operator had traded a flashlight for in Belém, Brazil, in a somewhat teasing manner. The explosion took place in the B-17 about seventy feet away from us while we were only a few feet from the rear entrance of our ship. Metzger was instantly killed. I suffered a bomb fragment that went into the pleural cavity. Members of my crew were all injured in some manner or other.

"We tried to get up and run away from the site at the instant of the explosion, but heavy clods of dirt kept pounding us to the ground. It completely destroyed the B-17, blowing a hole in the ground about 6 feet deep and 30 feet in diameter. My ship suffered a glancing blow from an engine from the exploded airplane just forward of the rear exit and the fuselage was punctured with holes throughout. Sgt. Cords had been in our airplane when the explosion took place and came out of the ship with multiple bleeding wounds and was a yellow ghost. Apparently a fragment had disintegrated a package of sea marker that was always carried on the ships and this powdered dye had him completely covered.

"It put about twenty in the hospital and killed eighteen. A rough beginning for the Group. Colonel Kessler visited me in the hospital, asked if I felt I could still fly, and of course I assured him of that. 'You are the new Squadron Commander of the 336th Bomb Squadron,' he informed me. So I was promoted to Major a short time later and that was the sequel to the Alconbury Explosion."

Clifford Cole wrote later: "Four other B-17s nearby were crumpled like old paper. Eleven others were written off with damage so severe they wouldn't fly again for months. The engines of the exploded plane were never found. The others, badly damaged, were blasted several feet into the ground."[12]

Leonard Herman remembers:

> One afternoon, Pilot Johnny Johnson, Navigator Tommy Lees, and I were sitting in the balcony of a movie house in the town of Alconbury. The shock wave of a giant explosion reached us. We jumped out of our seats and ran out of the film house. We caught the first Army transportation back to Alconbury Air Base. When we got there, the place was in turmoil. There was a big hole in the ground. As we walked across the field, every once in a while you stubbed your toe or you tripped against a piece of human anatomy. Mostly it was elbows, or arms, or parts of a leg. It was really an absolute disaster.
>
> Not only did it kill a lot of our men and destroy a number of our planes, it also brought home to us what our bombs were doing to the Krauts when we had a good hit.[13]

The "tragedy at Alconbury" as it became known, took a terrible toll in human life and in aircraft. Four B-17s were completely destroyed. Eleven others were damaged. Eighteen men were killed instantly, and one died later.

However, the group learned a valuable lesson. Writes Harry Conley: "We were loading fused bombs into our B-17s, which was our procedure then because it was fast and easy to fuse the bombs on the ground where we could readily reach them. . . . This was the last time we loaded fused bombs. . . . This was a very tragic and expensive lesson."[14]

The 95th would fly 321 additional combat missions, but it would never again experience such a tragedy on the ground.

The 95th flew a few more missions out of Alconbury before departing for a new air base at Framlingham, Suffolk. Navigator Ellis Scripture remembered that up until June 13, 1943,

> the 95th had flown to targets in France and Belgium, relatively close to the English Channel coast. We had also gone to Emden, Germany,

which was the deepest penetration to date, and we had also bombed a refinery in Wilhelmshaven, Germany. We had put up a relatively large number of airplanes into combat, and until 13 June 1943, the 95th Group had lost only four aircraft. During these first eight missions we had claimed thirty-six enemy fighter planes shot down. This would indicate, of course, that we had been under relatively heavy attack during each of these first few missions.[15]

Their next mission was to Kiel, Germany. There, the 95th would be nearly wiped out.

Mission Day

In addition to being on the front lines of the European air war, the American bomber base in East Anglia was quite similar to a small American town, albeit minus the women. The base contained all the essentials of life that the young Americans were used to, from dining halls to movie theaters, from chapels to sports teams, from bars to post exchanges (PXs) selling American products.

Today, if one wanders through what is left of the old base at Horham, one will find that lush English vegetation has reclaimed much of the area. Nissen huts are tumbled down, their foundations tangled with vines and trees. Roots as thick as a man's wrist writhe through rooms where once men lived, slept, and dreamed. Vibrant red poppies dance on a light breeze next to a runway that once thundered with the roaring engines of mighty Flying Fortresses. The silence of the landscape is in dramatic contrast to those tumultuous early mornings when one fully loaded Fortress after another raced at full throttle down the runway destined for a distant German city.

One would never know, driving down the narrow rural lanes near the airfield, that an American air base had thrived here in the 1940s. In the late afternoon amber fields of wheat and barley shimmer like ocean waves. A light rain drizzles down, nourishing the rich English soil and the foliage that will eventually cover the base completely.

The old control tower is gone, demolished, a victim of England's lean, unsentimental postwar years. Most of the surviving buildings on the base became storage sheds or garages for local British farmers. But what if one were to drift back through the mists of time, to a day in 1943 or 1944 when the air base was filled with life, noise, and motion? It is still possible, through the words of those who were there.

It is the night before a mission. The sun is low in the western sky. Flight crews are relaxing, sleeping, grabbing a beer, or playing cards. Ground crews and support personnel are hard at work getting the 95th Bomb Group's valuable airplanes ready for the morning. Though the mission is still many hours away, preparation has begun. It involves many men for each flier. And every man on the base knows that his job is important, from the lead pilot to the cook who fries the eggs at three o'clock in the morning.

The ground crews are giving the group's forty-plus Boeing B-17 Flying Fortresses, or Forts, a thorough going-over. Many planes will not be making tomorrow's mission because, as the base engineering officer Clarence D. Fields wrote in an engineering report on June 15, 1943, thirteen of the sixteen planes returned banged up from that day's mission. Gunfire damaged aircraft 42-29943's right horizontal stabilizer and elevator, and a 20mm cannon shell wrecked a blade of the number 1 propeller. Aircraft 42-3283 had a cracked bombardier's window and multiple flak holes. Aircraft 42-3331 had a punctured gas tank. Aircraft 42-30185 had damage to its radio, ball turret, the hydraulic system of its top turret, and Plexiglas. Ground crews and other sub depot personnel would be busy repairing it all before the next mission.[1]

To save time, many ground crews have built tiny shanties next to their Fort's hardstand. They live, work, and sleep there, rarely going to their assigned quarters. Local British children know where to find them, as do the local dogs, which come begging for scraps and hoping to get their stomachs scratched by crewmen homesick for their own pets back home. Men at the 457th Sub Depot take care of the big jobs, from engines to paint to sheet metal.

During the afternoon, the base Teletype machine begins to clatter insistently. An office clerk, an enlisted GI, rips the report off the machine and briskly takes the field order (FO), or "aerial bible," to Base Command. The commanding officer reads the order and nods tersely to the GI, who hurries out to the flagpole in the squadron area. He hoists a red flag that everybody knows means "Mission tomorrow."

When flight crews spot it, they wander in and check to see who is flying the next day. If their pilot's name is on the blackboard, it means no carousing that evening. Some men wander over to the flying NCOs' Red Feather Club to relax and talk with friends. Sometimes, a movie provides a welcome distraction.

The section heads and the air executive go over the FO, which has been decoded. Their target is coded. The order gives the bomb load, the number of planes to be used, engineering and communications details, specifications for intelligence and aerial camera installations, and the zero hour, or start time.

Operations clerks phone every strategic point on the field, keeping the sections up to date. Briefing, taxi, and takeoff times are figured out, and the FO gives the time—to the minute—for assembly and rendezvous points with supporting fighters. Each Fortress's spot in the formation is diagrammed on a schematic with the name of its pilot and its serial number.[2]

The S-2 requests maps from the map room. The briefing officer collects information on flak areas to and from the target and other important details the flight crews will need. Other personnel inspect the escape kits for each crew member, pack the parachutes, and prepare equipment for checkout to the individual flights' crewmen.

In early 1944, a young reporter for *Yank* magazine visited the 95th BG and filed a report on the living conditions of a typical bomber base "somewhere in England." Published in the January 30, 1944, issue, his article covers the day's procedure during the hours leading up to the 95th Bomb Group's deep penetration mission.

First he pays a short visit to the Officers' Club, where only beer is served on a mission's eve. He notes a large sign: "Members of the World's Best Air Force Are Served in This Bar." Afterward the reporter walks down a narrow winding lane to a single-story building where the mission is being planned. He writes:

Large maps of the fighting fronts adorned the walls and colored marking indicated the important enemy targets and other information about them. Except for the maps, the intelligence room might have been any board of directors' office. In the center was a long, well-polished table surrounded by eight comfortable leather chairs. In the corner was a radio playing softly. An S-2 lieutenant relaxed in one of the chairs, his legs slung over its arm. A staff sergeant walked in and out of the room incessantly, always looking very serious, always carrying what appeared to be important documents.

The sergeant walked out of the room, then returned. "The FO is in, sir," he said. "Okay," replied the Lieutenant. "Call the Colonel." Three other members of the S-2 staff walked in—Major F.J. Donohue, chief of the group's intelligence section, a former Washington, D.C. lawyer; Captain Wayne Fitzgerald of Kalamazoo, Mich., the group bombardier; and Captain Ellis Scripture of Greensburg, Ind., the group navigator.

The three men sat down and watched as the sergeant tracked a narrow red tape from the spot on the map that represented the base in Britain to the enemy target that was to be bombed the next morning. The tape followed the exact course as directed by the field order.

Presently, a tall, middle-aged man walked in. He was a good-looking guy with a friendly smile. This was Colonel John Gerhardt [*sic*] of Chicago, commanding the group. With him was Lt. Colonel David T. McKnight of New York, the air executive officer of the group. McKnight was a short and personable fellow that made friends quickly. . . .

Colonel Gerhardt [*sic*] stood before the map and studied it. Then he asked for a copy of the field order. A cat strolled lazily by. Lt. Colonel McKnight stroked her back until she lifted her tail and purred.[3]

The reporter leaves the meeting and strolls down to the base theater, which also houses the chaplain's office and serves as a church on Sunday. The theater is filled to capacity that night. "The sergeant gunners and officers laugh a lot and occasionally somebody whistles," notes the reporter, adding that they are watching the movie *Duke of West Point*.

Next stop is the Aero Club, run by the Red Cross. Enlisted men read hometown newspapers, play billiards, or stand in line at the long counter for an evening snack. A round-faced sergeant named Vincent Barbella drinks a Coke as he tells the reporter that tomorrow's mission is number 12-B for him. Then he laughs. "To hell with it. I won't call it 12-B. I'm not superstitious. I'll call it straight number 13. I certainly hope we go tomorrow, though. This will make it about the sixth time I've been trying to make my thirteenth."[4]

Through the inky darkness of the blackout in the outdoor squadron area, the reporter finds his way to the 412th Squadron. There is no electricity in there tonight. A group of lieutenants sits around inside their quarters and chats by candlelight. Four of them—Lt. Robert W. Sheets of Tacoma, Washington; Lt. Jack W. Watson of Indianapolis, Indiana; Lt. Elmer Wong of Roachdale, Indiana; and Lt. Joseph C. Wheeler of Fresno, California—joined the squadron only last week. They had been in a Fortress that buzzed Yankee Stadium in New York during the 1943 World Series. "All that looks funny now that we're going into actual combat," says one. "It's the first mission that counts. Once over the hump I'll gain my bearings. I'm just itching to get that first one in."

A first lieutenant called Hapner interjects, "I know just how you feel. You change a lot after the first five missions. I don't know how to put my finger on it, but you sort of become more human. You become more appreciative of the men you fight with and the men you live with. It's particularly bad when you lose some of the men from your crew, or if one guy finishes his ops ahead of you and leaves the crew."

The reporter recounts that Hapner goes on to tell the story of pilot Kit Carson. Carson's first crew went off on a mission without him; none came back. He transferred to the Johnny Johnson crew as copilot. "Johnson was married at the time and had a helluva pretty wife in East St. Louis, Ill. On a raid over Kiel, a 20 mm exploded against Johnny's side and killed him. The Brass Rail nose-dived about 4,000 feet and everybody in it thought they were goners. . . . By some miracle, Kit was able to level the ship off. Except for Kit that whole crew would have been goners. He got the DFC [Distinguished Flying Cross] for that. I really miss that guy."

The new lieutenants listen carefully. They had met Carson just before he left the squadron, but up to now they had not known his story. When one of the lieutenants comments that Carson was never one for tooting his own horn, Hapner replies, "Neither will you after a while. Combat does something to a man. You'll see."

As the flight crews try to bed down for the night and catch some much-needed shut-eye, the ground personnel continue their hard work through the night. Armament men holding flashlights walk quietly from their huts to arm the ships. "Maybe we won't have to unload again for a change," says one man. "It looks too good tonight, even for English weather."

The reporter checks in at the kitchen in the combat mess. Two cooks are standing by a stove with frying pans in their hands. It is 4 a.m. The reporters notes, "They were frying eggs for the men scheduled to fly that morning. 'I don't know what it is,' the short cook said, 'but about every dog in England seems to have found a home on this base.'

"'You'll find the same thing is true on all the bases,' the other cook said. 'Even the RAF has its share of dogs. Some of them have seen more combat than a lot of guys.'"[5]

Pilot John Walter lies on his bed, staring at the curved ceiling of his Nissen hut. Years later he writes:

I doubt that anyone kept records on the amount of 100 Octane gas that was used preflighting engines. Soon after the Group was alerted for a mission it would begin. At first, you could hear one or two engines start up, then slowly accelerate to 1000 rpm [revolutions per minute] for a five to ten minute warm up period. Once the engines were warmed up, the magneto, propeller and full power checks would follow. This was repeated for each of the approximately 160 engines potentially involved for the next day's mission. Usually, the ruckus started around 2300 and lasted well into the early morning. This chorus of Wright Cyclone R-1820's didn't make falling asleep any easier for the combat crews. It was more a portent of bad things to come rather than a lullaby"[6]

Bombardier David Webber listens to the engines and makes an entry in his diary. "I'm getting a mania to fly these damn missions. The excitement & thrill of being shot at is rather appalling. This mania almost frightens me because after the war what will I do to fulfill any desire of danger & excitement such as I feel now? Strangely enough I have no desire for rest from combat."[7]

Crews pump fuel from underground storage tanks into trucks, which then rumble from one hardstand to another and pump gas into the planes. The men cart rows of bombs over from the bomb dump and carefully load them. Armorers go over the guns and ammunition.

Others test the aerial cameras before loading them on the Forts, knowing photographs of the mission will be stored for future intelligence use. Still others preflight the Norden bombsights and carry them out to the planes.

Now that the planes are ready, an enlisted man with a flashlight rouses the men who will fly in them. Men grumble and stumble out of bed. In the winter, they can see their breaths in the chill. They begin their pre-mission rituals. Some are based on hard logic. John Walter takes the time to shave before each mission. "Given our youth, a daily shave was not always necessary," he says. "However, a smooth face made six or more hours of wearing an oxygen mask a little more bearable."[8] Some men put on lucky socks or religious medals; others kiss photos of wives or girlfriends back home. A few, feeling that their luck has run out, tell their roommates in hushed tones what to do with their belongings if they don't come back. A few men scratch out quick letters and leave them next to their beds.

Breakfast on mission day is usually very good, if you can eat it: real eggs, coffee, toast. More than a few men wonder if it is, indeed, their last meal. Their faces are taut, with too many lines for men so young.

Pilots then head to their briefing. Navigators, bombardiers, and enlisted men go in groups to their own. Copilot John Chaffin is nervous as he waits for the curtain to be raised on the map showing the day's target. He tells himself:

Maybe we'll have a "milk-run" today. Perhaps someplace in France or Belgium. Maybe it will be just four or five hours. Maybe we will have fighter escort. Maybe we will have a good position in the formation instead of "Tail-End Charlie" in the high squadron. Please God don't put us with Captain X. The bastard can't fly an airplane. Oh, hell, we are in "Purple Heart Corner." Why should we have to fly that position? After all we are veterans now—we have already put in seven missions. Damn![9]

Crewmen try to concentrate as they sit through the briefings. Slides of the target are flashed on the screen. Flak and fighters are discussed.

After their briefing, the enlisted crewmen ride by half-ton truck down a narrow lane to armament sheds where they wrap their .50-caliber guns in burlap sacks, to keep them clean and greased, before heading to the hardstands. Each crewman is issued a .45-caliber sidearm and two clips "to fight our way out of Germany in case we went down," recalls Bob Brown. Above their heads in one shed is a sign: "Without Armament There Is No Need for an Air Force."

At the Supply Depot, each crewman is issued his flight gear. Besides an electrically heated flight suit and gloves, he receives fur-lined boots, leather pants, and tops; parachute and harness; Mae West (life jacket); oxygen mask; and escape kit.

Each bomber crewman has specific duties on mission day. Each man knows his job. He can do it in his sleep, but he pays full attention as he works in the predawn hours. After all, his life and the lives of his fellow crewmen depend on it.

On the hardstand before takeoff, a tail gunner listens in at the hard-stand briefing. Then he requests the formation sheet from the pilot and goes on to check the ship's oxygen, Aldis signal lamps, flare pistol, walk-around oxygen bottles, and flak suits. He distributes the POW kits, checks with the radio operator for interphone reception, and checks the Aldis lamp's red slide, which would be used, if necessary, to abort the mission. Depending on visibility, and to identify the formations, the tail gunner's job also involves sending Aldis lamp signals to other ships in the formation.

The top turret gunner/flight engineer served as the mechanic and troubleshooter on the aircraft. He checks the flares, the oxygen systems, the turret meter for freedom of movement, the main fuse box for proper fastenings, the bomb bay door heaters for connections, the radio for inter-phone reception, and the bomb bay crank and extension in the cockpit.

The radio operator is responsible for obtaining the flight's approximate estimated time of arrival (ETA) and estimated time of return (ETR) and the times to each check point on the route. He's been fully briefed on winds to be encountered. Now he checks chaff release points with the navigator; affirms the crew's position in the squadron, group, and wing formation in the bomber stream with the pilot; and contacts all crew members on the interphone. He makes sure the liaison transmitter units are tuned and easily obtainable, ensures the radio room has two walk-around oxygen bottles, and sees that the heated flight suits are functioning properly.

The two waist gunners look over all the emergency equipment, checking oxygen readings and the waist fuse box for spare fuses, first aid kits, and all other necessary equipment. They also consult with the pilot on the day's flare colors for the group and wing.

The ball turret gunner makes sure his guns are mounted and ready. He enters the plane through the waist, where he will ride during takeoff, assembly, and landing. The Sperry ball turret hangs only fifteen inches above the runway, and a landing gear accident means certain death to a gunner stuck inside. The ball gunner trusts his waist gunners. William "Dub" Vandegriff remembers what happened to one of his buddies on a mission a few weeks ago. The guy became stuck in his turret when the mechanism jammed. He panicked. One of the waist gunners, a big burly man, worked him free manually. When the ball gunner refused to go back into the ball on any more missions, the big waist gunner put his hand on the smaller man's shoulder and vowed that if he became stuck that the waist gunner would go down with him while trying to get him out. Hearing that promise, the ball gunner went into the turret for the next mission.

The pilot and copilot huddle, going over a lengthy checklist, printed in microscopic print on a blue wallet-size card. The pilot's preflight duties include inspecting seats and various controls. He must ensure the fuel transfer valves and switch are off; intercoolers, off; gyros, uncaged; fuel shut-off switches, open; gear switch, neutral; turbos, off; idle cutoff, checked; throttles, closed; high rpm, checked; autopilot, off; deicers and anti-icers for wings and prop, off; cabin heat, off; generators, off; and cowl flaps: open right, open left, locked.

The copilot's preflight warm-up includes making sure the brakes are locked, trim tabs are set, and propellers are exercised. He also ensures that the generators are checked and turned off and that each of the four great engines run up in turn.

Each navigator knows every turn and every point on the mission that requires a change of course or altitude or both. Each bombardier knows the types of bombs carried, has looked at photos of the target, and hopes that the sky above the target will be clear so that he can drop his bombs accurately and not scatter them away from the primary target.

Their preflight duties done, crew members lie on their kits and wait. This waiting for takeoff is long and often the most trying part of a combat mission. Usually one hears a great deal of talk and banter, but the suspense is thick now. Sometimes, as the men wait, nervously smoking cigarettes, they watch the local farmer peacefully harvesting his crops in the field at the edge of the runway. A few men fulfill pre-takeoff rituals, such as urinating on one of the Fort's huge rubber tires.

The *Yank* reporter visits the Rodney Snow crew as it waits. It's five minutes before "Stations," and he's in time to see Snow make his ritual trip to stand behind the tail in silence for a few moments, gathering his thoughts. According to *Contrails II*, the 95th BG's pictorial history,

> Snow's bombardier, Lt. George Lindley of Seattle, Wash., was smoking a cigarette and telling the left waist gunner about his baby son. The baby was born October 6 and Lindley was sweating out a picture that was supposed to be on the way over. The mission didn't seem to bother him, but the absence of the baby's picture did.
>
> Some days, the crews wait for an hour or more as takeoff is delayed. Occasionally, after waiting, and its inherent nervous tension, a mission is scrubbed, leaving the men bundles of nervous energy. All the bombs and ammunition must be unloaded.
>
> As takeoff time approaches, flying control gets into high gear. The control tower operator is in radio touch with all planes. Instructions are given for taxiing. The planes jockey into position, one following the other in prescribed order. The tower jeep buzzes around as a mobile control. The group is ready for flight.[10]

When the pilots receive the takeoff order, slowly the Forts begin lumbering toward the runway in neat rows. They weave back and forth so that their pilots can see the taxiways. Since the Fort is a tail-dragger, pilots crane their necks out their side windows to keep the planes on course.

Takeoff. Flying Fortresses thunder into the air at thirty-second intervals. John Walter pilots one of the planes: "After a short roll, the throttles are full open. My copilot began to call off the air speed as we seemed to move very slowly down the runway. We had between forty-two hundred and six thousand feet to get 60,000 plus pounds of airplane, people, fuel and bombs up to flying speed."[11]

"The aircraft are heavily loaded," remembers pilot John Chaffin. "Four thousand pounds of bombs, ten men, full fuel tanks, and thousands of rounds of fifty-caliber ammunition. Sometimes a plane did not make it. Sometimes only skillful pilotage and luck saved the plane, such as the time we had a tire blow out during the takeoff roll."

"It's off they go, but more often into a thick, grey mist than a wide, blue yonder," reports *Contrails II*. "The control tower checks each off by plane number. It's a heavy load, bombs and gas, and the take-off is long with a gradual rise and turn. Elements of three will gather in the air and form into Squadrons of three elements each, four Squadrons to a Group."[12]

If the sky is overcast, pilots must rely on instruments and a strict climbing pattern to avoid a terrifying and usually fatal collision with another plane. A quick flash, a boom, and a shower of parts and bodies signifies the end for two B-17s and all twenty crewmen to those below at Horham.

Pilot Richard Smith says, "I am lucky to still be here. My most persistent memory is of morning takeoffs in the fog, when you couldn't see one end of the runway from the other."

Climbing through clouds with zero visibility is a nerve-wracking experience. Pilot John Walter remembers wondering how far he was from being a "nice, big bright flash in the dimly-lit early morning sky. On one mission, we went into clouds at 800 feet and didn't break out on top till 23,000 feet. That seemed like an eternity. About an hour and three-quarters of 'screwing' upwards through a blanket of clouds full of circling, climbing airplanes. For over 100 very long minutes we sat there wondering where the other 35 planes of the Group were."[13]

Each Fort climbs at a predetermined heading at a 250-foot-per-minute rate of climb at 135 miles per hour for a specific amount of time, usually five minutes. Then the plane makes a 180-degree turn and maintains climb and airspeed for the same amount of time as the first leg. Thus, through a series of switchback maneuvers, each aircraft works its way up to rendez-vous altitude. This pattern minimizes the chance of midair collisions. However, they still happen. When they did, according to Walter, particularly in the dark, a tremendous flash lit the sky as six thousand gallons of gasoline and seven tons of bombs ignited. Survival by anyone was improbable.

Pilot Les Lennox recalls seeing a map of assembly formation over East Anglia, showing each group's climb pattern for group assembly.

> It was an amazing map to look at, very similar to the pieces of a gigantic jigsaw puzzle. The intelligence officer stressed to my Co-pilot, George Marks, and me the absolute necessity of staying within our climb pattern, guided by Buncher radio transmissions from the ground, and not straying into someone else's pattern. . . . I'm sure everyone can recall climbing through dense cloud to assembly altitude and then suddenly hitting severe prop-wash, instantly knowing that you had just passed close behind an unseen aircraft and had experienced another near miss.
>
> The people in air traffic control today would be absolutely appalled if they could see our only method of controlling all these bombers. Taking off at thirty-second intervals and climbing through all types of weather, in daylight or in darkness while maintaining radio silence. When two aircraft have a near miss today it makes national news. We had so many each day that we thought nothing of it.[14]

Making things more difficult for the 95th is the fact that there is no clear route straight out and straight back from the base that can be used for assembly. Any direction brings them close to another group's assembly route. Because of this limitation, the 95th's method of group assembly is to fly in a climbing spiral pattern, with the center of the turn being the base.[15]

"What a sight!" writes pilot John Walter. "Hundreds of airplanes appear to be milling about aimlessly in the early morning sky. Soon, out of this seeming chaos, orderly groups of aircraft begin to form. Then, as if by magic, the smaller groups merged into larger groups and then the larger groups fall into trail and head toward the rising sun."[16]

Three groups rendezvous and form the next organizational unit, the wing. The wing is, nominally, a strike force of 108 aircraft. The 95th now usually flies with the Thirteenth Combat Wing. The wing's other two groups are the 390th Bomb Group, based a few miles away at Parham near Framlingham, and the 100th Bomb Group, also down the road at Thorpe Abbotts.

On important missions, referred to as "maximum efforts," each element is expanded to four aircraft by adding a plane in the "slot." Sometimes two planes are added to an element. For group takeoff, the three squadrons' lead aircraft take off first as they are the nucleus for pulling the formation together once they reach assembly altitude. After the leaders take off, the high, lead, and low squadrons follow in that order.

Half the required mission altitude is reached over England; otherwise, the Forts would not have time to achieve bombing altitude when they reach the continent. Al Forrester remembers that assembly could take two hours. Once the groups and wings are in proper order the bomber stream heads east toward occupied Europe. The ball turret gunner descends into his metallic cocoon. Ball gunner Ed Morrison remembers that a ball turret gunner could be wedged inside the ball for six of the eight hours on a long mission and four of the six on a shorter one.

Over the English Channel, gunners check their guns. There are five types of cartridges in the chains of ammo: incendiary, armor piercing, tracer, lead, and general purpose.

Ahead, the pilots see Europe through their cockpit windows. "From five miles up, the earth below has become a patchwork quilt of green and brown," writes Chaffin.

The involved aircraft change from man-made objects of aluminum, steel, copper and rubber to creatures which are alive with their own specific personalities. Some of them move with the rapier-like thrusts and jabs of a skillful, lightweight boxer. Others, more cumbersome, move slowly like a punch-drunk fighter. . . . Guns of various sizes protrude from different parts of the machines. . . . The occupants of these machines—the warriors—have strange-looking equipment covering them. Helmets of leather cover their heads; faces are covered with rubber masks which have hose connections to strange-looking little boxes beside them. From the helmet come wires that also connect to little boxes. Surrounding these creatures is a great array of light, switches, knobs and gauges. . . . They [the crew] all wear ill-fitting yellow vests and strange-looking harnesses of cloth webbing and steel buckles.[17]

At ten thousand feet, an order crackles over the interphone and the crewmen hook on their oxygen masks. The masks tend to clog with ice, and the resultant anoxia renders the affected man light headed and giddy, and can lead to a permanent sleep. Frequent oxygen checks of all crew members are needed to prevent this tragedy.[18]

As the bomber stream slices through thin, cold air, it often leaves a calling card. Explains John Walter,

These lines are more commonly known as contrails. The "con" is an abbreviation for condensation. Among the various gases emitted in the engine exhaust is water vapor. They are nothing more than miniature man-made ice crystal clouds. We despised seeing them for two reasons. First, the screening effect of the contrails would allow enemy fighters to approach unseen from the rear. Second, from the ground, they clearly indicated our presence and, from our apparent heading, gave a clue as to our intended target. If you could be objective about them, they were spectacular. And, it was fascinating to watch as adjacent ships spun them.[19]

Enemy aircraft are sighted. The Fort shakes with the concussions of .50-caliber guns firing in all directions. The pilots move their wingtips closer to their neighboring aircraft's waist. The closer the formation, the more protection from fighter attack—but also the greater the danger from midair collisions. Within minutes, the pilot and copilot are drenched with sweat as they try to keep the Fort in tight formation.

Flak. Shot from 88mm guns twenty thousand feet below, antiaircraft ammunition is fused to explode at altitude. The contrails point the flak gunners directly at the tiny green or aluminum specks in the sky. "During parts of the air battle some of the airspace will be filled with thousands of small black puff clouds. Sometimes if one is looking in the right direction, he will see one of these little clouds form. At first it is a bright orange flash; then gray for a brief instant and then black. If one is close to the formation of the little cloud, he will hear a muffled sound like a distant boom of thunder. Finally the airspace will be filled with enough of these little clouds that, from a distance, they'll look like a single, large, black cloud. Death lurks in these places," remembers John Chaffin.[20] Time after time, bomber crewmen describe the sound of jagged shards of flak striking the thin aluminum shell of their aircraft as very similar to that of someone throwing gravel into a tin pail. Each 88mm flak shell weighs twenty pounds and contains dozens of sharp pieces of heavy metal. The shell leaves the gun muzzle at twenty-six hundred feet per second and is effective up to twenty-six thousand feet.

Germany has been rapidly building up its flak guns around the Allies' prime targets. These guns, and their crews, operate twenty-four hours a day and use prodigious amounts of ammunition, creating a real drain in terms of money and manpower. By the summer of 1943, no fewer than eighty-nine flak batteries guard the German capital of Berlin. According to one historian, the German 88mm flak gun required an average expenditure of sixteen-thousand-plus shells to bring down *one* Allied aircraft flying at high altitude.[21]

"The air battle may last as long as three hours or no more than thirty minutes," Chaffin recalls. "The ferocity of the engagement is determined by the number of defenders which, in turn, determines, to a great extent, the losses sustained by the aggressors. Aircraft fall like giant wounded birds fluttering to earth. Aircraft are set on fire but continue on for a while. Aircraft disintegrate before your eyes. These are all machines. There is little sense that within them are young men dying."[22]

At fifty degrees below zero an ungloved hand will freeze in seconds. Without oxygen, a man will die in minutes. In such conditions, even simple tasks are nearly impossible. Ball turret gunner Bob Capen remembers: "You couldn't eat or drink. Liquids would freeze. I know some guys took candy bars but I don't know how they ate them unless they stuck them under their armpits. It was anywhere from 45 to 55 below zero."

"Everyone received a package of gum and a candy bar," remembers Bob Brown. "That was the food for the day until we returned. I haven't chewed gum since."[23]

Even a normally simple task such as relieving yourself becomes difficult. Men inside the plane have a relief tube, or a funnel connected to a rubber tube, to use for emergency urination. However, it freezes at altitude and the urine backs up. Another problem with the relief tube is that it dangles out of the plane right in front of the ball turret. On frequent occasions, the ball turret becomes coated with a layer of yellow ice, occasioning furious interphone calls from the ball turret gunner.

Ball turret gunner Ed Morrison writes: "We had a tube that we called 'The Gremlin' for urine release. It was difficult because of all the flight clothes and being in a sitting position with the Sperry's gunsight between our legs."

Ball gunner Franklyn "Frank" Coleman named his condition "The Ball Turret Blues": "You just couldn't pee. My kidneys have been weak ever since from holding it." Frank winced at the memory when he told me: "When drops of urine turn to ice on the tip of your penis it hurts. The ball turret gunner was sometimes a little damp in the groin region."[24]

The planes fight their way to the initial point (IP), defined as an easily distinguishable location to start a bomb run to the target. Then they prepare for the bombing run. Using the Automatic Flight Control Equipment (AFCE) mounted on an instrument control panel between the pilot and copilot, the pilot transfers control of the aircraft's lateral movement to the bombardier and the Norden bombsight for the bomb run. The bombardier can, in an extreme emergency, use his own auto turn control switch to perform an evasive action, but evasive action on the bomb run is frowned upon.[25]

Minutes tick by. The wait is excruciating, as the formation must fly straight and level to maximize accuracy, no matter how much flak is bursting around it or how many fighters are attacking. Finally, over the target, the bombardier announces, "Bombs away!" The Fort lurches upward, relieved of several tons of cargo. As the crews breathe sighs of relief, the formation turns and heads for England.

Sometimes, one or more bombs get hung up in the bomb racks. Once the run is over, the bombardier must inch his way out on the narrow catwalk, carrying a walk-around oxygen bottle, and dislodge those remaining. He tries not to look down through the open bomb bay doors at a city or fields twenty thousand feet below.

Each crew member who sees the bombs hit files the information mentally for the postflight briefing. The pilot informs the radio operator to send a strike report as soon as possible. The gunners report the positions of other squadrons to assist in the reforming of the groups. They also report missing planes, stragglers, or feathered engines; confirm kills of enemy aircraft; count parachutes from downed aircraft; check for damage to their own planes; and advise following groups about flak.

Planes still in formation wing together toward England. Stragglers drop to low altitude, using the ground or sea as cover, and make a run for it. In some Forts, wounded men fight for life. First aid kits contain only rudimentary equipment.

And then, back at the airfield, "Here they come!" Anxious ground crews count planes, group by group, as they circle the field, peel off, and start their landing procedure. Crippled planes and those with dead or wounded on board shoot off flares and are given preference. The "meat wagons" are readied in case something goes wrong. Flight surgeons in the hospital are ready for casualties.

The ground personnel turn out to await the group's return. They have been sweating out the mission for hours, ever since the Forts disappeared as mere specks in the English sky. Ground crews look for their particular plane. There is no worse feeling for a ground crewman than to stand at an empty hardstand, realizing his plane is not returning and wondering if a mechanical problem brought down the plane.

After taxiing to the hardstand, each crew climbed out and inspected the plane for damage. Then the men got equipment and guns, loaded into a truck, returned the equipment, and went to interrogation.

The flight crews trudge wearily to interrogation. They get a shot of whiskey and answer questions about the mission. Afterward, they munch on Red Cross doughnuts or cookies. The information is sent to division and then on up to Eighth Air Force headquarters for analysis. Film is developed and printed, reams of paper spin out of clacking typewriters, and the planes are taken back on the line and repaired for the next mission.[26]

Crews return to their barracks, glad to be alive but weary beyond belief. Back in the barracks, bunks may be empty this evening if another crew has failed to return. Some men shower, change clothes, and go to the mess hall. Many go to the Red Feather Club or the Officers' Club for a drink or two.

While the flight crews were away on their mission, the ground personnel went about their duties. Reports had to be typed, duplicated, filed, and sent. Patients had to be cared for in the base hospital. Meals for three thousand people had to be prepared in the kitchens. The base and its hundreds of vehicles had to be maintained.

As the sun sets on another mission day, the base disappears behind blackout curtains. German fighters occasionally come over during the hours of darkness, dropping bombs and keeping everyone's nerves on edge. Germany also launched V-1 flying bombs and V-2 rockets across the North Sea and the English Channel on a regular basis as well. One V-2 rocket landed in nearby Hoxne, causing a huge explosion. Another killed a herd of cows outside Horham village.

In the Officers' Club and the Red Feather Club, men unwind, drink a few beers, and listen to music or the propaganda broadcasts of "Lord Haw-Haw" from Germany. In the Nissen huts, men play cards and chess, write letters home, hold bull sessions, or read. The military policemen (MPs) stand at the entrances to the base, keeping a watchful eye for suspicious intruders. The base never completely sleeps, for too much work remains to be done. Tomorrow will bring another day, perhaps another mission. Nearby, the citizens of Horham sleep.

Then Came Kiel

Talk to any of the original members of the 95th Bomb Group and they will tell you the same story—not about the date when the 95th Bomb Group was nearly destroyed in the flames of battle but instead about when the group forged itself into tempered steel: June 13, 1943. "I think [that day] will have to go down in history as the day the 95th Bomb Group became combat ready," writes Ellis Scripture, "and it is probably the one day that many of the original crew members will remember most of all the days of World War Two."[1]

The 95th had moved from Alconbury to its new base at Framlingham, Suffolk, a few days earlier, still reeling from the Alconbury tragedy. Intelligence officer Joseph Florian remembers Framlingham as "a peaceful and picturesque country town . . . located about twelve miles from the North Sea coast, which didn't allow much time for air raid warning against low-flying German bombers and fighter-bombers that occasionally came swooping over."[2] Florian also enjoyed exploring the medieval Framlingham Castle, defended by sixteen-foot-thick stone walls, perched on a small rise above the village. In 1943, Framlingham also offered the young GIs a small cinema, a hotel, several pubs, a fish and chips shop, and a bicycle shop. The locals put their cars in storage and rode bicycles, as there was no gasoline.

When I visited Framlingham in June 2008, it looked the same as it did in the airmen's old black-and-white photographs taken in World War II. Surrounded by emerald-green fields and forests, its narrow, winding streets—some cobbled—twisted this way and that. The town reminded me of a scene in a Dickens novel. Framlingham Castle, now in ruin, stood silent guard over a lawn bowling tournament that echoed with the laughter of children and the competitive exuberance of the bowlers.

The men of the 95th had little time for exploring their new environs, however, before they were summoned to discuss what promised to be their biggest mission yet. Their first hint that change was afoot came in early June in the form of an immaculately uniformed, mustachioed officer striding confidently around the base. It was Brig. Gen. Nathan Bedford Forrest III, great-grandson of the legendary Confederate general Nathan Bedford Forrest. Thirty-eight years old and a graduate of West Point, Forrest was a career air corps officer straight from Washington, with no combat experience. He was, however, a respected aviator and had been sent to England to test his new idea of formation bomber warfare. The 95th had been chosen to try out some of his tactical innovations.

At this point in the air war, the best formation to protect the slow-moving and usually unescorted bomber formations from the skilled German Luftwaffe fighter pilots was still under debate. German fighters often waited to jump the bomber stream until the American or British fighter escorts were forced to turn back when their fuel ran low. The task of defending the bombers fell to the gunners on the bombers themselves.

Forrest thought he had a better idea. His proposed "Forrest formation" was in direct contrast to that already designed by Col. Curtis LeMay, arguably the greatest genius of the U.S. air war. LeMay was responsible for three of the most important advances in American bomber tactics during the European air war. First, he believed that contrary to the previously accepted doctrine of allowing pilots in formations to take evasive action on the bomb run, they could achieve improved results and be safer if they flew straight and level throughout it. The first trial of this new straight and level tactic, on November 22, 1942, proved that LeMay's technique conserved fuel, helped maintain the formation, improved accuracy, tightened bombing patterns, and saved lives.

LeMay's second contribution was to have a highly skilled lead navigator lead each wing and a highly skilled bombardier initiate each bomb drop, with all other planes dropping on his lead rather than independently. This strategy reduced the chances of bombing errors owing to faulty navigation or bomb sighting.

His third contribution was the creation of the "combat box." German fighter pilots had figured out that the best way to attack a B-17 was from the front and slightly above the bomber, in a position bomber crews referred to as "twelve o'clock high." Not only was the B-17 poorly defended from the front, but coordinated frontal attacks could kill or incapacitate its pilots, bombardier, and navigator. LeMay's combat box was a radical departure. Rather than deploying the bombers in "flat, two-dimensional, follow-the-leader formations that went straight back, LeMay placed his three-plane elements in three dimensions, high and low as well as back and to the sides."[3]

To prevent higher-flying bombers from dropping bombs on lower-flying ones, all planes had to drop simultaneously while in strict formation. Furthermore, the tighter the formation, the more protection each bomber afforded its neighbors. Thus pilots were admonished to fly "wingtip to wingtip" or to "tuck your wing into your neighbor's waist window." LeMay's innovative ideas had germinated during his many hours of combat missions over Europe in 1942 and 1943.

When Brigadier General Forrest met with the 95th Bomb Group's leadership, he confidently postulated a new defensive and offensive tactic. "General Forrest was convinced," remembers Scripture, "that we would gain better firepower if we flattened the formation and flew wingtip to wingtip so that we would be able to concentrate our firepower ahead, below, above, and to the rear. After a great deal of discussion, it was finally decided that we would fly that new type of flat formation on 13 June."

Lt. Bob Cozens was present at the meetings and remained highly skeptical of the new Forrest formation. However, he accepted his superior's command decision.

Bombardier Leonard Herman was also skeptical of the new formation. "Our original formation was a good one," he stated emphatically and angrily many years later. "LeMay had come up with it, and the planes were stepped up and down and included not only each element being involved but the entire bomb group. Forrest's formation had us flying in a straight line across, like the Charge of the Light Brigade. But it doesn't work when you're at high altitude and the Krauts are coming right at you with no back-up fighters and there is no coverage and no protection."[4]

Also, the B-17s' guns had been jamming at high altitudes. Brigadier General Forrest thought that switching to a different type of oil would solve the problem. Crews were directed to try the new oil on the mission.

The Forrest formation had its maiden trial on the June 13 mission. Its target was the German U-boat pens—gigantic steel-reinforced concrete bunkers—in Kiel, Germany. The U-boats were continuing to wreak havoc on Allied shipping. At 6 a.m., the 95th Bomb Group took off in two elements—one with eighteen planes and the other with eight. The lead aircraft was flown by Capt. Harry A. Stirwalt, and Brigadier General Forrest himself was strapped into the copilot's seat, flying as a passenger and observer. The 95th's top navigator, Lt. Willard "Bill" Brown, had also been selected to fly in the lead aircraft with Forrest.

In a 1977 interview, Willard Brown claimed that Brigadier General Forrest had a thing going with "Lord Haw-Haw," an English-speaking German propagandist who would taunt British and American soldiers on the radio. "Forrest would talk to him on the radio. Forrest was a climber and loved publicity. Lord Haw-Haw challenged him to fly on a raid to Germany and I think that Forrest told Haw-Haw he was coming. Thus the German Air Force knew Forrest was aboard the lead plane in the formation to Kiel on June 13."

Before the mission, General Forrest pulled Lieutenant Brown aside and asked for a favor. The married Forrest told Brown that if anything were to happen to him on the mission, he wanted Brown to make sure that his girlfriend in New York received certain items that he had on the base with him.[5]

After assembly, the group turned north, crossing the North Sea and approaching Kiel's submarine yards. Shortly after reaching the German coast, swarms of German fighters, both FW-190s and Me-109s, and some larger Junkers Ju-88s jumped the formation. In groups of three, the German fighters dived in from the front between eleven and one o'clock, their brightly painted noses of red, yellow, and black-and-white checkerboards distinguishing their fighter groups. Bursts of flame signaled the crews in the Forts that hundreds of rounds were streaking through the formation.

Bill Lindley, on *Zoot Suiters*, described the fighters:

[They appeared as] black dots on the horizon, thicker than gnats around the rear end of a camel. About the time I made the turn toward the Initial Point [the beginning of the bomb run], I told Grif Mumford, "Boy, we are in a heap of big trouble." Then all hell broke loose. The flak looked awesome but the Fw190s and Me109s would put the fear of God into anyone. . . . For the next fifteen minutes I was in a state of absolute and incredulous shock. Between the exploding flak shells, the burning aircraft going down, excited voices yelling over the radio, and those concentrated and continuous fighter attacks, I spent half the time with my head in my steel helmet ducked down behind the instrument panel.[6]

The bomber stream continued to fly straight and level toward the release point. In response to the withering fighter attack, gunners on board the Fortresses desperately tried to fire their guns, only to find that they would not fire at all or jammed almost instantly. Forrest's new lubricant was not working. Forty percent of the .50-caliber guns were unable to fire a single round in defense of the bomber stream.

The formation flew straight into the eye of the hurricane, as German fighters lined up to attack head-on. Because of the way Forrest had arranged the planes, those behind the leaders could not fire forward without hitting their own ships. Those aircraft in the front were therefore at the mercy of the German fighters.

Waist gunner Sgt. Arlie Arneson remembers, "There were B-17s out of control doing unbelievable aerobatics, exploding, on fire, going straight down in near vertical dives, shedding parachutes; one was hit so hard that the complete ball turret fell free."[7]

In pilot Johnny Johnson's plane, bombardier Leonard Herman sat in the nose and watched the horror unfold. To his dying day, Herman had only furious words for Brigadier General Forrest. "Kiel is past but not forgotten," he told me a few years ago. "Sixty years later I can still visualize the havoc and the absolute waste of both aircraft and men because some half-assed general thought he knew the score.

"Our plane started out at the back of the squadron and ended up next to the squadron lead. Of the seven planes the squadron had at the time, five did not come back from Kiel."

No plane was hit harder, however, than Captain Stirwalt's lead aircraft. The 95th's postmission report states:

> Enemy fighters in considerable strength and marked aggressiveness began their attack on the groups at a point approximately mid-way between Heligoland and the enemy coast. The attack continued to and over the target and was maintained on the briefed course back to a point off the enemy coast reported as 54 degrees 35 N and 08 degrees 30 E. In the attack before reaching the target the lead ship piloted by Captain Stirwalt, in which Brig. General Nathan B. Forrest Jr. [*sic*] was flying as a Combat Wing Commander, was seen to be hit. It was reported as continuing over the target with one engine, No. 4, smoking, dropping its bombs and then was attacked from the nose by a formation of three enemy fighters. The A/C [aircraft] was seen to slow down, to have been hit by several explosive shells and to go down banking sharply to the right. Lt. Conley, A/C No. 202, stated his belief that the lead A/C was not out of control and reported eight parachutes as having opened. Lt. Cozens pulled into the lead position of the group.[8]

In the lead aircraft, navigator Willard Brown knew his ship was in trouble. According to Brown, six or seven fighters of the Luftwaffe's Yellow Nose Group attacked before the bomb run and then broke off over the target. After the bomb run the formation turned back toward the sea, and the fighters returned. Suddenly, the entire nose section of the B-17 was shot away, killing the ship's regular navigator and the bombardier. With the aircraft at twenty-five thousand feet, Brown struggled to the exit and jumped out. He went into a free fall and waited a long time to open his chute, because the air at such a high altitude would have been too thin to breathe.

Brown landed in the shipping channel near Kiel in water that was so cold he had trouble staying awake and shivered uncontrollably in his Mae West. Brown stated in the interview that in his opinion, either the other men on the lead ship—Forrest included—opened their chutes too soon and suffocated, or if they were alive when they hit the water, they may have drowned. Also, a strong offshore wind may have prevented any other survivors from making it closer to shore and rescue. Brown floated in the frigid waters for three hours before a German vessel picked him up. He was imprisoned but escaped and returned to the States, where he delivered General Forrest's items to Forrest's girlfriend in New York. General Forrest was the first brigadier general to be killed in action in the war.[9]

Capt. John Miller was flying on Forrest and Stirwalt's right wing. On Miller's crew was a young ball turret gunner, Staff Sgt. Floyd L. "Chief" Thompson. A Cherokee Indian from Durant, Oklahoma, Thompson asked for help over the interphone during a momentary lull in the fighting. His electrically heated flight suit had short-circuited, and he had been in the freezing ball turret with no heat for many minutes. His feet were frozen. His crewmates pulled him up into the plane, took his shoes off, and rubbed his feet to restore his circulation. Before they had been working long, over the interphone came a shout: "Fighters attacking!"

As the waist gunners returned to their guns, Thompson crawled back to his guns inside the ball turret. He had left his jacket and his earphones in the radio room so he wouldn't be able to receive the order to quit his post.

After Stirwalt's plane went down and eight parachutes blossomed out, Bob Cozens immediately pulled his plane into the lead of the formation. In a postmission report, Cozens's copilot J. W. Reed stated that "the formation did not loosen up when Stirwalt went out. Without a moment's delay, Cozens pulled his ship up and into the lead of the formation." The intelligence officer added that Reed stated, "It was the most beautiful piece of flying he had ever seen."[10]

The battle in the sky raged beyond the coast. "In one instance," remembers Leonard Herman, "one plane flew up below another, and the lower plane received the bombs and blew up. There was a great deal of fire and—whammo—they were gone. . . . Those guys were going down like flies."[11]

Another B-17 in trouble was B-17F 229737, with navigator Lt. John Korman aboard. A flak hit pounded the plane, knocking out its oxygen system. The crew went on portable oxygen, but within minutes the supply in the smaller bottles began to run out. The men on board began to suffer from anoxia. Luckily, copilot Lt. Ralph Ziegler realized what was happening and jammed the control column forward, sending the plane into a steep dive.

One by one, the men began to regain consciousness, only to find themselves skimming over the surface of the North Sea alone and under attack by German fighters.

With their number 2 engine hit and number 1 smoking, the pilot lowered the landing gear, indicating to German fighter pilots the bomber's surrender. The crew prepared to ditch, but right before they went into the sea, the pilots spotted a small sandbar ahead. Pilot Lt. Laurier Morissette put the plane down on the soft sand, and the crew jumped out as fast as they could. By now the plane was burning, and ammunition was going off in all directions. There was nothing to do but watch the plane burn, and wait. After a while, the dazed crew noticed a tiny three-seat aircraft puttering over the water. It landed near the stricken B-17, and a German soldier with a submachine gun jumped out, followed by a German doctor and the pilot. Speaking English, the doctor told them that a boat had been sent from the mainland and would pick them up. They became prisoners of war.[12]

Back at Framlingham, the ground echelon sweated out the mission. Finally, a few battered and beaten Forts began to stagger back and make rough landings at the airfield. The official casualty list for the 95th runs eleven typed, single-spaced pages. Ten aircraft and a hundred men failed to return. Two more planes returned so badly damaged they had to be salvaged. One of these was Harry Conley's, written off after a crash-landing in a barley field near Rackheath, Norfolk.

Reading the casualty list of the Kiel mission is sobering and heartbreaking. Pilot W. C. Adams (aircraft 229675) and his entire crew were killed in action (KIA) and last seen west of the target. Pilot A. V. Stone (23286) and his entire crew were KIA after leaving the formation with three engines feathered and the tail damaged by flak. Pilot J. G. Peery Jr. (23106) and most of the crew survived and became POWs. They were last seen after turning off the target. Pilot J. L. Nunes (229680) and his entire crew were KIA and last seen over the target. Pilot W. D. Renaud (22964) was killed, along with his entire crew, and last seen west of the target. As noted earlier, pilot L. Morissette (229737) crash-landed, and all of the crew became POWs. Pilot C. Rubin (229763) was involved in a midair collision with Adams's plane or 230118, and all aboard were killed. Pilot K. C. Mason (229827) was listed as KIA along with all but two of his crew, who were last seen west of the target.

Pilot H. A. Stirwalt (230164) was also KIA along with all but two crewmen after parachuting into the frigid North Sea.

Further testament to the fierceness of battle is the ammunition expenditure, which the Office of the Armament Officer published the day after the battle. It reported that the eleven returning planes had shot 114,100 rounds of .50-caliber ammunition in air combat.[13]

Surviving crews returned in a state of shock. "When we landed," remembers Leonard Herman, "we went to the interrogation building, and I kept saying to Russ Kelley, our squadron adjutant, 'Kelley, they're all gone. They're all gone.' Kelley tried to comfort me. When crews got shot down, a personnel officer—I believe it was Russ Kelley—would go around and take all the letters, all the pictures, all the booze that the guys who went down had left behind in their barracks. There was some guy, an S-2, that all he did was go through personal effects and weed out all the letters and photos that suggested these guys had girlfriends in England or were scoring in the combat zone. Only after these personal effects had been gone through very carefully would they be sent home to the next of kin. They'd come and take everything away. The bed would sit there empty. It was like the guys had never existed. And then someone new would take that bed.

"After the Kiel mission, it was terrible to think that most of your friends wouldn't be with you anymore. Only one or two of the original crews were left. There was the Johnny Johnson crew and the Cliff Hamilton crew, and Cliff went down on the next mission."

Lt. William Isaacs, a 336th Squadron navigator, described his feelings upon return. "I recall how quiet and lonely it was in our barracks that night with twenty of our close friends missing. I sincerely felt that I couldn't possibly survive my tour of twenty-five missions. The odds were simply too overwhelming." And Capt. John Miller of the 412th recalls Colonel Kessler listening to the surviving crews during debriefing, "his eyes brimming with tears and very obviously extremely distressed." All Kessler could bring himself to utter was: "What's happened to my boys? What's happened to my boys?"

Bob Cozens's bombardier, Earl "Basie" DeWolf (no relation to Ted De-Wolf), was close friends with Wayne Fitzgerald of Pilot Harry Conley's crew. They had a pact that if one of them was shot down, the other would ensure his belongings were returned to the man's family. After his return from Kiel, DeWolf was devastated; Conley's ship was missing. DeWolf sat on the side of Fitzgerald's bed, sifting through his friend's possessions. As tears streamed down his face, DeWolf divided up Conley's stuff. "One for Fitz's mama, one for me," he croaked, and it would have been funny if not for the tragic circumstances. "Suddenly, a truck pulled up out front, and Fitz walked in," laughs Bob Cozens. "You can imagine what that was like." Conley's ship had not gone down after all. It had crash-landed.

"Needless to say," writes Cozens, "the 'Forrest' formation was never again flown by the 95th or any other Group. General Forrest had demonstrated his conviction that his leadership would be beneficial to the Allied air war by personally involving himself in this ill-fated mission—a mission that cost him his life and, unfortunately, the lives of many, many of the 95th Bomb Group's stalwart air crew members."[14]

Kiel did not only affect the flight crews. The ground echelon also learned a valuable lesson, one that would help them cope with the heavy losses that the aircrews suffered in the war. Joseph Florian, for instance, remembers Kiel as a milestone for the 95th in a different way:

> The harsh realities of war were brought home to us all following the Kiel Mission. [It] was a date never to be forgotten. We waited tensely for our combat crews to return. Finally, we could see some of them in the distance, but as they circled the field we could only count half the number of planes that had taken off earlier in the day.
>
> After the surviving crews had been debriefed, we waited in vain for another three hours until all possible hope of any others returning disappeared. These missing men were close friends with whom we'd trained, swapped jokes, laughed and traveled. It left a void that was impossible to write or think about.
>
> Perhaps it sounds callous, but from that day on I made a silent resolve never to get to know aircrew members well again, because the heartaches that accompany the sudden loss of such warm friendships were too great to bear.[15]

It was tough on the surviving crewmen as well. William Irving remembers,

That morning our barracks had about thirty men in it. That night there were only about fourteen of them left. The place was more like a morgue than anything else. Why shouldn't it be? After all, men don't just pass out of your life like the snap of a finger. . . .

The one little guy down the way for instance who had the nightmares every night. He was gone. No more would we sit around and listen to him and his wisecracks and laugh at and with him. There was another fellow who I remembered well. He had sat around just recently talking with another fellow about some of his troubles. His father had just died recently and he was very much upset over that. He was married and very much in love with his wife. He showed me a picture of her. . . .

Most of all though I was going to miss McNeely, Palmer's tail gunner. He was a nice quiet sort of fellow and a darn good boy, who just a couple of short weeks ago we had been to London together. It just didn't seem right, that was all. It didn't seem right that you could wake up in the morning with a group of fellows, laugh and talk with them, go eat breakfast with them and then come back in the evening and find that they wouldn't be around anymore.

The next morning some of the boys from Supply came in to clean out their clothing and pack it up. The idea of an outsider coming in to do that job didn't settle quite right with us and some of the boys went to the Major to see if we couldn't take care of the job ourselves. He gave his consent and we lost no time in chasing the Supply fellows out. It wasn't that we didn't trust them or anything but merely that it didn't seem right for someone to come in and pack their things when they didn't even know them. It was a sad job and none of us enjoyed it a bit. All the clothes were packed in the proper bags and the personal items packed in separate ones. Items such as soap and cigarettes were all piled together and put in a box out in the middle of the barracks for the use of anyone there. All the personal things were supposed to be packed away at Supply and sent home to the next of kin after a reasonable time. That was the mission and the results of June 13th, 1943, a sad day for a good many persons.[16]

The reporters covering the war developed the same code, one of an enforced personal and professional distance. War correspondent Walter Cronkite, when he took fellow journalist Harrison Salisbury on a tour of a bomber base, advised: "Don't make friends with the kids . . . It's too much when they are lost, and most of them, you know, will die."[17]

Percy Kindred once farmed the land upon which the air base sat. He watched the planes take off in the mornings and come back in the afternoons. But the Kiel operation taught him the true sacrifices the young men, whom he knew as "nice fellows and extremely generous," were making. He remembers that on June 13, "the whole group took off for another mission to Germany. About half their B-17s returned, one crash-landed, and the remainder were literally shot to pieces. This was one of my first sights, virtually outside my front door, of what those men were going through. I was stunned and shocked. What I saw that day I won't forget, ever."[18]

Ellis Scripture had not flown with his crew that day, and all were lost. He was assigned as the group navigator. That night, Colonel LeMay phoned and asked how many planes the 95th had available to fly the next day. One, he was told, and one crew. LeMay answered, "Fine. You're on alert to fly, and I will be at Framlingham early tomorrow morning to fly with them." The group didn't end up flying on June 14, but as Scripture remembers, the crew was ready and so was LeMay.

"The words 'Remember Kiel!' became our rallying cry for the remaining two long and often bitter years of the air war in Europe," writes Scripture.[19]

As evening turned to night on June 13, the members of the aircrews lay in their beds, with empty beds around them, and wondered when their own turns would come. Few slept.

The British

For several years, the American servicemen of the 95th Bomb Group and the British locals lived side by side, became friends, helped each other, and even married each other. Bonds were forged in the early 1940s that remain as strong or stronger today. When the 95th arrived, Horham had at most 150 residents, if you counted farmers nearby. It was an ancient community with a few shops and pubs along a single winding street. With the Americans' arrival from their previous base at Framlingham, Horham added a sprawling "suburb" of three thousand men.

Even before the 95th's arrival, the hamlet had seen an influx of new faces. Several British searchlight units were stationed nearby. A number of new residents were evacuees, seeking to escape the Germans' bombing of the big cities. German and Italian prisoners of war lived at nearby POW Camp 231 at Redgrave Park and worked on area farms. Land Army girls, employed by the Ministry of Agriculture and Fisheries, supplemented the diminished labor pool while most of the able-bodied men were off fighting the war.

Alan Johnson was born in 1936 in a stone house built in the thirteenth century by the village's Norman priest, named Jernigin. Appropriately, the house is known as Ancient House. Alan lives in the house to this day, and when I visited Horham in June 2008 I stayed there with him. English people in the 1200s were small, and every time I walked through a doorway, I hit my head on the doorframe. Weathered, dark wooden beams supported the walls, and in the front part of the house, where Alan's cousins live, a section of the wall was left open to show the original wattle-and-daub construction.

While Alan was a boy, his father was Horham's postmaster, and the post office was in the house itself, as it is to this day. Now Alan's cousins David Spall and his wife, Irene, run the post office and a small but well-stocked store. Just across the street is an unused building named the Green Dragon, which served as a pub during the war. A five-minute walk along the narrow sidewalk takes one past the Church of St. Mary, whose graveyard is filled with wildflowers and tall grass that ripples in the breeze. Across from the church is the village green, which Alan mows every week. In front of the redbrick wall around the church sits one of the original red British telephone booths, and beyond it is the Old School, now a social club open several days a week. Alan and I attended the club each evening, and I conducted a number of interesting interviews in its cheery, cramped interior. We walked home each night, a little unsteadily, in the pitch dark, our way illuminated by Alan's trusty flashlight.

During my weeklong visit to Horham, I took the chance to get to know many of the English people who had lived in the village during the war. Without exception, the villagers were a friendly, welcoming lot, quick to share a story and a pint. Most of the folks who remember the 95th's sojourn in their midst were either children or teenagers, as many of the older residents have passed away.

The people of Horham had known war for a number of years before the Americans arrived. Only a short distance from the North Sea, the area was well within range of German fighters, bombers, and rockets. As did most of the British people near the coast, Alan's family had a Morrison shelter in their house to protect against German bombing. A Morrison shelter was basically a box with a steel plate roof and mesh sides to safeguard the occupants from rubble. When a raid was imminent, the Air Raid Precaution (ARP) wardens in Horham would go house to house and warn everyone.

The occasional German raids were both exciting and scary for Alan and the other village children. Alan remembered standing outside his house with his father one night, watching the Germans bomb Ipswich eighteen miles away. "The whole sky was lit up by explosions," he said. Another time, he dived behind a wall as a German Messerschmitt roared low over-head, emptying its guns into the train station three hundred yards up the road. "Ten seconds later, a Mosquito [bomber] came over. Even as a little child, I felt pride, and the Mosquito shot it down before it got to the coast."

Many of the locals have grimly funny stories about German attacks. One old farmer recounted that during one attack, "when that bomb hit, my shirt-tail rolled up like a window blind!" Another farmer was milking his cows in his milking shed. Suddenly, the cow went completely rigid. Won-dering why, the farmer looked up, only to find that the roof of the shed had been blown off!

Later in the war, Alan recalled a V-2 rocket landing in nearby Hoxne, a little more than two miles away. "There was a massive explosion. The tree leaves shimmered and the birds stopped singing for a long time." Some cows on a local farm were blown to bits by German bombs.

Before the United States entered the war in December 1941, the Brit-ish people faced the German juggernaut alone. Many fully expected a Ger-man attack to be imminent. Older British men served in the Home Guard, though "the old boys could not have prevented an invasion," Alan said.

The British government initiated a Secret Army, whose units primar-ily recruited local men who could live off the land and knew the terrain. Sworn to secrecy for fifty years, these men, many of whom were farmers and thus exempt from military service, were trained to wage guerrilla war-fare against the Germans should the "Huns" manage to invade England. The Royal Engineers constructed underground bunkers, accessible by a concealed door on the surface, and in the event of an area being overrun, teams of four men were to drop everything, rush to the bunkers, and stay in dark, damp underground shelters by day, their only link to the surface a periscope. At night, they were to emerge and commit acts of sabotage and wreak as much havoc as possible. Three thousand to four thousand men joined that force during the war.[1]

After the Battle of Britain in 1940, the British people began to breathe a little easier. The German invasion of Britain was abandoned for Hitler's newest project, the invasion of Russia. Residents in Horham, meanwhile, were under strict rationing during the war, as almost everything was need-ed for the war effort. Pubs displayed signs announcing, "No cigarettes. No beer." People made do with their prewar clothing and subsisted on staples. Parents often went without to ensure their children had enough to eat.

Noel Leader was fourteen when the Yanks of the 95th arrived. In 2008, at age seventy-six, he was one of the village characters and a frequenter of the Old School Social Club, ruddy faced, with bright dancing eyes and a flashing smile, clad in a tweed sports jacket. "I watched the base get built," he said to me, his hand wrapped around a glass of cold beer. "And I watched it pulled down." Noel's family actually lived on the base, and each family member had a special pass allowing them base access. "It was wonderful!" Noel enthused. "We had plenty of food not available previously. We lived better than we do now. I'd get clothes for my mother to wash, and we could go to the PX.

"We were always around the air and ground crews," Noel remembered. "We'd go out to the planes and have a look around. I taxied around in the planes sometimes. I got to know a lot of the guys. I'd watch them leave, and a lot of them didn't come back. Several planes went down right over us. There were so many planes circling and assembling in the air at a time. I saved everything the Americans gave me, even the gum wrappers." The children commonly asked the American GIs during the war, "Got any gum, chum?" Of course, the Americans carried plenty simply for that purpose.

Alan Johnson's Aunt Marjorie Ward worked at the grocery store in nearby Stradbroke. She'd married in 1943, and her husband was off to war. One of her jobs was to deliver food to the base using the store's van, a tiny vehicle even by British standards. "I had a pass to take groceries to the base," she told me. "On November 16, 1943, I was on the perimeter track of the runway, and we saw a B-17 coming. My passenger said, 'You're going to hit that plane.' I didn't think so. The plane swung around and hit the delivery truck! The passenger had jumped out by that time and was almost to the hedge when it hit me."

The plane's propeller sliced into the side of the van, tearing off one of the doors, but luckily, Marjorie was not injured. "We couldn't get insurance for the accident because cars are not supposed to hit airplanes, are they?" she told me drily.

Alan went to the base nearly every day to visit his friends, most of whom were ground crewmen living in the dispersal huts near the hardstands.

Many other local children also befriended the Americans. Noel Leader's sister Ann was a little girl when the Yanks arrived. She made friends with an American by the name of Jack Kelly. Kelly wrote a letter to his wife back in the States, asking her to send a doll and a tea set for his girlfriend in England, little Ann. Ann was thrilled when he gave them to her a short while later.

"Every Sunday the Americans came and took us out to the mess hall," Ann recalled. "I can remember the first time I had turkey. Another flight crewman taught me how to dance, with me standing on his toes. He was shot down. He came back later especially to say good-bye and to tell me that he had got free and was all right."

Accustomed to strict war rationing, Ann was always amazed at the amount of food on the base. "When Glenn Miller came to play, there were hot dogs all over the floor. I couldn't believe the waste."

Enid Wheeler was a young girl barely into her teens when the Americans arrived. "I rode my bike to Eye Grammar School each day. Suddenly, all of Horham was a huge aerodrome. We had to stop at a sentry box, and the sentry would say, 'Stop, we have forty-eight B-17s taking off on a mission.' The road was at the end of the runway, and they shut it down for the planes. We would have to wait to bicycle on. We would wave to them as they took off. One took off, we waved to him, and this particular plane didn't quite make it and it crashed three fields away. It was the most horrendous nightmare of a thirteen-year-old girl's life."

Some Americans died in the skies over or near Horham, often while the locals watched in horror. Alan Johnson watched one day as a B-17, a straggler from another group, flew over his school playground while the kids were out on their three o'clock break for recess.

"It was a foggy day," he remembered. "I heard it coming, and I looked up. Just then, a P-47 Thunderbolt came in from the north and ran into the B-17, cutting it in two. The front section headed down immediately. The tail section began spinning down. The kids yelled, 'Get out, get out!' And the tail gunner did get out, but he was spinning, and his chute never had a chance to open. He fell to his death right near the playground."

Young Eddie Coe's mother did washing for several aircrews. He recalled,

In collecting the washing I became friendly with navigator Russell Cook, bombardier Anthony Braidic and other crew members on the Lionel Sceurman crew. I remember Lt. Braidic cycled over to Redlingfield to ask Father's permission for me to visit London and him giving consent. To a 12-year-old who had never been on a train, and certainly never been to London, this was wonderful. We went on Saturday April 28th 1945. It had been a cold night and there was a sprinkling of snow, which disappeared as we travelled onward. On arrival in the big city, we ate at Grosvenor House. In the evening I went with Lt. Cook to see the play *Tonight And Every Night* starring Rita Hayworth. On Sunday April 29th we took a tour by taxi to see the sights and the bomb damage, then a train back to Diss railway station. Back in Redlingfield my Mother made me sit down and write a "thank-you" letter to thank Lt. Cook for taking care of me. He kept this among his possessions.

On Monday May 7th Lt. Cook was navigator on B-17G 44-8640's flight to drop food to civilians in German-occupied Holland. Despite these missions being given safe conduct by German authorities it is believed that it was fired upon by an anti-aircraft gun. The plane limped home and almost made it, cartwheeling into the sea just off Benacre Ness. There were only two survivors. Lt. Cook was not one of them. B-17G 44-8640 was the last aircraft of the Eighth Air Force to be lost in Europe during World War Two.

My thank you letter was found by Lt. Cook's Mother among his possessions, and she kept it until her death. It was eventually found and copied and sent back to me years later.[2]

When Enid Wheeler was ill with the chicken pox, some Americans visited and asked if the family needed anything. "I wanted pears," remembered Enid. "The next day, some men came by with seven one-pound tins of pears and seven one-pound tins of ice cream." At her school, the 95th's commanding officer handed out the school prizes. Enid kept an autograph book of all the American airmen she knew. "The Americans gave us so much comfort," she said.

Some of Horham's older residents saw the base as a cash cow, where the rules of rationing could be circumvented. Farmers were allowed to go on base and get swill for their pigs made of the leftover food from the messes. One farmer named Barney Cook rode off the base with a bucket of swill over each handlebar. "No MP would ever reach down into a barrel of swill to check it," remembered Alan. "When Barney got off the base, he reached down into the barrels and pulled out three pints of whiskey from the bottom of each bucket."

One of the local pubs, the Worlingworth Crown, took advantage of the airmen by overcharging them and watering down the beer, much to the consternation of the other villagers. In fact, after the war, one villager refused to deal with the now-wealthy pub owner. When the man came to his shop wanting to spend some of his gains, the villager told him, "I haven't seen you all during the war. You were too busy stealing from the Yanks. Now take your money and f——k off!"

One day during the war, the locals and the Americans got their revenge on the greedy pub owners. It was a Sunday, and by law the pubs had to close at 2 p.m. The locals and the Americans drank in the Worlingworth Crown until then, and after the pub shut down, they sneaked into the nearby storage barn and found the beer stores. They knocked the bung into the barrel, went outside, and plucked some sheep's parsley, which has a hollow stem. Each man cut a piece, creating his own personal straw. They then took turns drinking out of the barrel until they had drained it. At this point, they took the empty barrel and threw the keg into a nearby moat. In memory of this small revolt, a ditty was composed titled "Have a Drink with Anna."

Pilot Ed Jacobson remembers one enterprising young woman whose backyard was only feet from his B-17's hardstand. "One day as I was running up the engines, I noticed that I'd blown her washing off the clothesline. She ran over waving her arms and I tossed her a few pounds out of the pilot's side window. After that, any time she needed money, when she saw us coming to the hardstand, she would go out and hang up her wash. I noticed she used the same basket of clothes every time. I guess I gave her too much money the first time."

Visits to the American air base were not limited to humans, either. A young Jack Russell terrier by the name of Basil paid the base a daily visit. "He was of the short-legged variety, and it took lots of steps for him to get to the base," said Alan Johnson. "He lived at the Athelington Rectory just up the road from us, about a mile away. He found out where the base canteen was, and every day he walked past our house on his way to the canteen. After he was full, he walked home." Driven by a strong sense of purpose and an empty stomach, Basil learned to appreciate the Americans as much as any human in the village.

Aircrews were not averse to having fun at the locals' expense on occasion. One dispersal area was near a small straw hut that belonged to a local. The crew chief would direct the B-17, after returning from a mission, to turn the plane around so that the prop blast would lift the little house right off the ground.

Alan remembered his visits with the ground crews well. "The ground crew had a tent there where they cleaned the guns. We didn't really know the flight crews. They lived in a different part of the base. They came back and went to their barracks. We weren't allowed to cross the main runway, so we weren't allowed to go visit them over there."

The stationmaster at the Horham railway station during the war was a man named Albert Borrett. In his unpublished memoir, he wrote of the incredible amount of material that came in and out of Horham station every day while the Americans were there. "We used to receive forty wagons [train cars] daily for the air base, and an average of ten out. Practically all the airmen's clothing, boots, parachutes and so forth came in to Horham by train." Borrett also writes of the somber task of sending out "personal belongings of airmen who had been killed or wounded in combat."

Occasionally, the Americans caused problems in the village. On one occasion, a pub owner noticed that his sign was missing one of the wooden arms that held up a frothy beer. He walked up to the sentry box nearby and said to the MP: "I know your friends have been bringing you beer. I know you've been drinking on duty. Your fellows have some of my property. If I get it back, nothing will be said." The arm was returned in short order.

Clifford Anthony was an RAF direction-finding operator stationed off the end of Horham's main runway during the war. He remembered that one day, his ex-wife's father, Charles, was traveling to Catchpole and was stopped at a railroad crossing. He went into the crossing hut to pass the time with the rail employee. Suddenly, they heard a huge explosion in the sky overhead. Charles ran outside, and parts of a plane began raining down. A body came down out of the sky and hit a wire, sparked, and crashed through the roof of the crossing hut where he'd been standing only moments before.

The British in the area formed a group called the Welcome Club. The club's purpose was to foster friendly relations between the British and the Americans. At meetings, the two groups would get together and socialize.

Marvin Casaday was a young American armorer/gunner who in 1943 flew on many dangerous missions. "I found the English quite hospitable during World War Two," he remembers. "In fact, I stayed overnight at an English family's house at Christmas, 1943. I had received some bananas, fruit, sugar and took a box of chocolates my mother had sent me. The family would take one banana, one piece of chocolate, and cut them into four pieces to make them last longer. It had been five years since they had had these delicacies." Watching the family so carefully divide this meager treasure reduced Casaday to tears.

Some of the dispersal hardstands were literally in the backyards of British houses in Horham. The crews whose planes were in a family's backyard often adopted the family and shared packages with them. However, with the 95th's heavy losses in the summer and fall of 1943, many families learned a hard lesson about getting too close to the American flight crews. Horham farmer Dick Flowerdew remembered that several American crews were quite friendly with his family, visiting their house and bringing food from their stores for his wife to cook. "We got to know them very well as time passed, but when they went out on a mission and didn't return it was most upsetting. This happened to three or four crews who used to come regularly. Finally, it became so upsetting that my wife couldn't face it anymore so, very reluctantly, we had to stop inviting the crews as our guests."[3]

Basil Rodwell was Horham's village blacksmith. He also operated a small bicycle repair shop frequented by British and Americans alike. On one occasion, the Americans smuggled Basil on base for a meal. When the duty officer approached, the men quickly stashed the diminutive Basil in the mess hall's large walk-in refrigerator. After the coast was clear, they opened the door and found Basil calmly devouring a large bowl of ice cream.[4]

Thanks to Basil's bicycle repair skills, any nice evening in the Horham area would find small groups of young airmen from the base peddling along the country lanes and on their way to various local pubs, such as the Grapes at Hoxne or the Green Dragon in Horham, and to outlying village pubs, such as the Worlingworth Swan or the Crown and the Plough in Southolt. Men also rode to Saturday dances at Dennington Village Hall.[5]

Eddie Coe from Redlingfield said, "When the Americans came to Horham they found Redlingfield's small village pub and made it their local. They swarmed across the fields and drank the place dry. 'The Crown' was tiny and there was no room inside so they would sit along the verge. It must have seemed very quaint to them, as we had no electricity in the village. The pub was lit by oil lamps and, with cigarette smoke as well, walls and ceilings were very grubby—but they loved it.

"There was a Military Police post in Redlingfield and we became friendly with those on duty. We ended up doing laundry for some of the men. Once, I was given a sandwich which I thought contained cheese—it was in fact butter. Our butter was rationed and to see so much in a sandwich was unheard of. We were also given sweets and chewing gum. Mother was given soap for washing."[6]

When the weather was good, the locals would lift up their heads from whatever they were doing and listen as the planes flew overhead. Not only were planes taking off and landing at the base at Horham, but by the end of the war they sometimes saw more than a thousand heavy bombers and hundreds of fighters in the air over East Anglia.

As a schoolboy Ian Hawkins, whose father was killed in action while serving in the Royal Navy, looked up in the sky and watched "the stunning spectacle of over one thousand four-engined B-17 Flying Fortresses and B-24 Liberator bombers in precise formation, all heading east in a clear blue morning sky, five miles high, appearing like so many small silver crosses. . . . Nothing was as reassuring or as inspiring to me in the final three years as the truly spectacular sights and sounds over Suffolk, England. The sight was unforgettable for a whole generation of East Anglians." Hawkins was so inspired by the sight of the heavy bombers that he later became a military historian and is the author of some of the greatest books about the Eighth Air Force, including *Munster: The Way it Was* and *B-17s Over Berlin*, which is the oral history of the 95th Bomb Group. Hawkins served as a collaborator and expert on this book as well.

Originally from Yorkshire, Clifford Anthony was a Brit who actually had a military role on the base. The RAF first sent him to Horham to work as a direction-finding operator for the RAF, then for the Canadians, and finally for the Americans. He had three American servicemen for assistants. They lived their own separate existence in a small wooden hut surrounded by a blast wall and directly in line with the end of the main runway, in the nearby town of Stradbroke. Their mission was to assist B-17 navigators if they got into trouble. In such a circumstance, the B-17's radio operator would contact Anthony's detachment and request a bearing to fly home. Holding the Morse key down on the radio, they would send a continuous note to Anthony and his men, who would rotate a 360-degree knob with a pointer until they couldn't hear the signal. This reading would give them the necessary heading, based on the distance traveled from four aerials set up to the north, south, east, and west of their position.

It was also possible to transmit information. This system, called Oboe, could direct bomb drops to a target.

The men had a plum job. No one from the base ever bothered them, and they never had to endure inspections or other inanities of traditional base life. Their hut had two bunk beds, and they lived on their own. Every so often, men from the base drove a Jeep over to them and delivered rations, and they cooked their own meals. Rarely did anything exciting happen. The job could be tedious, as they had to transmit every fifteen minutes, twenty-four hours a day. Other than the occasional lost aircraft from another base, they weren't called on often for navigational help.

Anthony remembered that he occasionally "scrounged tinned fruit from the base and mailed it by post to my parents—but never from the local post office." After the second bombing of London, though, Anthony had his family evacuated to Stradbroke. His father died and is buried there, but the rest of the family eventually returned to London. Anthony, however, lives in Stradbroke to this day.

"I got along well with the American soldiers," Anthony said. "They were noncoms. One was nearly forty. He used to stand in front of the wash basin mirror and watch himself play the violin."

Anthony met and became engaged to a girl in Stradbroke. They married near the end of the war and went on their honeymoon. "When I got back, there wasn't a soul there. Everyone had gone home." Anthony became the longest-tenured serviceman on the base, being the first to arrive and last to leave.

Just like that, the Americans were gone. The base sat empty, the hardstands silent. The lush Suffolk vegetation began to reclaim the airfields, hardstands, and buildings. The farmers returned to their land, and the buildings became storage sheds. The English blew up the control tower as they considered it to be a safety hazard. Horham was once again a tiny village of 150 souls. It took a long time for its residents to get used to the new quiet.

Occasionally, an American wandered into the village, and it almost invariably happened he was a former airman from the base. These visits were few and far between. The majority of the airmen had returned to America and were building their postwar lives: working, buying a home, getting married, and raising a family. Most were trying to put the war behind them. It was too early to feel a great deal of nostalgia, and the pain of lost friends still forced many to push the war years to the deeper recesses of their memory.

Meanwhile, in England, confronted by the abandoned and derelict base and the constant reminders of the lively presence of three thousand young American airmen, it was harder to push the war years aside. Alan Johnson worried about the brilliant murals painted on the brick walls of the NCO Club, called the Red Feather Club. Painted by a young 95th staff sergeant named Nathan Bindler, they depicted scenes right out of medieval and Renaissance English literature.

"We used to go up there and play after the war," remembered Alan. "And by the nineteen seventies, you couldn't see the buildings for the trees, shrubbery, and rubbish. A chicken farm had been built next door to the Red Feather Club by a farmer named Mr. Mager, and the club buildings were in ruins, some used to rear rabbits and chickens and others to house

Mager's farm machinery. The structures gradually fell into disrepair, the corrugated sheets on the roofs rusted, [and] deterioration became even more rapid."

In 1981 a group of local enthusiasts called the Friends of the 95th bought the buildings from Mr. Mager. They raised money to reroof and insulate the room containing the famous Bindler murals, which were still in good condition despite the elements.

That same year, some American veterans returned to the base, visited the buildings, and saw the murals. A small team of volunteers kept the site tidy. Alan Johnson remembered going over to the land during the next fifteen years, cutting the grass and doing routine maintenance. The former group flight surgeon, "Doc" Steele, became interested in the project. Alan promised Steele he would keep forging on. And when locals questioned his commitment to the project, asking him why he was interested in what happened sixty years ago, Alan responded, "Six hundred and seventeen young lives."

Over time, Alan gathered a small but dedicated cadre of locals interested in the project. With his friends John Blott, Andrew Castleden, Frank Sherman, and others, he set out to rebuild the collapsing Nissen hut that housed the Red Feather Club. It was a daunting project. The hoops that held up the hut's metal roof had fallen in a tangled, twisted heap, so they had to straighten and weld new bottoms on all the hoops. They also had to manufacture new doors and windows, trying hard to use original material for everything. Referring to photographs, they researched the original building and painstakingly reconstructed the building and its rooms as close to original as possible. This effort included building a new wall that a farmer had demolished so that he could store his combine harvester in the building.

In 2000, the Suffolk County Council passed a local initiative titled "Friars to Flyers" to publicize the area's airfields and priories. A new nonprofit group called the Horham Airfield Heritage Association was formed, and Andrew Castleden chaired it. The group applied for and received a lottery Heritage grant of £20,000 and promised to match labor costs. Volunteers donated seventy thousand hours of labor to the Red Feather Club project. The association held its first "Open Day" for the public in October 2000.

In 2003, the group applied for a Local Lottery Heritage Initiative grant. The money would allow the group to fully restore the buildings. The Friends of the 95th Group and the Horham Airfield Heritage Association merged and became the 95th Bomb Group Heritage Association.

During my 2008 visit, the group recently had received word that it had been awarded a grant to construct a large building on the front of the Red Feather Club that would be used for dances and other community activities. In the spring of 2009, the building opened with a big band dance.

Today, the Red Feather Club lives again as a museum and meeting place. It even has the original bar. The lovely murals are haunting and spectacular on the interior walls. Its museum collection of 95th Bomb Group items continues to grow, and tourists make their way to see it each week. Several times a year, the group holds an "Open Day," when the public is invited to visit for free. Each May there is a Grand Open Day, often with a flyover by a real B-17. Local schoolchildren come to the museum on field trips. Artist John Blott has painted the outline of a B-17 on the floor, and the children sit in the different crew positions of the aircraft as they learn about it.

Another committed Englishman is Tony Albrow, who with his wife Val purchased the derelict remains of the old 95th Bomb Group Hospital from a local farmer. The buildings had been used as chicken sheds, a pig shed, a grain store, and finally as a mushroom farm. The Albrows bought it and began restoring it to its wartime condition as a museum. Tony took me through the Hospital Museum in 2008, each of fourteen rooms filled with original equipment and lovingly restored to as close to original as possible. It was quite evident that it's been a labor of love for him. One can wander through the dentist's office, the infirmary, and even the mortuary and get a feel for what the hospital was like during the war.

Bob Capen, a ball turret gunner in the 95th, explained to me how the community and the base were linked through time. "The British really appreciated us Yanks. . . . I've had British strangers shake my hand and thank me for our help during the war—even youngsters. They seem to spend more time learning the history of the war than our kids do, though that seems to be changing recently somewhat."

Today, the village of Horham is a sleepy hamlet once again. But a chance visitor to the village would know fairly quickly that Horham was once attached to the U.S. Air Force. Across from the Church of St. Mary, separated from the village green by a small hedge, is a marble monument in the classic swooping shape of a B-17 tail dedicated to the 95th Bomb Group. If you walk across the street and into the church, you will notice the needlework on some of the kneelers has colorful Eighth Air Force wings or a Flying Fortress or even a red feather, the group's heraldic symbol.

Though the war years are fading into the distant past, the 95th Bomb Group is still very much alive and well in Horham and in the surrounding Suffolk countryside. The 95th lives on in the memories of villagers, in the restored buildings, the memorial, and the bells in the Church of St. Mary. And if one has time, one can trudge through grasses, ferns, and vines and past ancient trees to the remains of the old base. On a still day, one can hear the sounds of laughter, the scraping of wooden chairs in the briefing room, and the whispers of ghosts.

7 Cold Sky

Instead of breaking the spirit of the 95th Bomb Group, the June 13 Kiel mission turned the group from greenhorns into a collection of highly motivated, deeply integrated, and more cynical young men. The 95th had been dealt two potential knockout blows in a short time—first the tragic accident at Alconbury, then the battle over Kiel—but in both instances, the men of the bloodied group picked themselves off the floor and got on with their grim business.

Though the American press heralded Kiel as a great victory, the group's official assessment of the bombing's results was "poor to good." Roger Freeman writes that "bombing at Kiel was suspect, only 16 aircraft having dropped in the harbor area." And it wasn't until late in the war, when Allied armies had overrun the sub pens, that they discovered the bombs dropped on Kiel had done little damage to the bunkers or the submarines inside.

"A sense of shock pervaded the bases of the 94th and 95th Bomb Groups [the evening of June 13]," writes Freeman. "The boisterous youngsters of a month previous, or rather those who remained, reached a state of psychological disquiet far quicker than the airmen of the pioneering Groups the previous winter. After only nine missions, nearly half of the original crews and aircraft were gone, and many a young airman at Bury [St. Edmonds] and Framlingham could see no future beyond the next few missions: morale was but a word."[1]

On June 15, the 95th BG moved, en masse, from the base at Framlingham to the new base a dozen miles away at Horham. Roger Freeman attributes the move to the uncompleted condition of the Framlingham base, which later became the base for the 390th Bomb Group. Horham was the 95th's home for the rest of the war.

According to *Contrails II*, "The 95th moved by road, and with their own motor power. The Ground Echelon packed up everything from shirts to large hunks of machinery into Jeeps and trucks, climbed in on top and set out. Villagers for miles around gaped at the winding caravan. MPs stationed at every crossroads showed the way. They arrived in style, set up in a hurry and prepared to put new pages in their combat diary."[2]

Joseph Florian, normally a ground gripper, was invited to fly to the new base with one of the aircrews. This flight provided him "with the opportunity to view the earth's pattern. A green patchwork of fields and dense, wooded areas. Red poppies appeared vividly from several fields and roadside verges during the short flight to our new airfield."[3]

William Irving of the *Yankee Queen* also remembers flying the short hop from Framlingham to Horham, combining the move with a one-hour practice mission, though the flight to Horham only would have taken five minutes. "Our first concern upon landing was to get to our area and pick out a bed before all the choice spots were taken. . . . One good feature about the place was that there was barracks for Ground Personnel" rather than tents.[4]

On June 22, 1943, the group was shaken by the news that its beloved commanding officer, Col. Alfred A. Kessler, was being promoted out of the group. His replacement was Lt. Col. John Gerhart, formerly of Brigadier General Eaker's Command Staff and one of the original officers assigned to the Eighth Air Force upon its establishment in January 1942.[5] Kessler, the wily old World War I veteran and pioneer military pilot, had taken and molded the disparate group of young men into a cohesive and proud fighting unit. His men would never forget him. *Contrails II* calls Kessler the "Father of the Ninety-Fifth."[6]

Florian recalls East Anglia as "a totally unspoiled area of England, gently undulating farmlands, quaint Old World villages, founded on the wealth of trade with Europe dating back to the Middle Ages, with half-timbered houses and ancient churches. It has immensely wide skies and a network of rivers and tributaries that meander quietly past tree-lined fields and marshlands to wind their way into the North Sea."[7]

On June 22, the 95th took off for the city of Hüls in western Germany. Replacement aircraft and crews had arrived, and twenty aircraft thundered off Horham's broad, 6,337-foot-long runway, surrounded by dancing red poppies and ripening wheat. Curious villagers turned out to watch as the Fortresses rose into the morning sky at 7:20 a.m. Sixteen made it to the target, a plant that produced 30 percent of the reich's synthetic rubber. Roger Freeman writes that this bombing run represented "the first large-scale penetration of the Ruhr industrial pocket. A quarter of the bombs dropped exploded in the factory area, rendering the plant inoperative for a month."[8]

Four enemy aircraft attacked pilot Joel Bunch's aircraft and shot off 230211's nose and tail right after it dropped its bombs. Bunch was able to level the craft out at 5,000 feet, and the entire crew parachuted out. They became POWs.

Bunch, the 95th's Group operations officer, remembers: "Very shortly after 'bombs-away' we took a hit and things began to happen. Our aircraft . . . was seriously disabled; Lieutenant Harold King, our navigator, was mortally wounded; we were forced to leave the Group's formation; and the order was given to abandon the plane." Bombardier John Pearson pushed the seriously wounded King out of the nose hatch, pulled King's rip cord, and hoped the Germans on the ground would give King quick medical attention. Pearson then bailed out but struck the still-open bomb bay doors with his legs, one of which German doctors would have to amputate later. Bunch hurt his back when his chute opened, and hitting the ground worsened his injury. He crawled into some trees, but German sentries captured him, stripped him of his clothing, beat him up, and threw him into the city jail at Wesel. He spent the next sixteen months as a POW at Stalag Luft III in Sagan.[9]

On the mission, 170 B-17s dropped 1,202 five-hundred-pound bombs and 242 thousand-pound bombs. The mission report later noted that the crews' morale afterward was quite high.

Throughout the rest of June, the 95th flew three more missions: numbers 11, 12, and 13. Number 11, on June 25, targeted Bremen with no losses. The twelfth mission, on June 28, was to Saint-Nazaire, France. The Fort piloted by W. R. Thomas, 23267, was so badly damaged that it ended up crash-landing in the English Channel. Luckily, the crew was rescued and returned to duty. A similar fate, also with a happy ending, befell the R. M. Smith crew, though two crewmen were wounded.

During the Saint-Nazaire mission, pilot Robert "Spook" Bender had managed to baby his plane 23026 back toward England after losing an engine. The crew also discovered that the refueling crew at Horham had not filled their long-range "Tokyo" fuel tanks, and the men began throwing out everything they could to lighten the load as they crossed the Channel. When the plane ran out of gas, Bender ditched about sixty miles short of the English coast and forty miles off the French coast of the English Channel. Once aboard the life rafts, a head count showed they were missing a major from Wing Headquarters who had flown along as an observer. They spotted him standing on the wing of the sinking plane and yelling that he couldn't swim. Copilot Don Merten and another crewmember, Willie Isaacs, took off their clothes and swam to his rescue, but as the major was climbing into the raft, his knife punctured it.

Merten dryly reports: "Eventually we got the leak plugged with the repair kit, as 'Spook' gave our 'super-cargo' a non-stop verbal barrage while the major held his thumb on the leak." The men coaxed their box kite with an antenna to fly, and the radio operator tapped out distress signals as the others ate chocolate or took turns vomiting over the side.

Finally two British motor torpedo boats rescued the men, and eventually they returned to Horham. However, "Spook" Bender would not fly again. As Merten recalls:

> He'd lost a lot of weight and was usually shaking like a leaf. Who could blame him? All he could talk about was "all them Focke-Wulfs" and "all that flak". About this time Bill Lindley and "Spook" went to see a movie in the nearest big town, Ipswich. They sat in the first row of the balcony but the projectionist made a big mistake when he showed the latest newsreel before the movie, with nothing but German fighters attacking B-17s of the Eighth Air Force. "Spook" went slightly berserk. He crouched down behind the rail of the balcony and kept screaming for his gunners to "SHOOT! SHOOT! SHOOT!" Bill managed to calm him, get him outside, and then they took a taxi back to Horham.[10]

On June 29 the group bombed Le Mans with no losses, but the stress of combat was affecting many aircrews by this time. After the intense fighter and flak attacks they encountered on nearly every mission, the weary crews brought many Fortresses home that appeared more sieve than airplane. Tails and parts of wings were shot off, engines were blown, or propellers were missing.

Ground crews toiled day and night to have the planes ready should they need to go up the next day. The ground crews and support personnel had a high esprit de corps. Art Watson, who worked in bombsight maintenance, told me, "Our job was to put up the best airplane on every mission. We usually had guys in our shop twenty-four hours a day."

In its first two months in combat, the 95th flew fifteen missions, losing twenty aircraft—ten on Kiel alone—and 207 men, and were credited with destroying seventy-one German aircraft. It was a rough start. The men on base, both air crewmen and ground personnel, braced themselves for an even tougher summer.

 # DNIF: Duties Not Involving Flying

The transient aircrews, which were made up of only about five hundred of the three thousand men on base at any given time, would arrive, fly their missions, and leave after around six months. Meanwhile, much of the ground echelon at Horham showed up at the beginning of the war and stayed for the duration. The ground personnel—also known as ground grippers, ground pounders, or paddle feet—were thus able to forge strong bonds with each other and with Horham. As for the feelings between the airmen and the ground personnel, one has only to go to a reunion and listen to the conversations and the toasts to realize how much the flyboys appreciated the men who kept both them and their planes ready to fly day after day.

Grif Mumford writes: "As in most war stories, the men who flew in combat get the most space, attention, and acclaim; but the people on the ground, the people who handled the million details and who made sure that men and planes would fly, deserve much more credit than they ever received."[1]

Pilot Marion Turner of the 335th Squadron wrote to me in 2010. He noted that at a reunion in the early 1980s all the stories related to combat crews, mission losses, and so forth. "I finally asked at a group meeting, 'Does anyone ever talk about our support people like aircraft mechanics, armaments people, administrative staff (ground pounders) and medical personnel?' I got a standing ovation. I think there are so many of the smaller heroes like cooks and bakers and truck drivers and Charge of Quarters that have never been given enough credit. They must feel no one remembers them or is aware that they were also an important part of our Bomb Group. It is too late to rectify these omissions to most of them personally—they're gone! But I do hope you will give due credit in your history to convey their contributions and vital support to our missions."

Bob Cozens, who as a squadron commander spent more time than most did with air crewmen at Horham, goes out of his way at each reunion to thank the ground personnel in attendance, and at reunions distinctions between rank and flight status are tossed out the window. Everyone is treated as family.

It took roughly twenty ground personnel to provide the logistical support for one Eighth Air Force combat flier. Each base had men working in no fewer than sixty-eight key operations, ranging from mechanics and sheet metal workers to cooks and military policemen. Art Watson, who worked at Horham as a bombsight and Automatic Flight Control Equipment technician, said it best: "What made the 95th as effective as it was is that the group functioned as a team. Everybody worked together. It was a very professional outfit, from the top to the lowest rank. Everybody did their job and everybody helped others do their job when help was needed."

The ground echelon at the Horham heavy bomber base was organized as follows. At the top of the ground hierarchy was the 95th Bomb Group Headquarters Staff, responsible for managing the day-to-day operations of the base and planning the missions. Also on base were the 8th Base Station Complement, the 18th Weather Detachment, the 49th Service Group, the 64th Service Squadron, the 215th Finance Office, the 271st Medical Dispensary, the 433rd Headquarters and Base Service Squadron, the 457th Sub Depot, the 683rd Air Matériel Squadron (Armament), the 859th Air Engineering Squadron, the 879th Air Chemical Company, the 1029th Ordnance Company, the 1210th Quartermasters Company, the 1285th Military Police Company, the 1676th Ordnance Supply and Maintenance (S&M) Company, and the 2022nd Engineers Fire Fighting Battalion.[2]

Because Horham was so close to the North Sea, Luftwaffe fighters frequently attacked. Air defense and security forces manned searchlights, stationary antiaircraft guns, and mobile .50-caliber guns mounted on the backs of Jeeps. The 1285th Military Police provided routine security, patrolling the base on motorcycles and in Jeeps.

The 2022nd's firemen protected the base and its surroundings from the ever-present danger of fire. Planes crashed with disturbing frequency, often loaded with high-octane aviation fuel and tons of bombs. When there was trouble, the firemen "would roar out of their fire house with a flourish, their wire-haired mutt poised on a coil of hose, his tail curling in the breeze," relates *Contrails II*.[3]

The Service Squadron provided "recreation, entertainment, information, and on occasion a little fatherly advice. They maintained a roadside stand where the soldiers might find out when the next truck to the train station departed, what was the next train to London, [and] what pubs were likely to be open in Norwich. They also provided a theater with movies and shows, sponsored an athletic program and in general busied themselves dreaming up ideas for the soldier's leisure hours."[4] Photos show men lined up for a "liberty run" to London or Norwich and in language and typing classes, and a well-stocked Orientation Room and library.

Training personnel kept the airmen's skills sharp. The base had its own Link flight simulator, a boxlike contraption mounted to repeat the movements of an aircraft when controlled by a pilot. It also had a turret trainer and radio school. Crews spent many hours in sometimes dull but nonetheless important training school sessions.

Sending up balloons and taking readings, the 18th Weather Detachment monitored atmospheric conditions. The 879th Air Chemical Detachment ran gas mask drills and had a special vehicle for decontaminating aircraft or personnel. The 215th Finance Depot handled payroll for the entire Thirteenth Combat Wing. At the peak of the war, the depot handled over a million dollars of payroll.

The 1210th Quartermasters kept the group well supplied with everything from blankets to uniforms. The company had departments for transportation, communications, ordnance and armament, flying control, and a Parachute and Dinghy Shop.

The 271st Medical Dispensary ran the base hospital, which was equipped to handle everything from common illnesses to emergency room trauma. A small fleet of ambulances—commonly referred to as meat wagons—were on hand at every takeoff and landing. Dentists filled cavities and pulled teeth.

The 457th Sub Depot, originally formed as the 64th Squadron of the 49th Service Group, trained in Walla Walla, Washington. It joined the 95th Bomb Group and accompanied the group overseas. The 457th was in charge of two large hangars; all major repair shops, including sheet metal, instruments, and parachutes; and performed much of the battle damage repair on the group's aircraft. Each plane had a designated ground crew to service and fiercely protect it.

On mission day, one could find most of the available ground personnel sweating out the mission. First, the men wandered over and watched the Forts thunder one by one down the runway and disappear as small specks in the sky. Hours passed. The men knew when the planes were supposed to return and, in the final hour before the first specks appeared, walked over to the runway, coughing nervously, looking for that one plane that held a friend or an acquaintance.

Ground personnel also learned early on to keep a certain personal distance from the fliers. As noted previously, they found too many of the young airmen simply did not return from missions, especially in the beginning of the war. There were exceptions to this self-imposed distance, however. Bombardier Leonard Herman became friends with a man named Abe in the parachute-rigging department. After returning from his twenty-fifth and final mission, Herman felt an uncomfortable lump under his pillow when he retired for the evening. Reaching under his pillow, he found a bottle of champagne. The parachute rigger had bought it for Herman to celebrate the end of his tour. Herman treasured the rigger's gesture so much that he saved the cork, which is now in the 95th Bomb Group's Red Feather Club Museum at Horham.

Neal Connelley Jr. worked in Group Operations at 95th Headquarters. Connelley typed up reports for the group navigator and bombardier. "We'd check late in the evenings for any mission alerts," he remembers. "We'd do the preliminary work on the navigation routes that came from Third Division Headquarters. If a mission wasn't scrubbed, we'd contact the lead bombardier and the lead navigator. They would come down and go over the work we had done. Then we'd go with them to the briefing for air crews in the early morning.

Frank Knox also worked at Group Headquarters in communications. "There were the four squadrons, each one having an assigned communications officer. What we did was to divide up the major tasks, so that one officer was responsible for the maintenance of radios aboard the planes, and another officer was responsible for maintenance of the radio school. We had to provide refresher instruction to the radio operators and give them an opportunity to maintain their Morse Code speeds. We also were responsible for operating the telephone system on the base. It had been installed by the British Post Office. We had to provide personnel to operate it so that we would have crews on duty at the switchboard to answer the phones and direct the calls. We also had a Teletype system that needed an operator. I had a Staff Sergeant and a couple of other airmen to take care of office work.

"In addition to all of this, I was ultimately responsible for the Radio Direction Finder Station on the base. I went out once a month to that station to inspect it and to report in my monthly inspection sheet that it was operating satisfactorily. Most of my work during the war seemed to be evening or nighttime work, because I was responsible for briefing the crews. When a Field Order came in, about eight o'clock in the evening, we all went to work to do our part in preparation for the briefing—mine on radio aids to navigation.

"We had what is known by the crewmembers as a flimsy, which was a transparent, rigid case with a hinged lid inside of which you could place a sheet of rice paper. On that rice paper was typed all of the necessary information on radio aids, frequencies and the like. You could use both sides of the paper. When a crew was shot down, it was their responsibility to dispose of that sheet of rice paper, usually by eating it."

Dr. Jack McKittrick was one of the 95th's flight surgeons. "We had a lot of problems [with aircrews] early on," he recalls. "A big problem was frostbite, especially in the waist [of the plane] because of its open windows. If the gunners removed their gloves their hands froze. Battle fatigue was another problem. I administered Sodium Pentathol to relieve memories."

Some of McKittrick's own memories are gruesome. Starting in mid-1944, McKittrick observed frequent midair collisions in the area. (According to McKittrick, they happened nearly every day.)

If I was Officer of the Day I'd have to go and pick up whatever was left. Occasionally I found that I'd known some of the crewmen that were involved. A mid-air crash is the worst crash in the world, and you compound that with 500-pound, high-explosive bombs. I can remember going along and picking out a perfectly dissected human heart from a bush. The twisted remains of a crewman would resemble a gnarled tree trunk. It was horrible. The first time I did it, I couldn't eat for a week.[5]

Adam Hinojos was an enlisted man who worked at the 457th Sub Depot. "This group did all the heavy repairs on the B-17s and all the heavy transportation equipment," he remembers. "The crew chiefs of each aircraft did the minor repairs, but the Sub Depot did the main repairs on the planes, such as armory, gunnery, radio, engine replacement, bombsights, painting, parachutes and so forth. It also kept track of all fuel and parts, and supplied the parts needed to the individual crew chiefs.

"By the end of the war, 95th Bomb Group aircraft had flown enough miles to take them around the world twenty-five times, consumed thirty-five million gallons of gasoline, flown 321 combat missions and numerous practice missions, and dropped nearly 20,000 tons of bombs.

"A comprehensive range of highly skilled specialists, tradesmen, and their assistants made up from well over 2,000 ground personnel made the accomplishments of our flight crews possible—all played an important part in the very complex organization that was the 95th.

"During one ninety-one day period between 1 April and 30 June 1944, men on the base often worked round the clock to do general maintenance on 570 aircraft (of which 205 were battle damaged) . . . and changed 153 aircraft engines. The engine-change time—including hanging, pre-oiling, and ground-testing time—averaged one day." Hinojos also made daily mail deliveries by Jeep all over the widely dispersed base.

Ted Lucey spent the entire war with the 95th. Lucey wanted to join a flight crew and tried several times for a job as a radio operator/gunner. Though he asked for waivers on the age and color-blindness rules, the service turned down his request. Instead, he was relegated to ground duty. He remains proud of his service, however. "You did what you were told to do, with only a normal amount of bitching. You were no hero . . . but neither were you a slacker.

"If you'd been assigned to a B-17 or B-24, you'd have flown. If the selection process had put crossed rifles on your lapel badge, instead of a propeller and wings, you'd have slogged along in the infantry. If your uniform had been blue, you'd have taken your chances with [a] U-Boat or kamikaze. If your basic training had been at LeJeune, you'd have been at Guadalcanal or Iwo. You did your bit, whatever form it took.[6]

Carl Voss was an airplane engine mechanic who arrived in England in March 1943 and stayed until August 1945. The only mechanical training he had prior to the war was fixing his own car. He admits that most of his training was "OTJ—on the job." "I was strictly an engine mechanic," he told me. "I started as the cleaner. The lowest-ranking man would always get that duty because we had to clean outside. I first went over there as a PFC [private first class]. I forget when the next guy came in, and I got off that and moved up to the engine itself, working on changing accessories.

"The engines would be shipped to Horham in a box. We'd take it out of the box, put it on the engine stand, take the old accessories off of the old engine, repair them, and put them on the next engine. Then we would stack them, line them up. They were all different. They all had different assemblies for the position that they were in on the aircraft. When we saw an aircraft coming back with a feathered engine, we would run back to our hangar, get an engine, take it to the hardstand where that aircraft came in, take the engine off, put the new one on, pre-oil it, run it up, and turn it over to the Crew Chief for the next day's mission.

"When an engine had a hole in it, or had flak damage, or had a damaged hydraulic line, or had a cylinder missing, or exhaust pulled out, we would clean them. Then we would put them on the new assembly."

To get a new or repaired engine onto the plane itself, Voss and his crew used an A-frame. "The A-frame had a hand crank on it. A couple of your buddies would help you. Sometimes we used a Jeep or some sort of carrier we'd hook up to it, and push it up to the aircraft. We'd take the old one off, and then hang the new one. It was really something how crude the engines were at that time, as far as engine repair. Now you go out and work on your car, it's got lock nuts and so forth. We used to drill holes ourselves and then safety-wire them with 35,000-pound safety wire. The Wright-Cyclone engines they used on the B-17 was a good engine, though.

"Sometimes we worked around the clock. We worked when we had to work. When work had to be done, everybody was there.

"We lived in tar paper shacks. We had a sergeant who had a wire-haired terrier. We'd be playing cards around the pot-bellied stove. This dog would hear the German buzz bombs first, and he would head for his room and hide under the bunk. That was our cue to head for the bomb shelters."

Voss fulfilled his dream of flying combat when he flew on one of the last combat missions of the war. He also flew on several of the Manna/ Chowhound missions that delivered food and supplies to the starving Dutch people at the war's end.

Dr. Elvin D. "Doc" Imes, another member of the 95th's ground echelon, flew missions but only so that he could understand how the men he treated were affected physically and psychologically by aerial combat. According to Joel Bunch, Imes "was never too busy to tend the lowest in rank as quickly as the brass. His risked his life to participate in several tough bombing missions to learn, and experience personally, the effects of high altitude, freezing temperatures, combat fatigue, strain, and other factors that the combat crews experienced."[7]

With the job title of bombsight technician and automatic pilot technician, Art Watson was a specialist who worked on some of the most delicate and secret components on the B-17, including the Norden bombsight, and was trained in all AFCE. He received eight weeks of specialized training from Honeywell Corporation, the company that produced the Norden bombsight, at a training school at the University of Minnesota. Watson learned how to clean the servomotors and amplifiers and to balance and adjust the gyros inside the sight.

"Early in the war, every aircraft was equipped with a Norden bombsight," remembers Watson. "They were top secret. I couldn't go anywhere without a guard during training. As the war went on, only the lead aircraft had a bombsight. The other planes had toggliers, men who would drop on the lead plane's command." Toggliers had replaced bombardiers in these planes when it was decided that all bombs would be dropped on a single lead bombardier's cue.

The Norden bombsight was a technical marvel. It was linked to the aircraft's autopilot, and while the plane was on the bomb run, the bombardier technically flew the aircraft. The Norden was also immune from the jarring bumps and jolts common in a combat aircraft, as a series of gyroscopes held the sight steady.

Before each mission, Watson and his crew visited each aircraft and adjusted the Norden and the automatic pilot. Watson soon became known as an expert technician, and when the Eighth Air Force ran into a serious problem with its B-17 superchargers at high altitudes, they sent Watson to a special training school in Blackpool, England, again run by the Honeywell Corporation.

A supercharger is a mechanism mounted on the engine that forces air into the intake manifold so that more oxygen is available. This is vital at the high altitudes where the B-17s commonly flew. The B-17 supercharger was of the turbo type. It had a turbine, or impeller, driven by the engine's exhaust gas, which in turn drove a fan that forced more air into the manifold and supplied the needed oxygen to the carburetor. Pilots in the cockpit controlled a waste gate that could either increase or reduce the amount of exhaust gas directed through the impeller and thus the amount of oxygen being forced into the carburetor.

Early model B-17s had a flaw in the waste gate system. Since the superchargers operated hydraulically, they tended to work sluggishly at high, cold altitudes. In 1944, the B-17s' superchargers were upgraded to an electronic rather than a hydraulic control system. The electronic system was immune to the vicissitudes of cold and altitude; however, a new problem developed. Flight crews noticed that the manifold pressure tended to oscillate at high altitudes on one or more engines, threatening the performance of the aircraft and creating the very real hazard of a blown cylinder head.

In mid-1944, the 95th flew Watson to Blackpool to figure out what to do with the new supercharger. After review, Watson discovered the problem was in the electronic supercharger control overspeed circuit. "I redesigned the circuit and reassembled the supercharger and reinstalled it on the aircraft. After much testing, I made out a technical order, which explained the change to Division Maintenance. It was forwarded to Honeywell and they approved and implemented the design change. It was henceforth installed on all new aircraft coming off the assembly line."

Brig. Gen. N. B. Harbold awarded Staff Sgt. Art Watson the Legion of Merit on April 7, 1945, for his contribution to making high-altitude bombing safer. The Legion of Merit is given to service personnel who have distinguished themselves by exceptionally meritorious conduct in the performance of outstanding services. As do most of his brethren in the 95th, Art Watson deflects accolades. Though he is proud of his contribution, he says that in the end, he was simply doing his job.

Before the war, George Betts had worked as an upholsterer. Because aircraft at the time were partially made of fabric, his knowledge of fabric and sewing machines helped him advance quickly during his time in the Eighth Air Force. After entering the service in June 1941, Betts was sent to Fresno, California, where he and others took a test to determine who would end up as job foreman. Because of his civilian training, Betts received the best grade and after only four months in the air corps was promoted to department head. Betts was assigned to the 95th Bomb Group's 457th Sub Depot.

He writes, "We were in England for 27 months. When the planes came in after a mission the ground crews examined them. If they could be made ready to fly the next day they had to be repaired. Since the ailerons, elevators, and rudders were covered with fabric that was our job. If there were just small flak holes that could be repaired we did that so they could fly. If they were badly damaged they would be removed and replaced. If possible they would be rebuilt by the Sheet Metal shop and then we would replace the fabric. Eventually we had a wall in our hangar almost covered with spares.

"I had a paint shop and a sewing room. After we had been there a while the Yankee ingenuity began to surface and many of the men in the shop came up with ways to make money, as they were all craftsmen. It wasn't hard; they made all kinds of cigarette lighters, picture frames, and letter openers. As there was a constant supply of new customers in the flying personnel, two of the men in my shop also became very accomplished on the sewing machines. We had a large steam iron for the fabric and the men were soon running a pressing and alterations business."[8]

One of Betts's jobs involved designing and building plush booths with recessed lighting for the Officers' Club. A young artist on the base named Nathan Bindler visited Betts's shop on a regular basis. "He came in a lot because I had access to all the paint," remembers Betts. Bindler made extra money on base painting aircraft and the crewmen's leather flight jackets. He then began his most ambitious and lasting project, painting the large murals on the walls of the Red Feather Club. Sadly, Bindler passed away without seeing the later efforts to restore his work; in fact, he never returned to England after the war.

The men on the ground who supported the 95th had many interesting stories. The bottom line remains: no member of a World War II heavy bombardment group is unimportant, and truly a group is only as successful as its weakest and strongest links. What made the 95th Bombardment Group such a distinguished and effective unit in World War II was the commitment of its men, from top to bottom, to excellence and teamwork.

From Kiel to the Eve of Regensburg

During the final weeks of July 1943, the U.S. Army Air Force joined the night-bombing Royal Air Force for the first time in a sustained bombing of targets beyond the Rhine River. By taking the air war deeper into enemy territory, however, the Fortresses of the Eighth Air Force became even more vulnerable to the elite units of the German Luftwaffe. The P-47 Thunderbolts and British Spitfires had insufficient range to accompany the Forts this deep into enemy territory. And if a bomber went down on these runs, the crew's chances for escape or evasion were slim.

The first mission for what would become known as Blitz Week occurred on July 24, when a large force of bombers attacked targets in German-occupied Norway. Though at takeoff the skies over England were shrouded in clouds, a new navigational aid known as Splasher beacons allowed the planes to assemble in heavy overcast with less risk of collision. The Splasher beacons were British medium-frequency radio stations situated at intervals across the East Anglian countryside that allowed the bomber force to take off, climb on instruments, and assemble in group formation around one of three beacons.[1] A total of 324 Fortresses took off from English bases. The First Bomb Wing attacked a newly constructed German nitrate factory at Herøya, Norway, and it was out of commission for more than three months.

The 95th's Fortresses, equipped with long-range Tokyo tanks, were assigned more distant targets—the harbors at Bergen and Trondheim, 950 miles away. This job would become the 95th Bomb Group's longest overwater mission of the war.

At the briefing, the crews found out they would be flying at only 2,500 feet while crossing the North Sea to save fuel. The force would climb to its higher bombing altitude when it neared the targets—153-by-111-meter bunkers that resupplied German U-boats after their long underwater missions in the Atlantic.

At Trondheim, the bombing destroyed *U-622.* The first U-boat to be sunk in the Allies' campaign against the bases, it was also one of the only U-boats sunk by high-altitude bombing in World War II.[2]

Flying with pilot Johnny Johnson, bombardier Leonard Herman remembers it as "a hell of a long journey." A famous USAAC photo from this mission shows their plane flying on three engines. The fourth is on fire, and flames are slowly burning through the trailing edge of the wing and the rear stabilizer.

"I was sitting up in the nose, praying," remembers Herman. "I always carried my Jewish prayer book on missions, and I prayed when I could. Nothing fancy, just 'God, please get us home alive. Please let us live through this mission.'"

Three FW-190s had jumped Johnson's plane, *Ten Nights in a Bar Room/ The Brass Rail,* so the pilot dived until it was skimming the icy waters of the North Sea. This maneuver prevented the German fighters from making an attack from in front and below, and Johnson's tail gunner, Sgt. Donald Crossley, shot down one of the attackers. Crossley finished his tour as the top aerial gunner ace of the Eighth Air Force.

When the Johnson crew landed at Horham, "over half our stuff had already been taken," remembers Herman. "They thought we were never coming back so they started helping themselves to everything that wasn't in our locked footlockers. We had to go around and get them all back again!"

The next day, the 95th went on another mission and went back to the city that had been its Waterloo—Kiel. Twenty-seven 95th aircraft took off. The first B-17 lost was 23277, with all on board, after its wing and engine were ripped with flak. Pilot L. L. Mauldin managed to pull the ship out of the formation shortly after unloading its bombs. It rolled over in a tight spin and suddenly exploded.

The Johnny Johnson crew's luck ran out as well. "We had dropped our bomb load when we got hit by a fighter," Herman remembers. "This lone fighter came in from ten o'clock high. He was firing at our nose and cock-pit. I was hit in the forehead, and tiny splinters of metal and Plexiglas embedded themselves in my forehead and face. I remember thinking, 'Well, Leonard, so this is how it is.' We started to go into a slow spin, and I could see the topography turning and spinning slowly below us.

"I worked my way up to the cockpit. Johnny had been hit by a 20 millimeter that went through his left arm and embedded itself and blew in his right thigh. Oh, it was a mess. The shock knocked Johnny against the wheel. As we dived, Randy Cowan jumped down from the upper turret and with the help of copilot 'Kit' Carson got Johnny back out of the seat and carried him to the little catwalk between the nose and the cockpit. Randy took Johnny's place at the controls. Blood was all over the place, but he sat down and helped Carson bring the plane back on an even keel.

"[Johnny's] arm was hanging by a few tendons and his leg had a gaping hole from the 20 millimeter cannon. When it exploded, it tore his thigh apart. Tommy [Lees] tried to save him. He gave him shots of morphine and put a tourniquet on him. But Johnny had lost too much blood. He shut his eyes and started calling for his wife. He took one deep breath, and went to his maker. He didn't suffer much."

Blood dripping from his own wounds, Herman crawled back to his station in the nose, where he was greeted with the unwelcome smell of cordite and gunpowder. The same bullet that had grazed him had embedded itself in an ammo can and the .50-caliber shells were beginning to smolder. Desperately, Herman pulled the smoldering rounds from their link and threw them into the spent-shell reservoir. Fortunately, none of the rounds exploded.

Back at Horham, an ambulance carried Herman and the deceased Johnson to the base hospital. In the examining room, Flight Surgeon Doc Imes plucked one splinter after another out of Herman's body, dropping each in a metal pan. Herman lay there and listened as each splinter was dropped into the pan with a "plunk."[3] By the time the *Brass Rail* crew finished its tour, all but one member had been killed or wounded in combat.

Tragedy continued the next day as the group bombed Hannover, Germany. Four aircraft from the 95th BG went down on the July 26 mission. The S. Foutz crew all perished after being hit with flak. Three other crews—those of Robichaud, Quirk, and Massey—were lost as well. That quickly, forty men were gone.

After a day off, the group flew to Oschersleben, Germany. Of the twenty aircraft that took off, three were shot down, and ten returned with damage. One plane had to be salvaged. The J. F. Rivers crew became POWs. However, the crews of pilots H. D. Hodges and F. J. Regan were not so fortunate. All twenty men on these crews were killed on this mission.

After such heavy losses in the stretch of four days, the group was only able to send up nine planes on July 29. On that mission to Warnemunde, the crewmen of the *Yankee Queen* had reached their limit for stress and combat fatigue. Radioman William Irving wrote in his diary: "The past few days have been darn hard on ships as well as the men. Our crew had flown four ships in five days and all four of them had been grounded for some time after. Three of the ships had been shot up and the fourth needed an engine change because of a runaway prop. For that reason, or reasons similar, our Group had a grand total of nine ships that could be put in the air that day. During the course of the mission, five of those nine ships had to abort for mechanical reasons and we ended up by going over target with but four ships from our Group.

"The worst part of the trip came just as we were coming to the English Coast. We were just about two miles from the coast and everyone was coasting along taking things nice and easy. I happened to be in the nose of the ship at the time, for some reason, talking to the navigator and bombardier, when one of the ships a short ways from us became caught in the prop wash of the planes ahead of his and flipped over on his back. It just turned him nose over tail . . . and he ran into another ship.

"We weren't flying at over two thousand feet, if that high. One of the ships blew up on the spot and the other broke in half, exploding when it hit the water. There wasn't a man who got out of either ship. All of us were pretty much on edge at the time from going so much and that seemed pretty much to clinch the deal. As soon as we hit the ground and saw our Squadron C.O. [commanding officer] we asked that we be sent to a Rest Home for a few days. As much as anything else we were afraid for our pilot though I guess we had no cause to be. We knew darn well that he wouldn't say anything no matter how tired he was and we sure didn't want him cracking up. He was getting to the point, as we all were, where he gave some rather short answers at times. At any rate the C.O. agreed to send us. We had flown eleven missions in a little over a month and had just cause to be ready for a rest."

The next day, the CO had the unpleasant task of informing the crew that all rest home, or "flak house," leaves had been canceled. Instead, the men received a standard forty-eight-hour leave. Upon their return, the disappointed crew sat around for thirteen days, waiting for the next mission: "Of course we had a nice long rest there on the base . . . but to really do any good you have to get as far away from the whole thing as possible. I think those thirteen days were harder on us than if we had been pulling missions right along."[4]

On July 30, only seven aircraft were able to take off on the mission to Kassel, Germany, and only three completed the mission. The R. B. Jutzi crew, flying 230192, was hit about ten miles inside Holland. With their oxygen out and three engines feathered from flak damage, part of the crew bailed out before the remaining crewmen decided to stay with the ship and try to make it back to England. The Fort incredibly managed to stagger to within six miles of the coast of Dover when it lost altitude and ditched in the English Channel. Sadly, of those men who elected to jump, the radio operator and the tail gunner were killed, and the others became POWs. Those who chose to remain with the plane lived to fly another day.

The 95th airmen had now flown only twenty-three combat missions. However, they already had lost thirty-two Forts and most of the group's original cadre.

10 Replacement Crews

Experiencing such heavy losses, the bomb groups always needed more aircraft and the crews to fly them. Arriving replacement crews found that their break-in period was short. After processing at the replacement clearinghouse at Bovingdon, crews were randomly assigned to one group or another based on each group's needs. They arrived without the camaraderie that had galvanized the original cadres. They were expected to hit the ground running, and most of them did.

In 1943, most replacement crews flew over in their own aircraft from the States, thus killing two birds with one stone—aircraft delivery and crew delivery. Occasionally, they would have their shiny new B-17 taken away upon arrival only to find themselves flying the worst bucket of bolts in the group.

Radio operator William Irving arrived via the North Atlantic in 1943. While at Bovingdon, new crews attended classes to prepare them for combat. The intensive classes lasted two full weeks. "For the first time during our training the instructors were men who had, for the most part, actual combat experience," he remembers. "Few, if any, of our instructors in the States had any actual experience and so really knew nothing more than we did except that they knew it better." Officers and enlisted men took general classes together on subjects ranging from oxygen to first aid, and there was a heavy emphasis on enemy aircraft identification. Then the men were divided according to specialty, and Irving, a radio operator, discovered that "all the training [I] had in radio might as well have been scrapped and thrown out the window. About all that remained was our code."[1]

John Walter, pilot of a replacement crew, also remembers his time at Bovingdon and the cultural lesson offered in how to get along with his English hosts.

We attended classes to acquaint us with some of the British customs and habits. In one of the sessions, the Briefing Officer gave a good example of differences between British and American views of their environment. The intent was to prepare us so we would foster good relations between the two peoples. The example he used went something like this:

"If you had a visitor from Britain in your home town and you wanted to show him around, where would you take him? You would take him to see the NEW high school, the NEW post office, the NEW department store and anything else NEW. On the other hand, if you were to visit him, in his home town, he would show you the OLD town hall, the OLD cathedral, the OLD castle and other OLD things.

"The point of all this," the Officer concluded, "is this. Do not brag about your new possessions and other things and do not disparage his buildings and customs." For me, this was very good advice.

We also began our acquaintance with the British currency. The only thing in common with U.S. currency was the word penny. And the pennies were almost the size of a silver dollar!! From then on it was a real mind boggler. Twelve pence (pennies) made up a shilling. Only the shilling was usually called a "bob." It took twenty shillings to make a pound. But to help "clarify" things, in addition to the shilling coin, there was a myriad of other coins. Such as: a half crown coin. (Only half crowns, no crowns. A half-crown was equal to two shillings and six pence.) Farthings (one quarter of a penny), half pennies (ha'penny), three pennies (threepnee bit), six pennies (six pence), and two shillings (two bob) and half a crown. And if that were not enough, one pound plus one shilling, or 21 shillings, was a guinea.

[As far as paper money, they were all a different size.] The higher the denomination of the bill, the larger the bill. The five-pound note was printed on white paper. We called them bed sheets. They were rather scarce. In fact, at times the establishment taking the "fiver" would ask you to sign the back. In spite of its watermark, that bill must have been quite easy to counterfeit.[2]

After indoctrination, crews received their assignments to various bomb groups. Upon arrival at Horham and other fields, they had to try to blend in with crews who had already flown missions. The new replacement crews felt as though they were young high school boys who found themselves surrounded by worldly and tough older men. The old-timers, most of whom were no more than twenty years old themselves, tended to treat the newcomers with a mixture of aloofness and scorn. Old-timers considered the newcomers cocky but with no reason to be, and the former had seen enough replacement crews come and go that no one bothered to get too close to the newcomers until they had been around for a few missions.

The newcomers alternated between dreading that first mission and wanting to get it over with so they, too, could say they had been bloodied in combat. Irving remembers that his first night on base, his crew talked to the old-timers and tried to make some new friends. "We soon found out the Group hadn't been on combat operations very long. None of the boys had more than four or five missions. At that time though five missions over Occupied Europe seemed like a wonderful accomplishment to us."[3]

When ball turret gunner Robert Fay arrived with the Hiram Griffin crew in September 1944, the crew's enlisted men were assigned to the 334th Squadron's Barracks 13. Two other enlisted crews were already living there, and both crews were lost on missions within weeks. One of the men had been sick the day his crew went down. "The one fellow left in there was really in trouble mentally," remembers Fay. He and his mates changed the barracks' address to 12-A and completed their tour.

Navigator Bob Sullivan's replacement crew arrived at Horham after crossing the North Atlantic on the *Queen Elizabeth*, which, as noted earlier, had been converted to a troopship. All beds and furniture had been removed from the suites. He writes, "We arrived in England in November 1943 and were shot down February 10, 1944. Our total stay in England was during the winter months. It was solid overcast and foggy every day. The only time we saw blue sky was when we flew above the overcast. It felt colder than Wisconsin, my home state, as it was so damp and chilling to the bone. Many of us slept in our sheepskin-lined flying suits.

"It was dark when we arrived at Horham Airfield and we were met by a member of Base Personnel. He said the Group was just starting to take off on a mission and so we all sauntered over to the main runway to watch. Everything went according to procedure except the last remaining plane was obviously having a problem. After several seconds of revving up his engines, he started down the runway. Possibly because he was late, he started to bank to his right before gaining proper speed and altitude. He kept banking right into the ground with a loud explosion. What a way to go for ten young men—and what a welcome for us to our new air base."

Sullivan's pilot Hank Wilson and copilot Charlie Prince went through about one week of training on formation flying, takeoffs, and so forth before the crew was cleared for combat missions. Sullivan was a man of humor and showed an amazing amount of self-assurance when, at the end of the briefing for his first mission, the colonel asked if there were any important questions. "At this point it was still dark outside. I raised my hand, stood up and stated that I preferred to 'sleep-in' in the morning and would it be possible to schedule these missions later—like 10:00 or 11:00 a.m.? I think his answer was 'No.'"[4]

Replacements were common even among the 95th BG's leadership. The group had no fewer than six different group commanders: starting with the group's founder, Colonel Kessler, and followed by Col. John H. Gerhart; Col. Chester P. Gilger; Lt. Col. Robert H. Stuart; Col. Karl Truesdell Jr.; and Col. Jack E. Shuck. Men at all levels in the chain of command came and went.

Col. Noel T. Cumbaa spent the first part of the war as commanding officer of a primary pilot training school at Augustine Field, later renamed Bruce Campbell Field, in Madison, Mississippi. After the air force closed the school, Cumbaa was sent to Sebring, Florida, where he trained in the B-17. During the month he was there, Cumbaa racked up 105 hours of flight training. Shortly after D-Day (June 6) 1944, he was shipped along with eight thousand to ten thousand other troops on the *Queen Elizabeth* to England for combat duty. Once in England, Cumbaa was assigned to the

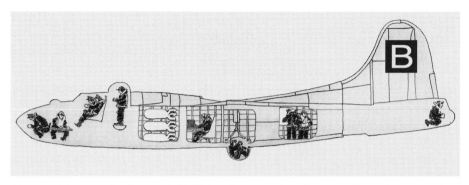

Crew positions on the Boeing B-17 Flying Fortress. (Credit Paul Dillon, drawn for this book and used with his permission)

95th Bomb Group Headquarters staff officers, U.S. Army Air Base, Rapid City, South Dakota, January 27, 1943. *Left to right, row 1:* Maj. F. J. "Jiggs" Donahue, S-2 (Intelligence); Lt. Col. L. E. Burt, Ground Executive; Col. A. A. Kessler Jr., Group Commander; Maj. J. H. Gibson, S-3 (Operations); Maj. E. P. Russell, S-1 (Adjutant). *Row 2:* 2nd Lt. Joe Florian, assistant S-2; 1st Lt. R. F. Knox, Group Communications; Capt. Cliff Cole, assistant S-3; 1st Lt. "Sandy" Ballwin, assistant S-4. *Row 3:* 2nd Lt. Charles J. Brickley, phys. ed.; Capt. Bob Petraitis, dentist; 1st Lt. George Myers, chaplain; 2nd Lt. David Olsson, statistical. *Row 4:* 1st Lt. Leonard "Joe" Dawson, bombing officer; Capt. Bill Harding, surgeon; 1st Lt. W. W. Brown, navigator; Capt. C. D. Fields, S-4 (Engineering). (95th Bomb Group Memorials Foundation [hereafter cited as 95th])

Waldo Cleveland on high snowdrifts after the April 1943 blizzard in Rapid City, South Dakota, where the 95th Bomb Group trained during the winter of 1942–1943. (95th)

At Alconbury, England, the 95th BG's first temporary base, on May 27, 1943. In a grim reminder that the air war can be deadly on the ground, a bomb loading accident killed nineteen men dead and seriously wounded twenty others. (95th)

Nissen huts at Horham became each man's home away from home. Drafty, wet, and often cold, they were not designed for comfort. (95th)

In their hut on Army Air Force (AAF) Station 119 at Horham, (*from left*) bombardier Frank Mago, navigator Joe Blagg, navigator Ed Charles, and pilot Robert Kroeger. (William "Ed" Charles, 95th)

Overview of 95th's headquarters and technical support buildings, Horham, England. (95th)

Sweating out the mission. (95th)

95th BG mission briefing. (Eddie Liggett, 95th)

Horham control tower. (Thomas DeHart, 95th)

Planning the mission. (95th)

Gary Anderson, Robert Anderson, and two other *Worrybird* crewmen load up for a mission. (95th)

Aircraft coming home after a mission, 1944. (Ed Charles, 95th)

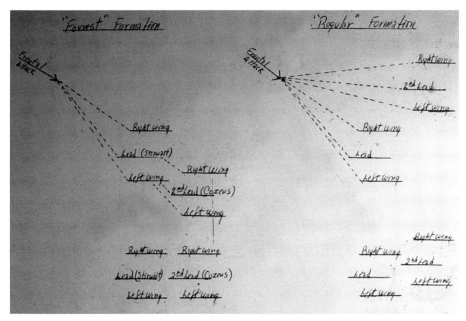

The Forrest formation, flown on the Kiel raid June 13, 1943, and never again (L) and the LeMay combat box (R). (95th)

Horham Post Office, Ancient House, during the war. (95th)

Horham village in 2008. (Rob Morris)

[Top] Sheep on the 95th BG's airfield, with Church of St. Mary in background. (95th)

[Right] Ground crewmen Pollos and Dunbar with two local English boys at Horham. (Adam Hinojos, 95th)

British-American Friendship Club, Stradbroke. (95th BG Heritage Association)

Marjorie Ward's grocery delivery van after it was hit by a B-17 at Horham. (95th BG Heritage Association)

DeWayne Willis Long with the Gyford Dance Band during the war. (95th BG Heritage Association)

DeWayne Willis Long (*seated*) is reunited with his trumpet mouthpiece by James Mutton, Tucson, Arizona, in 2008. Alan Johnson is standing behind Long. (Rob Morris)

Mechanics at work on an engine. (95th BG Heritage Association)

Bomb dump, Horham, 1944. (95th)

Damaged B-17 on hardstand, 1944. (95th)

Art Watson receiving the Legion of Merit for improvements to the B-17 supercharger making the aircraft safer to fly. (95th)

[Top] Ted Majer (*back row, third from left*) and other members of Horham's champion ping-pong team, September 1944. (95th)

[Left] Horham's control room. (Ed Charles, 95th)

[Bottom] The Alps as seen from the nose of a 95th aircraft during the Regensburg mission. (95th)

[Top] Pilot John Walter (*top row, far right*) and crew were replacements to the 95th BG. (95th)

[Left] Robert and Patsy Ann Cozens on their wedding day. (Robert Cozens)

Bettylou and Robert
Capen on their wedding day.
(Robert Capen)

Geri Delbern Marshall in 2009.
(Geri Marshall)

Geri and Fred Delbern shortly
after their wedding and before
he shipped out to England.
Geri would never see him
again, as he went missing in
action. (Geri Marshall)

95th Bomb Group. His arrival was no more feted than that of any other replacement. After being assigned to quarters, he found himself unpacking in the dark during the nightly blackout. As he finished, the air raid alarm sounded, and Cumbaa dived under his bed and hoped for the best. A German buzz bomb had puttered directly over Horham. The next day, another buzz bomb flew over in daylight. "Flying just above tree-top level in the direction of London, its tail section looked like a red-hot pot-belly stove and the putt-putt sound of its engine was similar to a motorcycle without a muffler," he remembers.

Cumbaa became a squadron commander shortly after his arrival, and later he was promoted to group operations officer, a position he held until the end of the war. In this capacity, Cumbaa coordinated bombing missions by scheduling crews, bombs, ammunition, and aircraft. He also flew nineteen missions as a command pilot on the Flying Fortress.[5]

By the time Julian Meyer and his mates on the Vergene W. Ford crew received their orders to the 95th Bomb Group in early October 1943, they had already seen many of their comrades die in the United States. Training accidents were common there during the war. Roughly fifteen thousand men died in aircraft accidents during training, or about 12.5 percent of the total air force casualties in the war.[6]

Meyer's crewmate Robert J. Evans kept a wartime scrapbook, and among its pages are articles that covered the obvious concerns of most replacement crews. One article states that air combat crews in 1944 had a 66 percent chance of finishing their twenty-five-mission tour of duty, but in comparison with the figures of late 1943, only 36 percent were expected to finish. Even better news, claims the article, is that an air crewman going into combat in 1944 has an 80 percent chance of surviving the war. On the crew's first practice mission, flying in tight formation as a group, two aircraft collided, killing all on board.

"We reached Horham on October 20th, 1943 just as the Group was returning from a mission. The base was a hub of activity. Just as we pulled up outside Group Operations the planes returning from the day's mission began to peel off. As they did one of the Forts zoomed down to roof-top level and buzzed the buildings housing Base Headquarters and Operations, shooting off flares as it went by with a thundering roar. This was the ship named *Darlin' Dolly*, piloted by Captain [K. S.] Knowlton. Knowlton was the first pilot in the 95th to finish the required number of missions—25."

Several replacement crews made the headlines in the States before they ever faced combat. After finishing their final training in Florida, four newly minted crews flew north to make the North Atlantic crossing to England. Three of these crews—those of pilots Jack Watson, Robert Sheets, and Joseph Wheeler—would end up at Horham with the 95th, but only after the mayor of New York City decided not to insist they be court-martialed for buzzing the Opening Game of the 1943 World Series between the St. Louis Cardinals and the New York Yankees.

It was October 5, 1943, and the crews had been on their way to Bangor, Maine. While airborne, Lieutenant Watson remembered that it was opening day of the World Series. With Watson's Fortress in the lead, the four planes took turns buzzing the field. The low-level buzz job angered Mayor Fiorello LaGuardia, himself a World War I pilot, and he demanded that the crews be grounded and court-martialed.

When the four crews landed at Bangor, they found themselves in a heap of trouble. Though LaGuardia wanted the air corps to throw the book at the men, the leadership decided that too much time and money had been sunk into the crews' training at a time when flight crews were being shot down almost as fast as replacements could arrive. Instead, the men were given hefty fines of several hundred dollars and sent on their way to England. LaGuardia later sent the crews telegrams telling them all was forgiven.

Once in England, they faced a new set of problems. William Irving remembers: "Every night, we listened as some of the more experienced men in their barracks had nightmares. During the still of the night one of them would yell out something like 'Here comes one in at five o'clock! Get 'em, get 'em, get 'em!' It was also the first time in my life that I talked to a bunch of guys and had them come right out and say they were scared of something. They really meant it and weren't in the least ashamed of it. There wasn't any of this deep horror business or nervous twitching of muscles but just a good honest fear of being killed. At that time we couldn't really appreciate what they meant. It wasn't something you can explain to someone and have them truly understand it. You have to go through the same thing yourself and then, and only then, can you fully appreciate what they mean."[7]

Navigator William "Ed" Charles of the 336th Squadron tells a particularly poignant story. In the middle of the night, a replacement navigator was shown into the Charles's barracks by flashlight. Charles introduced himself to the new man, named Spencer, and then they both went to sleep. At two o'clock, the door swung open again, and the charge of quarters told Spencer that a navigator was needed on that day's mission. Spencer roused himself and left for breakfast.

Spencer never came back. His Fort was shot down, and he became a POW. Charles noticed Spencer's brand-new A-2 flying jacket lying on his bunk and appropriated it. As for Spencer, he entered 95th BG legend as "the man who came for breakfast."

Sixty-six years later, I met Spencer at the 95th Bomb Group Reunion in Dallas, Texas. Trim and looking twenty years younger than his eighty-plus years, Melvin Spencer chuckled when we talked about Charles's story. He told me, "Well, it's a great story, but it's not completely accurate. In fact, I'd been on the base since early January 1944. I'd flown six practice missions and then three missions with a pilot named Connolly. That day, I was assigned to the Anthony Tuberose crew because Tuberose's navigator was flying as lead navigator . . . and Tuberose needed someone to fill in. That was me." Spencer ended up in Stalag Luft I in Barth, Germany, as a POW until May 1, 1945.

James Gregory remembers that replacement crews to the group rarely flew their own planes; instead, they were assigned a plane on a mission-by-mission basis. "If replacement crews survived long enough, their seniority often allowed them to 'adopt' an airplane."[8]

A little-known aspect of the air war concerns the so-called bastard gunners, men who had no regular crew but filled in as needed on existing crews. One such bastard gunner was Stewart McConnell. After spending the early part of the war as a gunnery instructor at Nellis Air Force Base, Nevada, McConnell was transferred in June 1944 to the 95th Bomb Group's 335th Squadron. "I had no crew but filled in as needed. I served as ball, tail, waist and togglier/gunner for whoever needed me. I completed thirty missions, plus several aborted sorties, at least two missions with the 100th

Bomb Group, and one with the 486th Bomb Group. Crew members who flew as bastard gunners led a lonely existence."[9]

Tragically, many new crews were lost after the first few missions, including some on their very first, though the fickle hand of fate had as much to do with it in some cases as inexperience did. Basil Lyle Shafer, a replacement pilot in the 390th Bomb Group, told me that in 1944 some replacement pilots were raced through training and expected to learn on the job and in combat. One month he was flying the twin-engine AT-10 trainer as a cadet, the next he was copiloting a sixty-thousand-pound, four-engine B-17 over occupied Europe.[10]

One of the most fascinating stories of a late-war replacement involves not a flight crew member but a ground gripper. Walter Stitt arrived in England on D-Day and landed on Omaha Beach two weeks afterward. He was assigned to a tank crew in the army's Third Armored Division as a loader.

Stitt's Sherman tank was one of the first to roll into Germany. On September 19, 1944, a German shell hit it, killing the gunner and the tank commander and wounding Stitt in the legs. In November, the new tank to which Stitt had been assigned was destroyed in a minefield. After getting yet another tank, the crew participated in the Battle of the Bulge. On January 6, Stitt's tank was hit by a German Panzerfaust, killing the tank commander and wounding Stitt in the head. Patched up and returned to combat, Stitt became sick and was moved to a hospital near Bristol.

"In March, I was sent to the 95th Bomb Group on 'limited service,'" Stitt told me in 2009. Upon arrival at Horham, Stitt was assigned duty as an armorer and bomb loader, but he discovered, "I couldn't get my arm over my head or my shoulder went out of joint! So they sent me to work in the PX. It was wonderful! Any time I had money (they didn't really need me in the PX) I took off for London. A *big* experience for me was being on a pass in London on VE [Victory in Europe] Day [May 7, 1945]! After the fliers and support troops started home I was put in charge of the Enlisted Men's Beer Hall, another job to die for."

Considering the number of aircrews that came through the 95th Bomb Group and how few of the early crews survived, replacement crews fought much of the war. These men quickly became veteran crewmen and acquitted themselves with skill and courage until the war's end.

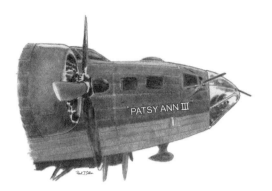

11 Wives and Mothers

Because of the relative youth of the men who ended up in the air corps, the vast majority of 95th Bomb Group personnel, both flight and ground crews, were single. However, a few had married before their combat tours.

The wife of an USAAC bomber crewman fought her own battles, and though not life and death, her struggles required all her reserves of inner strength. Many worked, and some were pregnant or had small children to rear. In addition to the normal fears of any young married person about fidelity and long separation, she also dreaded, day by day, the knock on the door that brings bad news. She could not escape the troubling realities of war. The daily newspapers carried dark headlines about the air battles over Europe. If she went to the movies, the opening newsreels showed footage of aerial combat, with German and American planes plunging from the sky.

Despite being bombarded daily with war news, the airman's wife received little that was specific. Wartime secrecy allowed her only to know her husband was "somewhere in England," and letters came from or were sent to U.S. Army postal codes, not real places. Letters were censored. They often came after only long delays and sometimes not at all. Letters from a prisoner of war could take months. Letters informing spouses of injury or death contained only spare details.

In addition to couples who had married before the war, some young American servicemen found the loves of their lives while stationed in England. Many of these men were ground personnel, who stayed in Horham for the entire war and had more of an opportunity to become a fixture in the local communities. Some seventy thousand to a hundred thousand young British women fell in love with and married American servicemen, most leaving the country of their birth and traveling across the sea to build a new life in a strange land.

Given the many available and interested women in England, not all men were faithful to the girls they left behind, though it appears the majority of the married men were, based on my informal discussions with veterans. This fidelity is all the more commendable considering what Leonard Herman acknowledged was intense pressure on the early 95th flight crews. The men clearly realized that a twenty-five-mission tour of duty was little more than a delayed death sentence. "Morals were different there," he remembers. "Many a man went out and partied away because he didn't know where he'd be the next day. Many of them never came back from their missions. They were killed in the air, killed on the ground, or became POWs. Attraction and companionship meant a great deal more to us, married and unmarried."[1]

The American crewmen were highly sought after by some English women. The Yanks were well paid, well dressed, and available at a time when most English servicemen were posted elsewhere around the world.

American Patsy Ann Hamrick became Patsy Ann Cozens the same day her new husband, Robert, received his pilot's wings. She followed him through many of his phases of training with the 95th Bomb Group and then saw him off to war. The day Bob and his crew landed their Flying Fortress in England, April 17, 1943, Pat gave birth to their first child, having hired a taxi to get herself to the hospital.

Pat's friend from Rapid City, Jerry Stirwalt, lost her husband, lead pilot Harry Stirwalt, on June 13, 1943, over Kiel. In an instant, Jerry was left to rear her young child alone. Pat Cozens tried not to think that Bob might be next.

"I wrote Bob every day," she remembers, "even though I didn't have much to say. I had an 8mm camera and we took footage of the baby and sent it over to England so Bob could see his new child. They couldn't find an 8mm projector anywhere to show the film. Finally, they tracked one down in the Group Photo Section. But they had to watch the movie one frame at a time." It was the first time Bob had seen his new baby.

For his part, Bob wrote as often as time permitted using Victory mail. An ingenious invention, V-mail saved precious cargo space and resources for the war effort. The sender wrote his or her message on a special stationery sheet that had a glued flap and folded into a marked envelope. After the mail was opened and censored, it was photographed and reduced to the size of a thumbnail and combined with hundreds of other letters onto a hundred-foot-long reel of 16mm film. These microfilm reels were then shipped overseas, where the messages were enlarged and delivered to the addressees. Each roll held up to seventeen hundred letters and weighed only 5.5 ounces, including its metal container. A sack of mail holding the original letters would have weighed 50 pounds.[2]

Writing was often frustrating. "I couldn't say where we were going," remembers Bob. "I *could* say we were going on a big one, and then Pat would watch the paper and try to match them up." He also tried to keep her advised of his mission totals as he crept toward the coveted number twenty-five.

"Other than the newspaper, I didn't know how bad the odds were," Pat told me in 2009. Bob added: "After Kiel, she had some idea that it was dangerous."

"I worried about it every day and every night," says Pat. "I tried to keep busy, to keep positive. And I did a lot of praying. I was very happy I had a child because if Bob were lost, I'd have a little piece of him."

The war was also hard on Bob Cozens's mother. Three of her four sons were military pilots. Dick Cozens crashed and died in B-24 training in Oklahoma. He'd been married six weeks. Tom Cozens was killed when his plane crashed in a thunderstorm in New Mexico.

On December 22, 1943, Pat received the telegram she'd dreamed about: Bob had finished his tour. He was alive. He would be coming home to build the life they'd planned together. More than sixty-five years later, the Cozens are still together.

Another member of the original cadre of the 95th Bomb Group was navigator Ellis Scripture. Scrip had married a girl named Peggy in his small hometown of Greensburg, Indiana, shortly before the United States entered the war. Peggy Scripture remembers, "When war was declared on December 7, he said to me, 'You know, I'll want to go. Will you release me?'

And I thought he wouldn't be able to leave me so I said yes. He enlisted the day after war was declared. We'd only been married a little over a year.

"He went to Santa Ana, California, for basic training as a navigator. I followed him there and lived in a residential hotel in Los Angeles. When Scrip got his navigator's wings, I followed him to Spokane, Washington. Another girl and I rented a room from a single lady and had breakfast privileges. Whichever of our husbands was in town, the other would move out for the night.

"From there, we went to Rapid City, South Dakota. We wives drove from Spokane to Rapid City in two cars. It was an adventure. Because the war was on, there were almost no cars on the road and almost no filling stations. We got to Rapid City on Christmas Day. As we drove into town, the men flew over in the planes and dipped their wings at us. We had a lot of fun times in Rapid City.

"One family we got to know very well was the Lincoln Borglum family. Lincoln's father, Gutzon, had started the Faces on the Mountain, now known as Mt. Rushmore. When Gutzon died in 1941, Lincoln took over and finished the project, and then stayed to oversee the new monument. Lincoln and his family were very interested in the 95th Bomb Group. He'd come in with his wife and a young toddler, who would run around the hotel lobby with a baby bottle in its mouth. We became great friends. In fact, Jay Shaatz named one of his sons after Lincoln Borglum, Lincoln Shaatz.

"The Alex Johnson Hotel charged us $2.75 a week for a room, but if our husbands stayed with us, the rate went up to $4.50. So there were a lot of guys sneaking in. They'd get up early in the morning and make the bed so the maids would not know they'd been there.

"Jackie Mumford and I each got a little black cocker. Jackie named hers 'B-17' and Scrip named ours 'Flaps Down.' We spent a lot of time training them. The wives also knit. It seemed like half the wives there were pregnant. And then in April, they shipped the men overseas for combat.

"Scrip sent me an awful, smelly leathery purse that turned out to be camel! I was afraid to get rid of it because it would cause bad luck. We agreed I'd throw it away when he got home, and I never carried it."

Peggy returned to Chicago and went to work for the Red Cross. Officially, she worked for the Home Service of the Red Cross, initially at the organization's main building on South Michigan Avenue and later at its

Oak Park branch. Her job was to visit relatives of service people and find out if there was a financial or physical need in the families.

"I did my best to keep busy," she remembers. "I wasn't lonely. I'd go and visit an older couple who lived in my apartment building, and in the evening, the man would escort me home, very courtly. I kept happily busy.

"There were sad times at work. After the Battle of the Bulge, many of the wives in our office had husbands fighting in the army in Europe. One lady got word that her husband had been killed in the Battle of the Bulge. Another lady was told her husband was missing. Even with all of our contacts with the Red Cross we did not know for three months if he was alive or dead. Finally, we found out he was a POW.

"Scrip was given a one-month leave. He came home and we and three other married couples went to Atlantic City, New Jersey, and stayed near the beach. Two of the husbands were fighter pilots. One, Joe Legan, went back to Europe and was shot down and killed the day he went back into combat. He and his wife had a little boy. She was pregnant when he went back, but she miscarried.

"When Scrip returned home at the end of the war, he was out of touch with life in the States. For the first time in a while, I knew more than he did. And once he was home, he put the war behind him. He didn't talk about it until his retirement. I'd saved all his V-mail, but water leaked into our basement and all the letters got wet. I laid them out to dry and Scrip came home and read them. He ended up burning most of them. I guess they embarrassed him. I managed to salvage a few for the kids. He's sorry now that he did that."

Another original pilot in the 95th was Johnny Johnson of East St. Louis, Illinois. Johnson was newly married and had a small child. After Johnson was killed on the Kiel mission, his wife was only told that her husband had been killed in action on July 25. Desperate for more information, she wrote a letter to Johnson's bombardier Leonard Herman and navigator Tommy Lees. Dated August 4, 1943, it reads in part:

Dear Herman and Tommy,

I suppose you were expecting a letter from me sooner or later. I hardly know what to say except that I have been fully informed of Johnny's death. That is between the newspapers and the government I know pretty well what happened. I'm including some of the newspaper clippings. What it says are all the details I know.

I'm writing you because I thought you might be able to tell me what Johnny said during the hour before he died. In fact, I'd like to know as much as you two are allowed to tell me. You cannot imagine how terrible it makes a person feel to sit and not be told anything but what the clippings say and the short telegram from the government. . . .

There's no use telling you of my sorrow. You know. I'm afraid you know too well.

Johnny did not want me to write you boys in case anything happened. He did tell me to write Major McKnight. I would rather write you two, however, as I feel you will tell me what you can.

I guess I have no more to say. You boys keep right on pitching. You must fight so there won't be too many broken hearts like mine and hundreds of others.

The best of luck to all of you. Tell the rest of the crew I said so and I'll remember all of you in my prayers.

Herman was so moved by this letter that he kept it for more than sixty years. The original is now in the 95th Museum at Horham.

Another touching letter gives readers insight into the anxiety that the mothers of the 95th's airmen felt. Charles Shaughnessy was a navigator with the 95th Bomb Group who was shot down in 1944 and ended up as a prisoner of war. Shaughnessy's mother wrote a poem titled "A Mother's Outburst to Her Four Distant Soldier Sons" around this time. It reads, in part:

> *Today I've lost my heart of jazz,*
> *And found a sober self.*
> *Especially when I see their things*
> *Strewn out upon a shelf.*
>
> *Our soldier sons you are today*
> *You once were little boys,*
> *When mother held you close and dreamed*
> *While sharing all your joys.*

I mustn't doubt this tangled web,
With peace there will be dawn.
But while the night is very dark
Please help me carry on.[3]

As a high school senior in Kansas City, Missouri, Bettylou Capen told me, she played tenor sax in an all-girl, ten-piece band called the Western Sweethearts. The man who managed the group also oversaw a ten-piece men's harmonica band that was losing its members to the draft, and the two groups played gigs together in the summer of 1942. Playing in the harmonica band was a fellow named Robert Capen. Bob, five years older than Bettylou, worked in a factory as a metal spinner.

Shortly after the two started dating, Bob went off to the service. "When he was at Aircraft Mechanics School at Shepherd Field, Texas, I took the bus down to meet him," Bettylou told me. "I'd been working at the Montgomery Ward's in Kansas City, as an auditor, and had been making fifty cents an hour. I had a little vacation time so I went down to visit. I got off the bus, and Bob took me to the base. He told me he'd be there for a little while and then would be shipping out overseas and I wouldn't see him for a long time. We then decided to get married there. We were married at Shepherd Field in Base Chapel #4, and the other fellows in Bob's class were in attendance."

Bettylou took a job in the Montgomery Ward's near the base, working as a shipping clerk. In January 1944, Bob was shipped overseas from Camp Kilmer, New Jersey, on the *Aquitania*. Bob's crew, piloted by James Sheller, were assigned to the 95th Bomb Group at Horham. Because of his small stature, Bob ended up as the ball turret gunner. "My first mission was May 19, 1944, and we finished up September 19, 1944," he remembers. Missions during this period were particularly dangerous. Flight crews had to deal not only with German fighters but also with the increasingly heavy flak from the 88mm guns that ringed most of the 95th's bombing targets.

Meanwhile, Bettylou returned to Kansas City and worked at a music store, and the two wrote regularly. She also sent Bob boxes of popcorn, comic books, and canned shrimp, which he shared with the crew. "Those comics really got passed around," remembers Bob.

Because of wartime secrecy, Bettylou did not know specifically where Bob was based or when he flew his missions. However, she went to the movies and watched the RKO News that preceded the main feature. "They only said general areas such as the South Pacific or Europe. That was about as specific as it got. But from the RKO News and from the papers, I could tell how hard the war was on the flight crews.

"We chose not to have children until after the war," says Bettylou. "I didn't want to become a widow with children. I worried Bob wouldn't come home. I knew he was in combat."

Finally, in September 1944, Bob and the rest of the Sheller crew completed their last mission. Bob and Bettylou have now been married for sixty-five years, second in the 95th Bomb Group to Bob and Pat Cozens, who married in 1943. Bob and Bettylou faithfully attend the annual reunions; an inseparable couple, they are small in stature but huge in presence. Their love has survived constant moves, lengthy periods of separation, and deadly combat, becoming stronger and long lasting.

Of course, not every husband returned.

It's been nearly sixty-six years since Geri Marshall said good-bye to her husband, pilot Lt. Frederick A. Delbern Jr. She never saw him again, but he remains the great love of her life. Geri, now ninety years old and living in Duluth, Minnesota, readily admits that every morning, when she wakes up, her first thought is about the man she married on May 2, 1942. "I think of him all the time, every day," she says.

One day in 1939, nineteen-year-old Geri, a pretty girl with rich brown hair and sparkling eyes, was walking to her home on Eighteenth Avenue West in Duluth. "My brother was walking ahead of me," she remembers. "He was with several friends. I recognized one of the men with my brother, but not the other man. I overheard the other man say, after looking my way, 'Wow, that's for me!' They were going up the stairs to my apartment. He had no idea that I lived there, too. I followed him right up the stairs into the apartment, and my brother introduced me. I didn't have much to say. We were both pretty embarrassed. He had no idea that I was his friend's sister when he said it."

It wasn't love at first sight for Geri. She admits it took several weeks to fall for the handsome young man. Fred Delbern had been an outgoing, happy student in high school who excelled in football. His yearbook photo caption read, "He's an athlete but he sure loves fun!" Fred had been good enough to win a football scholarship to the University of Minnesota, and he'd spent two years there before returning to Duluth.

"We got married at St. Clement's Catholic Church on May 2, 1942, at a nine o'clock Mass," remembers Geri. "Jobs were scarce. I worked in a factory that made boxes. Fred worked for the railroad. We got a little apartment on Eleventh Avenue."

Fred had been bitten by the flying bug in his teens. He'd flown small single-seat aircraft as a hobby in the Duluth area. One day, without consulting Geri, he went and enlisted in the U.S. Army Air Corps. "When I found out, I didn't like it," says Geri. "I wanted him to wait and be drafted like everybody else. But he was crazy about flying, and he enlisted.

"We were sent down south to Montgomery, Alabama. After Montgomery, we spent time in Decatur and then Valdosta and Macon, Georgia. We were in each place for about two months for training. Finally, we went to Sebring, Florida. That's where the flight crews were put together and Fred was given his assignment. We had a short furlough to Duluth and then went west, spending time in Moses Lake, Washington, and also in Spokane. I stayed at a hotel in Spokane while Fred trained with his crew. They did an awful lot of training. Sometimes, the fellows from his crew came over to the hotel and played poker, and then we'd go down and have a drink. Everyone on the crew was so nice, and they were all so young. Of course, I was very young, too.

"The last time I saw Fred was in Spokane, Washington. He then went to Nebraska with the crew, and they were issued their cold weather clothing. He called me from Nebraska. I had gone home to Duluth after Spokane."

Fred's crew continued its training in England, preparing for its first combat mission. The young pilot was now given the awesome responsibility for a heavy B-17 Flying Fortress and the lives of the nine other men on board.

Fred took his responsibilities as the crew's leader seriously. "We were lucky to have Fred Delbern for a pilot," remembers crew member Loren Dodson. "He loved those big awkward B-17 planes and was at the height of his glory when he was at the controls. He cared very much for his crew, and he was always looking for ways to make our lives a little more comfortable. He asked me several times if were we getting enough to eat, was the food good, was our barracks comfortable? He would always say, 'Tell me the truth, don't lie to me. If they are not right we will get them right.' All the crew had the greatest respect for him and was glad to have him for our pilot."

On December 16, 1943, Fred prepared his crew members for their first combat mission. They paused for a moment in front of their plane, the *Lonesome Polecat II*, and had their photo taken.

A short time later, while the *Lonesome Polecat II* was preparing to drop its bombs, a burst of flak hurled jagged shards of metal through the plane's thin aluminum skin, hitting both Fred Delbern and copilot Don Neff and wounding waist gunner Staff Sgt. Charles J. Schreiner. The plane began to fall behind the protective cover of the bomber formation.

Then two Me-109 fighters jumped the *Polecat*. Copilot Neff was hit again—one account has him dying instantly, while others surmise he survived it—though he remained seated upright in his copilot's chair. At this point, it appears that Delbern knew the plane would never make it back to England and that he began looking for a place to set it down. He hit the bailout bell. Three crewmen jumped. The plane was so damaged, however, that the men in the rear of the aircraft could not hear the order. They continued to fire furiously at the attacking fighters, filling the smoky air with the acrid smell of cordite.

Delbern struggled to keep the Fortress in the air. With the plane approaching the Dutch coast, he knew that the chances of surviving in the icy-cold North Sea were next to nil. Alone, gripping his injured arm with one hand and flying the plane with the other, Delbern struggled to keep the plane level.

The plane lost altitude and was limping along at between three thousand and four thousand feet. Delbern must have been unsure of where they were; a solid layer of clouds obscured any sight of the earth's surface. In reality, the *Polecat* was passing over the small island of Texel, about 166 miles from Bremen.

Delbern finally managed to get word to the remaining crew to jump. Radio operator Eugene Darter was too injured to attach his parachute or pull his rip cord, so ball turret gunner Doral Hupp buckled Darter's chute on him upside down so Darter could pull the cord with his good arm. After Darter jumped, the rest of the crew in the back did the same. Tragically, Darter landed off the shore of Texel and was presumed drowned. The other men landed on the island and become prisoners of war.

Pilot Fred Delbern's final moments were likely very lonely. He'd been hit in the arm, leg, and abdomen. All of his crew but his dead copilot were safely out. The sea was coming closer and closer to his windscreen. What was he thinking? Was he thinking of his wife, Geri, the love of his life? Was he wondering why he had not received a *single* letter from her since he had been in England?

Aboard the *Lonesome Polecat II* with the body of his copilot, Delbern piloted the severely damaged B-17 over the village of De Koog and then two rows of high, brush-covered sand dunes before crashing into the sea and disappearing beneath the waves. Neither Delbern nor Neff was ever found.

Back home, Geri had thought about Fred daily. She had faithfully written and mailed a letter to him every day. On New Year's Eve 1943, the phone jingled in Geri's apartment. It was Western Union. "They called and then started to tell me something, and then all of a sudden, they hung up," remembers Geri. "I lay down on the davenport, and put a record on the phonograph. I had been getting ready to clean but I lay down and I must have dozed off.

"I saw Fred. He was right next to me. He put his arm over mine, and touched my right arm. He had a big smile on his face. It was so real. I was sure I was not sleeping. From then on I was certain he would be coming back.

"An hour later, there was a knock on the door. It was a Western Union messenger reporting that Fred was missing in action. It was heartbreaking. I called Fred's family immediately. Fred was an only son. His mother idolized him. They were very, very close. Fred's mother asked if I could come up and be with her, and I said I'd come up the next day.

"It was awful. I just couldn't believe it. A year went by, and they still didn't know if he was alive or not. I knew nearly all of the crew, and so I wrote Charlie Schreiner to write me a letter describing to his best knowledge what had happened to Fred. He did so, and this letter was of great consolation to me because Charlie was the last to bail out. He described how he watched the plane flying toward England and leaving a trail of smoke. . . . It was not until just recently in February of 2009 that I found out from the brother of Eugene Darter that the plane was found just off the coast of Texel Island and that they had apparently spotted the shoreline and swung around and crash-landed in the North Sea.

"I got letters of condolence from President Roosevelt and then from President [Harry] Truman. But they never found him. I could never let go of it. I carried him with me all these years. I never got over how much I loved him.

"I went to my Catholic priest about my dream. He said, 'People don't come back. Only saints come back.' But it was so real. I believe what I saw. I've heard of such things happening."

Geri had no body to bury and no grave to visit. Five years passed. Geri met a man at a dance named Joseph R. Marshall—a quiet, serious man— and they married. The couple never had any children. Joseph and Geri were married for sixty years until he passed away in December 2008. Then, Geri took out the old photograph of her first love, Fred Delbern, and placed it on a chest of drawers where she could look at it every day. "I look at that photo, and it brings me peace," she says. "I wake up every morning, and the first thing I do is think of him. I think of him all the time. It doesn't hurt as much as it did when I was young, because I now realize that we all have to pass on, but I still think about him and I still love him."

Out of respect for her second husband, Geri had little to do with Fred's family, with whom she had been so close. "I was in touch for quite a while after the war," she says, "but when I remarried, I dropped away. When Fred's mother was sick, I went to visit her. When she died, I went to her funeral. She cared for Fred so much. She never got over his death."

Before we ended our conversation, Geri told me she would send me her wedding photo. "A few years ago, I pulled it out and showed it to my nephew. I said to him, 'Do you know what happiness looks like? This is what happiness looks like.'"

Each morning, as Geri goes about her daily routine in her apartment in Duluth, she sees Fred's smiling, handsome face, and she feels a mixture of sadness and peace. She knows that he isn't really gone. He's inside her heart and has been for seventy years.[4]

12

Sudden Death

To Horham's aircrews, it often seemed the Grim Reaper lurked around every corner and behind every tree. As much as the men of the 95th Bomb Group hated to see their comrades die in combat, it was even worse to lose a friend to a simple accident. Airmen and villagers alike were exposed to a regular dose of horror throughout the war, especially in the later months when every mission involved hundreds of bombers and fighter escorts and the skies resembled Piccadilly Circus at rush hour.

The 95th's first loss to accident came early, while the group trained in South Dakota, and the last occurred with the crash of a military transport plane carrying a load of crewmen back to the States after their tours.

Living in the shadow of death for months at a time took a heavy toll on combat crews. Copilot Robert Brodersen of the 336th Squadron remembers desperately wrestling the controls from his screaming, sleep-deprived pilot shortly after takeoff on D-Day and narrowly averting a fatal crash. A week or so later, Brodersen wrote: "Our pilot has been getting worse. We talked it over and he agreed to go see the flight surgeon. He was sent to a hospital in England, and through the use of drugs and tests they determined for sure he wasn't faking it." The pilot was relieved of command, and Brodersen became the aircraft commander. The pressures of being in command now haunted him instead.

On July 31, he looked in the mirror while shaving. "It really worried me what I saw in the mirror. My eyes were completely black. I looked like a broken man, and it scared me. After a bit, I got hold of myself, and made up my mind I had the stuff it took to hang on, and I wouldn't let my crew down. This is the closest I ever came to breaking down."[1]

Tail gunner Edwin LeCorchick 334th Squadron also felt the pressures of facing death on a regular basis. Having survived one crash, he became increasingly distraught as he prepared to return to flight status. "I was going to refuse to fly anymore. Yes, I was scared, but when I saw the rest of my crew was going to finish out I knew I couldn't quit on them. When the time finally came for our first mission after the crash, I was right there with the crew."[2]

Ted Lucey remembers one incident as clear as day. "I was working in the radio shack when I heard much yelling. Looking out the window, I saw a B-17 break through the mist, about a mile away. The plane's tail broke off and the fuselage turned downward. One figure dropped from the stricken Fort. Moments later a parachute blossomed. I ran outside but in the few seconds that took, the Fortress disappeared behind some trees. Immediately afterward there was a big explosion and a pattern of smoke and flame shot up hundreds of feet. I saw a second chute floating down: some fellows counted four in all. Two unfortunates dropped with closed chutes.

"No more than fifteen or twenty minutes earlier, though I didn't know it at the time, another Fort broke up and fell a short distance away. Frank Norley and another telephone man were off base when this happened. They watched in horror as several fliers fell nearby with closed chutes, feet kicking in futility on the way down.

"One chute did open, however. The flier came down near them. They picked him up and rushed for the base hospital. The flier was conscious, though cut about the face. He said the plane had been weakened by flak and came apart.

"On the way to the hospital, the second plane crashed and the poor devil who'd just been through the experience was hysterical as he watched others drop with closed chutes."[3]

Bombardier Bill Green's journal is a litany of loss.

> 4/12/44: Field day today. Lost five planes—not over the Continent, but right over our field. We had just landed from a practice mission, when all hell broke loose. No sooner climbed out of our plane when two planes collided overhead—big explosions—then BOOM—lots of smoke—what a mess! Only saw three chutes open up.
>
> Started back to the briefing room, when a B-24 crash-landed. The nose was completely shot out. Lost the nose gunner—literally

washed him out. The bombardier was severely injured. Well, that was enough, so we thought. Came back to our hut and stood looking out the door, looked up and saw another B-17 in trouble. The entire tail fell off, and a few seconds later the tail gunner leaped out of the falling wreck. Only two other chutes opened. One boy leaped out, but his chute never opened.

   The remainder of the plane went into a flat spin—what a terrifying noise that crash made. Waiting for that plane to hit gave me the most sickening feeling I've ever had. This will take some getting used to. What the devil could have happened? Will we have to sweat out our practice missions, too?

Green witnessed all of these tragedies before he had flown a single mission. He continued to record his experiences:

4/22: Heard that Richmond crashed on takeoff yesterday. Keagy, his bombardier, went through Childress with us—nice guy. Only found pieces of the plane. Keagy was married just before he came over.

5/2/44: Saw another B-17 fall apart this afternoon—only one chute opened.

5/23/44: Early this morning a Ju-88 bombed our field—Results— killed seven cows and woke everyone up—except me. Another collision—B-24 and B-17 this time.

5/29/44: On our return our Group ran into a mess of B-24s. All of our planes managed to get out of it, but two 24's collided and dropped down on a third. All three then exploded; they never had a chance. Someone sure had their head up you know where. Hours over the target and then get killed when you are almost home.

6/20/44: Saw two 24s collide when we took off this morning and one crash when we landed. We have lost more over England than we have in combat, I think. Seems there could be a better system.[4]

Death could come on the ground as well. The men of the 95th knew it as well as anybody after the Alconbury ordnance explosion in early 1943. Bob Evans of the 335th Squadron writes: "My pilot V. W. Ford had completed his tour and I was assigned to fill in as waist gunner on Lt. Bruce

Henderson's crew on April 1, 1944. This was my twenty-fifth mission. After six hours in the air we were recalled and returned to base with a full load of bombs and a lot of fuel. When we landed we ran off the end of the runway into the mud. Over the intercom we were told that a plane was right behind us and to 'Get out fast!' Top turret gunner Max Lipchitz jumped out of the bombardier's escape hatch right into the propeller. Just then the plane following zoomed overhead to go around. I believe he died on the way to the hospital."[5]

Perhaps the most thoroughly documented accident at Horham is that which befell the Fortress piloted by Lt. Kenneth B. Rongstad on November 19, 1943. The crash, now commonly known as the Green Farm crash, happened close to the base. Each year, the farmers at Green Farm unearth more artifacts from the Rongstad aircraft.

Harry Conley watched that morning as the Fort began its takeoff run.

As Rongstad's plane lumbered along gaining speed near the end of the runway, it just barely rose off the ground and apparently started its bank to the left. But it was still too close to the ground! The plane stalled and its left wing hit the ground. The plane spun around and crashed! It started burning right away.

I jumped into my Jeep and drove as fast as I could over to the crash. I could see that Dave McKnight and "Doc" Imes were also driving madly over there to the end of the runway to help the crew. When I was less than 50 yards from the burning wreck—WHOOM!—the whole thing exploded big time! I tried to drag a couple of the boys out of there, but they were all dead.[6]

Flight surgeon Doc Imes remembers the incident as well. When the plane crashed,

I was on the balcony of the tower, and I immediately jumped into my ambulance. Dave McKnight had a Jeep he was driving himself. My driver knew all the roads around Horham and Redlingfield, and we took off at top speed for the wrecked airplane, with McKnight right behind us in the Jeep. We arrived at the scene of the crash within three or four minutes.

We stopped the vehicles about twenty-five feet south of the house. We could see the plane burning, and all the time there had been only the one explosion that had occurred on impact. As I got out of the ambulance there was another explosion, a bomb I suppose, and a large piece of engine cowling landed about six feet from me in the road.

We went into the house, and there was a crewman lying on the ground at the corner. I could see no marks on him, and I didn't know whether he was alive or dead. I took hold of his feet to pull him around the corner of the house. At that point there was another explosion; the blast knocked me off my feet. When I got up and looked around the corner of the house again the crewman was partially decapitated.

Inside the house I found Lieutenant Colonel McKnight comforting a very pregnant woman and a small child, both of whom were frightened and hysterical. . . . There were still sporadic explosions as bombs were going off, and it was a complete nightmare.[7]

Ruby Gooderham lived with her husband, Victor, and two-year-old daughter, Ann, in the small cottage across the lane from Green Farm. She distinctly recalled what happened when part of the plane crashed into her cottage, She heard

a terrific high-pitched screaming sound of a falling plane. I was standing by the open kitchen window . . . I just stood there, frozen with fear. Then I was hurled bodily backward against the kitchen table. Falling plaster from the walls and ceiling filled the room with clouds of choking dust, doors were blown from their hinges, the thatched roof of our cottage was set on fire, large trees outside our home were flattened in an instant by a tremendous blast, chunks of white hot metal from the exploding bombs were flying and falling everywhere. It was an absolute miracle that Ann and I were mercifully unharmed. She appeared to be stunned as I picked her up and rushed her outside to safety and her pram.

Victor rushed to the scene and "saw the dreadful sight of the pitiful remains of the bomber's crew. A few heads, arms, and legs, all blown to pieces and scattered haphazardly among and near the burning wreckage were all that remained of what had been ten human beings a few minutes earlier."[8]

Meanwhile, the wreckage of the aircraft continued to burn at Green Farm, consuming the large farmhouse across the street from the Gooderham's cottage. The Gooderhams lost nearly everything but escaped with their lives. Ruby Gooderham gave birth to a baby boy less than a month later. The American government fully compensated both the farmer at Green Farm and the Gooderhams for damages from the crash.

Meanwhile, those who knew Rongstad remembered him as a good pilot who had amassed 263.9 hours in the B-17. However, the accident report attributes the crash to pilot error: "Too steep a turn attempted after take-off before sufficient altitude attained. Aircraft stalled, crashed."

When I visited Horham in June 2008, James Mutton and Alan Johnson drove me out to the sight of the Green Farm crash. It was a sunny day with blue skies, and the narrow lane to the farm was edged with thick shrubbery and mature trees. The Green Farm today is a large modern farmstead, built on the spot of the burned farmhouse. The farmer took us behind the house to a densely wooded area where the plane had come down. A few weeks before, the farmer had gone into the grove with a shovel and unearthed many artifacts from the crash, including live .50-caliber ammunition, scraps of metal, rubber from the massive tires, and pieces of gauges and instruments. The museum at the Red Feather Club has a case full of artifacts from the Green Farm crash. Perhaps because the crash happened literally on the base and because it affected the local civilian population, the Green Farm crash continues to hold a special fascination for Horham's people.

Though the Rongstad crew flew their final mission for only seconds, the mission has passed into 95th lore and legend. In 2010, a memorial was placed at Rongstad crash site.

For the men of the 95th, death could come at any time and strike without warning. Either a man learned to deal with it, or he would end up removed from combat. Despite the terrible sights of fellow airmen falling from the sky, nearly all of the young air crewmen somehow steeled themselves to climb back into their deadly machines time and time again and take off into a sky that even over England could become unfriendly in the blink of an eye.

13 Entertainment and London

The war that the flight crews of the 95th fought was a strange one. One moment, a crewman might be twenty thousand feet in the air and in temperatures at fifty degrees below zero, fighting for his life against German fighters and flak. A few short hours later, that same crewman might be dressed in his Class A uniform and standing in the middle of bustling Piccadilly Circus in downtown London with a lovely young woman on his arm.

Each crewman crawled out of clean sheets, had a hot meal, faced down death over Europe, then returned to another hot meal and a familiar bed. It was a mentally disconcerting way to fight a war. It played serious games with a man's head.

The tiny village of Horham had little to offer in the way of entertainment besides the Green Dragon pub. Though the men's living quarters were only a few minutes' walk from the village, connected to it by a series of narrow, winding roads, some flight crews never set foot in Horham at all, preferring to spend their days off in London.

Because the base at Horham was widely dispersed, the weather mild, and the terrain relatively flat, many 95th flight and ground personnel had bicycles. British bikes operated differently from the American ones. For one, their pedals continued to turn even when the rider would have preferred to coast, resulting in a number of accidents, some serious. The men rarely locked up their bikes, and as a result theft was rampant, though the preferred term was "requisitioned."

As noted, one could socialize in the various clubs on base, depending on rank. The Officers' Club, though an ordinary Nissen hut on the outside, had a fireplace and comfortable overstuffed chairs, a piano, and a bar. The flying enlisted men's club, the Red Feather, was also quite cozy and outfitted with soft couches, a fireplace, and a bar. The Aero Club, run by the Red Cross, served the base's nonflying enlisted men. It had a pool table, ping-pong tables, a library, and areas to play cards or read.

The base had a large theater that showed newsreels and recently released Hollywood movies. Later in the war, it showed movies almost nightly. The theater also hosted live stage acts. Industrious airmen added cushioned seats and indirect lighting.

Attending a movie at the base theater could be a trying experience. Pilot Eugene Fletcher remembers the projector as

> an antiquated job suspended in a box from the ceiling with loudspeakers tossed around any place where somebody is apt to sit.
>
> The lights are put out and the machine is started. The next five minutes are spent trying to focus on the screen. Finally the job is accomplished and you've missed the introduction to the movie. Things run along pretty smoothly now for three or four minutes, then the picture doesn't appear on the screen but the talk goes on anyway. The operator immediately remedies this. The picture comes back and the sound track quits. So the operator makes a few more adjustments. Everything is all set now. Then what happens? The first reel is finished and we have to rewind and set up the second reel.
>
> The whole process is continued until the last reel has been shown. By that time you are completely worn out mentally and physically for the benches are very hard and your neck is so stiff from bobbing your head around that you welcome the chance to get up and go home. Each time I swear it's my last but I always wind up going back.[1]

The 95th also had its own dance band, which included members who had played professionally in civilian life. The occasional dances on base were enjoyable. Women were trucked in to serve as dance partners, and the rafters shook with the big band sounds as the young men and women tried momentarily to forget the stresses of war. Bombardier Leonard Herman recalls that early dances were pleasantly lacking in decorum. "Good lingerie was quite scarce during the war and many of the fellows were quite happy that there was not enough material to go around." Finally an order was issued that banned tossing women without undergarments in the air. Still, the events were loosely controlled, beginning with a couple of six-by-six trucks loaded with girls lurching into camp. "Some girls stayed over, had a hot breakfast, and left in the morning," he remembers.

Herman recalls the 335th Squadron had a tiny puppy as its mascot. "We spoiled this little dog. Everybody missed their dogs back in the States. At one of the bashes, a gal stayed over." To the chagrin of the squadron, her date gave her the squadron mascot. "So the story began, 'Lt. Bombardier X traded his little puppy for a little pussy.'"[2]

Occasionally, important visitors or entertainers came calling. Col. Curtis LeMay spent the early years of the air war on and near the base before being assigned to the command of the B-29 Superfortress units in the Pacific. World War I flying ace Eddie Rickenbacker addressed base personnel from the balcony of the Horham control tower. Lt. Gen. Jimmy Doolittle, hero of the first American bombing raid over Tokyo and commander of the Eighth Air Force, visited Horham after the 95th became the first American daylight bomber group over Berlin. Roman Catholic archbishop Francis J. Spellman paid a call, and Glenn Miller and his band played at the group's 200th mission bash in March 1944.

Group chaplains cared for the base's spiritual needs. Catholic chaplain Edward P. Nolan and his colleague Father Christopher J. Hinckley said Mass for the base's Catholics, while Chaplain George Myers handled interdenominational Protestant services. The base also held specific services for Jews, Christian Scientists, and Latter-Day Saints. Religious holidays such as Christmas and Easter were bittersweet for the homesick men, but these services were packed, especially midnight Mass on Christmas Eve.

Sports provided needed exercise and relieved boredom and stress. The 95th fielded one of the top basketball teams in England throughout the war. One member of the team was tall, gangly navigator William "Ed" Charles of Indiana. "We had a good team," he told me some years ago. "I was one of only three flying personnel on the team. The flying personnel turned over too fast for any continuity." The core of the team began playing together while training in Rapid City. Stateside, it went undefeated, winning twenty straight games, scoring 758 points, and winning the Rapid City Army Air Base Basketball title.

Once overseas, the team became known as the Gallopers and walloped opponents all over England, winning the Eighth Air Force Basketball Championship, the Third Air Division Basketball Championship, the Bury St. Edmunds American Red Cross Basketball Championship, and the Norwich American Red Cross Championship.[3] The following year, the team successfully defended all its titles except the Eighth Air Force championship, which it lost by two points in the final forty seconds. Photographs of the team show a muscular and determined lot, ranging in age from teenagers to men in their early thirties.

The 95th's table tennis team "went on to whatever kind of glory such an enterprise leads to," according to the *Contrails* reporter, who was obviously not a fan. The team won ninety-one out of a hundred tournaments in two seasons and was twice crowned Third Air Division champions. "The way they played that innocent-looking game would make you think it was organized mayhem," the reporter concludes with grudging respect.[4]

Ted Majer worked in the 412th Squadron, handing out and collecting aircrews' flight gear on mission days. The quiet, bespectacled Majer was also a member of the 95th's ping-pong team. When asked years later how he helped win the war, the unassuming Majer told family and friends he'd helped win the war by playing ping-pong.

The 95th fielded a baseball team as well. Known as the 95th Bombers, the team won the Third Air Division championship one year and went to the Eighth Air Force baseball championship three straight years, but it never won the big one. The team also has the distinction of playing in the longest baseball game in the history of the United Kingdom (UK), an eighteen-inning game at High Wycombe. The team also traveled to Belfast, Northern Ireland, and beat the Eighth Composite Command 3–0. After the obligatory pub crawl, the team returned home.

For those not quite at this caliber of play, usually fellows would join a pickup game of some kind. Other sports opportunities included horseshoe pitching, quoits, volleyball, and tennis.

If a man was not up to the physical exertion required on the diamond or the court, a rousing game of cards could be found in nearly any barracks most nights. Prodigious amounts of money changed hands in these friendly but cutthroat contests. Pilot Robert J. Brodersen and a buddy won so big in a base high-stakes poker game that they decided to pool their money and buy a horse. A local refused to sell them a fine-looking horse, but he agreed to sell them an older one in its stead for £65. The duo took the mare, whom they named Queenie, to Basil the blacksmith and then rode her triumphantly back to the base.

"We found a long rope and tied Queenie behind the barracks," remembers Brodersen, "as there was grass everywhere. Every day that we didn't have to fly, we'd harness her up and go for a ride to town or to the local pub, which was about two miles up the road. She was a very gentle horse, and smart, too. When coming home from the pub, after dark, she would take all the correct turns back to the barracks, without any help from the driver. Whether home or away, someone was always petting her and she loved it."

In July 1944, Brodersen notes with concern in his diary that Queenie had begun losing weight. "The English farmers thrashed their oats, so she hasn't been getting any oat bundles any more. While eating breakfast with Hal this morning, we were discussing what we could find Queenie to eat, as grass wasn't enough to keep her in shape. For breakfast in the mess hall there was always a big box of Corn Flakes on the table, and we got the idea that Queenie might like them. We took a box back to the barracks for her, and she just loved them. We tore the top of the box open, and we couldn't get her head out till she ate them all. We brought her a box every morning, and in a few days she started getting her strength back. It was a miracle!"[5]

Many men, especially those from rural areas, loved to hunt and fish, and most did not understand the concept that in England, the land belongs to the queen and is off-limits. Pilot Bill Lindley hunted regularly on the queen's reserves, as did many others, and as far as this author can tell, no one was ever fined.

Some of the best entertainment on base was spontaneous. Ribbing and practical joking, both good natured and otherwise, was a common tension breaker. When a bunch of energetic young men get together, in close proximity to firearms, high-octane fuel, and live ammunition, they have all the ingredients for fun. It wasn't long before flight crews began blowing things up, both intentionally and accidentally. Tossing bullets into the stove proved an enjoyable diversion. Men also discovered practical uses for the fuel and tapped into supplies regularly. Leonard Herman used it to dry-clean his uniform, and John Walter used it in his cigarette lighter. Explosions were always good for a laugh and future kidding.

With men packed into cramped Nissen huts, there was bound to be some tension. Robert Inman remembers that some men in his hut insisted on playing chess after lights-out. Inman wreaked his revenge one day while the offenders were flying a mission. He took a red-hot poker and burned a hole in every other square on the painstakingly constructed chessboard. "I think it was several years before they talked to me again," he adds.

Sometimes the ribbing resulted from funny things that happened in the air. Top turret/engineer Earle Bogacki remembers that shortly after takeoff one day, his plane took a direct hit on the Plexiglas nose. Marvin Markus, the togglier, came back to the cockpit, his face ashen, his chest covered with blood. Closer inspection determined he was slathered with bird guts from an enormous raven or crow. Once the scare was over, this incident was good for "a few chuckles now and then," remembers Bogacki.[6]

Another hilarious character was a young radioman/gunner named Hon Quan Lee, who had lived in China until age twelve and consequently spoke fluent Chinese. When Lee became excited during missions, he would jabber away in a mixture of Chinese and English, cracking up his crewmates. On one mission, the excitable Lee managed to shoot the aerial off his own aircraft!

Also good for a laugh were incidents involving in-flight urination and defecation. Often a crewman urinated into the B-17's rubber relief tube and coated the front of the ball turret. Soon it would be covered with a layer of yellow ice. Occasionally a crewman was forced to use his flak helmet as a commode. In the heat of battle, he would forget and clamp the helmet onto his head. The resulting story was bound to be told and retold as long as the witnesses were around, even sixty years later at reunions.

The ultimate recreation for airmen in England was the long-awaited trips to London. Upon acquiring the necessary pass to the bustling capital, men were ferried to the train station at Eye in a two-and-a-half ton truck. "Eye was the closest town that had direct trains to London," remembers pilot John Walter. "The trains were often full and the men had to stand during the trip." Walter used to remove his gas mask from its bag and take the bag, minus the mask, as a carry-on.

Sometimes the drinking and fun began before the train even arrived in London. Leonard Herman remembers one trip where his pilot, Johnny Johnson, already "in his cups," had climbed up into the overhead luggage rack in the crew's compartment. "There were eight guys in that car, along with their liquor, and one of us took Johnny's shoes and socks off and threw his socks out the window of the moving train. Then he put Johnny's shoes back on. Johnny was so stoned he didn't even budge."

Once in London, the tipsy crew loaded into and onto a cab. When Johnson was seated, he looked down and noticed he wasn't wearing socks. "How could I have gotten dressed without my socks?" he asked his straight-faced companions. "He kept marveling at it, wondering how he could have done such a thing," remembers Herman. Sadly, Johnson was killed several months later without ever resolving this conundrum.

"When we went to London on the train, there were some places we really enjoyed," Herman remembers. "The Grosvenor House was a fine place to have a drink while the ladies drank tea. One day some of us were there when we heard a commotion. Flying through the door was none other than Clark Gable, being chased by a pack of screaming women. Fortunately the elevator operator opened the door, Clark entered, the door shut quickly, and up he went."

London had been heavily bombed for nearly four years by the time the American airmen began arriving in strength. Its people were by now resigned to a life of rationing, air raid sirens, and sudden death. The city was blacked out nightly, an eerie sight to Americans whose own country was safe from enemy bombs. At night, one had to feel one's way around the streets, a strange thing to do in a city of that size and with so much night-time activity. It was said that whores ran their hands up a serviceman's pant leg not as a come-on but to check the fabric. Varying qualities indicated whether the man was British or American, and officer or enlisted.

The most popular area in London for American servicemen was Piccadilly Circus. Navigator William Gifford of the 336th Squadron remembers:

"Piccadilly Circus was *the* gathering place in London, and though the statue of Eros had been [encased in concrete] for safety reasons, its influence was still felt very strongly. The English pound was pegged at $4, which was very deceiving. A shilling was worth 1/20th of a pound and spent by the GIs as they would normally spend a nickel at home. Needless to say, the Americans fouled up the local economy just as they did everywhere they went.

"The Windmill was *the* burlesque theater in London, and had the distinction of never missing a performance throughout the entire war. . . . The shows were elaborate, well-staged, and quite ribald. Costumes were so skimpy, it was necessary to cage one's eyeballs. British law allowed total nudity as long as the person did not move. The skits were well populated with female 'statues.'"[7]

John Walter recalls that "Piccadilly Circus was the major center of activity in London. At night, the sidewalks around the concrete-barricaded statue of Eros were heavily populated by girls. The word 'girls' could be changed to 'whores' without erroneously describing the scene and only slandering a very few."[8]

After visiting Piccadilly, many red-blooded Americans went in search of like-minded women, which in wartime London were not difficult to find—or catch. Leonard Herman reported, "There were always plenty of women. They loved the air corps uniforms, and of course they knew we made a lot more money than the Brits. There were very, very few eligible English men around, so the Yanks had a pretty good deal. As the English used to say, we were 'over-paid, over-fed, over-sexed, and over here.'"

The American soldiers, in fact, made five times as much as their British counterparts did. It was an exciting scene for the young men, many of whom had never been in a big city, let alone been surrounded by so much to see and do. In Soho, they were bombarded with "very explicit, very descriptive sex ads, including very explicit pictures, [that] were displayed on bulletin boards, doorways, and telephone booths," remembers Gifford.

Prostitution in wartime London was big business. The corner news vendors hawked condoms along with their traditional papers and racing forms, and the women plied their trade in the open. The general term for a prostitute around Piccadilly became "Piccadilly commando," and many a B-17 was so named during the war.

Gifford recalls: "It was said that English girls did not consider themselves prostitutes unless they laid down to have sex. In a black-out, opportune trysting places were unlimited. Favorite locales included telephone booths, doorways, taxi cabs—you name them, they used them. To quote an unknown: 'There is no such thing as bad sex. Just some is better than others, and any beats none at all!'"[9]

According to John Walter, "Prices ranged from two pounds ($8.70) for a 'quickie' in a nearby alley to ten pounds ($47.50) for all night." (Neither Walter nor his crewmates ever succumbed to temptation.)

Ted Lucey remembers: "In Piccadilly, a Yank needs only hold up his hand with one or more fingers extended. He'll immediately be besieged by the notorious 'Commandos'. Number of fingers indicates how many pounds Yank will pay for certain 'quality' of woman. These gals, formerly available to such British forces as are here, curse them now and won't have anything to do with them, because the Yank has money and is carelessly generous with it."[10]

Prostitution by itself was not a serious problem for the military, but the venereal disease (VD) that often resulted from it was bad for the war effort. By the end of 1943, there was a VD epidemic in the United Kingdom, and the Americans introduced a new prophylactic kit, called a Pro-Kit, that contained two condoms and a tube of sulfathiazole and calomel to stem the tide.

Pinched by rationing and with husbands or boyfriends stationed far away in other theaters of war, many young women were willing to provide company, and sometimes more, to the American airmen and soldiers. In an economy so tight that women drew false seams on the back of their calves with eye liner to simulate silk stockings, a good dinner and a movie with a handsome young American seemed a fair trade for an evening together.

Tail gunner Daniel L. Kinney, in his reminiscences, recounts an unusual but touching incident. "As I came out of the Universal Brasserie, a restaurant and bar, it was about 10 p.m. and pitch black. I'd had a lot to drink, and I couldn't remember the name of my hotel. I was wandering down the street, trying to figure out what to do, when I was accosted by two British GIs who attempted to mug me. I hollered bloody murder for an MP, who came running as the Brits disappeared. Almost immediately, I was approached by two elderly women, who asked me where I was going. I could not tell them because I still could not remember the name of my hotel. Anyway, they took me home with them, tucked me into bed, and when I woke up the next morning, I found myself in bed between them. No hanky panky involved, just two lovely women who felt sorry for me. I put a five pound note on their table and left, heading back to the base."[11]

Another popular stop near Piccadilly Circus was the Red Cross Club at the corner of Shaftesbury Avenue and Denman Street known as Rainbow Corner, complete with an exact replica of an American corner drugstore in the basement. At Rainbow Corner the men could listen to the jukebox, dance, shower, get a shoeshine or a haircut, change money, play pool or ping-pong, and book tours. Adele Astaire, whose brother was the famous movie star, volunteered at Rainbow Corner and could be found there most days.[12]

Many young men had no interest in the prostitutes and wild nightlife of London. Bob Cozens was a married man, and on his rare forays into London, he says, "I went straight to the Dunhill Pipe Shop when it opened and grabbed all I could get." Other young men satisfied themselves with seeing the many historic sites, sketching, visiting museums, and generally soaking up the ambience of one of the world's great cities. Places to visit included Westminster Abbey, St. Paul's Cathedral, Buckingham Palace, Madame Tussauds Wax Museum, Hyde Park, and London's many museums.

John Walter remembers: "The movie houses and theaters, although the marquees were dark, were very much in operation. Among the shows we saw were *Arsenic and Old Lace* (new at the time), *Strike It Again* with Sid Field, *Is Your Honeymoon Really Necessary?* and Sir Lawrence Olivier's *Henry V.* This latter film was most spectacular for two reasons. First, it was in Technicolor (still somewhat novel in 1944), and second, because it had been made in wartime England."

Tom Hammond was another young pilot who loved London for its cultural activities. His monthly pay of $225 a month was, for Tom, "a princely sum, considering he had been earning about forty-four dollars a month working in a textile mill" back home. "London sure does cover a large area," he writes, "I believe it would take me a year to learn how to get around here. The English cities are not built in orderly fashion like ours are. They are built very haphazardly and the streets run in every direction but the right one. There is also a very elaborate underground railway, but you almost need a guide in order to make use of it."[13]

Ted Lucey visited London in October 1943 and noted "hundreds of civilians camping in subway stations for the night. Little children sleep somehow, oblivious to the noise and bustle going on around them."[14]

Some airmen belonged to private clubs in London. They cost a few pounds to join, allowing the proprietors to be selective of their clientele, and featured booze, food, music, and sometimes a floor show. Ed Charles was a member of several. His entry card reads: "The New Nut House, 96, Regent St. W. 1. Mr. David Finer requests the pleasure of the company of William Charles at a Private Party held nightly at the above address. From 11 p.m. onwards. Holder's Signature: _____ This invitation must be presented at the door." Flip side: "This information is for your protection. Under the Defence Regulations, excessive drinking is forbidden and anyone abusing the premises will have their card withdrawn. All our parties are held in strict accordance with the law."

While visiting the city, quite a few men from the 95th experienced what had become commonplace in London by the time the Americans had joined the war effort—that is, attacks on London by German bombers and V-1 buzz bombs, which were essentially cruise missiles. One night, while Leonard Herman slept with a lovely young lady in a London hotel room, they were awakened when antiaircraft fire started from the roof. Herman recognized the distinctive sound of the German planes' de-synchronized engines as they approached. His girlfriend jumped up and exclaimed: "My God, they're bombing! Let's get out of here!"

As he recalls, "I said, 'Are you crazy? If we have to go, let's just get it in bed. If we have to go, that's the way to go.' She agreed with me, and that's exactly what we did."

William Gifford recollects a similar attack: "I was already in bed when I heard the sirens, followed by an ominous putt-putt-putt. The butterfly valve on the engine that propelled the V-1 Flying Bomb made a very distinctive noise. As long as you could hear the pulsing sound, the bomb continued on its flight. When it ran out of propellant, silence. The Flying Bomb glided down to earth and exploded. The psychological effect of the unpredictability of its target made the bomb an awesome weapon. Those that made it across the English Channel created stark terror throughout the English countryside."[15]

Bombardier William H. "Bill" Greene of the 95th was in London on June 30, 1944. "Went to London for the last time," he writes. "Blitz-bombed. Knocked out of my bed. Often wondered what it is like during a blitz. Joe Eldracker (waist gunner) and I were lying in bed sleeping when—WHAM!— we found ourselves on the floor. The room was full of flying glass and plaster. Blew the door out and part of the wall. Joe was hit in the leg by flying glass and bleeding like a stuck pig. The Regent Palace was a madhouse. Screams, shouting, cries for help. Finally I got Joe to a hospital at Charing Cross, where he was sewn up.

"They started bringing in people from cars, G.I. trucks, ambulances. . . . Never saw so much blood in my life. We were put to work carrying stretchers. Never thought people could be so cut up and live. Finally had to turn them away at the hospital—truckloads of them. Learned that one 1,000-pounder hit the top of the hotel and one 2,000-pounder hit the rear. Thank God for no fire. I think it might be safer at the base."[16]

By mid- to late 1943, however, it was becoming apparent to the flight crews that, in the words of reporter Harrison Salisbury, "to fly in the Eighth Air Force was to hold a ticket to a funeral. *Your own.*"[17] Base surgeons were seeing more and more cases of men with stress-related symptoms ranging from insomnia and nausea to intense nightmares. Though men joked about being "flak-happy" or that they had the "Focke-Wulf jitters," they actually had classic cases of what would later be diagnosed as post-traumatic stress disorder.

Unlike the Royal Air Force, the U.S. Army Air Forces had no set policy in dealing with stress cases. The RAF tagged such cases as "lacking in moral fibre" and dismissed them in shame from the service.[18] The American military took a more compassionate approach, dealing with each flier on an individual basis. In the winter of 1942, the Eighth Air Force's chief medical officer, Dr. Malcolm Grow, had suggested to Brig. Gen. Ira Eaker that men be rotated out of combat duty after fifteen missions. Though Eaker refused, he did agree to limit combat missions to twenty-five. As the war progressed and fighter escort improved, the mission requirement was raised to thirty and later to thirty-five.

Flight surgeons treated combat stress with the few remedies at their disposal in bomb group hospitals. A shot of sodium amytal sent a fatigued flier into a deep sleep that could last forty-eight to seventy-two hours. Surgeons also used sodium thiopental to force repressed anxieties to the surface and help the patient deal with them.

When a crew appeared to be flak-happy, the flight surgeon also could recommend to the squadron or group commander that a crew be sent to a "flak house." These homes catered to airmen, providing them a soft bed, hot bath, privacy, and manicured grounds to relax in and roam.

Bogacki remembers flak leave at Southport, England, near Liverpool: "We went sightseeing, horseback riding on the beach, and of course bar hopping with plenty of ice cold beer, a rarity in most small pubs over there."[19] Many estates had butlers and maids. Men could hunt; play tennis, croquet or golf; or simply sit under a tree and read or rest. Many men found it difficult to adjust to the slow pace, and frequently, they cut their flak leave short to return to combat.

Throughout the war, American airmen learned to love the tranquility of the English countryside and the urban excitement of London. Their leisure activities allowed them to forget, albeit briefly, the dangers they faced on missions if they were flyboys and the sheer drudgery and grueling hard work if they were ground pounders. Many men took the opportunity, in later years, to return and see everything anew. Some places had changed. However, the Church of St. Mary still watches over the village green in Horham, the peals of Big Ben still reverberate over London city streets, and Piccadilly Circus still hums with activity. Sometimes, one can go back and recapture a part of the old magic of the war years.

14 Regensburg Shuttle Mission

On August 14, 1943, exactly one year after the United States had flown its first tentative combat mission over Europe, the Eighth Air Force launched one of the air war's most daring missions. Seven groups of the Fourth Combat Wing, including the 95th, would strike aircraft factories at Regensburg while the First Air Wing would simultaneously attack ball bearing factories at Schweinfurt. Underscoring the importance of the mission was the fact that none other than Curtis LeMay would lead it himself. Equipped with long-range Tokyo tanks, the planes of the Fourth Combat Wing would then cross the Alps and the Mediterranean Sea and land in North Africa, while those of the First Wing would return to England the same day. The planners hoped that this "double-strike" mission would split the Luftwaffe's witheringly effective fighter response.

Planning began in July, when a lead crew from each participating bomb group was called to Wing Headquarters and notified of the mission. These crews were sworn to secrecy and removed from mission status until the raids took place. The rest of the crews would not be informed of the raid until right before the mission.

Radio operator William Irving remembers waking up at 1:30 a.m. on August 14 and eating breakfast at 2 a.m. "While we were eating, a couple of Officers came into the mess hall and made an announcement that set us all wondering and speculating. We were told to pack certain articles of clothing, blankets, canteens and mess kits and several other things. Some of us, in fact most of us, had the thought that we might land in Africa or Sicily that night." When his speculation was confirmed at a later briefing, Irving's concern over the mission's riskiness was trumped by the fact that "none of us wanted to miss it."[1] Pilot Bill Lindley, flying *Zoot Suiters*, was excited to get going: "This mission was my kind of action. You never knew what would happen, but you looked forward to a change of scenery." Hoping to capture some exciting fighter attack photos, he appointed his copilot Orville Tigerman as mission cameraman.

Morning mist delayed takeoff, a worrisome detail because the Regensburg force could not be delayed more than ninety minutes if it was to reach North Africa in daylight. "For a while, it looked as if Command might cancel the mission, but gradually the mist thinned and the 4th Wing was ordered off."[2]

The planned 5:30 a.m. takeoff actually occurred instead at 7:15 a.m. Twenty-four 95th Bomb Group aircraft began their tedious climb to altitude, as did the aircraft of the Fourth Wing's six other groups, including the brand-new 390th, stationed at the 95th's old base at Framlingham. Some groups took nearly two hours to form up, burning precious fuel that they would need to reach North Africa. Mission planners again discussed calling off the mission but decided to press on. By 9:35 a.m. the groups completed their assembly and droned across the English Channel in clearing skies.

Now other elements of the plan began to unravel. The First Wing, stationed farther inland, could not take off owing to the weather. For a mission whose success relied on every element working like a precision watch, this start was inauspicious.

Four groups of P-47 Thunderbolt fighters had been assigned to provide cover for the Fourth Wing, which was expected to draw heavy concentrations of Luftwaffe fighters. The Allies' plan anticipated the German fighters would take on the Fourth Wing, then have to land and refuel. Meanwhile, the First Wing was supposed to be overhead, relatively unopposed by fighters. However, the First Wing's late start meant that the German fighters would have time to engage the Fourth, land, refuel, and be ready when the First appeared overhead.

By the time the 95th reached the continent, the visibility was good, up to twenty miles. "Enemy fighters pecked away at our formation for two hours, never very many, but with continuous replacements," reported Bill

Lindley. Meanwhile, his copilot was snapping excellent shots of the incoming fighters, or so they thought. When Tigerman was almost out of film, Lindley noticed that though the sight on the camera was above the windshield, the lens was below. Not a single photo came out, much to Lindley's disgust and disappointment.[3]

Two groups of P-47s were scheduled to meet the formation as it entered Germany. By this time, the formation was widely dispersed; fifteen miles separated the lead and rear boxes. One P-47 group showed up on schedule and provided cover for the lead boxes. However, the second group miscalculated the timing, and the rear boxes, straggling far behind, had no fighter protection whatsoever.

The Luftwaffe wasted no time in taking advantage of the situation. The 95th, flying lead in the rear box, fared slightly better in the devastating attacks than the low group, the 100th, which bore the brunt of the fighter attacks.

General Eaker had assigned Lt. Col. Beirne Lay Jr., who was training to take over a group, to accompany the 100th Bomb Group on missions to prepare for the job. The high-ranking observer thus had a front-row seat to the furious air battle that ensued ten miles from the German border. "The sight was fantastic and surpassed fiction," he wrote in the mission report. "I fought an impulse to close my eyes, and overcame it. I knew I was going to die, and so were a lot of others."[4]

Within minutes, the German fighters had shot down six Forts from the 95th and 100th. Lay watched in horror as a German fighter pilot stepped out of his burning plane, folded himself into a ball, and somersaulted through the middle of the 100th's formation.

Finally, the first group of P-47s, returning from escorting the lead boxes, began to pass the carnage occurring in the rear box. As the Thunderbolt pilots watched helplessly, their fuel reserves expended, Forts began to fall from the sky.

"The battle moved over Germany at 180 miles an hour, its course marked by flashes, flames, smoke, the debris of disintegrating aircraft, parachutes and men, the noise indescribable," writes Roger Freeman.[5]

Harry Conley records: "We met around 300 fighters, and for a little over two hours the battle raged. It was a terrible fight, even worse than Kiel in my opinion."[6]

William Irving writes: "The fighters did not come in one or two at a time but came through the formation a squadron at a time. At one time in particular a squadron of fighters came through the formation and took out three B-17s just as fast as the snap of a finger."[7]

Navigator E. A. Backa reported: "Before the target, at about 11:30, an Me 109 came in at 10:30 o'clock from about a thousand yards. I fired several bursts as he came in. At about 500 yards away burst of flame in engine and explosion and both wings came off. Plane and parts fell down to earth."[8]

Second Lt. M. R. Neel Jr., a bombardier on pilot R. L. Yuenger's crew, shot down a German fighter as it attacked. "Just as he started [a] portal attack my tracers hit him. There was an explosion and the ship fell in two separate flaming pieces—motor separate from rest of ship. Came to within 800 yards—no one bailed out. It was an FW 190 and was hit head on."

First Lt. W. H. Powell, on another Fort, observed: "EA was within 200 yards of me. My tracer was surely going into his nose. At 200 yards it started to flame. A short time thereafter EA disintegrated with thousands of small pieces of AC coming off in flames."[9]

During the furious aerial battle, the 95th's gunners expended 100,000 rounds of ammunition. William Irving remembers that the men in the nose of his aircraft were firing so much ammunition that they were running out. The wooden 265-round boxes were too heavy to carry, so Irving opened the boxes and started pushing the belted rounds up the catwalk to the bomb bay, where the engineer grabbed them and hustled them down to the nose.[10]

After fighting off enemy attacks for an hour and a half, the sky became strangely quiet shortly before the target. In the preceding firefight, seventeen Forts of the initial force of 143 had gone down. Thirteen had come from the rear combat bomb wing.

The bombing results at Regensburg were good, according to most sources. Col. Curtis LeMay claimed that the objective was totally destroyed. Bill Lindley also reported that the strikes were on target. The official mission report, written by operations Lt. Frank Imand, states that "visual reports of the bombing were reported as excellent." Navigator Basie DeWolf, who flew with Bob Cozens, filed the lead bombardier's report. He states that the bombing, carried out from 18,000 feet at an indicated airspeed of

153 miles per hour, hit the target but dust obscured the results. However, a high-flying photo reconnaissance aircraft reported several days later that nearly all the bombs fell either on the factory or the adjacent airfield.[11] Roger Freeman adds that unknown to the airmen at the time, the raid destroyed most of the fuselage jigs (frames) for Germany's top-secret fighter, the Me-262.[12]

Their bombs dropped, the Fourth Wing banked away from Regensburg for the seventy-mile leg to the Swiss Alps, covered in snow and bathed in bright sunlight under a blue sky. "Minutes later we were over the Alps," remembers Bill Lindley. "Visibility was forever and never have I seen anything, before or since, that could rival that magnificent picture of majestic splendor."[13]

Once across the Alps, LeMay had the force drop to low altitude to conserve fuel and make for the North African coast at Telergma and Bone, Algeria. While over the northern tip of Italy, the group made two or three 360-degree turns to allow stragglers to catch up before it crossed the Mediterranean. The Italian Air Force elected not to engage the formation over Italy or the Mediterranean. Many of the stragglers were dangerously low on fuel. Irving watched as one B-17 lost altitude and prepared to land at a small airstrip in Italy. "He appeared to be making his final approach and was almost on the ground when for some unknown reason, the ship exploded."[14] He could do nothing but watch helplessly.

The 95th lost four aircraft and crews. Besides the Hayden crew, the J. L. Sundberg crew, the W. A. Baker crew, and the R. C. Mason crew were lost for the duration, with five killed and the rest taken prisoner or evaded. Other aircraft were going down in the sea, some because of battle damage while others ran out of fuel. Navigator Nathaniel Mencow with the 390th BG told me years later, "As we went across the Mediterranean, every fifteen or twenty miles there was a B-17 in the water."[15]

Irving remembers that "ships started running out of gas and a good many ships hit the water that day. I was standing by on the distress frequency and heard more SOS calls that day than I have ever heard before or since."[16]

The Regensburg mission was also unkind to the 100th Bomb Group, which had flown in the vulnerable low position in the rear box and borne the brunt of the relentless fighter attack. The group lost ten B-17s.

"These first anniversary raids occupy a prominent place in the history of the Eighth Air Force for a number of reasons," writes Freeman, "not the least of which was the loss of 60 bombers (the previous high was 26 on the June 13th Kiel raid). Against this gunner claims ran to an even more staggering figure of 288 enemy aircraft destroyed." According to the operational records, the 95th claimed 25 of the Fourth Wing's 140 confirmed kills. Freeman asserts, however, that if indeed 288 Luftwaffe fighters had been shot down, it would have constituted every plane the Germans had put up that day. Claims were later reduced to 148, with nearly another 100 damaged or probables, and still represented a crippling blow to the Luftwaffe.[17] Subsequent investigation put true German losses at 27 fighters in a battle that nevertheless was one of the most heated and intense of World War II.

One by one, the Forts and their dog-tired crews staggered into Algeria, only to find that the airfield at Bone was unmanned. "The Allied forces that were supposed to meet and refuel us had moved on to pursue the retreating Germans and Italians. The place was deserted!" remembers Bill Lindley. "Curtis LeMay was visibly upset when he called Lieutenant General Carl 'Tooey' Spaatz, the Commanding General of the 12th Air Force, yelling into the microphone, 'Hey, Tooey! We're at Bone. Where the hell is everybody? Goddamnit! There's no one here to service our aircraft!'"[18]

He continues: "Bone had a few tents and mud shacks where we could sleep on the ground. Almost everyone opted for underneath the wing of their aircraft. The tent bar was going full blast, with plenty of whisky and a piano. There were a few Australians around, and the Aussies sang songs that made the British look like nuns in a convent."

"After fighting in the skies all day—eleven hours and twenty minutes of recorded flight time with about three of it under the fiercest of all fighter attacks—our crew arrived in North Africa," writes Eldon Broman's copilot John Chaffin. "Broman and I make a bed on the wing of the airplane. It is hard; not level, and there is the possibility of falling the ten or twelve feet to the ground. We are so tired, however, we have no trouble sleeping."[19]

The next day, some men decided to venture into the nearest town, a place called Constantine. John Chaffin made the trip. "The fascinating ancient city sits on the top of a large stone mountain which juts up vertically from the desert floor to a height of about eight hundred feet. Centuries-old buildings and shops line narrow, winding streets. Old men sit in the shade on the sidewalks. Merchandise of all kinds is sold from the small side street stands and open shops. Most of all, however, are the hoards of little children. Within seconds you are surrounded by dozens of little eight-to-twelve-year-old urchins. They are dirty and look undernourished. They beg for money, candy, gum or cigarettes. Many are hustlers for prostitutes: 'Hey mister, come home with me for chicken dinner and fuck my sister!'"[20]

"We had a wonderful time in North Africa," Harry Conley wrote his mother. "The greatest treat of all was that we got all the fresh eggs, vegetables, and fruit that we could eat. Also white bread (French), which is unheard of in England. For a week we just laid around in the nice warm sun and swam and ate and went to town.

"We had lots of fun trading soap and mattress covers to the Arabs for eggs, chickens, watermelons, and some of our boys even got a donkey and took him back to England. For one bar of Army soap, we got nine dozen eggs! The Arabs love the mattress covers. They cut a couple of holes in them and wear them."[21]

William Irving remembers that the destitute Arabs showed up at the base with wheelbarrows. They picked through the garbage and took food home to their families.

Meanwhile, the men had to wait for the necessary fuel to be shipped in so that they could refuel their planes and finish their shuttle. Not only did the base not have any fuel, but also it had no workers to refuel the planes. The aircrews solved the problem with typical American ingenuity and not a little griping.

Remembers John Chaffin: "Early in the morning on August 15, fifty-gallon drums of gasoline are left at our airplanes along with a hand operated pump. We are to refuel the plane by hand—*twenty-seven hundred gallons*!" Pilot Eldon Broman picks up the story: "They brought us . . . drums of what was supposed to be gas. I looked at it and thought, 'That doesn't look like gas. It's pretty oily.' But we put it in."

"With ten of us to take turns on the pump, even in this heat, it is not too tough," remembers John Chaffin. "We pump a few barrels and I'll be a son-of-a-bitch if some ground crew guys don't come back and say, 'Sorry as hell to tell you guys this, but some of those damn barrels are kerosene instead of gasoline. We use it around here for fueling our cooking stoves and lighting system. Sorry, but you will have to pump it all out and start over.'"[22]

William Irving recalls, "One man would have to stand on the wing and hold the hose in position and keep an eye on the tank. A couple more men would have to hold the pump in position while another man worked the handle. The whole thing was run in relays. It was too hot for a man to spend too much time on the wing. The metal became so hot that it was just about [to] blister his feet in no time. During that time they were also bringing around the bombs. We were to carry ten 500 pound bombs. We had to load and fuse them ourselves." A truck pulled up and the truckers simply pushed the bombs off the truck, each landing with a dull thud. "By all rights none of them was supposed to explode as they were not yet fused or anything but nevertheless none of us was any too happy. We were relieved when the last one had hit the ground and stopped rolling."[23] Especially relieved, one might imagine, were the men who had been at Alconbury.

"While our shuttle aircraft were being refueled at Bone," remembers Harry Conley, "one of our crews traded a bunch of mattress covers for a donkey and a cart. When their plane left for England with us on the shuttle return flight, they brought the donkey and cart with them. I remember looking out the window at that plane and I could see the donkey with an oxygen mask over his snout. His large ears were quite visible. They successfully got the donkey and cart safely back to Horham, where they later gave donkey cart rides to many of the local children."[24]

The North African donkey was unable to acclimate to the cold English climate and sadly succumbed to pneumonia or distemper during the winter months of 1943–1944. The crews decided to send their departed animal friend out in true 95th style. The deceased was fitted with his own surplus air corps uniform, complete with dog tags, and was dropped (sans parachute) near the initial point on a mission. "Unfortunately no one can record the confusion and consternation of the German people assigned to grave registration," remarks John Storie.[25]

Eldon Broman's crew, meanwhile, bought watermelons to take back to Horham as a treat. Fruit was very rare in wartime England.

On August 24, the 95th BG's eight flyable B-17s flew the return leg of the shuttle, a milk run over Bordeaux, France. Broman remembers: "The

French made us fly all the way around by way of Spain and Gibraltar, then east to Bordeaux. There were only about 80 of the 147 B-17s left by this time. Ten to twelve fighters met us before Bordeaux. Our gunners were shooting at the German fighters and all of a sudden the plane began to buck and shudder. Somehow, our inflatable life raft had deployed, and it was stuck on our horizontal stabilizer! That slowed us way down, and the 109s came after us." Broman jettisoned the bombs and then began fishtailing the Fort back and forth to shake the life raft loose. After several agonizing moments, the raft ripped and fell free.

The bombing results at Schweinfurt were somewhere between fairly good and negligible. The Regensburg-Schweinfurt double-strike mission was in the books, one for the ages, and it was time for High Command to learn from its successes and failures. It was becoming evident that without fighter escort, the B-17s were going to continue taking a heavy beating at the hands of the Luftwaffe. Gen. Henry "Hap" Arnold issued orders that the Eighth and Fifteenth Air Forces be given priority in ordering the new P-51 Mustang long-range fighter. A disappointment when introduced in 1940, the Mustang became a veritable tiger when Rolls-Royce Merlin engines replaced the original Allisons. The P-51 was the first American fighter with the range to accompany or rendezvous with the heavy bombers deep into Germany. The improved Mustang, with disposable drop tanks, could reach thirty thousand feet and fly 455 miles per hour, making it the equal or better of every fighter currently in Germany's arsenal. The introduction of the Mustang would be one of the main turning points in the air war in Europe.[26]

The impact of the Regensburg-Schweinfurt mission on the German leadership was devastating. On August 18, Luftwaffe chief of staff Hans Jeschonnek placed a gun to his temple and blew his brains out. German fighter pilot losses had skyrocketed from between 6 and 9 percent a month in early 1943 to 12 percent in May and 16 percent in July. In the first half of 1943, 67 percent of all crews had been lost. July and August nearly broke the back of the Luftwaffe fighter corps. Aircraft losses were huge, reaching 31.2 percent in July and 32 percent in August. In addition to combat losses, the Luftwaffe suffered extraordinary noncombat losses of between 40 and 45 percent, a problem that also plagued the U.S. Army Air Forces. In 1943, the USAAF had 20,389 major accidents in the continental United States, killing 2,264 pilots and 3,339 other flight crew members. The next year would be only a little better.[27]

At this juncture in the air war, Adolf Hitler made a grave miscalculation, changing his focus from air superiority to retaliation for Allied bombing raids on Germany. He began sinking precious German capital and resources into the army's V-2 and the Luftwaffe's V-1 retaliation weapons. One historian writes: "Unfortunately for Germany's cities, the critical production choices that German air strategy faced in the summer and fall of 1943 were made by individuals who did not possess the background to make intelligent decisions. Hitler, while he knew much about army weaponry and the conduct of ground operations, did not understand the technology or conduct of the air war. The fact that he consistently relied on [Hermann] Goering did nothing to enhance his knowledge, for the Reichsmarschall's technical expertise was severely lacking."[28]

For sheer audacity, the double-strike mission became one of the legendary aerial battles of World War II. Because of its performance on the shuttle mission, the 95th Bomb Group won its first Distinguished Unit Citation. The award would not be its last.

15

Black Week

The raid on Munster on October 10, 1943, posed new moral and ethical dilemmas for the American bomber crews. Until Munster, the air corps had been committed to a concept of daylight precision bombing, limiting targets to military and industrial facilities. The British had tried and rejected daylight precision bombing as too costly and dangerous. The Royal Air Force switched instead to nighttime saturation bombing, though British losses continued to be heavy. American planners took great care to avoid targets with a high probability of civilian collateral damage. On the rare occasions when American airmen had been put in the position of dropping bombs on general rather than specific targets, it had really bothered them.

Throughout the war, airmen knew that the Norden bombsight's vaunted "pickle barrel" accuracy was overstated. Bombardier Maurice Rockett had no illusions about collateral damage. He writes: "The only people who uttered the propagandistic expression 'pickle barrel' really did not know what they were talking about. To get a perfect hit essentially demanded ideal conditions which rarely prevailed in combat. . . . I rarely saw the target area; therefore, it was every person for themselves on the ground."[1] Flight engineer Daniel Culler of the 44th Bomb Group writes: "I knew my ancestors came from Germany and at one time wondered how many of my relations were killed when we bombed Germany."[2] However, both men, despite their misgivings, attest to the fact that they felt that killing civilians was necessary.

The combined bomber offensive, also known by its code name Operation Pointblank, officially began on June 10, 1943. Losses had been incredibly high in subsequent months. Brig. Gen. Ira Eaker insisted that the bombers needed long-range fighter escort in order to succeed, but his superior Gen. Hap Arnold felt that the problem was not a lack of fighter escort but a lack of equipment and military will. Thus began a serious fracture between these two men who made USAAC policy. Eaker was worried that continued losses of aircraft and trained personnel in the skies over Europe, and the subsequent drain on military expenditures to replace them, might lead to the dismantling of the Eighth Air Force. One of Eaker's main worries, he confided to Arnold, was that officials at the highest levels might not be able to tolerate the combat losses.

On September 6, 1943, after continuous pressure from Arnold, Eaker launched a massive raid on Stuggart, well beyond the range of Allied fighter escorts, resulting in the loss of forty-five American bombers. At this point, Eaker appears to be unwilling to engage bombers outside fighter range and instead launched missions against German targets in France. In the meantime, he continued to advocate for long-range fighter escort with drop tanks.[3]

Historian Max Hastings concludes that General Arnold's belief that more planes would solve the great attrition rate was proven false after the heavy damages suffered on the Regensburg-Schweinfurt missions. And no one knew this situation better than the airmen themselves. The 95th's fellow group at Thorpe Abbotts, the 100th, had lost nine planes and ninety men on the Regensburg mission.

It took time for the bomb groups to recover from the heavy losses of the Regensburg shuttle mission. For several weeks, the 95th flew shorter raids to France and experienced light casualties without any lost aircraft. It wasn't until September 6 that the group flew over Germany again, this time to Stuttgart. Of twenty-three aircraft four were lost with their crews: J. A. Cabeen, all POWs; G. A. Tyler, all POWs; G. F. Ransom, POWs and evaders, with one KIA; and N. S. Rothschild, who was able to stagger back across the Channel before ditching and being rescued. Mission 36, on September 15, saw the loss of another crew, that of J. H. Noyes. Sadly, the plane was only a few miles from the English coast when it disappeared. All on board were lost. After thirty-six missions, the group had lost forty-four aircraft.

Missions 37 through 44 saw slightly lighter losses for the group. In those three weeks, the R. B. Jutzi, M. L. Crowder, and R. W. Eherts crews were lost.

Munster, an ancient German city founded in 804, was famed for its lovely architecture. After its mostly Catholic population had pelted Hitler with rotten eggs and fruit during the 1932 election, he had vowed never to return. The city was famed for its medieval cathedral with its stone sculptures and lovely surrounding Westphalian countryside. But Munster also had sprawling railroad marshaling yards that employed hundreds of workers. Through these yards came such raw materials as iron and finished goods for the war effort: tanks, ammunition, and trucks.

Mission orders directed that the 95th would lead fifteen other groups of the First and Third Air Wings in an attack on Munster. Six fighter groups of P-47 Thunderbolts, now equipped with seventy-five-gallon pressurized drop tanks, would escort the air wings the entire way to the target.

At 7:15 a.m. on October 10, intelligence officer Maj. "Jiggs" Donohue briefed the airmen. "Your target today, gentlemen, is Münster," he told them as he removed the curtain from the mission map. "However, unlike all previous military and industrial targets attacked to date by the 8th Air Force, today it will be different—very different—because today you will hit the centre of that city, the homes of the working population of those marshalling yards. You will disrupt their lives so completely that their morale will be seriously affected and their will to work and fight will be substantially reduced."[4]

The aiming point for this mission would be the front steps of Munster's ancient cathedral, in the heart of the city. Historian Ian Hawkins describes "stunned silence in the briefing room as the enormity of this sudden and complete change in strategy was set before the men in such cold and clinical terms. . . . It was hard to believe that here in this quiet sleepy Suffolk village plans were being made, and instructions issued, for a city's destruction in the centre of Europe that very day."[5]

Navigator Ellis Scripture recalled his response:

I'd been raised in a strict Protestant home. I was shocked that we were to bomb civilians as our primary target for the first time in the war and that our aiming point was to be the front steps of Munster Cathedral at noon on Sunday, just as Mass was completed. . . .

I approached Colonel John Gerhart in the war room and told him I didn't think I could fly this particular mission and explained my reasons. His reaction was exactly what one would expect (in retrospect) of a Career Officer and a very fine Commander.

He said something like, "Look, captain, this is war—spelled W-A-R. We're in an all-out fight; the Germans have been killing innocent people all over Europe for years. We're here to beat the hell out of them, and we're going to do it. We have, to date, been very diligent and concentrated all our efforts in U-boat yards, aircraft plants, oil installations, and other industrial targets, but it has become very apparent to the Allied leaders that we must now carry the war to the German people and make them realize there is a war going on and that they are the victims of their own military leadership in Germany. Now, I'm leading this mission and you are my navigator. . . . You have no option! If you do not fly, I'll have to court-martial you. Any questions?"

I said, "No, sir," and that ended the incident.[6]

Copilot John Chaffin remembers hearing the news. "For months we had been flying missions, priding ourselves on our pin-point bombing with the Norden bombsight where, by contrast, the British flew at night and did only saturation bombing. We felt like we bombed true military targets and they were bombing civilians. Now we too were going to bomb civilians— and on Sunday! Although we agreed with General Sherman's definition of war it somehow didn't seem quite right."[7]

In his memoir, pilot Harry Conley writes: "[When we] found out the aiming point was the cathedral in the very middle of the city, there was amazement and consternation. Several of our pilots, speaking for themselves or for their crews, said for the first time that they had problems reconciling this bombing objective with their moral senses."[8]

Copilot Lt. John Perceful, however, felt only a momentary qualm "because by October, 1943, our Group's losses were almost 100 %. . . . In the early days we might have had second thoughts, but not at this point."[9]

This assignment would be the 95th BG's third mission in three days. The men were dog tired. Bill Lindley and the *Zoot Suiters* would lead the entire Thirteenth Combat Wing, with Ellis Scripture as lead navigator.

Two hundred sixty bombers set off for Munster, three hundred miles away. Lindley's *Zoot Suiters* lifted off Horham's runway at 11:15 a.m., followed by the rest of the group. The drop time had been moved from noon to 3 p.m.

John Chaffin recalls, "It was a beautiful, clear fall day. Assembly and the formation and flight to the target area were without incident. We had P-47 escort all the way to the IP."[10]

The group passed over Schouwen Island, encountering flak, and soon was over occupied Holland with a panoramic view of the land of dikes, windmills, and windswept canals. P-47 Thunderbolts of the 352nd Fighter Group rendezvoused right on schedule, weaving back and forth in the sky above the slower Forts. Near the target, they began to jettison their belly tanks through the bomber stream, meaning they were headed off to engage German fighters. Finally, at 2:48 p.m., near Dorsten, Germany, the P-47s turned back to base. As soon as the P-47s peeled off to return to England, the German fighters swooped in like raptors, ready for the kill.

Lindley saw the initial point ahead, as well as a huge swarm of German aircraft barely out of the group's range. At 2:59 p.m., Scripture radioed Lindley that *Zoot Suiters* was over the IP. Chaffin writes: "'Bro' [Eldon Broman] and I had been following our usual method of dividing the flying task by flying fifteen minute intervals. My turn to fly came again just as we neared the IP. I recall seeing the P-47s turn to return to England and from the other direction came the German fighters, many of them, in a head-on attack. Flak was very intense and the fighters seemed almost to ignore it."

At 3:03 p.m. ("and, as predicted, as accurate as hell," reported Lindley in his post-mission briefing), the lead plane released its bombs on Munster's city center. Pilot Rodney Snow remembers the bomb run as being quite long, more than six minutes, during which time the crews were unable to take any evasive action because they had to ensure the bombardiers could sight the targets accurately.

Chaffin continues: "As we left the target we made a turn to the left, which put our Squadron on the inside of the turn, making our required speed slower than the Lead Squadron. It was just about at this point that our tail gunner reported that the 100th Group, which was flying Low Group, was being wiped out. When the formation returned to level flight, our Squadron Leader, who had feathered an engine, could not maintain air speed and we began to fall back. I asked 'Bro' if he wanted us to stay with him and he said we should not leave him alone.

"I could see a string of fighters coming head on for our Squadron Leader like so many little arrows and remember thinking, 'You poor devil, they see that you are in trouble and they are going to shoot you down.' He peeled off and went down, and the crew started bailing out."[11]

The mission report summarized the activities that followed. "The 3rd Bombardment Division encountered the most violent and concentrated attacks yet made upon its formations. The attacks lasted forty-five minutes and from 200–250 enemy fighters were engaged. The concentrated attacks occurred from the I.P. through the target until fighter escort was picked up. The enemy fighters were FW-190s, Me-109s, Ju-88s, Me-210s, and Me-110s. In attacking they concentrated on one group at a time, first flying through the lead group to attack the 100th Group. The attacking A/C flew parallel to the formations, out of range, in groups of 20 to 40 stacked in echelon down. They then peeled off, singly, or in pairs, in quick succession to attack the lowest members of the formation. Two minutes after the concentrated attack on the 100th began, the formation was well broken up and in seven minutes the entire group was completely destroyed or dispersed. Twin-engine fighters appeared to remain out of range, firing explosive cannon shells from 200–1500 yards. Ju-88s attacked with rockets from 800–1000 yards. A new feature was the use of enemy bombers, [Dornier] DO-217s and DO-215s, which flew parallel to the formation and fired rockets from 1500 yards."[12]

Capt. Leslie Kring, flying *Rhapsody in Flak*, reports that Sgt. R. W. Cunningham, his tail gunner, "called me on the interphone and yelled 'move this damn airplane around a little! Jerry is behind us shooting rockets! I can't reach him!'" As Kring began evasive action, he watched an air-to-air rocket streak past, about a foot above the left wing. "My heart skipped a beat. Cunningham called that one, and saved us all a lot of grief."[13]

Kring's navigator, James Goff, recalls that he shot sixteen hundred rounds of ammunition from his gun position in the nose. "It seemed like a blurred nightmare. Wave after wave of enemy fighters, pieces of aircraft littering the clear blue sky, ugly black smoke of flak bursts, men drifting in parachutes, burning bombers and fighters all around us, twenty-five minutes that lasted an eternity."[14]

A few minutes after the bombing run, a 95th Fort commanded by Lt. Lionel Correia, came under severe concentrated fighter attack. Nine parachutes were observed before the plane exploded, but radio operator Jerome Schneider was unable to get out. The rest became POWs.

Ellis Scripture recounts the mission: "Never before had we seen the great concentration of enemy fighters—nor would we in the months ahead. They were everywhere, attacking from every direction, every level. It was similar to fighting off a swarm of bees. This continued literally from the Dutch-German border to the Initial Point, to the target, and the withdrawal to the rendezvous with American fighter cover near the Dutch border."[15]

Pilot W. E. Buckley's Fort, *Patsy Ann III*, was next to go down. Most of the crew managed to jump, but four men were killed. Navigator Lt. Robert Bartow reports: "We received a direct hit, either by flak or rocket, that broke off the entire tail assembly, and the plane went into a spinning dive. Our bombardier, Lieutenant Ed Janney, and I bailed out through the nose exit hatch. I later saw our aircraft crash and explode in a corner of the same field where I landed."[16]

Lt. Paul Perceful, copilot on B-17F 230218, recalls "seeing a B-17 [*Patsy Ann III*] that had simply been cut in two halves by the concentrated cannon fire from a German fighter. . . . The Fortress came apart at the radio room. The front half of the fuselage, wings, still functioning engines, and the cockpit, seemed to slowly rise upward, completely separate from the rear fuselage and tail unit. Then both halves tumbled down and away."[17]

Near the rally point, flak hit *Miss Flower III*, leader of the group's low squadron. With an engine on fire, gears down, and its propeller feathered, Capt. John Adams held the Fort steady until all the crew had bailed, then he jumped over the rally point of Emsdetten, Germany.

The last plane to go down was *Fritz Blitz*, piloted by Eldon Broman and copiloted by John Chaffin. This author has had the good fortune to interview Broman, Chaffin, and tail gunner Richmond "Red" Dillon extensively. They shared their experiences as the last crew down over Munster, providing more details and conveying the intensity of the combat and the visceral reactions of those involved.

Fritz Blitz had been fighting for its survival for many minutes when the plane met its end. Ball turret gunner "Red" Dillon remembers the German fighters were so plentiful and so close he simply could not miss, and that if he'd had something to throw at them he could have hit them. He could see the German fighter pilots' faces and even the yellow scarves the men wore as they flew through the formation.

Three German fighters approached *Fritz Blitz* from below, flying wingtip to wingtip. Left waist gunner Frank Dean desperately tried to swing his .50-caliber down far enough to get in a shot at them, only to find that his gun would not fire that low. Dean watched as the cannons and machine guns flashed from the German aircraft, and he knew that in another moment, *Fritz Blitz* would be sawed in two from the overwhelming offensive barrage.

In the ball turret below Dean, Dillon only had time to think, "Oh, shit!" Then he put his optical gunsight on the nose of the fighter in the middle and fired a short burst. It blew up, and the concussion or debris from that fighter either hit or caused his two wing men to peel off and break away. Dillon frantically kept his ball turret swiveling and found that no matter where he turned, a German fighter filled his vision. He fired and watched as one after another exploded and went down in smoke and debris.

In the Fort *Situation Normal*, directly to the right of *Fritz Blitz*, left waist gunner Staff Sgt. Everett Lewis watched Dillon's ball turret spin like a dervish, flames licking from its guns. He counted as Dillon knocked one plane after another out of the sky. Lewis counted ten and then looked away for a moment. Dillon believes at this point that he may have hit an eleventh fighter. In the confusion of battle, an Me-109 flew directly into his line of fire, and Dillon shot off its vertical stabilizer. What he did not see was the Me-110 out of gun range that began firing rockets into the formation.

Seconds later a rocket fired from the Me-110 exploded near *Fritz Blitz*'s cockpit. "There was a tinkle of broken glass behind my head and then an explosion," remembers Chaffin. "The next instant I was slapping flames off my helmet and shoulders. The cockpit was suddenly a glowing pink. I leaned over and got the small fire extinguisher from under my seat and turned to work on the fire. Around the turret and hydraulic system everything was a mass of flame. The tiny stream of carbon from my extinguisher seemed useless against that roaring inferno."

Broman tugged on Chaffin's arm, motioning downward: Jump! The communications were shot out. Chaffin recalls: "It took only an instant to straighten back in my seat, unbuckle my belt, and then drop down to the catwalk. I knelt there and buckled on my chute, then crawled on the hatch. I blacked out as I dropped from the hatch, because when I had turned around to fight the fire, I had pulled my oxygen mask loose. At 24,000 feet it takes only a very short time to pass out from lack of oxygen, and I had been without it for about two or three minutes."

Fortunately for Chaffin, he came to in time to pull the rip cord. He wrote the following passage in a bound, blank book he received at Stalag Luft III shortly after his capture: "How strange this is. I'm in a parachute drifting downward at a thousand feet a minute toward German territory. My left boot came off when the parachute opened, my helmet, goggles and oxygen mask are gone. I can hear the sound of machine-gun fire fading away into the west, and then silence. Just a few minutes before I had been fighting a roaring inferno in the cockpit of our B-17 *Fritz Blitz*. And now, nothing but quiet. No sensation of falling. I can't see any other parachutes anywhere. This is about as alone as I've ever been in my life."[18]

Chaffin's long free fall had separated him from the rest of the crew. "I landed all by myself, almost with one foot in Holland and the other one in Germany. I landed in a pine tree and crashed through it, my right leg taking the force of the crash. My right leg hurts to this day from that." Because he delayed pulling his chute, Chaffin landed far away from the rest of his crew, whom he would not see again until after the war.

Four of *Fritz Blitz*'s regular enlisted crew, noticing the overcast, rainy weather the previous day, had gone to London without permission. They were replaced for the Munster mission by fill-in gunners, all of whom went down with the ship. One, Sgt. Roy Rightmire, was killed over Munster; the other replacements became POWs.

For the other aircrews, it was time to head home. Every plane still flying was damaged. According to Harry Conley, "Not one of our ships returned from Munster without at least a dozen holes." An air-to-air rocket's shrapnel had hit Conley inside *Holy Terror*. "A large chunk of very hot metal struck me at the base of my neck on the left side. It felt as if someone had hit me with a baseball bat but all the damage it did was to give me a stiff neck, a slight burn from the hot metal, and a big black and blue bruise. It must have hit me with its flattest side as it ended up on my lap. I subsequently used it as a paperweight in my office."[19]

Ellis Scripture writes: "On this mission, calm prevailed in the planes. When planes were going down, we heard their pilots say over the command radio such things as: 'We're hit badly . . . We're going down . . . Carry on. We'll be okay . . . We'll see you later.' No panic, but rapid talk, men doing a difficult and hazardous job and doing it well, the calm way young men reacted to extreme danger stands out as a lasting tribute to the men of the Eighth Air Force."

The Germans had badly mauled the 95th's accompanying groups—the 390th and 100th. Though the 95th had lost five planes, the 390th had lost eight, and the 100th had lost all but *one* of its thirteen planes.

Lt. Marshall Thixton, in *Liberty Belle*, waited tensely as his plane limped for home on three engines and with most of its Plexiglas nose shot off. He fully expected to end up in the North Sea.

The shot-up formation returned to England to find landing conditions extremely challenging. In addition to the extensive damage to the planes, many carried injured crewmen who needed quick treatment, but low clouds and patchy ground fog blanketed most of East Anglia. Two P-47s, returning earlier in the "soup," had crashed, and both pilots had been killed. Thirteen of the 95th's surviving B-17s managed to find their way back to Horham, though, arriving between 4:32 and 4:52 p.m.

Pilot Rodney Snow recalls:

> As we approached the vicinity of our base the weather was rapidly deteriorating. Visibility was extremely restricted. We were in bad shape because of our shot-up condition, our near-empty fuel tanks, and the inevitable fatigue, which had begun to set in.
>
> After we had cranked the right landing gear down manually because of a lack of hydraulic pressure, we prepared to land. We saw a runway, and I tried a big right-hand turn to line the plane up with it. Suddenly the waist gunner yelled, "Pull up, Cap!! Pull her up!! You're heading straight for a church steeple!!" With a violent maneuver to the right we only missed hitting the church spire, which

had been obscured by mist and fog. We then completed the turn, and saying a little prayer, let down at an unidentified base.

While we were taxiing back to a hardstand, the Tower told us we were at Thorpe Abbotts, home base of the 100th. The Commanding Officer of the 100th then inquired as to the whereabouts of his Group as they should have at least been in radio contact with the Tower at that time. The Colonel refused to believe me when I told him, "I'm sorry to say this, Sir, but I don't think that you will have anyone from your Group come home today."[20]

Several planes from the 390th Bomb Group also landed at Thorpe Abbotts, and finally the 100th's own Robert Rosenthal landed *Royal Flush* in the gathering mist there. A 20mm cannon shell from a German fighter was found rolling around inside one of the self-sealing wing tanks after landing. Copilot Winfrey "Pappy" Lewis pictured a German slave laborer "risking his all to sabotage and secretly turn out defective rounds of ammunition." In fact, this author recalls speaking to an airman and hearing that another dud shell was opened and found to contain a note that read simply, "We are with you."

Another 100th plane, *Stork Club*, landed a short time later, and the wing's final Fort to land in England came into RAF Wattisham, Suffolk, at 5:20 p.m. The pilot crash-landed, breaking the plane in half but luckily without causing any injuries.

After interrogation, the 95th crews staggered to their barracks or retired to the base bars for a drink. It had been a long, hard day, with heavy losses for the wing. Twenty-nine planes from the six groups had gone down. One crewman had returned to England dead, 14 returned wounded (including five from the 95th), and 296 men were missing in action: dead, POW, or evaders. Fifty-one men from the 95th were MIAs.

Back in Munster, the city continued to smoke, and rescuers scrambled madly to dig out survivors buried in the rubble. In addition to many industrial and commercial buildings, 526 residential buildings were destroyed or severely damaged. Twenty-five thousand civilians were homeless. Munster police casualty reports for October 10 state 391 dead, of which 60 were soldiers. The Munster City Council issued a summary in 1954 stating that the October 10 raid killed 473 civilians and around 200 soldiers. Ian Hawkins reflects that "it is highly probable that the exact figures will never be known."[21]

October 10, 1943, the date of the Munster mission, later became known as Black Sunday. It was the greatest air battle to date in World War II, with 229 bombers and their fighter escorts against more than 300 German fighters clashing over 800 miles of sky for more than three hours. Only 33 American bombers returned undamaged. Of the 2,900 crewmen involved in the raid, there were 642 casualties, or more than 18 percent of the force.[22] Frank Murphy, a 100th BG navigator shot down at Munster, summed it up: "The performance by the men of the 100th, 390th, and 95th could quite rightly be considered the United States Air Force equivalent of The Charge of the Light Brigade in the Crimea or General George Pickett's charge at Gettysburg during the American Civil War."[23]

The weary crews barely had time to nurse their wounds before another big raid was launched on the morning of October 14, 1943. This raid would become known as Black Thursday and would also enhance the legend of the Eighth Air Force. The morning dawned overcast and damp, with a thick fog blanketing the East Anglian countryside. After a predawn breakfast, the assembled crews were told that the day's operation would be the most important air operation yet conducted in the war: "The target must be destroyed. It is of vital importance to the enemy. Your friends and comrades [who will be lost today and] that have been lost are depending on you. Their sacrifices must not be in vain. Good luck, good shooting, and good bombing."[24]

The target—the German ball-bearing factories at Schweinfurt, Germany—produced most of Germany's antifriction ball bearings used for everything from planes to tanks to precision instruments. Schweinfurt produced 42 percent of Germany's bearings. Its closest competitor was Stuttgart, with only 15 percent. Ball bearings were literally the mechanical lubrication of the entire German war effort, and its war industry consumed fantastic numbers. Germany produced millions every month, and each one was considered precious. A typical medium bomber used more than a thousand bearings per engine; an 88mm flak gun had forty-seven; and a single 200cm searchlight used ninety.[25] If the mission could eliminate the ball bearing industry at Schweinfurt, it could cripple Germany's war effort.

Hitler's minister of armaments and war production, Albert Speer, concurred: "The principle followed was to paralyze a cross section, as it were—just as a motor can be made useless by the removal of the ignition."[26] The Germans were well aware of the vulnerability of the industry. Speer writes in his memoir: "As early as September 10, 1942, I had warned Hitler that the tank production of Friedrichshafen and the ball-bearing facilities in Schweinfurt were crucial to our whole effort. Hitler thereupon ordered increased antiaircraft protection for these two cities. Actually, as I had early recognized, the war could largely have been decided in 1943 if instead of vast but pointless area bombing the planes had concentrated on the centers of armaments production."[27]

Speer's assessment contradicts that of British air marshal Arthur "Bomber" Harris, who dismissed ball bearing and other "bottleneck" targets as "panacea targets." He continued to pressure the United States into joining Britain in area bombing.[28]

For the second Schweinfurt mission, the 95th was only able to put eighteen aircraft into the air after suffering such heavy losses of men and equipment at Munster. In one of the planes lumbering into the gray sky that morning was the Kit Carson crew. His bombardier Leonard Herman remembers his feelings on take-off: "Schweinfurt would be the twenty-fourth mission for the crew of *The Brass Rail*. Our original pilot, Johnny Johnson, had been killed during a mission to Kiel on 25 July and several of us had been wounded, but the majority of the original crew was still together."

As they neared the target, German antiaircraft batteries filled the sky with flak. Leonard Herman remembers:

Flak we can't do anything about. We fly our course, stay in formation, and pray we don't get hit. At least with fighters you can shoot back. We are busy . . . busy watching them as they line up to attack our tight formation, busy following them as they swoop in, crazy busy, short bursts, short bursting them to death. We're on pure oxygen and can feel the adrenaline flowing. There's no fear at this time because we're too busy to think about anything but doing our job. We see planes hit, we count the chutes as our buddies bail out, and we wonder when the hell the fighters are going to stop coming.

We're on the bomb run, flying straight and level. Then it's "Bombs away! Bomb-bay doors coming up! Let's get the hell out of here!"

We peer down seeing the bombs hit, watching the explosions, the flames, and the smoke boiling up from the largest ball-bearing manufacturing complex in Europe. Now the purpose of our mission is complete. Good, bad, or indifferent. We know one thing—we're going home. Our planes will fly faster on the way back. Sure, there are going to be plenty of fighters and flak to fly through and there will be further losses, but somehow we got through and back. That was Schweinfurt.[29]

The 95th Bomb Group came through Schweinfurt and lost only one aircraft, that of W. R. McPherson, whose crew ended up as POWs. In pilot L. L. Kerr's plane, three men were wounded: the tail gunner and the two waist gunners. Everybody else made it back alive and without serious injuries.

Other groups were less fortunate. The Eighth lost 60 B-17s missing—along with their 600 crewmen—as well as 5 B-17s that crashed in England upon returning because of battle damage, 12 others written off after crash-landings, and 121 planes in need of some level of repairs. In addition to the missing men, 5 dead airmen were unloaded back at their bases along with 43 wounded. Only 33 bombers landed without any damage. Ironically, the only group without a single loss was the "Bloody Hundredth."

Although acclaimed as a major victory in the British and American press, Schweinfurt became a Waterloo for the strategic bombing policy up to that time. Losses over Schweinfurt were almost double the Eighth Air Force's acceptable loss figure. Sixty of three hundred planes had gone down, or 20 percent of the attacking force. Of the 2,900 men who flew the mission 648 were dead, wounded, or missing, or more than 18 percent of the force. Morale was plummeting. Even with the twenty-five-mission rule, most American airmen statistically had little chance of finishing their tours without dying or being shot down. Though the 186 German planes lost at Schweinfurt was high, it was also obvious that the Luftwaffe had developed tactics that allowed it to break up the tightly knit bomber boxes by focusing on one bomber formation at a time, "dispersing it by firing rockets from beyond the effective range of defensive guns, and then repeatedly pressing attacks with single-engine fighters."[30]

Minister Speer took a call from Hitler the evening of October 14 while he was in a meeting at Prussian Headquarters. Hitler was in good spirits. Speer writes:

> "A new daylight raid on Schweinfurt had ended with a great victory for our defenses," [Hitler] said. The countryside was strewn with downed American bombers. Uneasy, I asked for a short recess in our conference, since I wanted to telephone Schweinfurt myself. But all the communications were shattered; I could not reach any of the factories. Finally, by enlisting the police, I managed to talk to the foreman of a ball-bearing factory. All the factories had been hard hit, he informed me. The oil baths for the bearings had caused serious fires in the machinery workshops; the damage was far worse than after the first attack. This time we had lost 67 percent of our ball-bearing production.
>
> My first measure after this second air raid was to appoint my most vigorous associate, General Manager Kessler, as special commissioner for ball-bearing production. Our reserves had been consumed; efforts to import ball bearings from Sweden and Switzerland had met with only slight success. Nevertheless, we were able to avoid total disaster by substituting slide bearings wherever possible. But what really saved us was the fact that from this time on the enemy to our astonishment once again ceased his attacks on the ball-bearing industry. . . . The Allies threw away success when it was already in their hands. Had they continued the attacks with the same energy, we would quickly have been at our last gasp. As it was, not a tank, plane, or other piece of weaponry failed to be produced because of a lack of ball bearings.[31]

Why did the Allies decide not to return to Schweinfurt for what Speer considered the death blow to German industry? Speer writes:

Not until after the war did I learn the reason for the enemy's error. The Air Staffs assumed that in Hitler's authoritarian state the important factories would be quickly shifted from the imperiled cities. On December 30, 1943, Sir Arthur Harris declared his conviction that "at this stage of the war the Germans have long since made every possible effort to decentralize the manufacture of so vital a product as ball bearings". He considerably overestimated the strengths of the authoritarian system, which to the outside observer appeared so tightly knit.[32]

By their presence alone, American and British bombers were wreaking havoc with Germany's war materials planning. Speer laments in his memoirs the great cost of protecting Germany's skies from Allied bombers.

In the Reich [empire] and in the Western theaters of war the barrels on ten thousand antiaircraft guns were pointed towards the sky. The same guns could have well been employed in Russia against tanks and other ground targets. Had it not been for this new front, the air front over Germany, our defensive strength against tanks would have been about doubled. Moreover, the antiaircraft force tied down hundreds of thousands of young soldiers. A third of the optical industry was busy producing gunsights for the flak batteries. About half the electronics industry was engaged in producing radar and communications networks for defense against bombing.[33]

Meanwhile, historian Martin Caidin observed,

The battle fought on "Black Thursday" stands high in the history of American fighting men. It will long be remembered, like the immortal struggles of Gettysburg, St. Mihiel and the Argonne, of Midway and the Bulge and Pork Chop Hill. . . . It was a battle in which we suffered unprecedented losses, and a battle that we cannot in honesty remember as having produced the results we had hoped for, or that hurt the enemy's war effort as much as we had believed. Yet it is an aerial struggle remembered with great pride, for it demanded the utmost in courage, in skill, in carrying on the fight in the face of bloody slaughter.[34]

In only three days of operations, the Eighth had lost eighty-eight heavy bombers and 18.4 percent of its available air crewmen. It had no choice but to stand down for a few days.[35] The 100th Bomb Group had lost twenty bombers and more than two hundred men in one week. Because of its performance over Munster, the 95th Bomb Group was awarded its second Distinguished Unit Citation.

Some historians believe that the Schweinfurt mission was the turning point in American policy concerning unescorted bomber streams fighting their way in and out of enemy territory. However, a few Eighth Air Force leaders, such as Curtis LeMay, and some current historical scholarship postulate that the Eighth Air Force leaders fought with what they had available and that the appearance of the drop tank on P-47s and P-51s in late 1943 and early 1944 was the reason for the change in tactics. Lt. Gen. Ira Eaker stated as late as October 22, 1943: "We must continue the battle with unrelenting fury." He later admitted that he and Brig. Gen. Frederick Anderson "would have gone right back into the heart of Germany, even without long-range fighters, if weather had permitted."[36] The week of the group's missions to Munster and Schweinfurt became known in World War II histories as Black Week because of the heavy losses inflicted on both sides. The men needed time to repair the aircraft and recover psychologically so they could forge onward. Fortunately for the men of the Eighth and the 95th, the weather did not permit another mission immediately back into Germany. The 95th flew only one more mission in the month of October, to Duren, Germany, when the hard-luck crew of Lt. K. B. Rongstad ditched in the English Channel and was rescued.

One final mission of the period that deserves mentioning is the long-distance bombing mission to Norway on November 16, 1943. With the weather up north suitable enough for a visual bombing attack, the Third Air Division, including the 95th, attacked a heavy water plant at Rjukan that many believed was an integral part of the German nuclear weapons program. The Allies' aerial attacks came on the heels of several daring sabotage missions against the 60-megawatt Vermork hydroelectric station that harnessed the power of the Rjukan waterfall in Telemark. The first assault, code-named Grouse, kicked off when an advance team of four Norwegian saboteurs landed on the Hardanger Plateau in October 1942. The following month, in Operation Freshman, British paratroopers were supposed to rendezvous with the Grouse team and destroy the dam; however, after the paratroopers' gliders crashed, the Gestapo captured and executed the survivors. In February 1943, a team of British-trained Norwegian commandos successfully sabotaged the production plant in one of the most daring missions of World War II, Operation Gunnerside.

After the Eighth Air Force's bombing raid in November, Germany gave up on the Rjukan facility and attempted to move its remaining heavy water to Germany. Forces in the Norwegian resistance intercepted and sank the ship carrying it at Lake Tinnsjø, effectively ending the heavy-water threat in Norway.

The 95th emerged from the devastating Black Week raids without many of its original cadre in the formation any longer. New planes and crews arrived to fill the empty hardstands on the airfield and the empty beds in the barracks, respectively. Though countless air battles were ahead, few would be as intense or as costly as the fierce combat fought in the skies in the second half of 1943. Those men who had survived looked ahead, through the ever-worsening British winter weather, and resigned themselves to the fact that few of them would see another spring.

16 POWs, Part I

Although hundreds of airmen from the 95th Bomb Group ended up jumping from their aircraft, virtually none had ever made a single practice jump. They received only rudimentary training, such as how to exit the aircraft, how long to wait before pulling the ripcord, and how to land. Navigator Bob Sullivan wrote later: "There was nothing in our training that prepared us for that awful feeling of descending into unknown enemy territory."[1]

Upon arrival at Horham, each airman was photographed wearing civilian clothing. These photos became part of the escape kit issued to each crewman before a mission. Should the crewmen have to bail out of their planes over occupied Europe, the Underground or resistance fighters could use the miniature, black-and-white photographs to forge identity documents for the fliers. Bombardier Leonard Herman remembers that every man in the group wore the same suit and tie, and it wasn't difficult for the Gestapo to figure out where a prisoner was from. For variety, Herman knotted the tie into a bow tie the size of a small propeller.

In addition to the photos, Herman remembers that each escape kit had candy, gum, a razor blade, a silk escape map, and some currency. It also included a tiny magnetic compass that could be hidden in one's anus and removed with an attached string.

Because flying boots were dead giveaways and not made for walking, many crewmen took an extra pair of shoes on missions in case they were shot down. Herman carried a pair of white tennis shoes. Men were also issued a .45-caliber pistol. "We were told not to get captured with our .45, but the underground loved to get them and encouraged us to hold on to them," remembers Leonard Herman. "Of course, the Germans would shoot you if you had it."

The first obstacle facing a crewman in a doomed airplane was escape. Imagine trying to get out of an airplane as it plummets to earth. You are wearing many layers of bulky flight gear. Centrifugal force pins you to the walls. The plane may be burning and filled with choking, blinding smoke. You may be wounded as you fumble to clip your parachute to its harness and then try to squeeze through a tiny hatch and fall free. In a few brief seconds of sheer terror, your life hangs in the balance. Up in the cockpit, the pilot and copilot struggle desperately to keep the aircraft as stable as possible so that the crew can bail out. Then they, too, must fight their way through to the escape hatch as the plane continues it death dive.

Navigator Bob Sullivan of the Hank Wilson crew went down on his thirteenth mission. A large group of Me-109 fighters jumped his plane and shot it up so badly that it instantly veered out of control. As the copilot tried to right the plane, the wing ripped off, and the plane began spinning downward so violently that the copilot was knocked off the flight deck. Sullivan and the bombardier found themselves alternately stuck to the fuselage like magnets and floating free in the cramped nose section. As did most airmen, Sullivan had his parachute next to him. He clipped it on and prepared to jump; however, the pack was snared on equipment. As precious seconds ticked away, he struggled to free himself. Finally he fell free.

"No sooner had my chute opened than another B-17 plunged nose down towards the ground with its belly towards me. It was so close that I felt I could have reached out and touched it. It passed me by with a sound I can only describe as a loud WHOOSH! In a split second it was past me and down into the clouds below—and then silence. Then and still today I can't believe that the plane did not catch a part of my chute and drag me down with it." A circling German fighter directed ground troops to his location, and they captured him shortly after he landed.[2]

Sometimes a crewman was so severely wounded that he was unable to bail out. In many instances, his crewmen put their own safety second and attached a chute to their wounded comrade, placed the rip cord in his hand, and pushed him out before jumping themselves.

Bailing out was itself dangerous. A man could spin back and slam into a wing or tailplane. If his chute had been near the flames, he might open it only to see to his horror that the life-saving silk was on fire and being consumed. Many a man became a "Roman candle" and plummeted to earth under a fiery chute. Mercifully, anoxia would usually render them unconscious well before impact, making them look strangely peaceful as they fell and slammed into the earth. The violence of the fall could only be noted in the foot-deep impression a man's body made in the earth.

The parachute opened with a jerk so violent that it yanked many men's boots off their feet. The harness dug painfully into a man's groin. Once a chute opened, a man was surrounded by unbelievable stillness. Many commented that they had no sensation whatsoever of falling, no reference point to mark their plunge. A man had at most twenty-five minutes to come up with a plan for escape and survival in a hostile country.

John Chaffin, copilot on Eldon Broman's *Fritz Blitz*, went down on the Munster mission. "It took almost twenty-five minutes for me to descend. I was pretty busy giving a lot of thought about what would happen when I got on the ground. We were supposed to try to escape—to try to get in the hands of the Underground if possible. I didn't have the slightest idea how to go about that. I began to look for hiding places as I drifted down onto the German countryside. I could see groves of trees, fields, and finally I saw a barn.

"Whoosh! Bam! Suddenly with a roar of wind in my ears, I am on the ground. My parachute is caught in the pine trees at my side. The ground is soft sand but I have hurt my ankle.

"[I tell myself,] 'Come on, now. Get that chute down. Get the Mae West off and hide them. You've got to hurry. There are a bunch of people coming down that road. Hurry! Hurry! Cover this stuff up with leaves; now run!'"[3]

The biggest danger facing a crewman once he landed in enemy territory, especially in Germany, was being attacked by hostile civilians who had lost homes, families, and friends to the bombers and were fed daily propaganda about the *terrorfliegers* (terror fliers) or *luftgangsters* (air gangsters). Though Luftwaffe chief Hermann Göring had issued instructions early on that all downed airmen were to be protected, "by early 1944 . . . official German policy had begun to shift ominously, at the insistence of the führer. In late May of that year, [Joseph] Goebbels published an editorial in a Nazi Party paper condemning Anglo-American air attacks against 'defenseless' women and children as 'naked murder', not warfare. In the future, Germans should not be expected to protect 'enemy man-hunters' from the righteous wrath of the people."[4] German civilians also had tacit permission from Goebbels to kill any terrorflieger they managed to capture.

Gunner James Gregory of the 95th BG's *Full House* was shot down on August 16, 1944. As he descended in his parachute, he noticed the plane was burning on a house. One of the children living in the house had been killed in "yet another tragedy in an era of tragedies."

Once on the ground, he was approached first by friendly civilians, but then a man appeared, raving wildly, and shot him at point-blank range in the hip with a handgun. "The shot and the shock put me on the ground again," remembers Gregory. "But the shock was not mine alone. A sudden look of disbelief filled the circle of faces of that small audience on that distant field."[5] Luckily, a German soldier arrived, disarmed the agitated civilian, and found a children's wagon to transport Gregory.

Pilot Clifford Hamilton bailed out on August 12, 1943. Only his Mae West was recovered, punctured over and over, apparently by pitchfork thrusts.

Water landings were extremely hazardous. In the cold North Sea and English Channel, death came in minutes. Willard Brown somehow survived for three hours in the Baltic Sea after his plane was shot down near Kiel; the rest of the crew died. Later in the war, when the badly wounded young gunner on his first mission, Eugene Darter, landed in chest-deep water off the Dutch coast and the wind filled his parachute, onlookers could only watch helplessly as it dragged him out to sea. His body was never recovered.

To its credit, the German Luftwaffe was often the unexpected savior of downed Allied airmen, rescuing them from angry civilians or more rabid military types such as the Schutzstaffel (Protection Squadron [SS]). The Luftwaffe was a conservative, merit-based, proud organization that predated the Nazi years. Many of its ranking officers were career military men who didn't necessarily see eye to eye with the Nazi regime. Ironically, it was often the Luftwaffe that appeared shortly after an American airman landed in occupied Europe to save him from the locals and the Gestapo.

An unwritten code of chivalry among fliers that went all the way to the top of the Luftwaffe protected the airmen. Göring, himself a highly decorated fighter pilot in World War I, and most of those under his command went to great lengths to protect captured airmen, to the point where even many Jewish airmen who made it into the Luftwaffe's hands survived their POW experiences and returned home after the war.

Jewish airmen knew that going down over occupied Europe posed special threats. On January 11, 1944, engineer and top turret gunner Irving Rothman went down over Germany with the J. E. Foley crew. The next morning a civilian policeman captured Rothman, a Jew, and used a dog chain to lead Rothman through the village to his home. "As I marched, he called after me, 'Juden! Baby killer! Juden!' He took me to his home, took the chrome-plated chain off of his dog, chained my hands, and put me in a corner. Then he let townspeople come see me. He didn't know that I spoke German, and he was telling people, 'I have an American gangster. See what he looks like?' It was a good twelve hours between my touching down and my being retrieved by the German Luftwaffe personnel. I didn't have as much as a taste of water the entire time, nor did I get any food as I was led to a nearby German airfield."

Jew or Gentile, the American luftgangster's life was not worth much until he was turned over to the Luftwaffe. Jim Gregory, the man shot by the angry civilian, bled profusely and was confined in a cow stall before a policeman took him to Camburg in a small car. He found the German civilians surprisingly friendly, though. In later questioning, the most common type of question was, "Do you know my cousin, uncle, aunt, etc., Franz, Heinz, Hildegard, etc., who lives in Chicago, St. Louis, Milwaukee, etc.?" writes Gregory dryly. "Also a common question was: 'Do you have any cigarettes?'"

Later that day he had interesting visitors: "Two veterans of the First World War dropped by, one of whom said he had been a prisoner of the Americans and liked them very much. I told them my father had served in France in 1918. I'm positive a clergyman came in, but I cannot remember any details of his visit. I received some harsh words from a lady who impressed me as possibly being a teacher. 'Why is a German boy like yourself dropping bombs on your relatives?' I told her I wasn't German, but Scottish."[6]

Some men were captured within moments of hitting the ground. Others managed to remain free, at least for a short period. Radio operator George Sulick of the 334th Squadron recalls: "'Go West' was firmly implanted in my mind, and I headed in that direction, staying close to brush and forest. I heard a train whistle. This was music to my ears. Intelligence always told us to follow railroad tracks. Following the tracks I came upon a small village railroad station with its name on the building. I checked my map for the location, but couldn't find any listing resembling the name. Traveling on, not too far from the station, I passed a farmhouse. People were sitting on the porch, so I waved as a friendly neighbor. Darkness was falling, so I found the next available haystack and fell asleep. When I woke up I found carrots, rutabaga, apples and pears at a nearby farm. Well supplied, but getting nowhere, I altered my course.

"I was more comfortable in the forest than out in the open along the tracks. I chose a wagon trail, which was a straight line versus a huge curve in the railroad tracks. Halfway along, I passed two German soldiers. They did not speak, so I kept my mouth shut. Quickly I found refuge and burrowed under a pine tree and stopped breathing! I'm not sure, but I believe I slept there for the night. Later it occurred to me that the German soldiers might have thought I was a tired woodsman, because I was carrying a large branch on my shoulder as a weapon."

Eventually, Sulick was captured and taken to a German military hospital, where minor wounds incurred in his bailout and landing were treated.[7]

Pilot Fred Kennie, who went down on the Munster raid on October 10, 1943, remembers: "At night, I used my Boy Scout training, looked at the stars, and started walking west. I figured I could be back at the base by Thanksgiving. Ten days later, I made Holland. There was nobody there to welcome me. The country was still occupied by the Germans."

Several young children discovered Kennie and took him to their farmhouse. "After I was fed, the family took me to the city hall. After a few hours, the Burgomeister, similar to an American mayor, brought in a gentleman who must have been brought up in England. He explained why the farmer had turned me in. Two weeks before, a British flyer had been helped by the people in this little town. The Nazis shot ten townspeople."

In 1992, Kennie returned to the farm where he'd landed. "They treated me like royalty. I also met the little boy, now a man, who had found me in the haystack. I'd given the Dutch farmer my GI watch. In 1992, I met with the Burgomeister of that little village, Eibergen, and the man gave the watch back. I still wear it."[8]

Some men did successfully evade capture for long periods or even completely. Their stories appear in chapter 18.

After being apprehended, the Germans took American airmen to the Wetzler transit camp in Frankfurt for their initial interrogation. The city had been heavily bombed by late 1943, and the citizens were none too friendly to the luftgangsters. Chaffin remembers arriving at the train station and then marching several miles with a group of other prisoners to the interrogation center: "About fifteen or twenty men and women, well dressed, gathered around us making hissing sounds and spitting at us. We had just one little corporal as an escort/guard, and I had very little confidence that he could control the mob if they decided to attack us."

Interrogations at Wetzler lasted from a few days to a week. The men were stripped and put in isolated cells, and the interrogators did their best to get them to talk. Most did not, despite some ingenious methods. A common method was to send in a man in suit who claimed to be from the Red Cross and needed information in order to contact the prisoner's family. There was also the threat of being turned over to the Gestapo if one did not cooperate. German intelligence officers did thorough work. Interrogators had newspaper clippings from hometowns, could describe events back at Horham, and gave the impression that they knew everything already. An interrogator left a large binder on the table in front of Chaffin, then excused himself. "He knew full well that I would look at it. I was amazed at the thick collection of personnel orders and copies of other military memos that I saw there."

Red Dillon also went down on *Fritz Blitz*. During his interrogation, he was asked when the next bombing raid was going to occur. Red said he wasn't sure, but he'd be happy to go back to England and ask. The interrogator was not satisfied with this answer and persisted. Finally, Dillon said, "I don't know, but I'll bet it will be somewhere in Germany." The interrogator's eyes lit up, and he called another specialist into the room. They began pouring over maps of Germany, looking for a town named Somewhere. "If it existed," chuckles Red, "it was the best-protected town in Germany for a few weeks."

After their interrogation at Wetzler, most men were loaded into box-cars and taken to various *stalag lufts* (air prisons). *Stalag*, the name given to German prisoner of war camps, is short for *stammlager*, which is itself a shortened version of *mannschaftsstamm und straflager* (team base and prison camp). Independent of interference from the more hard-core elements of the reich, such as the SS or Gestapo, the Luftwaffe administered the stalag luft camps, which housed only flying personnel.

The 1929 Geneva Convention reserved these camps for military pris-oners of war, and the camps should not be confused with camps used to detain civilians. In addition, the German stalag lufts were much more hu-mane places than prison camps for ground soldiers were. Even in the stalag lufts, however, conditions varied from camp to camp and depended a great deal on the commander of the camp and on whether the camp was for commissioned or noncommissioned officers. German camps for Russian and eastern European POWs were much worse. And none of the stalag lufts for air combat prisoners was anywhere near as terrible as the infamous camps of mass extinction, such as Buchenwald, Dachau, and Auschwitz.

Aircrew losses in the air war over Germany were staggering. Of the 32,263 combat aircraft that flew the 1,693,596 individual aircraft sorties, 55 percent were lost in action. Of the 94,565 American air crewmen who be-came casualties, 30,099 men were killed in action, and 13,660 were wound-ed and evacuated. The number of American airmen held in German stalag lufts was approximately 32,000 men, constituting a large percentage of the 51,106 American airmen who were declared missing in action, POWs, evad-ers, and internees.[9]

The U.S. Army Air Forces, aware that the Geneva Convention forbade officers from being used for agricultural or factory work, required that flight personnel be at least noncommissioned officers (sergeants). The pi-lot, copilot, navigator, and bombardier were either commissioned officers or flight (warrant) officers. The remaining crewmen—gunners, flight en-gineer, and radio operator—were sergeants.

German stalag lufts were segregated based on rank. All commissioned officers ended up together, as did all noncoms. Thus, cohesive bomber crews, who had trained together, fought together, and been shot down to-gether, were split up after becoming prisoners of war. Officers and non-coms often did not see each other again until the end of the war.

The senior officer in each officers' camp dealt directly with the German camp commandant, and his subordinates oversaw many of the more routine functions of daily life in the camp. In the NCOs' camps, a "man of confidence" was chosen by his peers and performed much the same function. Some of these leaders became powerful advocates for their men.

The stalag lufts designed for the commissioned officers tended to be a little nicer, generally speaking, a result of the Luftwaffe's class consciousness. Stalag Luft I was one of the early camps, opening in October 1942. Because few American bomber crews flew over occupied Europe at this stage of the war, almost all the early prisoners were British fliers. As late as January 1944, only a little more than 500 American airmen were imprisoned there. The vast majority of American POWs were captured in late 1943 and into 1944; so by the end of 1944, Stalag Luft I had more than 7,717 Americans and only 1,427 Britons.

As the air war progressed, existing camps were expanded and new camps were built. As the Russians advanced later in the war, the Germans evacuated all camps in areas threatened by Allied troop advances and force marched the POWs to more secure camps. By the end of the war, the surviving POWs were crammed into the remaining camps like sardines.

A typical camp was divided by barbed wire into compounds that housed the airmen by nationality. Movement between compounds varied by camp. A compound was further divided into blocks, with each consisting of around a dozen long, narrow wooden barracks. Each barrack housed as many as 150 men. Shortly after entering the camp in 1943, the Young Men's Christian Association (YMCA) furnished John Chaffin with a journal in which he assiduously wrote until the end of the war, and his entries provide a fascinating glimpse into the life of a 95th BG prisoner of war. As John Chaffin explains in his wartime log, "A barrack is a frame building approximately two hundred feet long and forty feet wide. There is a partition at the center of the building which divides it into two parts approximately one hundred feet by forty feet. At the outside end of each of these two sections, a space approximately fifteen feet wide is partitioned off to form (at each end) two rooms with a wide aisle between them. One of these small rooms on one end of the barrack is the living quarters for the barrack commander (a Captain who happens to be the ranking Officer in the building). The equivalent room on the other end of the building is used as a storage room, mainly for coal.

"The other room on each end is a kitchen which serves all of the Kriegies in that end of the building. [Kriegie was the slang term that the POWs used to describe themselves. It is a shortened version of the official German name for prisoners of war, *kriegsgefangener.*] This arrangement results in each half of the building being divided into a kitchen, a storage room or Commander's room, and the living space of approximately eighty-five by forty feet. The living space has an aisle down the center and the space on either side of this aisle is divided into three somewhat individual areas by the clever arrangement of tiered bunks. Each of these spaces is home for twelve to fifteen men and all of their belongings. We call these groups 'Combines.' The men who make up a combine live together, work together (doing those chores necessary for preparing meals and keeping our space orderly), and play together. Guys of each combine stay pretty much to themselves as long as we are inside the barracks. The rationing of food is done on a combine basis and not on an individual Kriegie basis.

"With [a] limited supply of coal, each combine has a coal manager. Early in our Kriegie life we did not do too well. Most of these guys had never learned how to cook or plan a meal. A certain number of them had been Boy Scouts and learned how to cook over campfires and a few, like myself, had not only the benefit of scouting experience but also a mother who believed that boys as well as girls should grow up with some knowledge of cooking."

A typical room consisted of double-decker or triple-decker bunk beds with straw mattresses, benches or chairs, a table at which one sat to eat or play cards, and a hanging bare light bulb. The barrack's latrine was only used at night after the barrack was locked. During the day, the kriegies used the communal latrines, or "aborts," that were housed in separate buildings in the compound. One of the camp's simple pleasures came the day when the aborts' contents were pumped into a large tank on a trailer pulled by horses. A large methane explosion resulted when the siphoning process began, eliciting loud cheers from the POWs.

The barracks were rarely insulated and became bitterly cold in the winter, especially in the northern camps. The Germans also built the barracks several feet off the ground, on stilts, to discourage tunneling and to allow English-speaking guards, known as moles or ferrets, to crawl underneath them and eavesdrop on the men inside. These guards kept the barracks' doors and windows closed and locked in the late evening and did not open them again until morning roll call, or *appel*. Guards patrolled during the night with fierce-looking Alsatian dogs, and searchlights swept the camp from watchtowers.

During the day, the prisoners could roam the camp freely as long as they did not enter any forbidden areas or cross the wire that was strung thirty feet inside the inner fence of the compound. Crossing this wire invited instant gunfire from one of the sentry towers where the guards, or "goons," watched every move in the camp. Compounds often had a recreation yard, a parade ground for roll calls, and communal buildings that could be used for libraries, theaters, or schools. Each camp also had administrative offices, a hospital, and storage sheds.

Because airmen were not allowed to work and because there was really nothing much to do "inside the wire," boredom (and hunger) soon became the POW's biggest enemy. With Chaffin's wry Texas humor, he describes "a day in a Kriegie Camp, POW number 3032, Stalag Luft III, Sagen, Germany": "A day in a kriegie camp is much the same as the previous one and no different than the one twenty-four hours hence. Life settles down to a set routine after one has been an inmate for two or three weeks. The opportunities for diversion are, to say the least, limited. The world awakens at 9:30 kriegie time, equal to 7:30 German Standard Time. The early risers get the fire going. After running to the wash house and brushing their teeth, they have just time to get a cup of Nescafe (a somewhat reasonable facsimile for coffee) and a couple of thin slices of black German bread with a little butter or jam, before falling out for appel (roll call).

"After we have fallen into something resembling military formation, the Goons go around and count us. 'Jerry' considers this necessary because there are some who become dissatisfied with their present life and set about making changes strictly on the QT [quiet, or in secret] (an extremely rare event). Appel lasts from twenty minutes to a matter of hours depending on the Goons' ability to count above ten and the contentment of the POWs. Eventually we're dismissed. From then until the noon meal, the choice of what to do is entirely up to the individual unless he happens to be a KP [kitchen patrol] or cook for the day in his combine. Some go to the reference library and study; others walk or trot around the compound for exercise. Afternoons are spent in much the same manner with reading and bridge and other pastimes. At 4:00 it is time to fall out for another appel.

"Supper is the big meal of the day and, for this, the cooks have been busy the whole afternoon. There is usually a meat dish which is either canned Spam, corned beef, lunch meat or fish loaf. With this, we will have potatoes and sometimes turnips. There is always dessert. It is either a cake made mainly from bread crumbs, a pie or stewed raisins and prunes.

"After supper the dishes are cleared away, the men play cards, chess, checkers or other games. Even though the light is not good for reading there are some who kill an hour with a book. The favorite pastime is arguing on any subject from women to politics inclusive. The participants make up for lack of knowledge with forceful words, far-fetched analogies and the ability to twist words. And thus the evening is passed.

"Around 10:00 we have 'brew,' coffee and tarts or bread, butter and jam, and then everyone talks until lights out. The lights are turned out at midnight but talk goes on for another fifteen or twenty minutes, gradually dying out as each man decides it's time for sleep. Another day, another ten dollars. I wonder what they are doing at home?"[10]

Food was scarce, and the situation only became worse as the war dragged on and Germany began to lose. Though the Geneva Convention required prisoners be fed 3,000 calories a day, 1,500 to 1,900 calories was the norm. The German food was supplemented with special parcels from the Red Cross. Full rations were one Red Cross parcel per man per week, but rarely did a man receive a full one and rarely were they delivered every week. One kriegie remembers that a full Red Cross parcel was a box about three inches deep and twelve inches square and contained the minimum amount of food required to sustain a man for one week at approximately 1,700 calories a day. In an American box were small portions of SPAM, corned beef, powdered eggs, jelly or ham, powdered milk, soda crackers, dried raisins or prunes, powdered coffee, cigarettes, sugar, a chocolate "D" bar, salt and pepper. Men rarely got their full parcels regularly, often waiting weeks in between, or having to split a parcel meant for one man several ways.[11]

The parcels provided for many of the prisoners' nonfood needs, as a lively barter system developed between the kriegies and with the guards. By the end of the war, the Red Cross parcels contained better food and cigarettes than the Luftwaffe guards were able to procure themselves. Many a clandestine radio part or other important survival or escape item was obtained by bribing guards with parcel contents. The parcels' powdered milk, made by a company named KLIM (milk spelled backward), came in cans that the men used for a variety of projects. Ingenious kriegies melted down KLIM cans, recast them, and constructed other metal items, anything from plates to parts for small bellows.

Kriegies dealt with a persistent, gnawing hunger most of the time. Red-blooded young American males talked as incessantly about food behind the wire as they had about sex before their capture. Hours were spent planning the perfect meal or debating the merits of various dishes and recipes. The kriegies figured out ways to make most of their favorite dishes using limited ingredients. Flour was made by crunching up the crackers found in Canadian Red Cross parcels. Since parcels didn't contain yeast, tooth powder containing baking soda was used.

John Chaffin's kriegie diary contains many recipes. One is for a chocolate pie that serves eight. First one made the crust: "Grind crackers into a fine powder. Over about half a bowl of the powder, pour a quarter-pound of melted butter. After mixing well, add milk until the dough is pliable; then put it in a pan and bake until brown and fully dried out."

For the pie filling: "Ingredients: one (1) *Klim* can of milk (dry), One *'D' Bar* or half can of chocolate, four tablespoons of sugar. . . . Shave *'D' Bar* into a fine powder; mix thoroughly with milk powder and sugar; then add enough water to make a thin paste. Boil mixture until thick; then pour into a crust and let set until cool."[12]

Some of Chaffin's other recipes include Barton's OO-LA-LA Cookies, Blood Sausage Sandwich Spread, Delta Delight, Kriegie-Style Grapenuts, and Prune Whip Pie.

Kriegies kept as busy as possible. Occasional packages from home brought welcome items. Some camps set up schools where prisoners used information from their peacetime occupations to educate their peers. Basil "Lyle" Shafer, a former POW from the 390th, told me that his interest in law and business began in the stalag school. He ended up as one of the top executives at National Cash Register Company (NCR) after the war.

In the summertime POWs could go outdoors. They played softball and touch football, exercised, and held boxing matches and track meets. The YMCA and Red Cross donated equipment for these events. Winters were tough. Temperatures sometimes were well below zero, and many men suffered from chilblains, a painful swelling of the toes and ball of the foot. Fleas and bedbugs shared the barracks.

Sulick writes: "It did not take much time to fall into the daily routine of life in the POW lager. We played bridge, pinochle or read all day. The bridge games were very serious business, non-stop all day, except for chow time. We were not allowed to exercise too much because it would make us more hungry and dirty. In the evening there was another roll call and lights out at 8 PM. As a new recruit, I listened to the many horror stories of my roommates. Daily rumors were abundant."[13]

Prisoners took advantage of their ample free time to draw and create various hobby projects. One man made a violin out of scrap lumber—parts from a bed, a chair, and a packing case—that played sweet and clear and had a beautiful satin finish. Another made a finely detailed B-17 from wood. Others painted. A few planned escapes, though very few American POWs managed to escape during the war.

Prisoners strived for a semblance of normality. They held religious services, complete with church choirs. They performed plays, with elaborate sets, and men in drag played the female roles. POW bands, such as the Luftbandsters, performed for their peers. Sometimes the German camp staff attended these functions.

And men waited with bated breath for mail call. Those who received letters shared with those who didn't. Letters were passed around, photos caressed and handled until ragged. All incoming and outgoing mail was censored, and although correspondence was limited, the letters from home kept many a young airman from going "around the bend."

The war dragged on. For the kriegies in the German stalag lufts, it was a different kind of war, fought not against German fighters and flak but against hunger, boredom, and the uncertain future.

17 Internment in Switzerland and Sweden

During the war, a total of 166 American bomber crews sought refuge in neutral Switzerland. Of these, 74 were flying B-17 Flying Fortresses and 82 B-24 Liberators. Because Switzerland was officially neutral during the war, American airmen landing there were not classified as prisoners of war. Instead, they were considered internees, meaning they could not leave; however, they were not subject to harsh confinement. Most lived out the war in relative comfort in resort villages high in the Swiss Alps.

A few tried to escape, and some ended up in the Swiss federal prison at Wauwilermoos, run by a sadistic Swiss Nazi named André Béguin. The Swiss sometimes shot down American aircraft if they ventured into Swiss airspace. In fact, twenty-four Americans died when Swiss flak guns or fighters shot down their aircraft.[1] One advantage of landing in Switzerland or Sweden, however—other than the obvious fact that the men would not be POWs of the Germans—was that valuable American aircraft and the secret equipment they carried would not fall into enemy hands.

A common misconception was that aircrews diverted to Switzerland to avoid combat. It likely originated from a misguided report to the U.S. Army Air Corps High Command from the American consul in Gothenburg, Sweden, William B. Corcoran, who suggested as much. In response to the report, Eighth Air Force commander Lieutenant General Spaatz ordered an air corps maintenance supervisor with a ground crew of five to fly to Switzerland and inspect the impounded American bombers at Dübendorf. According to Robert Long, the late head of the Swiss Internees Association:

"This supervisor remained in Switzerland until the end of the war. In a report from November 7, 1944, the supervisor wrote that 'no USAAF aircraft were in Switzerland without cause.'"[2] And the head of Office of Strategic Services in Switzerland, Allen Dulles, concluded that the charges were "ill-willed propaganda inspired by the Nazis."[3]

Most American planes entering Swiss airspace were directed by Swiss fighters, usually Me-109s, to a small, grassy airfield at Dübendorf. Once on the ground, the aircraft were stored for the war's duration. After the war, forty-one B-24s, thirty B-17s, and one P-51 were flown from Dübendorf to Burtonwood, England, where they were scrapped. The rest of the American planes were eventually scrapped in Switzerland.

German airmen who landed in Switzerland were allowed to wander the country freely. Moreover, 783 German airmen refused repatriation, choosing instead to live out the war comfortably in Switzerland. In contrast, nearly all interned American airmen were sent to one of three main villages high in the Alps—Adelboden, Wengen, and Davos—where they were confined for the duration and were punished harshly if they tried to escape. The Swiss chose these picturesque villages because their remote locations made escape difficult. Adelboden was surrounded by mountains on three sides and could only be reached by a narrow, winding road down a ravine. Wengen was similarly remote, perched on a jutting ledge below the Jungfrau Mountain and only accessible by a cog railway. Davos was more accessible, but it had a contingent of 400 guards to watch over 350 internees, who were housed in luxury hotels.

Historian Cathryn Prince writes about Swiss internment in her definitive work *Shot from the Sky: American POWs in Switzerland*:

> The strange thing about internment in Switzerland was that the fliers, most of whom had been under the tension of combat for quite some time, found themselves virtually plucked out of the air and plunked into a state of enforced idleness under conditions that fluctuated between privilege (by war standards) and privation. In Switzerland, time yawned endlessly before the fliers, who tried to fill their days and create some structure in their lives.
>
> Days consisted of exercise, both physical and mental; each camp had a "school" taught by fellow internees. In the afternoons, men

could do as they pleased. Many hiked, played baseball, skied or ice skated, depending on the time of year."[4]

Switzerland suffered from shortages during the war, and the internees felt the effects. The rooms were unheated. In the winter months, the water in the washbasins froze solid, and the men slept in their clothing. Food was scarce, particularly meat. Internees were restricted to 1,500 calories a day, the same as the Swiss Army. Often the meal consisted of beets, potatoes, tuna, goat cheese, and onions.

Ronald Grove was a young tail gunner on the Max Wilson crew and remembers his time in Switzerland well. The crew's one-way flight to Switzerland began on April 24, 1944, during a mission to bomb Oberpfaffenhofen and Friedrichshafen, Germany. Wilson's plane had an engine failure before reaching the target, but the crew forged on with a feathered engine. A FW-190 then scored a direct hit with a 20mm cannon that nearly knocked another engine off the plane. A third engine, hit by flak, began losing oil and became marginal. Rapidly losing altitude and with only one good engine, Wilson and copilot Lt. Felix Kowalczyk decided to instruct the crew to bail out, but the men discovered that two of the parachutes on board had been damaged. The crew talked it over and decided to ride the plane down. As it crossed the Swiss border, a Swiss Me-109 pulled up alongside and began shepherding the plane to Dübendorf.

Lieutenant Wilson and Lieutenant Kowalczyk brought the crippled plane in for a landing. As the plane touched down, the landing gear on the port side, weakened by flak and cannon fire, collapsed. As the plane skidded along the grass runway, its left wing dragging, the number 2 engine was ripped from its mounting, the propeller on engine 1 flew off, and high-octane fuel began pouring from the ruptured wing tanks. Careening wildly, the plane finally hit a wooden radio substation and an adjacent steel radio tower.

The Swiss Armed Forces were already on the scene as Lieutenant Wilson's airplane came to a stop. Miraculously, the crew had only minor cuts and bruises. As Swiss troops took the crew into custody, the men watched as Swiss youngsters climbed into the downed aircraft and began playing with the .50-caliber guns and live ammunition. After debriefing in Zurich and quarantine in Gurten-Kulm, near Bern, the enlisted men ended up Adelboden.

Tail gunner Grove, along with pilot Wilson, was the youngest crew member at nineteen years old. In a 2009 interview, Grove spoke of his incarceration: "The Swiss were pretty damn dirty to us, considering that they were supposed to be a neutral country. At the time, it looked like Germany might win the war. When it began to look like the Allies would win, the Swiss changed their tune. They started feeding us better and treating us better."

Grove spent time at both Adelboden and Wengen, but he quickly became bored and decided to escape in November 1944. As Grove tried to convince several other men to go with him, Sgt. Guiseppe "Joe" Piemonte overheard him. Piemonte volunteered to take off with Grove and had the added advantage of speaking Italian. Within fifteen minutes, the duo had a tentative plan of escape by sneaking onto the train.

Grove recalls: "As we were walking on the sidewalk toward the train depot, a Canadian came up behind us and began to speak. He said, 'You two Americans should not go to the depot. Just follow me. Stay fifteen paces behind. Don't say a word, just listen to what I tell you. If you go to the depot and get on the train they will pick you up in Bern. They will be waiting for you when you get off the train. They know you're supposed to get on it. Just follow me and don't say a word to anybody. If I ask you a question, don't even answer. I'll do all the talking.'"

The duo followed him for fifteen blocks until they met up with additional accomplices and a car. A Frenchman was driving, and an Englishwoman sat in the back seat. Once in the car, they received civilian clothes. As the Americans changed clothes, the car smashed through a Swiss roadblock. Now the military was in pursuit.

After plowing through a second roadblock, the car pulled up in front of the American Embassy in Bern, and the airmen were told to run for the door. Under international law, the embassy was considered U.S. territory, so once safely inside Grove and Piemonte had a good meal and a short night's rest.

The next day they were loaded into a truck and concealed under some boxes of freight that had been arranged to leave the men a small pocket in which to hide. The Swiss military stopped the truck but failed to find them. A short while later, two Frenchmen led them across the countryside to a lake, where they lay in the snow for an hour. Finally, a dinghy showed up, and two Poles on the other side of the lake pulled them halfway across. They got out and waded the rest of the way in the freezing water into France. The next day, a U.S. Army jeep picked them up and took them into U.S.-occupied Annecy.[5] Of the Lieutenant Wilson crew, only three crewmen served out the war as internees.

Sweden also managed to remain neutral during World War II. One hundred forty-one U.S. military aircraft crashed or made forced landings there during the war, including 69 B-17s, 61 B-24s, and 9 P-51s. Aircraft of other nations also ended up in Sweden, including 64 English, 125 German, and a number of Polish, Finnish, Russian, and Norwegian planes. All told, 1,128 American airmen ended up in Sweden after either flying in or evading capture in nearby nations once their planes had crashed.[6]

James Fournier was a bombardier in the 95th BG's 334th Squadron, flying with the W. S. Waltman crew on the B-17 *Smilin' Sandy Sanchez.* He had arrived at Horham in March 1944 and started flying combat the following month. On May 19, the crew flew a mission to Berlin. At "bombs away," an explosion hit the inboard engine on the starboard side, tearing off part of the engine. To make matters worse, a bomb was hung up in its shackle. While Fournier was trying to knock it free, he slipped on the narrow catwalk, losing his oxygen bottle. He narrowly avoided a 27,000-foot free fall by grabbing top turret gunner D. R. Gossman's legs and hanging on for dear life. He then passed out due to lack of oxygen while straddling the catwalk. As the plane descended Fournier recalled, "Gossman held onto me so I wouldn't fall out, and when we were at about three thousand feet, I came to. The bomb was still there. Gossman held onto my feet as I grabbed the bomb, jiggled it a little, and finally the bomb came loose. He pulled me back into the plane, and we cranked the bomb bay door shut."

By this time, they were all alone and vulnerable to fighter attack. Fournier continued, "We flew out over the North Sea and dropped our Norden bombsight and the Gee radar box into the sea. Then we flew for the Swedish coast. We had two dead engines by now, and we decided we had better drop the ball turret. We used the gun barrels to break the castings on the ball turret. We got rid of every loose item on that ship. We threw out all the guns and ammo. About this time flak came up through the Plexiglas and hit me in the left eye, partially blinding me.

"We all went into the radio room and braced for a crash landing. We had our wheels up and made a belly landing. The Swedes were firing over our heads as we came down. We hit and skidded along the ground to a stop.

"A Swedish officer walked up and said, 'Welcome to Sweden.' A horse-drawn wagon pulled up, and they loaded us into it and took us into the town of Ystad to a hotel. We were assigned two to a room at the hotel, and a doctor checked [James] Coppage, who'd been shot through the arm, and looked at my eye. At this point, we were just so happy to be there. They had a big table set out for the crew. I don't remember what we ate, but we had milk, and that was good.

"The next day, two Americans from the embassy came down from Stockholm. Then, the Swedes put us on a train to Stockholm, and we ended up at Falun, up north, which is an internment area. We stayed in a barbed-wire compound for two days, and the next day, they took us into Falun to buy clothes.

"Then they took us down to southern Sweden, to Lokabrunn. It was a new camp, with two men to a room. I was with my navigator. The nearest town was Karlstad. Every day, we'd have roll call; then we were relieved, and we marched down to a soccer field for some exercise. Then we'd have breakfast. The food was good. We often had oatmeal for breakfast and always had milk. After breakfast, we could do pretty much whatever we wanted. We could play cards, or go for a walk in the woods. There were two lakes nearby, and we could go swimming. The Swedes let us buy bikes, so we could ride bikes. There was no mail for four to five months. We did get to write but nothing came in. We were listed as MIA. The government told my family I was in a safe place, but didn't tell them where I was.

"Once a month, the embassy brought a box of supplies, and since I didn't smoke cigarettes, I could use my cigarettes to barter with the other guys. The embassy also gave us four hundred krona a month to spend. I think that was about twenty-three dollars.

"Later, the embassy came and got three people to go to the embassy and work. Eventually, the officers were taken to Stockholm. In November of 1944, they interviewed us and prepared us to go back to England. They put us aboard a B-24, and we flew back to the west coast of England. We did get back to the 95th Bomb Group, but because we had been shot down, they wouldn't return us to flying status. We didn't do too much. We'd go to the Red Feather, or go shoot birds with our .45s, which didn't work too well. We were there for about two weeks, then they put us on a DC-4 and flew us to Iceland, Labrador, and Washington, D.C. When we got to Washington . . . we were debriefed.

"In December 1944 we got our orders to go to Santa Ana, California, as our crew would be going to the Pacific. We trained in A-20s and B-26s and were still in training when the war ended."

Also on the Waltman crew with Fournier was ball turret gunner Russell Brainard of the 95th BG. He also discussed his time in Sweden. "We crashed just a hundred yards off of the Baltic Sea. We just barely made it. Once interned, we were treated nice and could get passes to get out, and we had civilian clothes. We had to buy all civilian clothes. The camp was run by the Swedish military. We had our own officers in charge of us, but the Swedes oversaw the whole situation."

Before Brainard entered the service, he'd been a copy boy for Associated Press. "I had knowledge of Teletype equipment as part of my training. The Swedes allowed me to go in and work at the American Embassy in Stockholm, running the Teletype. We had our own living quarters, a rented apartment. I was free to do anything that was available.

"I worked the night shift at the embassy. I came to work at seven or eight o'clock in the evening and stayed all night until seven or eight o'clock in the morning. It was a nice deal; I met a lot of people.

"When I did get out of Sweden, it was past D-Day, and things were advancing very well in Germany. It wasn't over yet. But they sent me back to the States."

Whether they ended up in Switzerland or Sweden, the internees of the 95th, as with their brethren who became POWs, found themselves in different kind of war. They became "guests" of countries that treated them with varying degrees of hospitality. Whereas Swiss flak and fighters occasionally shot at American planes in Swiss airspace, Sweden let American rescue planes land and "kidnap" interned Americans.

Gunner Sam Mastrogiacomo of the 445th Bomb Group was a young gunner who had been interned in Sweden. One evening in late September 1944, Mastrogiacomo and thirty-five other American internees were assembled for their daily two-hour walk but ended up walking considerably farther than usual.

As they crossed a railroad track, their guards told them to proceed over a small rise. Curious, the baffled men walked over the embankment and found a B-24 with engines running, waiting and ready for takeoff. An Allied Special Operations Executive (SOE) rescue mission, flown by a unit commonly called the Carpetbaggers, was offering a getaway to freedom. The Swedish guards warned the men that they would have to shoot at the bomber as it took off but assured them that the guards' aim would be very poor. The Swedes waved good-bye, then "opened fire on" the escaping POWs with machine guns and antiaircraft fire. The men heard the shells whistling past the plane. No hits registered, however, and the former internees were all returned safely to England.[7]

18   Escape and Evasion

Downed airmen were under direct orders to evade or attempt escape if at all possible, but few American airmen successfully escaped from German prison camps. A small number, however, did avoid capture and make it back to friendly territory. Others were able to evade for weeks—even months—before being captured and turned over the German authorities. The evasion stories are some of the most exciting stories of the war, often surreal and nearly always the stuff of movie scripts: intrepid airmen, incredibly brave civilians, despicable turncoats, and close calls. If an airman successfully evaded capture, he was not allowed to return to combat because if tortured, he could compromise the resistance movement.

Many downed airmen owed their lives to civilians who often took incredible risks to help them. The penalty for aiding a downed airman was usually death. British intelligence estimated "that for every downed flyer evacuated safely from Occupied Europe, one French, Belgian or Dutch helper was shot or died under torture."[1]

The total number of airmen who successfully evaded the Germans in occupied Europe in World War II is unclear. Figures vary. British MI9—the British military intelligence agency dedicated to aiding resistance fighters and to assisting and tracking troops behind enemy lines—estimated 7,046 total Allied evaders made it out of the western part of the continent and Italy. American sources claim 6,335 evaders from American forces alone. According to one historian, the correct figure may be as high as 30,000.[2]

Resistance movements in Holland, Belgium, and France were highly organized and expertly run, serving as a sort of "Underground Railroad" for downed fliers. The organized partisans worked in close concert with British and American intelligence agents based in London. Independent volunteers, not working directly for anyone, ran the most successful escape route, known as the Comet Line, which extended twelve hundred miles from Brussels to Gibraltar. They took downed airmen from Brussels, Belgium, to Paris, which was the central collection point for evaders. Small groups of men then set out for the foothills of the Pyrenees Mountains, where expert guides led them over the steep and often treacherous mountains. The guides turned the men over to the British in San Sebastian, where they were taken by car to British-controlled Gibraltar and thence back to England.[3]

An added danger of evading for the American and British fliers was that if they were captured without their dog tags and out of uniform, the Germans reserved the right to treat them as spies and summarily execute them. Some fliers solved this problem by sewing their dog tags into their clothing. Airmen were trained not to "act American." Tip-offs such behaviors as chewing gum, holding a cigarette between the second and third fingers, and jangling coins or keys in one's pocket.

When pilot Eldon Broman's Fort *Fritz Blitz* went down on the Munster mission on October 10, 1943, he bailed out and landed in the branches of a large tree in a wooded area. He released his chute and dropped to the ground. He recalled, "I ran through the woods until I was exhausted and then some more to get away from the telltale chute. I was still in the woods when I stumbled across what must have been an old foxhole. I rested there and buried my flight coveralls and flying boots. After taking a couple of Benzedrine pills from my escape kit, I started off in a westerly direction, navigating with my 'button' compass.

"I crossed several fences, which apparently was the Dutch/German border and continued westward until eventually I came to a large, busy highway. I deduced from the names marked in large lettering on the sides of passing trucks that I'd arrived in Holland."

As the sun set, Broman approached a farmhouse to ask for help. The woman there took one look at him and began screaming hysterically. Broman had burned his face severely, also losing his eyelashes and eyebrows. "I looked positively ghoulish, but I was so full of adrenaline that I was quite unaware of my injuries."

The woman's husband arrived, and Broman was able to explain to them that he needed to make contact with the Dutch Underground. The man hurried away. A half hour later, a young man named Patrick Laming showed up on a bike, pulling an empty bike alongside, and Broman rode it to a small camouflaged shack.

Laming, having been born in England and educated at Cambridge, spoke six languages. He had a Gestapo bounty of six thousand guilders on his head, dead or alive, and was disappointed Broman did not have his .45 pistol. Broman stayed with Laming for about three weeks while he recovered from his burns.

"Laming got me a picture ID," Broman told me in 2009. "I became a Belgian named Jean Séprinée. He also gave me one of his suits. He and I were about the same size." In late October, Broman began a long journey by bike, train, streetcar, rowboat, and "sometimes on all fours" to Liege, Belgium. He ended up in a second-floor safe house apartment with an airman from the 91st Bomb Group. Two other evaders soon joined them.

One day, as the men sat around, their resistance man told them he was going to go get them something to eat. "There was a stairway between our living room and the kitchen, and as he crossed the top of the stairway he yelled one word: 'Bosch!' He whipped out his 9mm handgun and emptied it down the stairs at the Gestapo. The Germans came up the stairs, firing back. After he'd emptied the gun, he threw it at them, ran through the kitchen, and dove through the second-story kitchen window, landing on the roof of a coal shed."

Meanwhile, Broman, who had dived behind a sofa, "saw the ominous barrel of a Luger pistol in the open doorway followed by the equally ominous and notorious skull and crossbones emblem on one of the S.S. troops' caps. The Gestapo had the area cordoned off, and they brought the resistance fighter back. He was injured, whether from his dive or from getting pistol whipped, I'm not sure.

"After capture, I got a ride in the biggest Mercedes I ever saw, from Liege all the way to Brussels, with a Gestapo officer on each side of me in the backseat. I was taken to St. Gilles prison, a Gestapo prison used for political prisoners dating back to the sixteenth century. They kept me in solitary confinement for thirty-two days and interrogated me twice a day. I was threatened verbally a lot but they never really hit me. They wanted to know everything I knew about the resistance movement." Eventually, Broman was sent to a German stalag luft, where he spent the rest of the war.

Leroy "Rocky" Lawson was a navigator in the 335th Squadron. On August 12, 1943, he was flying with pilot Cliff Hamilton's crew on a mission to Bonn, Germany, when the crew was forced to bail out. After landing in a cornfield, Lawson encountered a little boy, who crawled over to him and through sign language told Lawson that the Germans were looking for him and to stay put. After a while, a Dutch policeman arrived and took him into town, where he was treated for facial lacerations. The policeman then placed Lawson in a prison cell. "If the Germans came he would have to tell them he'd arrested me, but I was free to leave any time I wanted."

The next morning, after the locals fed him, Lawson set out on a bicycle, trailing his partisan guide. They met up with another evader, Virgil Jones, who had been Lawson's bombardier. They hid in a bakery in the Belgian town of Bree for three days. While at the bakery, a third crewmember joined them, flight engineer John Anderson.

The three squeezed into the back of a small Peugeot sedan and were driven to a large escape house in Brussels, the beginning of the official escape route for downed airmen. While there, Lawson was given a new set of clothes and issued fake documents. After a week, he boarded a train for Paris, shadowed by a partisan.

In Paris, he checked in to a small hotel called the Hôtel Bruxelles about three blocks from a train station. His guide told him to wait there. "After a few minutes the door burst open. In rushed three men in civilian clothes brandishing Lugers. 'For you the war is over,' one of them yelled."

One of the Gestapo men looked at Lawson's forged papers, identifying him as a Flemish traveling salesman for a plumbing company. "A very good likeness, Mr. Lawson," remarked the Gestapo agent.

"It was impossible to believe that I'd been on the loose for nearly three weeks and had gotten this far," remembers Lawson. He felt disappointed as he was led off to captivity in a POW camp.[4]

Group operations officer Clifford Cole had also flown on Lawson's plane. When he bailed out, Cole landed only twenty kilometers from Brussels. A young boy led him to a thick bramble patch that had been hollowed out in the middle. While Cole waited there, he wondered about his wife back in Illinois. She was expecting their second child. How would she know he was still alive?

Later, a man showed up on a tandem bicycle. He'd also brought Cole a complete set of civilian clothes and a pair of large wooden clogs. Though Cole's back was in severe pain, he climbed aboard and ended up spending the night in the man's attic. The following morning, a member of the Belgian Underground took him by train to Brussels. The man sat apart from Cole on the commuter train and told him not to let on to anyone that they knew each other. "No one paid any attention to me as I boarded although I couldn't help feeling extremely conspicuous," Cole remembers. "However, I found it amazing that at the interim stops, as people crowded by me, some of them gently and quietly touched and squeezed my hand to indicate they knew I was an evadee and that they were friends."[5]

In Brussels, after the Belgian Underground had verified that Cole was an American pilot, he was given forged identification papers, a passport, and another set of civilian clothes and shoes. The first safe house he stayed at was, amazingly, adjacent to the offices of the German Military Headquarters. He lived with a married couple. The lady cleaned the German offices, which allowed her to know what was going on. The man was a telephone lineman for the Brussels telephone company and often went out to "fix" the lines. He spoke fluent English, German, and French, and using his equipment he could climb a pole and tap into any telephone conversation he chose.

Cole changed safe houses several more times in Brussels. He met a member of the Underground who was Jewish. The man took him to dinner, and they even attended a soccer match together, where the unlikely duo cheered while surrounded by German soldiers and a uniformed German guard inspected and cleared his forged papers. In Paris, Cole stayed at the apartment of members of the French Underground. The man he was staying with worked at a factory that supplied trucks to the Germans. He told Cole that he and his fellow workers surreptitiously filed deep scratches in the cylinders, poured sugar into the gas tanks, and conducted other forms of sabotage. A few days later, Cole took a bus to the foot of the Pyrenees Mountains. There, at a small cabin, Cole and a few other downed airmen had a good dinner and were outfitted with heavy socks, rope-soled shoes, and warm clothing. Their guide was an elderly Basque man in excellent physical shape.

"I vividly recall the feeling of profound relief mixed with joyous elation as I pulled myself to a crest and saw the lights of a Spanish town, San Sebastian, twinkling in the distance. That night, a car from the British Embassy collected us and took us to Madrid, provided us with new clothing, identity papers, and shelter in the Embassy buildings. After a week in Madrid, a British Embassy guide accompanied us by train to Gibraltar, and the Royal Air Force flew us to London on 7 December 1943."[6]

Another airman, navigator Jennings Beck, also managed to evade over the Pyrenees Mountains. On a January 29, 1944, mission to Frankfurt, Beck's plane, *Old Dog*, lost two engines and dropped from the formation. As it neared the North Sea, five or six Me-109s jumped it. Pilot A. Roznetinsky put the plane into a steep dive. Beck heard the bail-out bell and jumped; unfortunately, the men in the back of the plane either did not hear the bell or did not have time to bail out. All the others perished.

Beck landed in an irrigation ditch. Soon some farmers arrived, stashed his gear, and gave him a pair of farmer's coveralls to wear, which were about five inches too short. Then they motioned him to follow them. Beck had injured his leg upon landing, so a young girl flattened her bike tire and told him to carry the back of the bike as if he were helping her, to disguise the fact that he was hurt. They walked through a village filled with German troops. The girl, Elsa Collins, took him to a bakery. That night, he was disguised as a girl, having rolled up his pants legs, put on one of Elsa's skirts and a jacket, and tied a babushka on his head.

Two weeks later, he was loaded into an ambulance to be taken to a larger city. One nurse knew who he was. The rest in the ambulance were told he was a mentally disabled person being taken to an institution there. "Accordingly, during the drive to the city I sat in the back jerking, slobbering and making queer noises. They didn't pay much attention, just laughed once in a while at me and talked among themselves."[7]

He was taken to the large home that belonged to a lady named Barbara Delporte. Delporte was an educated woman, a nurse by profession, from Holland. She had married a well-to-do Belgian industrialist named Bruno Delporte and had a twelve-year-old daughter. "Barbara was an expert at out-foxing the Germans. She volunteered at their hospitals where she continually played up to them. I suppose many Belgians thought she was a collaborator. In reality, she was in the Underground," remembers Beck.

Beck and several others were smuggled through Paris to a small French village, where they worked on a farm for four or five weeks. In early April as flowers were beginning to bloom, they were hustled onto a train and ended up seated in a car reserved for German soldiers. "It was very crowded so we stood in the aisles not ten feet from a German Army Colonel and a Gestapo Colonel as our group outside waved to us," writes Beck. After a nervous trip, they arrived in the town of Toulouse at about noon, and a man dressed as a woman, who later told them he was part of the Swiss secret service, questioned them there.

"The next day we were given backpacks and some food. I believe we left around noon on a train headed south toward the Pyrenees Mountains." Beck discovered that there were other evaders on board, including a young fighter pilot named Charles "Chuck" Yeager. They got off the train at a boarded-up railway station and hiked several miles on a dirt road into the Pyrenees. The group included a ten-man B-24 crew, three men from another bomber crew, Lieutenant Yeager, Beck and his crewmate bombardier O. M. "Pat" Patterson, a Belgian officer, and a young boy fleeing the draft. They were moved five or six at a time in a dilapidated 1927 Chevrolet taxicab five miles farther up into the mountains to a shepherd's cabin, where they spent the night.

At first light they assembled to hike across the mountains to freedom. "We were assembled in a single line of approximately 40 people with one armed guard leading and two bringing up the rear. We reached the tree line about noon and the crust of snow began to weaken under the spring sun. We were sinking in up to our hips in the snow. By the time we reached the top, it must have been mid-afternoon. Most of the Americans (except Yeager) were nearly exhausted."

The guides, being more fit than their charges, yelled constantly at the men for slowing them down. The guides also did not share their food. The hikers, hungry and exhausted, made it to a cabin in the woods on the far side of the mountain, where they waited for nearly a day. When they started out again, they found there was yet another high mountain to cross. As they climbed, the exhausted men ended up crawling on their hands and knees. Pat at this point said he could go no farther and was going to give up. From that point on, Chuck Yeager helped Pat. Without Yeager's assistance, Pat would not have made it.

At eight or nine o'clock the next morning when they reached the summit and looked down into a valley in Spain. "All I can say is that it was a beautiful sight!" remembers Beck.[8] At the bottom, everybody except Yeager went to sleep. Yeager hiked to a nearby village and reached the American consulate in Barcelona by phone, giving the names of everyone in the group.

When the rest of the men woke up, they hiked to the same village, but they had considerably less luck than Yeager had. The police, who appeared to be German sympathizers, picked them up; however, when the police found out that the American consulate in Barcelona had been notified, they put the men up in a small inn. While there, the men shared the restaurant with a German colonel and some of his staff. They felt brave enough to boo him, but the colonel just smiled and went on his way.

On the third day the group hiked to the next village and caught a bus. "As the bus neared Lérida, the effects of the Spanish Civil War were more and more obvious." All the bridges were closed to vehicular traffic, and they had to cross them on foot. When they arrived in Lérida, they were put in a jail for several hours until the American consul could collect them.

"The representative arrived and took us to the city's biggest hotel," Beck remembers. "There we were given a group of rooms on the top floor. Although it was Sunday afternoon, we were taken to a large department store and completely fitted with new suits, shirts, ties, shoes, underwear, toiletries and luggage. We stayed in Lérida for about a week until the first week of May. We really fattened up just lying around eating ice cream, drinking beer, and sleeping," The men had to be off the streets by dark, but otherwise they had considerable freedom.

They were then moved from Lérida to a resort village about a two-hour drive from Madrid. They spent some time there and were driven to Madrid, where they "went to the embassy, signed some book (we were within the first few hundred to evade this way), had lunch and went on our way to Gibraltar."

In Gibraltar, their brand-new Spanish civilian clothes were confiscated, and they were again issued GI uniforms. "In the evening of the third day we were hustled off to an airfield, loaded on a C-47, and headed for London. I don't know how late it was when we took off, but it was morning by the time we landed in London on May 25th. This had been a long mission. It had been four months from the time we had taken off to bomb Frankfurt in January."[9]

They waited at a hotel in London for someone from the 95th Bomb Group to come and identify them. Of the twenty-five crews that had come to Horham in November 1943, only one was still there. Its pilot, now a captain, arrived and identified Patterson and Beck. From then on, they were free. They went to Horham one day to visit the base and their few remaining friends. The rest of the time, they hit the London pubs, saw shows, and visited.

Their evasion friend and partner Chuck Yeager convinced the powers that be to let him return to combat status, and he became a fighter ace. After the war, Yeager was a test pilot of experimental aircraft, and on October 14, 1947, in the Bell X-1 experimental aircraft, he became the first man to break the sound barrier.

Keith F. Murray was one of the original 95th BG airmen. Murray, a bombardier on the G. F. Ransom crew, had already flown ten missions and had several close calls. "On my second mission something shot out my left eye," he told me. "One eye was looking straight ahead and the other was looking down. Now that was a funny sensation. But they were able to put the eye back in, and it still works." Murray spent three months recuperating from his wounds before returning to combat status. His luck ran out on September 6, 1943, when fighters jumped his plane. Murray landed in Belgium, where Allied sympathizers picked him up and gave him bread, cheese, wine, and cognac. Murray made his way to the foot of the Pyrenees Mountains, right as the bitterly cold winter set in.

"These mountains were tall!" he remembers. "It was fall, and it wasn't supposed to snow yet. We set off up the mountain. There were twenty-four of us. I had been given a pair of wooden-soled shoes with canvas sides to wear on the hike. The first day, the soles wore off. I was barefoot. All that was left was the cloth uppers. The hike was supposed to take one day. But we ran into a snowstorm. The snow was up to five feet deep in places, and we were barefoot. We climbed for three days through the snow." Finally, Murray staggered down the mountains into Spain and freedom. Of the twenty-four men who had started the journey, only three finished. The rest perished in the Pyrenees.

Upon his return to England, Murray was told he needed to take a mandatory class. When he arrived, he found out that the class, taught by a British officer, was about how to escape. Murray stood up and told the instructor, "I just did!" He was excused from the class.

Not all evaders made the trek over the Pyrenees. Pilot Richard Smith of the 95th BG's 336th Squadron went down on December 30, 1943, during a mission to Ludwigshaven, Germany. After bailing out and landing in a field, Smith hid in a hedgerow until dark, listening as German search parties combed the countryside. Three armed men arrived at his hiding spot, stopped, and dumped a bag of civilian clothing on the ground.

Smith followed them for about two miles to a small village in the Oise region of northern France. After meeting with the local police chief, "I was taken outside and crammed into the trunk of the smallest car I'd ever seen," Smith said. "After an extremely uncomfortable one-hour journey over rough country roads, we arrived at a large farmhouse, where I was overjoyed to be reunited with my copilot Bill Booher and Al Mele, our radio operator, who was of Italian descent and could speak a little French."[10]

Two days later, they were taken to Saint-Just and put up in a fully furnished house whose owners were out of town. Ball turret gunner Jerry Eshuis joined them at this point, a happy occasion for all. In mid-January the crew walked to prearranged spot in the center of Saint-Just and waited for their early morning transportation to Paris.

"What happened next could have been taken from a movie script, but it actually happened," recounts Smith. "A beautiful old limousine, from the late 1920s or early 1930s, appeared and glided noiselessly to a stop. Its driver, a large, unsmiling man, was the roughest, toughest, and meanest-looking individual I've ever laid eyes on, before or since. As we got in the car he gave each of us a loaded .45 pistol and told us if we got stopped by German authorities along the way we were to start shooting and run."

In Beauvais, the limo had to stop for a long, slow freight train. A German staff car pulled up next to them with four or five uniformed German officers inside. "They appeared to be in good spirits, laughing and talking amongst themselves. Had they looked sideways at us I'm certain our guilt would have been very apparent. It was an extremely tense seven or eight minutes."

The crew arrived in Paris and was billeted in an apartment at 34 rue de Madeleine. They ate well in Paris; the Underground appeared very well financed. Their host Alphonse even took them to a bar and a movie house.

Finally, Smith received documents identifying him as a discharged French soldier with papers to report to work in Germany in sixty days. A second set of false documents identified him as a French geologist. He took a train from the Gare de l'Est train station in Paris to the town of Saint-Brieuc on the Brest Peninsula. The town was crawling with Germans, and it appeared they were busily constructing coastal defenses there. Smith boarded another train in Saint-Brieuc, ending up in the village of Plouha. He settled in with a French family in a small house on the coast, waiting for the British Navy, which sent boats up onto the beach three nights a month when the moon was down. While he was waiting, the rest of the crew joined him.

The first two nights, the missions were scrubbed because of high seas. The third night, according to coded messages broadcast over the British Broadcasting Corporation (BBC) and picked up by their hosts, the Royal Navy was on its way. The men silently descended a steep cliff to the beach and saw blinking lights off the coast. Rescue! A longboat ran up on the shore, discharging supplies for the resistance and picking up the evaders. Once the evaders were safely on board the ship, the longboat returned to the beach with money, $15,000 for each rescued airman. On January 31, 1944, the happy crewmen made landfall at Plymouth, England. After a train ride to London, they returned to Horham and had a joyful reunion with their old bomb group.

Though there are stories of evasion, no airmen from the 95th escaped from German stalags. Not only was it hard to get outside the wire, but also once outside, there was nowhere to go and no friendly sympathizers. Men would have encountered only Germans who viewed the POWs as luftgang-sters. By October 1944, American prisoners received word through secret channels that Washington no longer required kriegies to attempt escapes.

19

MIA

In World War II, 78,773 American soldiers and sailors were reported as missing in action. The Eighth Air Force had its share. Some planes crashed into the sea or in isolated areas and were never recovered. Men parachuted from aircraft and were never seen again. The U.S. Eighth Air Force lost 4,148 bombers and 2,042 fighters; 43,742 airmen were killed or reported as MIAs. The 95th Bomb Group lost 583 men killed in action or killed in service (KIS), which included training and other accidents. Mike Darter, whose brother Eugene is one of the 95th Bomb Group's MIAs, found that 176 airmen from the 95th, or roughly 30 percent of the 95th's men listed as KIA or KIS, are still MIA nearly seventy years later.

The names of the 5,126 men and women who died in the European theater of the war but whose remains were never found or were not able to be positively identified are inscribed on a long, white stone wall at the thirty-acre American Cemetery at Madingley, three miles from Cambridge and sixty miles north of London. Most of the missing perished either in the Battle of the Atlantic or in the strategic bombing of the European continent.

The story of MIA Eugene F. Darter begs over and over the question "what if?" What if Darter had not been hit by an attacking fighter before his mates helped him bail out of their stricken Fortress? What if he had jumped out a few seconds later? What if the wind had been blowing inland rather than out to sea? What if he had landed at low tide rather than at high tide?

Mike Darter is Eugene Darter's kid brother. He was a newborn when Staff Sgt. Eugene D. Darter arrived home on leave in 1943. According to family legend, thirty-year-old Eugene, a former undercover police officer from Long Beach, California, put little Michael on a pillow and proudly paraded him around the neighborhood. The next day, Eugene left for combat in England.

Darter was the radio operator on the crew of the *Lonesome Polecat II*, piloted by twenty-four-year-old Fred A. Delbern. (The story of Delbern's wife Geri appears in chapter 11.) The crew arrived in the European theater on November 10, 1943, and was assigned to the 95th's 412th Squadron. Before the crew flew its first combat mission, some of the men came across three two-foot-long files of index cards on a desk in headquarters. Flight engineer Loren E. Dodson remembers: "Two of the files were filled and the other one about half full with names of those who were lost on past missions. Our bombardier, Lieutenant Junius (Ed) Woollen, thumbed through them before commenting: 'This doesn't look a *bit* good'. Was this an omen of what was soon to happen?"[1]

On a cold and foggy December 16, 1943, the Delbern crew took off for its maiden mission, an attack on the German North Sea port of Bremen. On board the *Lonesome Polecat II* were Delbern's copilot Lt. Don P. Neff, navigator Lt. Royal L. Jackson, bombardier Lieutenant Woollen, left waist gunner Staff Sgt. Charles J. Schreiner, right waist gunner Staff Sgt. Frank V. Lee, tail gunner Staff Sgt. Robert T. McKeegan, ball turret gunner Staff Sgt. Doral A. Hupp, flight engineer/top turret gunner Staff Sgt. Loren E. Dodson, and the "old man" on the crew, radio operator Staff Sergeant Darter.

Lonesome Polecat II was flying in the tail-end Charlie position, usually given to rookie crews, that put the plane in the back row of the low squadron. This position gave the *Polecat* the least protection of any plane in the combat box. As the flight approached Bremen, eight hundred German 88mm flak guns began lobbing shells through the clouds at the bombers. Several bursts hit the *Polecat*. One shell knocked a gaping hole in the right wing between the engines. Another shard from this burst damaged the bomb bay doors. Bombardier Woollen crawled back to the bomb bay, released the bombs with the emergency handle, and sent them tumbling through the closed bomb bay doors, forcing the doors open. Once the bombs were away, the doors remained jammed open, and the increased drag slowed the plane down considerably. It began to drop back from the rest of the formation.

Delbern feathered the number 3 engine, which had also been hit. The plane rapidly lost airspeed and altitude. To make matters worse, the bomb bay caught on fire. *Lonesome Polecat II* was now easy prey for German fighters. Two Me-109s attacked. *Polecat's* gunners shot down one, but the other shot out the left inboard engine. More Me-109s struck from the tail. A 20mm shell struck and shattered the top turret, bloodying gunner Loren Dodson's face. Darter, who had been shooting out of the top of the radio room, was badly wounded in the right arm and possibly also in his leg. He fell to the floor, bleeding profusely.

The Fort lost five thousand feet of altitude in ten minutes and now had only two working engines. Navigator Jackson and bombardier Woollen went up to the cockpit. Both pilots were injured. Pilot Delbern had been hit in the leg, arm, and abdomen, and was holding his wounded arm. Co-pilot Neff was flying the plane. Woollen told the flight crew that the bomb bay was on fire and it was time to bail out. After receiving this status report from Woollen, Delbern hit the bailout bell. Navigator Jackson was the first to jump, followed by bombardier Woollen. Both landed safely near Oldenburg, Germany. A few minutes later Dodson bailed out as well, landing safely near Leer, Germany.

Delbern and Neff apparently reached the conclusion that they could nurse the plane to a crash-landing back in England. American fighters arrived to escort the straggler as it limped toward home, preventing the German fighters from delivering the coup de grâce. Things appeared to be looking up a bit for the remaining rookie crewmen.

The *Polecat's* communication system had been destroyed by the flak or fighters, so the five crewmen in the back of the plane never heard the bailout bell and had no way of knowing that three men had already jumped. They were also unaware that both pilots were wounded. The plane continued to fly for another thirty minutes and 166 miles, crossing over Holland and then out over the Wadden Sea, a coastal area of the North Sea, toward England.

The *Polecat II* approached a small island called Texel. By now flying at only three thousand to four thousand feet and losing about three hundred feet per minute, the pilots realized that the plane would not make it back to England. If they flew on, ditching in the North Sea would mean certain death in the freezing waters.

Meanwhile, the five men in the back of the plane had no idea where they were. A thick layer of white clouds and fog obscured their view of the ground. Were they over land or water? They guessed that they must already over the main body of the North Sea.

Delbern managed to contact Doral Hupp in the ball turret, whose interphone was still functioning. Delbern told him to exit the ball and take stock of what was happening in the back of the plane. When Hupp came out of the ball, he saw Darter lying on the floor, seriously wounded. Blood was all over the radio room. Hupp rendered first aid and gave him a shot of painkiller and stimulant. He bound up Darter's arm as best he could. Darter revived a bit, and he stood up while Hupp helped him into his chest parachute.

Delbern, his face blackened by smoke, then walked back from the cockpit to check on his crew. When Hupp asked about copilot Neff, Delbern told him that Neff was mortally wounded. Delbern then returned to the cockpit, closing the door between it and the bomb bay. Hupp never saw him again.

Hupp struggled to buckle on Darter's parachute. He clipped it on upside down, because he didn't think Darter could pull the cord with his wounded arm. Darter spoke with him briefly, saying, "I'll be all right." Then Darter jumped.

Doral Hupp watched his friend as he fell, relieved when Darter pulled the rip cord. Within two minutes, the rest of the crew jumped from the back door, with the exception of the pilots. All expected to die in the freezing sea; instead, they were amazed to see land appear below as they broke through the underside of the clouds.

The plane flew for a short distance before crashing just off the coast of Texel. To this day, no one has found any sign of Sgt. Eugene Darter or of the *Polecat*'s pilot and copilot. All three were listed as missing in action and later declared dead, but for their families, there were no bodies, no proof, no closure.

One night in 2000, Eugene Darter's kid brother Mike was surfing the Internet when he came across a website that would change his life and give him the answers he had craved for so long. Within a day he was talking by phone with Doral Hupp, who had tried to save his brother's life, and, a day later, with Charles Schreiner, who had witnessed it. He also met with Loren Dodson. Darter wanted to know what happened to his brother's body. Had he perished before reaching the earth? Had he landed in the water and drowned?

After meeting with Hupp, Dodson, and Schreiner, he pored over the old Missing Air Crew Report (MACR) for clues. When Mike and I spoke many years ago, he was checking reports on bodies washed ashore around that time, on the outside chance that one of them had been that of his brother. He had also tracked down the four other surviving members of the crew and reconstructed the last fateful flight of the *Lonesome Polecat II* and the final minutes of his brother's life.

Darter visited Texel Island on many occasions in the ensuing years and found people living there who had witnessed the plane's last moments. Jack Betsema remembered a B-17 thundering at low altitude over his village of Oost, thus establishing the flight line of the aircraft in its final moments. A few months later, Darter received e-mails and a letter responding to a newspaper story that had run in the *Texelse Courier*. Two witnesses remembered hearing and seeing a low-flying B-17 over their village at De Koog that appeared to be attempting a crash landing on or near the beach.

But the real bombshell came in the form of an e-mail message from Cornelius J. Ellen, a lifelong resident of the eastern side of Texel:

On this day I (then age 17) am witness with eyes and ears when the airman with his chute above the dike about 150 meters (500 ft.) Before he hit the sea water I hear his (a shrill) clear voice: "Help me, Help me." He came down 300 meters (1,000 feet) out from the dike in the Wadden Sea (during high tide) standing in the sea water until his breast/neck. The chute at that moment was lying down on the water, but this poor airman did nothing to unsnap the chute. I ran away to get a rescue boat near the place. Half of the way to the rescue boat I looked behind me, and saw the wind is blowing into the chute and like a half-moon in the Wadden Sea, and it takes this poor airman with it. I am, after nearly 60 years satisfied to send you this.[2]

Ellen added that he believes Darter's brother was pulled into deeper water and eventually sank to the bottom in a deep crevice and was covered over with sand.

In June 2003 Darter returned to Texel with his brother's friend and crewmember, ball turret gunner Doral Hupp. Together, they interviewed witnesses, including Mr. Ellen, who had since placed a memorial marker consisting of a pole mounted on a concrete block at the spot where Eugene Darter splashed down in 1943. The visit provided closure for Mike Darter but made him sad.

> My brother came so close to surviving. Bailing out just a couple of seconds later would have landed him securely on the island. Or, if the water level was not at high tide he could have walked into shore from where he landed, as the Wadden Sea is very shallow there. As I stood on the dike sixty years after the event with Doral Hupp and Cornelius Ellen, the two people who last saw my brother alive, the moment will be etched in my mind forever. It finally brought closure for me and Doral and the other surviving crewmembers after so many years of uncertainty.[3]

Sometimes, the end of a missing man consists of nothing more than the paperwork of the bureaucracy that tries and fails to find him. The following case of 95th BG pilot Lt. Harold C. Coffman manages to be both poignant and personal despite being told entirely by documents. Listed in chronological order are the documents pertaining to his case:

- *Individual Deceased Personnel File for Harold C. Coffman, 1st Lt, O 765 226.*
    Lost over English Channel Dec. 16, 1944.
    MACR Extract, No. 189
    95th BG, 412th Squadron. Stuttgart. Cloudy. 9 crew members on board.

- *Combat Mission 249 to Stuttgart, Germany.*
    169th plane lost: H.C. Coffman-297232. Details of this loss are unknown at this time. Pilot Coffman, H.C. KIA, CP. Beadle,

L.W. Jr. KIA, N. Reid, T.J. Jr. KIA, B. Wediner, M.E. KIA, TT Gallagher, W.W. KIA, RO Lanni, D.J. KIA, BT Pellow, R.W. KIA, WG Hooser, W.E. Jr., KIA, TG Jones, J.J., KIA. (Mission Report)

- *Statement submitted by Captain David E. Olsson, Assistant Operations Officer* (reads as follows):

   B-17G 42-97232 piloted by 1st Lt. Coffman was not reported as to time and place of loss. On the route back from the target at 50 degrees 30' N 04 degrees 00' E clouds up to 23000 feet forced a turn northward. Because the aircraft of the group were low on oxygen and gas they broke off individually to return to base. This aircraft broke off as did the others and has not been heard from since. There was no contact made by radio at any time with this aircraft.

- *9/10/45 Effects shipped from Army Effects Bureau to Mrs. Coffman.*

   Contents include a short snorter (a piece of paper money signed by friends), souvenir money, souvenir dish (broken), 2 knives rusty, and photo damaged by moisture, a money order for 9.00 and a novel lighter.

- *Letter from Helen H. Coffman to the Effects Bureau in Kansas City, Missouri, Sept 22, 1945*:

   I received the personal belongings of my husband Lt. Harold C. Coffman, 0-765226 last September 15, 1945.

   I have reason to believe that there are some things missing. Whether they were misplaced while in possession of Lt. Coffman or afterwards I of course do not know. However, before I can sign a receipt of his property, I will have to have an itemized list of the contents, made at the time they were originally checked and packed at his own bomb group in England. I don't wish this to cause you undue trouble, but I think you will understand the position I am in.

- *October 1, 1945 from R.T. Brown to Helen Coffman*:

   This will acknowledge your letter of September 22, relative to the personal effects of your husband, First Lieutenant Harold

C. Coffman. In answer to your request, I have inclosed [*sic*] a copy of the Inventory and Effects of Lieutenant Coffman, which was prepared at his base overseas.

List of effects of Harold C. Coffman, 0-765226, 1st Lt., AC, Received at the Army Effects Bureau:

Class I	Class II	
1 assmt letters	1 blouse	1 wash cloth
1 photo and holder	1 field jacket	1 wool undershirt
2 pr wings	1 trench coat	2 wool drawers
1 set identification tags	4 caps	5 pr shoes
1 ribbon	2 belts	1 clothes brush
1 lighter	7 pr slacks	
3 novel lighters	7 shirts	
1 wrist watch	5 ties	
1 air medal	1 piece barathen cloth	
1 assmt antiques	2 hankies	
1 201 file	3 pr shorts	
1 #5 file	1 pr gloves	
1 assmt ribbons	16 pr socks	
1 wallet	5 towels	

The search for Coffman's remains comes up empty:

Field investigation returned negative results. Assumed plane went down in the water. Plane was last sighted in the vicinity of Brussels, Belgium, while en route back to its base. Captured German records reveal no information concerning this aircraft or its personnel and no information has been developed indicating that the aircraft landed on continental Europe.

Body of one of the crewman, 2nd Lt. Leonard W. Beadle, Jr. 0826852, AC, washed ashore at Zeutelande, Holland in May of 1945. No other bodies washed ashore after that, and no aircraft parts were recovered either.

- *Identification information.*

    Data on Remains not Yet Recorded or Identified: 5'10" 185 pounds Blue eyes blonde hair no fractures, breaks, tattoos or birthmarks. 26 years old. Ohio 20/20 vision.

    Dental Records: Flying Personnel Dental Identification Form, Office of the Dental Surgeon. 20th Aug, 1944. Shows ten fillings and . . . edge bite.

The military then checked Zeutelande for Coffman's remains:

May 2, 1947 Headquarters, First Zone 551st QM Group, American Graves Registration Command, APO 58 (Liege), US Army:

    Investigation conducted in the Zeutelande area failed to locate the remains of the eight (8) unresolved casualties of aircraft 42-97232.

    1947: Information from the Town Hall at Zeutelande is as follows: The Americans removed two bodies from the Zeutelande Military Cemetery March 14, 1946. Beadle, Leonard William . . . formerly buried in Row C, grave 24; [and a man from another crew] Both were found washed ashore at Zeutelande in May 1945. The town hall has no information concerning a plane crash of 16 December 1944. Also no further bodies have been washed ashore since May 1944, and no plane parts either. Had the police or civilians found a body or parts of plane it is compulsory for them to have reported it to the town hall.

Lieutenant Coffman was declared dead rather than missing. The following is a letter that the military sent to Coffman's mother:

26 August 1949
Dear Mrs. Duncan:

Almost four years have elapsed since the cessation of hostilities of World War II, which cost the life of your son, the late First Lt. Harold C. Coffman.

    The unfortunate circumstances surrounding the death of your son have been thoroughly reviewed and, based upon information presently available, the Department of the Army has been forced to determine that his remains are not recoverable.

W.E. Campbell, 1st Lt QMC Memorial Division

When Coffman's widow remarried, she received the following notification:

August 17, 1949
Pursuant to your request of July 20, 1949 the following data is forwarded for your information. The records on file with this office (VA) disclose that the veteran's widow, Mrs. Helen H. Coffman, has remarried and is now Mrs. Helen H. Jutzi, ——, Pico, California.

- *Battle Casualty Report, September 16, 1949. Killed in Action in the North Sea.*

 Aug. 26, 1949: The persons named below, of the 412th Bombardment Squadron, 95th Bombardment Group, were reported missing in action . . . 16 December 1944 by ETO Shipment 290 and were presumed dead as of 17 December 1945.

 1951: Above decedent and seven (7) others were crew members on an aircraft which was last seen 16 December 44 for purpose of memorialization presumed date of death 16 December 44. Area of death English Channel.[4]

Two stories—one told by a grieving brother who had to know the truth, the other told through official documents. As of the writing of this book in 2012, the remains of the MIAs on the *Lonesome Polecat II*—Delbern, Neff, and Darter—and of Lt. William C. Coffman have not been recovered. At this point it is unlikely that they ever will be found. Their stories are little different from thousands of others and serve as a stark reminder of the missing in action in World War II and in all wars.

20 Pathfinders and Aphrodites

The B-17 went through many modifications during World War II, but perhaps the Pathfinder and Aphrodite configurations are the most interesting. Both are tied in some way to the 95th Bomb Group, and a discussion of the group would be woefully incomplete without a chapter devoted to these two variants. Both programs showed typical American ingenuity in overcoming specific problems—in the Pathfinder's case the problem of how to continue daylight precision bombing through heavy layers of clouds, and in the Aphrodite's how to knock out Hitler's dreaded new rocket program.

Winter 1943–1944 put the U.S. policy of daylight precision bombing to the test. The skies over England and the continent were thickly overcast; in fact, they would mostly remain so until spring. A gunner with the 95th and later a Pathfinder crewman John O'Neil remembers: "There were only two or three days each month of clear weather over Europe which would allow navigation by dead reckoning and use of the Norden bombsight."[1]

The U.S. Army Air Forces leadership up to then had resisted the concept of area bombing. Would it be possible, however, to continue to practice pinpoint strategic bombing with targets hidden below the clouds? What if each bomber stream was equipped with an aircraft that could "read" the contours of the shrouded earth and direct the rest of the stream to drop accurately on an otherwise unseen target?

In 1940, after a study showed only one in ten British bombs was hitting its intended target, the British developed an air-to-ground radar system.

Early systems, named Gee and Oboe, relied on signals from the aircraft's base. The next step was to develop a system that could be carried in the bomber and operated independently of bases in the United Kingdom.

In 1941, an experimental radar known as AIS (airborne interception system on S-band operation) was tested, and the scientists found that it could successfully "read" terrain that was invisible to the bomber crews by bouncing radio waves off the ground. By late 1941, it could pick up the outline of a city from thirty-five miles away. In 1942, the Royal Air Force added the system to a blister on the underside of some bombers. The antenna inside the blister rotated and scanned the terrain, feeding the reflections to a display inside the aircraft. The rotating map display, known as the plan position indicator, resembled modern radar devices in which a line sweeps around a circular screen, highlighting items with light. The British first used the new system, dubbed H2S, in April 1942 on a Halifax bomber. In June, the prototype H2S Halifax crashed, destroying the system and the aircraft and killing one of the developers.

An added concern was that the cavity magnetron device in the H2S was difficult to destroy if a plane crashed in enemy territory. The copper core of the magnetron was virtually indestructible, and the Allies feared if the Germans obtained the device from a downed plane, they would easily duplicate it or develop countermeasures. Lord Cherwell, the head of the program, pushed for using a klystron device instead because its core was easier to destroy. However, given that the klystron was significantly less powerful, Prime Minister Winston Churchill opted for the magnetron despite the dangers.

The RAF first used the new system in combat on January 30, 1943, when thirteen radar-equipped British Stirling and Halifax bombers, nicknamed Pathfinders, escorted a bomber stream to Hamburg and marked the city with incendiary flares. A hundred Lancasters followed and hit the target successfully.

In February 1943, an RAF Stirling bomber equipped as a Pathfinder was shot down near Rotterdam, Holland, so the Germans now had one to study. Its display had been destroyed in the crash, so it wasn't until another set fell into their hands a year later that the German engineers realized what the device did. After the Germans set the H2S device up in one of their flak towers and turned it on, they were horrified. "The display recognizably showed Berlin's other flak towers and surrounding area. When Hermann Goering was shown this, Goering is said to have exclaimed, 'My God, the British really can see in the dark!'"[2]

The United States began working on its own version of H2S. Known as the H2X, the Americans gave it the code name Mickey Mouse and later shortened it to Mickey. Like the H2S, the Mickey device was attached to the belly of the bomber, immediately behind the chin turret. The Mickey system was not used until early 1944.

The 482nd Bomb Group (P) was created for the sole purpose of providing radar-equipped Pathfinder aircraft to the different bomb groups in England. Activated on August 19, 1943, at the 95th's old base at Alconbury, the 482nd had the distinction of being the only USAAF group to be activated outside the United States.

William "Bill" Owen was a pilot in the 95th's 412th Squadron when he was tapped for the new Pathfinder program. He remembered: "In November 1943 after our first seven missions with the 95th Bomb Group, which included four raids during the notorious 'Black Week' of mid-October 1943, my crew and I were sent to the 482nd Bomb Group at Alconbury to train on the Pathfinder blind-bombing technique being developed at that time, using British 'Oboe' and 'Stinky' radar equipment. Within a few short weeks, we were flying to the various Eighth Air Force bases in the middle of the night to join as lead aircraft for groups selected to lead the Eighth Air Force, a division, or a combat wing the following day."

The 482nd crews had learned how to read the beams of transmitted energy accurately. Pathfinder gunner John O'Neil writes: "The reflected signals gave a map-like picture on the unit screen in the bomber, with dark areas for water, light areas for ground, and bright areas for towns and cities. The actual navigation was done by comparison of the radar picture with a map."[3]

The USAAF's next big task was selling radar bombing to the American public. First it had to think of a way to explain that bombing a city through clouds was still precision bombing and not simply carpet bombing. The aircrews called it blind bombing, a term Gen. Hap Arnold despised. He preferred the term "bombing through overcast" or "bombing with navigational devices." Arnold saw not only the drawbacks of the policy change but also its distinct advantages. One of the greatest advantages was defensive; the bomber stream would be invisible to flak and much harder for German fighters to find. Another plus was that when poor weather was forecast, Pathfinders could be sent as insurance. If the weather cleared over the continent, the bomber stream could bomb visually.

The first mission to be led by the American Pathfinder Force (PFF) occurred on September 26, 1943, followed a feverish thirty-six-day training period. Four H2S radar–equipped B-17s from the 482nd flew to bases of the First and Third Air Divisions to lead the following day's mission to Emden. After its success, Pathfinders accompanied the groups back to base for debriefing, then flew to Alconbury.[4]

The Pathfinder program was a success. According to O'Neil, the 482nd Bomb Group led more than 80 percent of Eighth Air Force missions from November 1943 until late March 1944. The Pathfinders allowed the Eighth to fly missions that would otherwise have been aborted owing to bad weather. In fact, the Eighth flew more missions in the poor winter weather than it had in the previous summer and fall.[5]

Moreover, the 482nd was so successful that Allied commanders became worried that German intelligence would order a bombing strike at Alconbury. Such an attack "could have destroyed all the Pathfinder equipment of the Eighth. There was also a worry that the Germans would launch a parachute drop with commandos to destroy the Pathfinder airplanes as they sat on the hardstands," writes John O'Neil. However, the anticipated attacks never came.[6]

"By the end of March 1944, each Eighth Air Force bomb group was getting its own B-17s equipped with 'Mickey,'" remembers Bill Owen. "This, of course, meant the Alconbury Pathfinders (Stinky) were no longer required to fly combat. However, a radar school was established at Alconbury to train the Mickey radar operators before leading their own groups. Our navigator, Al Engelhardt, was in charge of this school. It was decided that radar maps, made up of individual scope pictures, would be of great assistance both during actual missions flown by the Eighth Air Force and in instructing the new crews at the school.

"This project was assigned to my crew because, I think, we were the closest to completing our tour. One of the Stinky B-17s was painted black,

[with] flame suppressors put on the turbo-chargers, and a camera, complete with an automatic timing mechanism, was fitted to the radar scope. The plan was to fly as high as possible, over 25,000 feet, during the eight or nine moonless nights per month that the RAF Bomber Command's heavy bombers flew at that time. We flew predetermined tracks with the camera taking the scope photographs at regular timed intervals, which enabled a map overlay to be produced. Flying at high altitude we would see much of Germany and watched each RAF mission develop in stages though the night. After flying only daylight missions over Germany, it was an incredible sight to behold."

The Eighth Air Force's decision to begin blind bombing had serious effects on the Luftwaffe. Its pilots had problems flying in poor weather. Gen. Adolf Galland admitted after the war that German aircraft were unequipped for bad-weather aerial combat, as they "had no instruments for blind flying, no de-icing of the cockpit, no safety arrangements for navigation or automatic pilots, and no knowledge of instrument flying or bad-weather methods of landing. Numerous German pilots were sitting in their completely iced-up cockpits, half-blinded, to become easy prey for the Thunderbolts. The appalling losses of this period were plainly due to the weather."[7]

With each bomb group's acquisition of its own Pathfinders, the 482nd became a Pathfinder training unit. Pilot Owen found it boring after a while, and he asked for a transfer back to the 95th, where he flew the few remaining missions that he needed to reach the end of his thirty-mission tour. In November 1944, Owen was detached to the Third Scouting Force, 55th Fighter Group, and flew P-51 Mustangs in reconnaissance. In all, Owen flew thirty missions in B-17s, both standard and Pathfinder types, and thirty-three more sorties as a P-51 pilot. He flew for twenty-two months, finishing up only when the war in Europe ended.

The Aphrodite program, meanwhile, had an entirely different goal than that of the Pathfinder and was considerably less successful. Although best known as the program that led to the death of Joseph P. Kennedy Jr., older brother of future president John F. Kennedy, Aphrodite was developed quickly to counteract what could have been a tragic turnaround in the German war effort. In 1938, a young socialite named James Henry

Rand III traveled to Germany to do research. Using his family connections—his father, James Henry Rand Jr., was the president of Remington Rand (incidentally the builder of the Norden bombsight)—he was able to visit high-level German officials. A fluent German speaker with aviation knowledge and connections, Rand ended up sharing an apartment with Ernst Udet, who ran T-Amt, the developmental wing of the Reichluftfahrtministerium (Reich Air Ministry). Udet would later become a high-ranking general in the Luftwaffe. A casual remark one day drew a stunning retort. Rand mentioned in passing that he'd heard the Germans were conducting experiments on television cameras. "I'm not going to tell you about that!" snapped Udet. "I could have you put in jail right now for asking such a question! Stick to your cancer research!"[8] Rand, however, dutifully notified the American Embassy that the Germans were developing something involving television to be used in wartime.

In 1941, while standing on a Liberty ship in the Mediterranean and observing a German bombing raid, Rand noticed one of the bombs was trailing smoke. As the bombs came down, Rand saw that they seemed to flatten their trajectories and move slightly from side to side as they approached their targets. The bombs were being steered! When he returned to Washington, Rand suggested that the U.S. military could equip missiles with a miniature, disposable television camera that could be guided by a controller in a nearby aircraft. The controller could guide the missiles to the target simply by watching a television screen that projected images from the missiles as they fell.

The first American guided missiles that Rand developed were called Razon (range and azimuth), but problems with their range led to a newer version called Azon (for azimuth only). Putting a television camera in the nose of each missile, however, was considered too expensive. Instead, the missiles were equipped with a million-candle-power flare in the tail that would be visible to a trailing aircraft. Rand used Azon with limited success before arriving at Horsham St. Faith airfield, near Norwich, Norfolk, to begin the new phase in his missile development, a top-secret program code-named Aphrodite.

Lt. Gen. Jimmy Doolittle called Rand into his office in the late spring of 1944. Doolittle said,

Jim, you've been shooting off your mouth about being able to guide a bomb right into a hole. The Germans have a whole lot of big concrete bunkers in the side of cliffs and hills, in the Pas-de-Calais, twenty-five or thirty miles across the Channel, and they're gonna use 'em to destroy London. We've got to knock 'em out and our bombers aren't getting the job done. We're losing five percent of our planes in missions against these sites. They've got four hundred guns around each one. I want you to figure out how to fly a plane into these things and blow them up. And I want you to do it fast. If you don't do it fast, London is done for, and maybe New York, too.[9]

Within days, Doolittle provided Rand with all the equipment he needed, as well as two aircraft with pilots. A card from Supreme Headquarters decreed that he was not to be interfered with by any military organization, that he was on a special government mission, and that he could commandeer any service or civilian transport, interrogate anyone, see any document, and demand any assistance he required, by order of General Eisenhower. Printed orders gave Rand's mission the highest priority in the northern European theater.

Rand recruited a small cadre of airmen sworn to absolute secrecy. One of these pilots, Lt. Fain Pool of the 385th Bomb Group, remembers showing up at the base commander's office at Great Ashfield airfield along with four other pilots. The commander asked them if they would be interested in a "hazardous, highly secret mission, one that involved flying a heavy bomber and bailing out over friendly territory. No crews would be needed; the Air Force only wanted pilots and radio technicians. Their reward for this one job: credit for five bombing missions."[10]

Of the five, only Pool—a veteran of fourteen prior missions—accepted. Ten hours later, he disembarked from a plane at an RAF repair depot at Honington, Suffolk, and a driver in a Jeep took him to a remote part of the base, where he met other recruits.

Pilots were instructed that the U.S. Army Air Corps was going to gut ten worn-out Flying Fortresses and fill them with twenty thousand pounds of nitrostarch, a highly explosive demolition powder, and a smaller amount of napalm. The Aphrodite drones would be equipped with remote control equipment that would allow them to be flown by radio from a B-24 mother ship. Several of the drones would have television cameras mounted in their Plexiglas noses, allowing the men in the mother ships to guide the planes into the target. Each drone would take off with a crew of two—the jump pilot and the autopilot engineer—who would fly it to eighteen hundred feet, put the drone into a gentle dive, set the autopilot, arm the explosives to detonate on impact, and then jump out over England through the only unbolted escape, a small hatch in the nose. The mother ship would then fly the plane remotely into the target, approaching below radar at six hundred to seven hundred feet.

The first Aphrodite mission took place on August 4, 1944, and its target was a German underground rocket site at Mimoyecques, France. The mission would use four drones, flying in pairs. Piloting the first aircraft was Lieutenant Pool, who whistled after getting into the plane and seeing it literally stuffed from floor to ceiling with high explosives. Pool's greatest concern at this point "was not that he was flying the most powerful single bomb ever assembled up to that time, but that he would be bailing out, at high speed and ridiculously low altitude, through a hole barely two feet wide."[11]

After a routine takeoff, Pool struggled to get the plane to climb. He finally had to bail out from five hundred feet. It crashed while still over England. The second drone exploded, killing the pilot. The second pair fared little better: none hit the target.

On August 6, the USAAC launched a second unsuccessful mission. On August 12, the U.S. Navy flew its drone version, a converted PB4Y that was a variant of the B-24 Liberator. The jump pilot was Lt. Joseph Kennedy, a veteran of more than fifty antisubmarine patrol missions. Minutes into the flight, Kennedy's plane exploded in a blinding fireball, falling over New Delight Wood, Suffolk. The bodies of Kennedy and crewmate Lt. Wilford Willy were never found. The probable cause of the explosion was a faulty remote control device.

By the time another mission was nearly ready, the Allied ground forces had overrun the mystery targets on the French coast. To their dismay, they found all the sites empty, filled only with rats and rubble. They hadn't been used for months, except as decoys to divert attention from the German mobile V-1 launching sites. The Aphrodites had been striking empty targets.[12]

The 95th Bomb Group was peripherally involved in the Aphrodite experiment. One of the first "Hangar Queens" tapped for conversion to an Aphrodite drone was none other than the 95th Bomb Group's *Ten Nights in a Bar Room/The Brass Rail*, which the Johnny Johnson and Kit Carson crews had used. The plane, B-17F 42-30353, flew as a drone on December 5, 1944, taking off from Knettishall for the marshaling yards at Hereford.

The other drone flying with *Brass Rail* was the 95th's *Darlin' Dolly*. A jump pilot and a technician flew in each plane. As the lead ship attempted to guide the two planes toward the target, it encountered heavy cloud cover and became lost. *Darlin' Dolly* exploded near Haldorf, Germany. The lead ship lost contact with the *Brass Rail*. Unknown to the former, the old plane began a gradual descent all by itself, coming in for a perfect landing in a muddy plowed field.

When Eighth Air Force Command found out, it scrambled Allied fighters to fly to Germany and destroy the aircraft; after all, it was packed with top secret equipment. While the Allied fighters raced to blow up the *Brass Rail*, German soldiers had discovered the plane. They had no idea that they were looking at a specialized aircraft. As the soldiers began their inspection, the *Brass Rail* exploded, killing them. As Roger Freeman wrote: "The Germans on the scene never had a chance to report what they found, and German High Command assumed it was a normal B-17 with a traditional bomb load."[13]

Even in death, the war-weary B-17F was able to rain destruction on the enemy. Its crew would have been proud.

21   Big Week

Eighth Air Force leaders intended to continue their long-range bomber attacks on Axis targets even after the disastrous Black Week raids, but as winter set in, the weather turned bad over the continent. In hindsight, that development was probably a good thing. On January 5, 1944, Lt. Gen. Jimmy Doolittle was named the new commander of the Eighth Air Force, replacing Lt. Gen. Ira Eaker. Two days later, Doolittle moved to his new headquarters at Wycombe Abbey, Buckinghamshire.

As Doolittle writes in his memoir:

> I inherited the 8th Air Force at a natural turning point in its history. Ira had left me a "going concern" that he had practically built from scratch. Due to the small number of aircraft and crews made available to him, Ira was never able to overwhelm the enemy's defensive force. Short on bombers and without long-range fighter escort, he had been forced to absorb prohibitive losses of upwards of 20 percent on missions against such targets as Regensburg and Schweinfurt. Rarely was he able to send out more than 200 to 300 bombers at a time. Hap Arnold had not been able to give Ira the crew and planes he needed in time. . . . [Even so,] Eaker had come heartbreakingly close to his goal when I took over.[1]

A huge issue in long-range daylight precision bombing was the need for escort fighters. In 1942, the best escort, the British Spitfire, had a range of only 175 miles. In May, the P-47 Thunderbolt took over escort duties, and by July, equipped with seventy-gallon belly tanks, it could escort the bombers up to 340 miles. When Doolittle arrived in England, Thunderbolts could go 426 miles using two belly tanks. By November 1943, the Lockheed P-38 Lightning and the North American P-51 Mustang that began to arrive in the European theater were capable of traveling up to 850 miles, a distance that was increased throughout the winter. The arrival of these two aircraft, but especially the P-51, completely changed the aerial balance of power over Europe.

Doolittle also radically altered the escort fighters' role in aerial combat. Up until his arrival, their mission was unequivocal: protect the bombers at all times. When Doolittle first visited Maj. Gen. William E. "Bill" Kepner's Eighth Fighter Command, he noticed a sign hanging on the wall in Kepner's office: "The First Duty of the Eighth Air Force Fighters Is to Bring the Bombers Back Alive." This directive did not sit right with Doolittle, because, in his words, "fighter aircraft are designed to go after enemy fighters. Fighter pilots are usually pugnacious individuals by nature and are trained to be aggressive in the air. I thought our fighter forces should intercept enemy fighters before they reached the bombers."

Pointing at Kepner's sign, Doolittle announced: "That statement is no longer in effect. Take that sign down. Put up another one that says, 'The First Duty of the Eighth Air Force Fighters Is to Destroy German Fighters.'"

Kepner looked at him in disbelief and asked, "You mean you're authorizing me to take the offensive?"

"I'm directing you to," replied Doolittle. Tears came into Kepner's eyes. For months he had pleaded with Eaker and Spaatz for permission to pursue the enemy fighters, and they had turned him down repeatedly. "As a fighter pilot myself, I knew how he felt," adds Doolittle. "I told him that he would still have to assign fighters for escort duty, but the bulk of them would go hunting for Jerries. 'Flush them out in the air and beat them up on the ground on the way home,' I said. In short, the doctrine was now one of 'ultimate pursuit.'"[2]

The bombardment group commanders were none too happy with Doolittle. "As soon as my decision was announced to the Bomb Groups, their commanders descended on me individually and in bunches to tell me, in polite terms, of course, that I was a 'killer' and a 'murderer.' I had taken away their 'little friends' and they were sure their bomber formations would now be picked off wholesale. There was no compromise as far as I was concerned, and many bomber crews remained very unhappy. Some still are." Doolittle refused to back down, and in his memoir he states that "as far as I'm concerned, this was the most important far-reaching military decision I made during the war."[3]

Doolittle realized he was really on the bubble as commander of the Eighth Air Force. He wrote his friend Brig. Gen. George Patton after learning of his appointment: "I don't know whether or not congratulations are in order. I have a bigger and more interesting job, but at the same time it is infinitely more difficult. [In North Africa] the problem was to make something out of nothing. Up here it requires an equal or greater amount of ingenuity to effectively utilize the almost unlimited resources at one's disposal."[4]

The 95th flew thirty-four missions after Black Week, which saw the October 10 Munster mission and the October 13 Schweinfurt mission and nearly broke the Eighth's back. Bombardier Maurice Rockett recalled the weather being atrocious from late December 1943 into February 1944. Owing to the poor weather, thirteen of the twenty-nine missions flown during January and February were to V-1 flying bomb sites near the coast. The bomb group flew in support of Operation Crossbow, which was initiated after the Allies discovered the sites around the Pas-de-Calais region and on the tip of the Cherbourg Peninsula. The men usually considered these Crossbow (also called Noball) missions milk runs, because they spent little time over enemy territory and encountered few fighters but increasingly thick flak. Hindsight shows that the Noball missions were ineffective; most V-1s were launched from mobile firing units. However, at the time, Allied leaders were justifiably worried that the launch pads could be used for the V-2 rocket or a feared V-3 supersonic rocket, which possibly had the ability to hit the U.S. East Coast.

Meanwhile, Doolittle did show compassion for his bomber crewmen on several instances in January 1944 and recalled the entire bomber force well into the missions because of concerns that the British bases would be fogged in upon their return. Lt. Gen. Tooey Spaatz called him on the carpet. "He really struck me where I was tender when he said, 'I wonder if you've got the guts to lead a big Air Force. If you haven't, I'll get someone who has."

Stung, Doolittle defended himself, saying that he did not want to risk the lives of so many men and a great amount of equipment. Spaatz countered that there would be no recall issued after the aircraft had crossed the enemy coast. Period. "The Germans are going to use every stratagem to turn us from doing our job," Spaatz insisted. "And one of those will be false recalls to our formations."[5] This tactic would become the major issue on March 4, 1944, when the leader of the 95th Bomb Group's Berlin mission, Grif Mumford, decided to ignore a recall and continue to the target, thus making the 95th the first American bomb group to hit the German capital.

Doolittle wasn't winning any popularity contests in his new job, with the exception of gaining the fighter pilots' respect. Another of his early decisions was to increase the number of required aircrew missions from twenty-five to thirty. As he recalls,

> By the time I arrived, which was coincident with the arrival of increased numbers of fighters and bombers, our losses were going down. The chances of an individual surviving one full tour were now greatly increased. It had been my observation that bomber crews did not reach an acceptable level of skill until they had about ten missions in, and had reached the peak of their efficiency just when they were being allowed to go home. It seemed wasteful to me when we were trying so hard to build up an effective force. As expected, my decision was greeted with a great lack of enthusiasm, especially by bomber crews.[6]

Despite the bad weather, the bombers flew several missions in the weeks leading up to Big Week. Pathfinder aircraft led three missions into Germany itself. The 95th suffered particularly heavy losses on a February 10 mission to Brunswick. Seven Forts went down and 70 men were lost. The Eighth Air Force as a whole suffered a 20 percent loss rate on the mission, or 29 bombers and 295 crewmen. But German losses were also heavy, with 60 Luftwaffe fighters downed in a little less than three hours.

The weather began to clear over the continent as spring approached. The lull had given the Eighth Air Force time to add much-needed fighter escorts, and the force in England numbered nearly 1,300 fighters, including more than 300 P-51 Mustangs.[7] Luftwaffe leaders had no idea that the Americans had finally solved their need for long-range fighter escort. By mid-February, the Eighth possessed 539 P-38Js, 416 P-47Ds, and 329 P-51Bs. German pilots noticed that Allied fighters now attacked them on sight and that the Eighth Air Force "went after the Luftwaffe wherever it existed."[8] The new P-51s, equipped with 150-gallon drop tanks, were capable of flying to Berlin in eastern Germany and back and at speeds up to 440 miles an hour. The Mustangs would have three times as many kills per sortie as the P-47s and twice as many as the P-38 Lightnings had.

The aerial battle that would become known as Big Week (also known as Operation Argument) began on February 20, 1944, after forecasters informed Doolittle that February 19 to February 25 would provide a seven-day window for visual bombing of German industrial targets. Big Week's main objective was for the U.S. Eighth and Fifteenth Air Forces and RAF Bomber Command to mount at least one maximum-effort bomber strike every day for a full week and seriously damage German industry. Big Week had a secondary goal that was no less important in the long run: to destroy the German Luftwaffe and ensure Allied air superiority for the eventual ground invasion of the European continent. To do so, the American bombers were to become the juicy worm on the baited hook, luring the Luftwaffe fighters into the air, where the long-range Mustangs would destroy them.

February 20 dawned bleak and cold over East Anglia. It was a Sunday morning, and those looking out of their windows saw low clouds and light snow. A thousand bombers thundered into the brisk morning air to strike twelve targets inside Germany, though the actual number hitting their targets was 823. In addition, a record 835 American fighters, equipped for the first time with 150-gallon drop tanks, participated in the attacks and shot down 59 German fighters and 2 Ju-88 bombers in a five-hour period while losing only 4 of their number.

The next day, the 95th BG's target was Diepholz Airdrome and the city of Brunswick, Germany. Of the thirty aircraft that took off, two crews were lost—those of Lt. M. R. Marks and Lt. J. P. McGuigan. Most of the men on board both planes were killed, and the rest became POWs. The 95th ended up dropping its bombs on Hannover, Germany. Overall, the Eighth lost 13 Forts and 3 B-24s, with a loss of 163 men, and another 7 planes were written off as scrap.

On February 22, aircraft from the Eighth and Fifteenth Air Forces launched attacks on Germany from two directions simultaneously; however, the majority of the former's sorties—544 of 799 Forts and Liberators—were either recalled or aborted owing to bad weather. "It was a day on which any self-respecting bird would not have flown," remembers Ed Charles.[9] Glenn Infield, in his book *Big Week*, calls February 22 Fiasco Day:

> An instrument takeoff required skill, experience and practice. Not all of the B-17 pilots attached to the Eighth Air Force were skilled instrument pilots. In early 1944, the need for bomber pilots was great, and many of the pilots passed the flight examination because of this need and not because of their proficiency. Consequently, when the B-17s of the Third Wing took off on the morning of February 22, 1944, and disappeared at one-minute intervals into the low-hanging clouds, a disastrous fiasco was in the making.[10]

Bombardier Rockett, hunkered down in the Plexiglas nose of his Fortress shortly after takeoff, "saw that dreaded flash in the distance indicating two planes had collided. As time went on, chaos soon developed. Pilots were changing their rate of climb and their pre-set directions. Icing was encountered. Startled pilots—and the element of fear—soon took over in many cockpits as planes altered their courses and descended through haze."

"LeMay was alerted to the problem, and he realized a major tragedy was in the making. Many of the monitored voices indicated the confusion and fright of the pilots. After several additional reports of mid-air collisions, LeMay knew he had no choice but to abandon the mission," writes Infield.[11] And despite all the stress, the day added nothing to his mission count, observed Rockett. Nor did it for anyone else.

The Second Wing forged on and dropped their bombs on Dutch towns by mistake. Overall on Fiasco Day, 38 B-17s, 3 B-24s, and 397 crewmen were lost. On a brighter note, U.S. fighters knocked down 57 German fighters, a Ju-88, and an Italian-made flying boat.[12]

On February 24, the 95th BG hit Rostock in a mission that lasted eleven grueling hours. One aircraft, piloted by Lt. E. J. Costales, was lost. Several of its crew were killed, while the rest became POWs. Overall losses for the day were 16 B-17s and 33 B-24s with 484 crewmen missing and 5 crewmen killed, plus 2 B-17s interned in Sweden.[13]

"Regensburg, February 25," Rockett wrote. "My last mission during Big Week. This trip took only nine hours. We enjoyed the scenic, snow-covered mountains seen below. It was not until after the target that we met up with an escort of P-51s."

Thirty-six 95th Forts took off and all returned. Big Week was thus concluded with 25 B-17s and 6 B-24s lost, 305 crewmen killed or missing, 3 B-17s written off, and 1 B-17 interned in neutral Switzerland. U.S. fighter pilots downed 25 German fighters and 2 Ju-88s. Bomber crews claim 30 downed fighters.[14]

In the final analysis, historian Roger Freeman believes,

the "Big Week" campaign undoubtedly deprived the Luftwaffe of many badly needed fighter aircraft but Allied estimations of the extent of this curtailment in German fighter production were over-optimistic. By February the German dispersal programme, initiated after the great raids of July and August 1943, was having a cushioning effect. Moreover, the small size of HE [high explosive] bombs carried by American bombers were not powerful enough to destroy vital machine tools. The Germans were often able to retrieve this equipment from the tangled ruins of their factories and put it back into production.

Nevertheless, German fighter production took a plunge after "Big Week" and the following month's total was less than half that planned. With the participation of two new Bomb Groups in the final mission of "Big Week," the Eighth Air Force reached another milestone; it had outgrown RAF Bomber Command in the matter of aircraft and crews available for operations. Thirty operational Heavy Bombardment Groups also made the Eighth the giant of the U.S. Army Air Force.[15]

Doolittle asked himself if Big Week had been worth the effort. As he recorded in his memoir,

> Initially, I thought it was. Historians tell us that we broke the back of the Luftwaffe and it never again equaled its prior performance. Even so, our later experience showed us that although we slowed them down, the Germans never did run out of airplanes and were still able to turn them out in underground factories until the end of the war. Some factories were again in full production by the end of June. The Germans reportedly produced an estimated 25,000 fighters during 1944, the highest number of any year of the war.
>
> What hurt the Germans most was the deterioration in the experience level of their pilots. The Germans lost an estimated 434 pilots during "Big Week" out of a total strength of about 2,200. According to General Adolf Galland, head of their fighter force, they lost about 1,000 pilots between January and April 1944.[16]

The total bomb tonnage dropped during Big Week equaled that dropped by the Eighth Air Force during its entire first *year* in operations. The cost, though, was high: the Eighth Air Force lost 137 bombers; the Fifteenth Air Force, 89.[17]

Big Week failed to curtail German fighter production as much as the Allies had hoped, although Albert Speer claimed the bombing had decreased production to a third of what it had been, at least for the months to come.[18] Postwar analysis, reports Speer in his memoirs, "showed that the almost ten thousand tons of bombs dropped on industrial targets during Big Week damaged or destroyed 75 percent of buildings that accounted for 90 percent of all aircraft production. Total impact of these February attacks on the German Air Force was catastrophic when actual air battle losses of more than six hundred fighters are considered along with plant production."[19]

Historian Wilbur Morrison claims Big Week did break the back of the Luftwaffe. He considers Spaatz's decision to launch Big Week one of the great decisions of the war. Moreover, Morrison feels that if Spaatz had not pursued the operation, Eisenhower probably would not have had the choice to invade the continent in June.[20]

22   "Big B"

The fortunes of the 95th Bomb Group and the German capital city of Berlin became irrevocably entwined on March 4, 1944, and the mystique surrounding the Berlin mission has grown with each passing year. On that day a minuscule force of twelve B-17s from the 95th Bomb Group, along with a 482nd Pathfinder aircraft and a few planes from the 100th Bomb Group, ignored a recall order and forged on to the German capital. In doing so, they became the first American daylight bombers over the city. The mission gave the 95th its identity and its rallying cry, "First B-17s over Berlin!" The American press covered it with much fanfare at the time, including an article and a two-page photograph in the centerfold of *Life* magazine.[1]

The first daylight raid on Berlin delivered a huge blow to German morale. On August 9, 1939, Hermann Göring had boasted: "The Ruhr will not be subjected to a single bomb. If an enemy bomber reaches the Ruhr, my name is not Hermann Göring: you can call me Meier!" Göring would live to regret his statement. He never fully recovered from the reversal to his prestige after American planes droned over Hitler's showcase city and littered it with bombs.

In 1944, Berlin was one of Europe's most beautiful cities. Its settlement dated back to the eighth century, when a fortress was built there for strategic reasons. In 1160, the Saxon Albert the Bear drove the Slavs from the region and gave the city its crest, a rampant bear. The city became a center of learning and culture in the early 1800s, and by the time Adolf Hitler came to power in January 1933, the world's sixth-largest city was arguably one of the great cultural centers of all Europe.

Until March 4, 1944, Berlin had not been bombed in daylight. It was a long way from the bomber bases in England, roughly six hundred miles, and a formidable array of flak guns and flak towers, as well as fighter aircraft, protected the city. The British had begun night bombings of Berlin on November 18–19, 1943, when 440 Avro Lancasters, accompanied by Mosquito fighters, bombed ineffectively through cloud cover. The first costly raid occurred on the night of November 22–23, when the RAF extensively damaged the city, killing 2,000 Berliners and rendering 120,000 homeless. In all, RAF night bombers visited Berlin sixteen times, losing 500 aircraft. Of their crews, 2,690 British airmen were killed over Berlin, and a thousand more became POWs. Losses were so severe that if they continued, the RAF bomber force would be wiped out before Berlin could be brought to its knees.[2]

Eighth Air Force staff began planning a daylight mission to Berlin in early 1944. As mentioned, part of the Allies' air strategy by this point in the war was to lure German fighters into the air to do battle and then to destroy them with the new long-range P-51 Mustangs. Planners anticipated the German High Command would do all it could to prevent aerial attacks on their capital. Roger Freeman writes: "Berlin offered important strategic targets but it was also very much one of prestige; to the man on the street in Britain or America it was the ultimate in German targets; bombing Hitler's capital was akin to piercing the heart of the Nazi machine."[3]

The 95th Bomb Group had been included in plans for a scrubbed bombing mission to Berlin in November 1943. A new mission on March 3 was launched, but the planes had to be recalled because of high and heavy clouds. The mission was pushed back to the following day, March 4, 1944. Al Brown's crew in *I'll Be Around* would lead the mission for the 95th, with Bill Owen's 482nd Pathfinder right behind in case the target was obscured.

The mission's field order from Eighth Air Force Headquarters arrived at Horham late on March 3 and predicted cloud cover in the Berlin area from 6 to 8/10 (60–80 percent) from twelve thousand to eighteen thousand feet. Ground crewmen bundled against the predawn chill preflighted the 95th's aircraft. Men rousted flight crews out of their beds at 3 a.m. for a

With his Brownie camera, Lt. John Miller took this photo of a B-17—cut in half and going down with ten men onboard—from his cockpit on a 95th mission. (John Miller, 95th)

A 95th aircraft flies through a thick flak barrage. (95th)

German bombs fell around the base frequently. This bomb killed some cattle in the 334th Squadron area. (95th)

In the Green Farm crash, all ten crewmen of the Rongstad crew were killed and several buildings on the ground destroyed after the B-17 stalled on takeoff and crashed near the base. (95th BG Heritage Association)

Bombs away! (95th)

Jiggs Donohue and other men enjoy their new donkey, purchased in North Africa. The donkey succumbed to the damp English climate and was dropped in full uniform over Germany. (Ed Charles, 95th)

[Left] Bill Lindley, pilot of *Zoot Suiters*. (95th)

[Bottom] On the way to Trondheim, Norway—a grueling twelve-hour flight into the Arctic—to bomb U-boat submarine pens in late 1943. (95th)

[Top] On August 17, 1943, the 95th Bomb Group received its first Distinguished Unit Citation for the bombing mission on Regensburg, Germany. The group flew on to North Africa. Bob Cozens flew the 95th's lead aircraft, *Patsy Ann III*. (95th)

[Left] Irving Rothman became a prisoner of war in Germany and survived many hardships before he was liberated. (Rob Morris)

William Waltman crew, with bombardier James Fournier (*second from left, kneeling*), interned in Sweden after crash-landing in *Smilin' Sandy Sanchez* on May 19, 1944. (James Fournier)

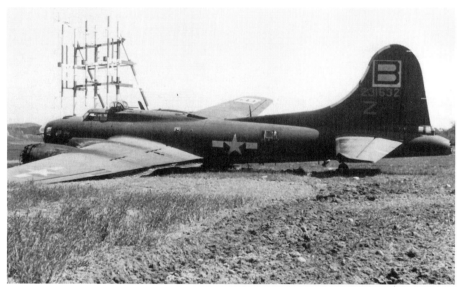

On April 24, 1944, B-17G 231632 of the 335th Bomb Squadron headed for the 95th BG's target of Friedrichshafen, Germany. Max Wilson's B-17 lost the number 4 engine with overheated cylinder heads on the way to target (feathered), the number 2 engine to FW-190 cannon fire, and the number 1 engine after flak damage caused an oil leak. Per Missing Air Crew Report 4264, the crew crash-landed at Dübendorf, Switzerland, hitting an airfield radar tower, and three were interned until the end of the war, the other seven having escaped after capture. (Swiss Air Museum/Fredy Peter)

Hit by flak and German fighters over Bremen on December 16, 1943, *Lonesome Polecat* and crew made it to Texel Island, the Netherlands. Pilots Fred Delbern (*top row, third from left*) and Don Neff (*top row, second from left*) and Eugene Darter (*bottom row, center*) became MIAs, leading to more than sixty years of heartbreak for their families. (95th)

Fighter pilot Chuck Yeager (*top right*) and Jennings Beck (*bottom, center*) were part of an Allied group that evaded and escaped over the Pyrenees Mountains. (95th)

Statue of an American airman at the Cambridge American Cemetery and Memorial, Madingley, England, honoring all those who collectively flew hundreds of dangerous missions over Nazi-occupied Europe from 1942 to 1945 and those nearly thirty thousand men who died. (Rob Morris)

IN PROUD AND GRATEFUL MEMORY OF THOSE MEN OF THE UNITED STATES ARMY AIR FORCE WHO FROM THESE FRIENDLY ISLES FLEW THEIR FINAL FLIGHT AND MET THEIR GOD. THEY KNEW NOT THE HOUR THE DAY NOR THE MANNER OF THEIR PASSING. WHEN FAR FROM HOME THEY WERE CALLED TO JOIN THAT HEROIC BAND OF AIRMEN WHO HAD GONE BEFORE. MAY THEY REST IN PEACE.

William Owen's crew of the first plane over Berlin on March 4, 1944. Owen's Pathfinder aircraft flew with the 95th on the historic raid. (95th)

After leading the first U.S. bomber attack on Berlin, March 4, 1944, Lt. Col. Harry "Grif" Mumford, mission commander, walks arm in arm with the crew of B-17 42-31320 *I'll Be Around* (*left to right*): Staff Sgt. Elmer Nutter (ball turret), Technical Sgt. Allan Smith (tail turret), Staff Sgt. Robert Raney (waist gunner), Staff Sgt. Dalton Addison (tail gunner), Staff Sgt. James Craddock (waist gunner), Technical Sgt. Frank Attebury (radio operator), First Lt. Forrest Flagler (bombardier), First Lt. Malcolm Durr (navigator), First Lt. Alvin Brown (pilot), and Lieutenant Colonel Mumford (mission commander). The 95th was awarded a third Presidential Unit Citation for this achievement, the only bomb group in the Eighth Air Force to be so honored. (95th)

All the returning men who participated in the March 4 Berlin mission line up for a group photo. *Life* magazine had a similar centerfold photo dated March 10, 1944, memorializing the 95th BG's leading the first daylight bombing of Berlin on March 4, 1944, "a feat for which it has already won world renown." (95th)

Lead pilot Lt. Col. Harry "Grif" Mumford (*left*), leader of the 95th BG's first daylight raid over Berlin, meets with Lt. Gen. Jimmy Doolittle (*right*), leader of the first daylight raid over Tokyo. (U.S. Army)

On the Russian shuttle mission to Poltova, August 8, 1944, a 95th BG crew dickers with the Russians for three bottles of vodka. (Ed Charles, 95th)

At Poltova, a Russian general arrives for a visit with the 95th BG brass. (Ed Charles, 95th)

"Smilin' Sandy" Sanchez, on top of the only B-17 named after an enlisted man. Sanchez went on to fly more combat over Italy, where he was finally shot down and MIA after forty-four missions. The tail section of his plane, found in a barn, is now displayed in the U.S. Air Force Museum. (95th)

The 95th BG flying food drops over Utrecht, the Netherlands, to supply the starving Dutch on May 5, 1945. The Nazis destroyed dikes and flooded the country as they retreated in defeat. (J. D. Bentz, 95th)

Although the 95th BG completed its 200th dangerous mission, leaving the enemies' war-making effort badly damaged, many of the finest young men of a generation were gone forever. (95th)

Glenn Miller and his famous Army Air Force Band play at Horham on September 10, 1944, as part of the 200th mission celebration. It was one of Miller's last concerts because he went missing in December 1944 on a flight over the English Channel to Paris. His name is on the Wall of the Missing at the Cambridge American Cemetery and Memorial in Madingley, England. (95th)

After fifty-four combat missions over Nazi Europe and six Manna/Chowhound food supply missions, the 95th BG's B-17 44-8640 tragically became the last aircraft and crew lost during hostilities over Europe on May 7, 1945. The B-17, filled with part of Lt. Lionel Sceurman's crew and observers, made its food drop over Utrecht and headed back to base. A Nazi coastal battery attacked the plane, which flew toward England and crashed into the North Sea a few miles from Bemacre Ness, Suffolk. Only two men survived. (95th)

Gale House's invitation to Buckingham Palace. (Photo courtesy of Gale House, 2008)

[Top] Dave McKnight flew many, many 95th BG missions throughout the war. (95th)

[Left] The 95th Bomb Group's memorial near the village green in Horham, Suffolk, with the Church of St. Mary in the background. (Richard Flagg)

[Bottom] Bradley Petrella Sr. stands behind the newly refurbished and restored bar at the Red Feather Club at Horham. In addition to his other duties as a member of the 95th during the war, Petrella was a bartender at the original Red Feather and the bar has been renamed in his honor. (Norman Feltwell)

[Top] The Red Feather Club,
Horham, before its restoration.
(95th BG Heritage Assocation)

[Right] One of Nathan Bindler's
murals in the Red Feather Club,
Horham. (Rob Morris)

Aerial view of the Red Feather Club, October 2009. (Richard Flagg)

UK's 95th BG Heritage Association officers, James Mutton (*right*) and Ian Hawkins (*left, seated*), holding a plaque from the US 95th BG Memorials Foundation citing the rebuilt Red Feather Club at Horham, Suffolk County, England, as the public museum for the 95th BG in the UK. (Norman Feltwell)

Kenneth Hutcherson returns to Horham several decades after the war. Many of the 95th's members have made similar pilgrimages. (95th)

The Rongstad crew, which was killed on takeoff from Horham in the Green Farm crash. (95th)

quick breakfast and preflight briefing. Five hundred planes from the First and Third Combat Wings would fly against Berlin and its formidable fighter defenses and twenty-five hundred flak guns. According to Sgt. James Johnson of S-2, "When the curtain was pulled aside revealing the route and the target . . . there was considerably more reaction and exclamations, whistles, groans, etc. from the crews than usual. Some of the boys were convinced that this was their last briefing and that they wouldn't be coming back. They left their personal belongings in safe hands."[4]

Nineteen Forts from the 95th were scheduled to take off from Horham and would be joined by two Pathfinders from the 482nd. Snow flurries caused a fifteen-minute delay. Takeoff began at 8:30 a.m., and the last plane was airborne by 8:53 a.m. Two planes failed to take off. At roughly the same time, nearly five hundred other aircraft from the First and Third Combat Wings took off into the snow and overcast. As the Forts tried to assemble in the dense clouds, it became apparent that conditions were too severe to continue. The First Wing called off the mission while still assembling over England, sending all its Forts back to base to wait for better weather.

The Third Wing continued to attempt assembly. The official mission report states that at 10:28 a.m. two elements of the 95th and the *A* element of the 100th managed to rendezvous near Clacton. At 10:52 a.m. the formation crossed the enemy coast at twenty-two thousand feet, its bombing altitude; however, encountering a hazy cirrus layer, it began a gentle climb to keep the low groups out of the clouds. Condensation trails from the lead group became so thick that the group continued climbing to twenty-five thousand feet.

At 11:35 a.m. and at twenty-five thousand feet, the mission report states that 95th crews noticed "all Combat Wings ahead turned to the left and took up a course for home. Contact was made with other two Group leaders in the 13th 'A' Combat Wing to see if the mission had been recalled, and as no one had received such a message the mission was continued as ordered."[5]

Recalled Pathfinder crewmen Marshall Thixton and John O'Neil,

As we approached the border of Germany, Sgt. Aken (our radio operator) said on [the] intercom that he received the radio message:

"Mission recalled." We watched as the groups ahead of us turned around to look for targets of opportunity to bomb and then head for home. Soon there were no groups ahead of us and [Harlan] Sours in the tail reported no groups behind us. We were sure that our leader would choose a target of opportunity, but it very soon became evident that we were going all the way to Berlin, come what may. Mac, our copilot, tried to reach the group leader [Mumford] on radio, "Red Leader One, Red Leader One, this is Red Leader Two, do you read me, over?" "This is Red Leader One, we are flying the course as briefed," replied Mumford. "Close up the formation, we can expect enemy fighters at any time."

Thixton had a disconcerting thought. By the time the tiny formation reached Berlin, only twenty-nine B-17s of the original five hundred bombers would face Berlin's fighters and twenty-five hundred flak guns![6]

The key moment on the Berlin mission was 11:35 a.m. Why did Colonel Mumford decide to continue on to Berlin even after seeing the rest of the Third Division peel off and head for home?

"All [of the division] turned back but one combat box," says navigator Ed Charles. "After a nervous silence the officer commanding the combat box, Lieutenant Colonel Harry C. Mumford, replied, 'We will continue to the assigned target.' Charles was stunned. 'It was suicide,' he remembers thinking. 'I swore softly. Had the colonel gone mad?'"

Charles seems to believe that there was a valid recall given that day. "Eighth Air Force Headquarters sent out over VHF [very high frequency] a recall signal. All the other formations immediately began 180 degree turns to return to base and attack targets of opportunity on the way home. It quickly became apparent however that Colonel Mumford, leading the 95th Group, wasn't turning around with the other groups. Our pilot Bob Kroeger and co-pilot Hearty Fitchko checked with our radio operator, George Green, and all were positive there had been a recall. Bob said, 'What's going on anyway? What's the guy doing?' Another pilot in the group broke the absolute silence radio code by calling on the command frequency, 'Colonel Mumford, there's been a recall.'"

Other pilots who flew the mission believed the recall to be genuine. Says William Owens: "Five hundred aircraft all got the same recall. They all thought it was a valid recall." Ed Charles remembers: "I'm sure there was as much aircraft intercom chatter in the other planes as there was in ours, but every plane in our formation continued on to the assigned primary target."[7]

Lt. Vincent Fox, navigator on *Spirit of New Mexico*, writes: "We soon had the chilling realization that we were alone in our undertaking. Our ball-turret gunner could identify squadrons with 95th 'Square B' tail markings and elements with the 'Square D' of the 100th Bomb Group still maintaining the integrity of the formation. It seemed incredible that our token force was still bearing east toward the German capital."[8]

In the Pathfinder aircraft, Thixton noticed:

Up ahead, we could see the reason why the mission was recalled. We were coming into solid cloud cover. We began a slow climb to get above the clouds—28,000 feet, then 29,000 feet—maximum altitude for formation flying. We were skimming the top of the cloud layer with occasional peaks of clouds blocking out the lead aircraft. The cloudy conditions made flying wingtip to wingtip extremely dangerous. This of course made us more vulnerable to enemy fighters, should any be able to find us in this weather.[9]

One of the PFF ships had aborted, but the remaining PFF, flown by pilot Bill Owen, was functioning well. From time to time he aided the wing leader in avoiding flak areas. "Then," writes Pathfinder pilot Owen, "the almost impossible happened, the sea of clouds parted and appearing below was a large town. We knew we were in trouble and it was not long in coming. The Germans opened up with several batteries of flak guns and they had the range. You could feel the aircraft bounce as the shells exploded all around us. The deadly pieces of steel sounded like hail as they hit the plane."

Owen had the feeling that "the Group Leader and crew were possibly not confident in accepting our radar fixes. Al Engelhardt, our navigator, knew exactly where we were at all times because of the radar, but most regular bomber crews knew very little about radar at this time and did not believe that it enabled us to see through clouds." In fact, Owen laughingly admitted to me: "When I first heard about it, I doubted it myself!" On future missions, Owen would ease his plane into the lead and nudge the groups to the correct heading.[10]

"We caught some ground checks," continues Mumford, "even though we were nearly five miles up. My navigator [First Lt. Malcolm M. Durr]—and believe me he deserves all the credit—saw enough ground points to set us up for a visual bomb run. But the clouds closed in again and the bombing was done through the clouds. I'm sure we hit the place."[11]

"Almost as quickly as it happened before," writes Pathfinder bombardier Marshall Thixton, "the clouds once more closed up. On we flew, courageously, brave and scared as hell. We wondered if our P-51 escort knew that a small number of struggling B-17s were still heading for Berlin, and whether the '51s would be at Berlin when we got there—or if the German Air Force fighters were waiting for us at Berlin, in which case it would be another Battle of Little Big Horn."[12]

He recounts,

When we reached the supposed Initial Point of the bomb run, the lead ship made the turn to the heading of the bomb run and turned the lead over to us to do a radar bomb run. The time was approximately 12:45 P.M., which was the flight plan time. However, we were by our radar about 47 miles from the actual I.P., and according to Al's map and Bill's notes, 20 miles north of course at this time.

This again confirmed our thinking that the lead crew had been navigating without full use of our radar fixes. We turned our small group of planes back on course to much loud dissent from many in the formation. Bill turned down the volume on the radio and gave full attention to getting the mission back on track. We flew approximately another 45 minutes to the true I.P. and turned on the bomb run. Bill put our B-17 on autopilot, and he, Al and Marshall coordinated for either a visual or radar bomb run.[13]

Thixton continues,

At last, we reached the city of Berlin and began our bomb run. As we approached the target area, we saw a small cluster of our P-51s circling overhead, but then noticed Me 109s as well, and at least twenty zoomed through the bomber formation, guns blazing. The P-51s dived in after them, barreling through the formation. Fortunately for us, two Eighth Air Force fighter groups, the 4th and the 357th, ignored the mission recall and were at Berlin when we arrived. This may well have been because of the P-51's limited VHF radios. By an incredible stroke of good fortune, P-51 Mustang fighters put in a miraculous appearance from nowhere and broke up the attack. How our little friends ever managed to find us through the maze of clouds that day is one of the incredible mysteries of air combat.[14]

Chuck Yeager, who had been shot down and successfully evaded the Germans only weeks earlier, was one of the young P-51 pilots with the 357th. He shot down his first German fighter over Berlin that day.

The first German attack through the formation reaped results. One Fort exploded and two more began to smoke and drop from the formation. Remembers Thixton:

As the bomb bay doors swung open, the fighters were on us once more. One fighter passed so close to us that that we could clearly see the pilot, and we were spared only because he was out of cannon shells and sprayed us with .30-caliber machine gun bullets. As the enemy pilot broke away from the formation, a hail of lead followed him from the ball-turret gunner, and he was reported going straight down. During this time the enemy opened up with his flak guns and anti-aircraft shells were exploding within our formation and their own fighters. Everyone was so busy with the fighters and the bomb run that the flak was almost unnoticed.

"In a cooperative effort, Al Engelhardt using radar lined up on the target, and signaled Marshall to drop," writes John O'Neil. "He was glad to report 'Bombs Away!'" The first American bombs were on their way to Berlin from the tiny force, and it looked as if even fewer planes would make the trip home. Meanwhile, because Lieutenant Colonel Mumford's bomb bay doors were frozen shut, the first bombs to drop on Berlin were those from Owen's 482nd Pathfinder.

According to the Pathfinder pilot, "The Berlin mission could have gone awry. If it wasn't for the radar and the lucky arrival of the P-51 fighters, there would be no story about the 95th being the first over Berlin. The Berlin mission would have come to nothing."

On their return flight, once the P-51s had scattered the German fighters, the airmen again noticed just how thick the flak was. "We turned the lead back to the 95th crew," writes Thixton. "But we were a little more insistent on using our radar navigational powers when needed. It was going to be very close making it home with not a drop of fuel to spare."[15]

Near Brunswick flak had hit the Fort piloted by R. P. Roehm, but the crew continued to the target. Shortly after the men released their bombs, Roehm's plane went down and the crew became POWs. Pilot M. J. Worthy's Fort left the formation shortly thereafter; all aboard became POWs. Pilot M. B. Dunham's plane dropped from the formation with a feathered prop, unable to keep up. The two waist gunners on this aircraft were killed; the rest of the crew became POWs. The last plane from the 95th to go down left the formation at 12:35 p.m. Most of pilot M. U. Brownlow's crew became POWs, but the radio operator and waist gunners were killed.

"We maintained an altitude of 11,000 to 14,000 feet the entire trip home," writes Thixton. "Presumably because of the extreme cold and high clouds, we did not see one enemy fighter on the trip back to England. We flew over Horham with the 95th, then peeled off and continued to Alconbury in the dark and cold. We were tired and . . . and as we crawled out of the plane and touched the ground, our legs were wobbly, but we were home and okay."[16]

Because the Pathfinder landed at its base at Alconbury instead of at Horham, its crew missed the rejoicing surrounding the completion of the U.S. Army Air Force's first daylight bombing raid to Berlin. "And I, for one, gladly missed it," says the reserved Owen. To this day he is unsure what the fuss is about. "We could have all been shot down if not for the fact that the P-51s had missed their recall. I know for a fact that the Eighth Air Force did not want to lose twenty-nine planes."

When the depleted little 95th formation returned to Horham, Ed Charles remembers: "We were taken to the debriefing room and found the area loaded with Eighth Air Force top brass, various other VIPs, reporters from leading newspapers and magazines, newsreel cameramen from Movie-Tone News, and overall confusion.

"The Group 'scuttle-butt' was that the top 'brass' had come to Horham to discipline Lieutenant Colonel Mumford for the direct disobedience of an order in combat. Whether this was actually true or not I have never discovered, but when they had confirmation that we'd actually become the first American Bomb Group to hit Berlin, the propaganda boost was immense and it was utilized to the fullest. General LeMay awarded the Silver Star to Lt. Col. Mumford in the debriefing room and the Distinguished Flying Cross to Al Brown."

Many crewmen who flew the March 4 Berlin mission do not remember it as much for being heroic as for being a snafu that turned from an ugly duckling to a beautiful swan only after its propaganda value was recognized. Bombardier Maurice Rockett flew the mission but was in the other element of the 95th that honored the recall. He said, "My crew could not believe, after aborting, that the rest of the gang went ahead to the assigned target. As I understand, formation Commanders were not to proceed unless Wing size in strength. I have said this before, and I will say it again, Mumford got the acclaim not because of what he did, but because we were doing so badly in the air war and needed something positive to proclaim as propaganda even though over dead bodies. By the way, if fighter support did not arrive, by *mistake*, the small party of planes could have easily been wiped out."

Navigator William Gifford writes: "The 95th had led the first American raid on Berlin. As was often the case in things like this, it was a fouled-up operation. Whether it was intentional or otherwise, no one will say. About halfway into the mission, orders were radioed aborting the mission, due to bad weather over the target. Our Group, accompanied by the 100th, 'failed' to receive these orders. Enemy fighter opposition was fierce, and the 95th suffered heavy losses. However, the raid was quite successful. Think what it did to German morale. In addition to a good chewing-out, it earned the Command Pilot a Silver Star, and the Group, a Presidential Citation. What fools some mortals be."[17]

"Everyone got the message except the Lead plane," argued Rockett. "Don't you think it strange, that with all the planes in the air that day, the

Lead's radio man was the only one to figure out, presumably, what was going on?"

What *was* going on? I posed the question directly to Colonel Mumford when we talked by phone on several occasions, and his story never wavered. Mumford claims that the Germans sent the radio message calling for the abort to foul up the mission. Mumford's assertion is shared by Mumford's radio operator, T/Sgt. Frank Attebury and Mumford's close friend, pilot Harry Conley. As Attebury writes:

> The recall message came in bomber code that consisted of groups of four letters without any particular sequence, but corresponded to a particular word. An example might be, PQAM, which might have been the code word for "obscured." The collective code word for the day was RZNC—the dash above the letter C meant that in our particular use of the International Morse Code the letter C would have an extra dash in it and to come across as "dash, dot, dash, dot, dash." The collective call sign was the call sign that our base station would use to call everyone on the mission. It was the greeting or salutation of the message.
>
> The actual decoding message came across as follows: ABANDON OPS, RETURN TO BASE, 1200 HOURS, RZNC (with overslash). The collective call was used as a signature to the message, which was an error, and there was no greeting call-sign used at all. I reported the message as received to the cockpit and later told the pilot that the message as sent did not constitute a recall per standard operating procedure.
>
> Upon returning to Horham, it was confirmed to me by Colonel Chester Gilger, 95th Group Commander at that time, that there had not been a recall sent from England. Where then, did the message come from? I am sure it came from an enemy radio transmitter in an almost successful attempt to turn back an historic event.[18]

Harry Conley concurs and writes:

> Shortly after the Wing crossed over into German territory, a Morse code message was received by all of our aircraft. It was encrypted properly for the day, and it appeared to have originated at Eighth

Air Force Headquarters. Because of weather conditions, it said, the original mission was recalled and the planes were given the options of hitting their secondary targets or returning to base. Most of the pilots heeded this recall. The radioman in the Lead aircraft noted some unusual things about the message and pointed them out to "Grif" Mumford and pilot Al Brown. First, the signal containing this message was strong, much stronger than normal for a signal coming from England. Second, the right code words were used, but in the wrong places. Could it be that the Germans were sending this message to head us off our target? Anyway, at this point, Grif decided that we were already close enough to Berlin to make it, and the weather wasn't bad enough to abort the mission. They tersely announced their decision by radio to the rest of the mission force, and kept on flying toward Berlin.

After everyone returned to England, no one at Eighth Air Force knew anything about any recall message. It had probably been a German trick intended to divert us.[19]

Conley, however, presents no evidence to back up the claim that a recall order had not been given. Nor has this author found any corroborating evidence in either the mission report, interviews, or other written evidence.

"One explanation given for the Lead crew ignoring the recall was that their radio operator had interpreted the recall as a fake radio message put out by the Germans," writes Marshall Thixton. "The Group Leader and the pilot of the Lead ship then made the decision to continue on to Berlin. However, the recall was accepted and interpreted as authentic by all of the other Bomb Groups on the mission, as well as our crew."[20]

Pathfinder pilot Bill Owen maintained that the "Eighth Air Force Headquarters gave the recall for a number of reasons. First, our leaders wanted the first Berlin mission to be a very successful, maximum-effort type of mission and the changing, deteriorating weather put this in jeopardy. The change in winds meant delays into the target, which could translate into fuel problems and a late, possible near-dark return by the bomber crews to England. There was also a possibility of poor weather in England preventing the takeoff of some supporting Eighth fighter groups."

Maurice Rockett stated bluntly: "I am convinced that if the U.S. was not so desperate for good news, what's-his-name would have been court-martialed." Instead, the Eighth Air Force had scored a public relations coup. Mumford subsequently posed in a publicity photo with Jimmy Doolittle, as newspapers and newsreels equated his effort with that of the Tokyo raider several years earlier—Doolittle being the first to bomb Tokyo and Mumford being the first to bomb Berlin.

General Doolittle admits in his memoir that he desperately wanted to go on the March 4 Berlin mission:

> I wanted to be in on this first effort and have the honor of being the first air commander to lead a raid over all three Axis capitals. I planned to fly a P-51 with one wingman ahead of the bomber stream over the capital city. To prepare for this, I sharpened up my fighter skills in the P-51 and then approached "Tooey" Spaatz to get his permission. I thought I might be able to persuade him to let me go, just as I had talked Hap Arnold into letting me lead the Tokyo Raid. Tooey finally gave in and reluctantly said I could go. However, just a day or so before our departure, Tooey changed his mind and said he couldn't afford to risk the capture of a senior officer who had knowledge of the invasion plans. So, contrary to what some have claimed for me, I did not participate in any bombing raids of Berlin. I admit, however, that I really wanted that honor.[21]

Ed Charles remembers, "The next morning photographers from *Life* magazine assembled all the surviving crews that had returned from the mission and took pictures of us all standing in front of and on top of one of our B-17s, *Berlin First*, Lieutenant Barksdale's ship, which had flown to Berlin and back."[22] The plane had been hastily renamed after the mission.

The March 27 issue of *Life* printed a centerfold photo that was more than two feet across. According to the copy:

> In this colossal portrait one Flying Fortress and some 130 young men commemorate an historic moment in the life of the U.S. Eighth Air Force. The men are the crews of a single formation of heavy bombers which on March 4 made the first American attack on Berlin. The

airplane is named *Berlin First*, not only because it took part in the raid, but also because all but one of its crew flew to Berlin on their first flight over the Continent.

In addition to being the record of a milestone, this picture partly overcomes a curious anonymity which has obscured fliers of the Eighth. For men who are making one of the greatest American offensive efforts of the war, little has been told about them. Only their heroes are known to the U.S. The *Berlin First* portrait is also a brief reminder of the human scale of the war in the air. The tight good-sized group of men shown above is just about enough to fly 13 heavy bombers.[23]

Two days later, the heavies returned to Berlin yet again, this time with a full complement of bombers in a maximum effort. The Eighth Air Force dispatched 504 B-17s and 226 B-24s against industrial and other targets in and around Berlin, and 474 B-17s and 198 B-24s attacked targets of opportunity through heavy cloud cover. The German Luftwaffe responded in force, downing 53 B-17s and 16 B-24s. Crew losses ran more than 700 men. The 100th Bomb Group lost fifteen planes, the worst loss to date for any bomb group. However, the P-51 Mustang fighters defended the bomber stream all the way to the target. A staggering 801 fighters accompanied the bombers: 86 P-38s, 615 P-47s, and 100 P-51s.[24]

On March 6, the 95th lost eight planes. Seven men were killed in action, including the four officers and top turret gunner on pilot A. J. Mailman's crew. Seventy-five 95th crewmen became prisoners of war that day.

While the March 4 raid put the 95th into the history books, the March 6 raid put many of the group into prison camps. However, from then on, the 95th became known as "First B-17s over Berlin," a name the group members cherish to this day. This author has found no official document—American or German—mentioning a phony recall order, so the mystery for now remains. As for Berlin, it was only seeing the beginning of the American bombing missions. Remembering Hermann Göring's comment that the German people could call him Meier if Allied planes ever hit Berlin, its citizens began bitterly calling Berlin's air raid sirens Meier's trumpets or Meier's hunting horns.

Jimmy Doolittle writes: "We learned after the war that Hermann Goering said he knew the air war was lost when he saw the bombers over the capital with their P-51 escorts."[25]

An important psychological milestone had been reached in the air war. For the Allies and the Germans, the Berlin raids showed that all of Germany was within reach of daylight bombers. Furthermore, no amount of Luftwaffe fighters or flak guns would thwart the Allied bombers.

23   D-Day

Everyone knew that an invasion of the continent was imminent. Bomber pilot Bert Stiles wrote in his journal: "We waited so long it turned into a joke. Each time they woke us up in the night somebody would say, 'It's D-Day.' But it never was. And then on the sixth of June, it was."[1]

When people think of D-Day, they envision thousands of ships steaming across the English Channel and recall the shaky camera images taken on the landing beaches as Allied infantry waded ashore under heavy fire. However, the land invasion of Fortress Europe would never have been possible if not for the efforts of the Allied air forces. For a ground invasion to succeed, Allied planes had to control the skies over the landing beaches and the coastal areas of France. As a result of heavy German fighter attrition in the previous months, the skies over the landing beaches were eerily empty of German defenders.

Doolittle's new policy of turning loose American fighter planes had excellent results. In addition to their air duels with the Luftwaffe, fighters attacked and strafed airfields, code-named Jackpots, and transportation hubs, code-named Chattanoogas. Luftwaffe fighter commander Gen. Adolf Galland said after the war that most of the airfields were so bombed he was unable to use them. Instead, Galland was forced to station his fighter planes much farther inland, making it considerably more difficult to engage the American landing forces and air forces on D-Day.[2]

Pre-invasion attacks began as early as February 1944, and through May 21, fighters destroyed 1,500 enemy aircraft and 900 locomotives, as well as railroad stations, bridges, barges, and other transportation targets. Improvements also allowed these fighters to fly farther; the 339th Fighter Group, based in Fowlmere, flew more than fourteen hundred miles on a May 29 mission to eastern Germany. On the eve of D-Day, the number of fighter aircraft available to support operations was 885 Eighth Air Force fighters, 1,000 Ninth Air Force fighters, and 1,900 RAF fighters. The Luftwaffe could send up only 1,500 fighters to counter them.[3]

Historian Roger Freeman writes that much of the Allied fighters' success in the months preceding the invasion resulted from the German air leaders' mistakes.

> The most damning was the failure to appreciate the threat of the long-range fighter escort and the lack of determined effort to counter until it was too late. Little was done about the first efforts of the American fighters in the spring and summer of 1943 thus allowing pilots to gain experience and become proficient in the unwieldy P-47s. Instead, it chose to concentrate on the bombers and finally found itself in a position where it was frequently prevented from reaching them. In addition, by D-Day, the average German fighter pilot entered combat with only a little over 27 hours of flight training, compared to 120 for their American adversaries.[4]

Another major blow to the German war effort took place on May 12, 1944. Albert Speer writes: "On that day the technological war was decided. With the attack of nine hundred and thirty-five daylight bombers of the American Eighth Air Force upon several fuel plants in central and eastern Germany, a new era in the air war began." After that date, Germany was unable to produce sufficient aviation fuel to keep the Luftwaffe in the air in strength over an extended period.[5]

Allied fighter-bombers also cut off most of Normandy and Brittany from the rest of France by the end of May, dropping seventy-one thousand tons of bombs on the French railroad system and smashing most of the railroad bridges. Heavy bombing of Pas-de-Calais convinced many German military leaders that the Allied invasion would be landing there rather than at Normandy. All bridges over the Seine River north of Paris were out of commission. A German commander on the ground described the roads leading to the Normandy beaches as *Jabo Rennstrecki* (fighter-bomber racecourses).[6]

By D-Day, fifty-one of eighty railroad centers had suffered major damage, with most completely knocked out of commission. French train crews refused to operate under such dangerous conditions, forcing the Germans to furnish their own crews. Even then, most rail traffic could run only at night.[7]

Tuesday, June 6, 1944, dawned sunny at Horham. A few hours before and only a short distance away, thousands of men loaded down with their equipment had clamored aboard the ships, planes, or gliders that would carry them across the English Channel for the long-anticipated amphibious invasion of the European continent.

By late evening on June 5, everyone at Horham knew a big mission was under way. Radio technician Ted Lucey remembers:

> The night was loud with the ceaseless roaring of thousands of planes going over. The invasion chatter was very prevalent, then confirmed when the early morning saw two missions, maximum efforts, one at 3:30 and the other 6:00. About 0800 hours, German radio announced Allied paratroop landings in occupied France. No official word from the BBC until later in the morning. When our ships returned, they were immediately serviced for a third mission, which took off about 5:30 PM and returned after dark. Returning crews reported thousands of ships of all sizes extended across the English Channel.
>
> Colonel Truesdell, our new Group CO, led the first mission of the three raids flown 6 June. The weather was beautiful here on D-Day, not a cloud in sight during the morning. Toward noon, however, it suddenly clouded over and except for brief appearances of the sun, we have had incredibly bad weather, even for England. Predominantly low ceiling and a thick blanket of dull, rain-filled clouds. Nevertheless, our B-17s fly even when they shouldn't. They must.[8]

The official Eighth Air Force Headquarters summary dated June 6 describes the day's missions:

Heavy bombers of the Eighth Air Force flew 2,362 sorties in four attacks on targets near the beach-head area. At the same time, 1,813
sorties were flown by VIII Fighter Command groups in patrols over
northern France and fighter-bomber missions against tactical targets. In the early morning a force of 1077 heavy bombers attacked
targets in the area of the landing beaches. In the early evening a
heavy force from all three bombardment divisions attacked tactical
targets in the coastal area. Bombers met no air opposition during
the day, while fighters reported no large engagements, attributing
the largest percentage of the 26 fighters lost to flak. Five B-24s were
lost and one crashed in England. One bomber crew was rescued
from the Channel.[9]

The first mission of the day for the Eighth Air Force was launched
between 1:55 a.m. and 5:29 a.m. to attack coastal targets in the area of the
invasion beaches between Le Havre and Cherbourg. Of the 822 B-17s and
543 B-24s dispatched, 659 B-17s and 418 B-24s dropped more than 3,000
tons of bombs in the beachhead area, including the town of Caen. One
B-24 was lost to flak. The second mission, involving 396 B-24s and 84 B-17s,
left England between 4:40 a.m. and 7:53 a.m. to attack targets inland of
the beachhead area. The third mission of the day, to Caen, dispatched 73
B-24s, 58 of which dropped 157 tons of 500-pound general purpose bombs
through cloud cover and with no fighter opposition at approximately 1:28
p.m. The Eighth Air Force's fourth and final D-Day mission sent 300 B-24s
and 409 B-17s, which hit twenty tactical targets on the Normandy beach-
heads. Visual bombing was possible on this mission, and 325 B-17s and
125 B-24s hit nineteen targets between 7:51 p.m. and 8:38 p.m. Again, they
encountered no fighter opposition, and results were rated good on seven
of the targets.[10]

The 95th's official mission report from June 6 also tells the tale. For instance, taking part in the fourth and final Eighth Air Force attack, thirteen
aircraft of the 95th's *A* group left Horham at 5:15 p.m. on June 6; dropped
bombs by Pathfinder at 8:19 p.m., with no fighter opposition; and saw the
last Fort touch down at Horham at 11:17 p.m. The *B* group took off at 5:30
p.m., bombed by Pathfinder at 8:27 p.m., and returned to base by 11:43 p.m.

It was a busy day of flying. Ball turret gunner Frank Coleman climbed wearily into his B-17 in the early morning of June 6. Through breaks in the clouds, he saw ships below in the Channel as far as the eye could see, churning their way toward the landing beaches at Normandy. He would fly not one but two combat missions on D-Day, landing in England only long enough to refuel and grab a quick bite to eat before taking off again.

Ed Charles was also amazed at the incredible armada of ships below him on D-Day. "You could have walked across the channel on the ship decks," he remembers. "I never saw a single German aircraft." In fact, ninety German fighters did manage to engage on D-Day, but they were almost totally ineffective.

Al Forrester writes: "On D-Day our target was a choke point in the town of Falaise, France. On our way over, we had a tremendous view of our invasion forces. I know that the men who were on the beaches will say that I know nothing about D-Day. They are right. I am thankful that my view was from five miles above. On the other hand, *every* mission we flew was a D-Day for us. There was a solid undercast at the target. When our target was in an occupied country, we did not drop our bombs unless the target was visible. We took our bombs back to Horham. Landing with a full bomb load makes everyone a little nervous."

Ted Lucey wrote in his diary on June 7: "Naturally, accounts of what's happening in France vary widely. The BBC claims Allied successes, while the German radio says otherwise. There's a girl with a sexy voice on German radio. This girl, Midge, has offered to go to bed with every Yank who walks down the streets of Berlin. She has certainly embarked on a very considerable undertaking!"[11]

The next two weeks saw bad weather and numerous tactical missions for the 95th, most days being "cloudy, gloomy, cold and with lots of rain," remembers Lucey.[12] Ed Charles recalls flying tactical missions for the next two weeks in support of the invasion forces.

The Eighth Air Force played a pivotal role in the success of the D-Day landings. Field Marshal Wilhelm Keitel contended that the Normandy landings only succeeded because of "our inability to bring up our reserves at the proper time. Nobody can ever prove to me that we could not have repelled the invasion had not the superiority of the enemy air force in bombers and fighters made it impossible to throw additional German divisions into the fight."[13]

Historian Donald Miller believes the Eighth Air Force won the Battle of D-Day in the five months leading up to June 6:

> In the five-month battle for air supremacy that made the invasion possible, the American Air Forces in Europe lost over 2,600 heavy bombers and 980 fighter planes and suffered 18,400 casualties, including 10,000 combat deaths, over half as many men as the Eighth had lost in all of 1942 and 1943. These airmen deserve an equal place in the national memory with the approximately 6,000 American soldiers killed, wounded, or missing in action in the amphibious and airborne assault on D-Day.[14]

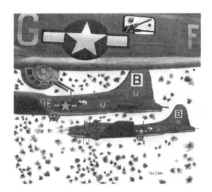

24 The Russia Shuttle Missions

One German response to the Allied bombing campaign was to relocate key industries farther from Allied bases. In late 1943 the Allied leaders met to discuss this development, deciding it would be necessary to build bases in Russia that American and British aircraft could use. Not only would these bases allow bombers to hit key industrial targets in eastern Europe, but they would also force the German Luftwaffe to spread its fighter defenses, in effect creating a two-front air war against Germany. Another benefit, according to historian and 390th Bomb Group veteran Marshall Shore, was that "if the Americans could develop full cooperation with the Russian Air Force in this matter they might also go along with our use of Russian bases in Siberia later when we completed our plans for the invasion of Japan."[1]

At a summit meeting in Tehran, Iran, in November 1943 Soviet leader Joseph Stalin gave his approval for the creation of three bases on Russian soil. It was quite a concession by the secretive Soviet leadership, allies with the United States by necessity but not particularly friendly. Stalin had concerns that the Americans would use the bases as a springboard to conduct espionage in the Soviet Union.

When Eighth Air Force Lt. Gen. Carl Spaatz arrived in England in early 1944, he started work on the Russian bases, which were completed in May 1944. The airfields were located at Poltava, Mirgorod, and Piryatin, all in the Ukraine in the southwestern Soviet Union. Six air divisions were selected to fly the Eighth Air Force's first shuttle mission to Russia on June 21, 1944. Five of them had flown the Regensburg shuttle, including the 95th,

100th, and 390th Bomb Groups. The Fifteenth Air Force had already made one Russia mission on June 2.

The plan, code-named Operation Frantic, involved 1,311 heavy bombers. Accompanied by bombers from the Fourth Combat Wing and a composite group from the Third Bomb Division, Fortresses from the Thirteenth and Forty-Fifth Wings would bomb Berlin. After the mission to Berlin, the Fourth Combat Wing and the composite group would return to England, but the Thirteenth and Forty-Fifth would fly on to Russia, escorted the whole way by seventy P-51 Mustangs of the Fourth and 352nd Fighter Group.

One ground crewman from each Mustang was assigned to a B-17 as a waist gunner. Each Fortress carried extra items, such as field rations and engineering kits. "The plane whose safe arrival was most desired was the one which carried our entire supply of toilet paper," remembers 100th Bomb Group navigator Harry Crosby.

Col. Joseph Moller, who flew with 390th Bomb Group and worked at Thirteenth Wing Headquarters at Horham, would be flying lead with the 95th Bomb Group on the shuttle mission. Moller earned his wings in World War I, and by the time World War II began, he was twice as old as the other pilots in the group. Assigned to ferry B-17s to bases overseas, he instead talked his way into a training command. Finally, he received an assignment to the 390th Bomb Group in England, where he flew forty-nine combat missions, the most by any senior officer in the Eighth Air Force.[2]

Moller remembers:

About 18 June 1944, we were alerted that we would shortly be flying a shuttle mission to Russia and returning to England via Italy after bombing a strategic target during each flight. A cadre of American Air Force personnel, commanded by General Robert J. Walsh, had been sent to Russia to resupply our aircraft with gasoline, oil, bombs and ammunition. In addition, they had communications capability with England and an Intelligence Officer. Knowing, however, that our aircraft repair and maintenance would have to be accomplished by our own task force people, we added one ground crewman per bomber, together with his tools, a few spare parts, and some P-51 parts, including spare belly fuel tanks.

The task force was led by the 45th Wing (96th, 388th, and 452nd Bomb Groups) under the command of Brigadier General Archie Olds; and the Thirteenth Wing (95th, 100th, and 390th Bomb Groups) led by Colonel Edgar Wittan, the Thirteenth Wing commander, who would be flying with the 390th Group. I was to lead the 95th Group and be the Thirteenth Wing deputy lead.[3]

Shore, who flew with the 390th Bomb Group as command navigator for the Thirteenth Combat Wing on the June 21 mission, remembers:

At 3:30 a.m. on the morning of June 21, 1944 the air was filled with high anticipation. We had been instructed to bring along our Class A uniforms. We were briefed not to get out of our airplanes in Russia until we had changed from our flying clothes to Class A uniform. We were scheduled to fly only the newer models of our B-17Gs that were bright aluminum and had not been painted a camouflage olive drab color. Who was trying to impress the Russians and for what reason?

With the usual secrecy, selected crews were given special indoctrination on Russian base facilities and language cards. Special escape packs were issued. Each of the 163 B-17s dispatched was fitted with a bomb-bay tank to increase endurance, and most carried a ground crew technician.[4]

In addition, each man was given a series of shots to immunize him against various Russian bugs.[5]

Near Warsaw, Poland, German fighters jumped the bomber stream. With the bombers' P-51 "Little Friends" flying escort, the Luftwaffe fighters inflicted little damage, and the Mustangs shot fourteen of them down.

Shore continues:

Our group landed at Mirgorod, another Russian airfield sixty miles west of Poltova. The fighters landed at Piryatin another fifty miles to the west. When we stepped down out of our B-17G, parked way to the side of the steel planked runway, we were met by a Russian soldier carrying a rifle. He was to be the guard for our individual aircraft. Not more than 300 yards away were three P-39 fighters. American Lend-Lease aircraft, these had been given to Russia earlier, and they were being serviced by young women wearing coveralls who appeared to be mechanics.

While standing around in front of our aircraft in Class A uniforms awaiting transportation to debriefing, we suddenly saw a German plane. Soon identified as a Heinkel 177 bomber, it was being used for reconnaissance and approached the field from the east. It was flying at about 12,000 feet and at maximum combat speed straight for the field. This photographic pass continued to the west in the direction of the German front lines.[6]

Shore was surprised when the three Russian women he'd observed servicing the P-39s jumped into their aircraft and took off in pursuit. "We had read in *Life* magazine about Russian combat pilots and now we were experiencing them first-hand!" However, right after sunset the pilots returned and reported that they had failed to catch the German plane.

Colonel Moller advocated an American pursuit: "We had several P-51s on the base. Ed Wittan and I agreed that we should request permission to send up two of our fighters and shoot the reconnaissance plane down, even though the German plane might have already radioed his home base where we were.

"Ed went to get the fighters ready for takeoff. I went to the Russian base commander and through an interpreter told him of our plan to send up our fighters. After a lengthy discussion with another Russian, he refused. I asked him why he'd refused; he replied that if we did shoot down the German plane, it would always be said that we'd had to defend ourselves on Russian bases. I then asked him how he proposed to defend us and our parked aircraft against a probable air attack. He had no answer except merely to shrug and turn away."

"By this time the German reconnaissance crew was reporting our arrival at the Russian bases. What a juicy set of targets they had found," writes Marshall Shore.[7]

Figuring that the group's whereabouts had been discovered, the leadership decided to move to another airfield. The 95th flew its Forts to a field at Kharkov, and the 390th flew to Zapororzhye. Colonel Wittan elected to stay at Mirgorod, and Colonel Thomas Jeffery of the 100th went to Kirovogrod.

The 95th landed in moonlight at Kharkov's grass field. Flight crews laid out blankets and sleeping bags under their planes and spent the night with their aircraft.

During the night, the Luftwaffe bombed Poltava. After illuminating the airbase with flares, the Germans dropped 110 tons of bombs on the field, destroying forty-six B-17s and damaging twenty-six more. Also destroyed was a huge fuel storage facility, which went up in a tremendous explosion. Only six planes were flyable from the entire 45th Wing. These losses, coupled with other losses over Germany the same day, resulted in the most costly twenty-four hours in the history of the Eighth Air Force—with eighty-eight bombers and twenty-two fighters destroyed and several more salvaged.[8]

The 95th had dodged a bullet by moving its planes to Kharkov. The next day, the aircrews took advantage of the free time to meet the locals, take photographs, and drink some strong Russian alcohol. The German army had destroyed Kharkov when it withdrew a few weeks previously, and aircrew snapshots show a city in ruins. Marshall Shore says that "only the walls were standing. The rubble of war was everywhere." When the Germans retreated, they tore up the rails and took them with them and set fire to anything combustible. They had also sabotaged the sewage and water pipelines, so the city had no running water. Residents had to collect water at a central location and carry it to their homes. The Russians had set up several large rooms with shower heads lining the walls, and men, women, and children all showered together, using only cold water. Moller asked permission for his men to use the shower facilities for several hours. While the grimy men showered, they were surprised to see "every window filled with the faces of giggling young Russian women watching the modest Americans taking their showers. This was the only time we were able to take our clothes off until we got to Italy."

The Americans were surprised to see that the Russian women did all the same combat duties as the men and that they could drink most American airmen under the table in short order. In addition to some wicked hangovers, some Americans also became ill with food poisoning. Crews had to be juggled to cover for illnesses.

The Americans watched POWs sweep the field for unexploded German butterfly bombs, which were used as an antipersonnel submunition. A row of prisoners lined up fifty across, and each held a fifteen-foot-long willow staff. When a prisoner located a bomb, it was marked with a stick for a blasting team to blow it up later. When a bomb went off near a prisoner and the man fell wounded, a trailing truck picked him up and replaced him with another prisoner. "The lesson seemed to be: don't let yourself get taken prisoner by the Russian Army," says Shore.

Shore attended a private party for high-ranking officers that resembled a gathering out of *Alice in Wonderland*. At the invitation of a Russian general, Shore and a few other American officers sat at a dining table in a building with no roof and amid a block of rubble. A picture of Stalin was hung on the wall behind the head of the table. The room had been freshly swept. Rubble was ten feet deep outside the open glassless windows.

"The General got up and gave a speech, waving his hands at a map on the side wall and talking about 'Mother Russia'. Suddenly the general grabbed his glass, held it high, and said in a loud voice, 'Viva Roosevelt'. Then he downed the contents of his glass. So did the other officers. Following suit, I put my glass to my lips and the taste compared to low grade fuel oil. Taking one swallow, I looked around into the staring faces of the Russian officer corps waiting for me to empty my glass. Opening my throat I poured the contents down, swallowing when it was all past my throat, a trick I had tried several times at beer parties in college. I knew I was in trouble when the fiery liquid started bouncing around my stomach.

"The butter on the table was, like the P-39s, a lend-lease item," Shore recalls. "Its wrapper identified it as being from a creamery in Ames, Iowa. The meal lasted an hour and more toasts were given. After dinner, the General made his way unsteadily out the door. The next three Russian officers all ran into the wall trying to go out the door." Shore felt his way out with his hands. "My cheeks and lips were numb. Never in my life had I been in such a condition." As the general went down the steps to the street, he missed a step and fell face-first on the pavement, but he jumped right up. Two drivers helped him into a Chevrolet staff car.

Shore then watched three young Russian girls dance to the accompaniment of a zither. He retired to the nearest building, where he vomited and fell asleep in the straw, only to wake up hours later covered with flea and lice bites. "I didn't fully recover from this binge until four days after we arrived in Foggia, Italy on the way home."[9]

Refueled and loaded with bombs, the force took off on June 26 and bombed an oil refinery and marshaling yards at Drohobycz, Poland. After bombing the target and flying for nine hours, the Fortresses landed at air bases near Foggia, Italy, which reminded the men of the Waldorf Astoria after the primitive conditions in Russia.

Lyle Scott remembers fondly that some of the men went swimming in the Adriatic while ground crews made the necessary repairs for the return trip to England. On July 3, the bombers flew a mission out of Foggia to Arad, Romania. Bob Capen remembers being in Foggia for nine days.

On July 5, more than two weeks after the 95th had taken off from Horham for the shuttle mission, the "Square B" Fortresses droned into sight over Horham after bombing the marshaling yards near Marseilles. Participating crews had seen Russia and Italy in a few short days and had received credit for three combat missions. It had been quite an adventure, one that its participants would never forget.

Frank Coleman, a ball turret gunner, sent the author an amusing news article from the July 19, 1944, edition of the *New York Daily News*. Headlined "Nude Welcome to Russia Shocks Pilots," Coleman discovered his name is mentioned. In a note, the devout Mormon added: "How would you like to see *your* son's name in the paper with this headline? Some girl in New York read the paper, saw my folks' address in the article and sent the article to them."

The article recounts the experiences of some American airmen near the Russian base who stumbled upon a party of men and women bathing nude. "Purely from a pinup point of view they saw a lot more of Russia than they bargained for," reads the text. Yankee fliers, accustomed to the taboos of America and the surface primness of England, were also baffled by Russia's forthright handling of the boy-meets-girl situation. "In Russia," one of the fliers reported, "each soldier is allowed to visit official Army brothels every so often. It's more or less the same way we go to the Post Exchange and get our weekly ration of cigarettes and razor blades. Russian soldiers don't pay anything if they stick to the regular ration, but if they want to make more frequent visits, they have to pay a fee."The article continues in the same prurient vein by telling now-breathless readers how men and women soldiers sleep in the same barracks and "lead a completely clubby existence."[10]

The 95th participated in a second Russia shuttle mission on August 6, 1944. Thirty-eight B-17s with the Square B, together with thirty-seven bombers from the 390th Bomb Group, took off for the Rahmel aircraft factory near Gdynia, Poland, a city on the Baltic coast. No fewer than 154 P-51 fighters from the 55th and 339th Fighter Groups escorted the bomber stream to Gdynia.[11] The P-51s turned around after the target and returned to England. At the time, it was the longest round-trip fighter mission of the war in Europe, or 1,592 miles.

Charlie Gallagher was a young gunner on this mission. He recalled, "We took off and bombed an aircraft repair facility, and landed at Poltava in the central Ukraine. This was a long mission, over ten hours. On the way over, we had two British Mosquitoes being flown by American pilots. Just north of Gdynia we heard one of the pilots say, 'Stop shooting! I'm friendly!' There was a pause, and then we heard the pilot say: 'Too late. Good-bye.' Another group had shot him down!

"As we flew over Poltava, a city of sixty thousand people, we could see into the basement of every building in town. The town had been leveled. We landed on a steel runway. It slowed us down because it kind of bunched up in front of the tires. However, when you took off, being slowed down is not such a good thing! We had barely gotten parked and the props had barely stopped spinning when a big four-by-four full of husky Russian women starting ramming ramrods down the barrels of our guns."

After landing, Gallagher and others took advantage of the fact that the "medicinal liquor" in the infirmary was unguarded. "This was good Irish whiskey. There was a ditch between the infirmary and our barracks, and when we crossed the ditch, you didn't even have to step down. It was filled up with guys who'd sampled the whiskey and passed out!"

The next day, August 7, the 95th bombed an oil refinery at Trzebinia, southeast of Warsaw, Poland. The mission took ten and a half hours. The number of heavy bombers was diminished to fifty-five, and the formation had only twenty-nine P-51s protecting it. After dropping 134 tons of bombs on or near the target, the men returned to Poltava tired and mighty glad to be done for the day.

"The next day, August 8, we went and bombed an airfield at Buzau, Poland," remembers Gallagher. "Buzau was near Ploesti. After nine hours in the air, we landed in Foggia, Italy. We stayed in Foggia at a base belonging to the Fifteenth Air Force, from August 8 to August 12, preparing to assist in the southern French invasion. While in Foggia, we went swimming in the Gulf of Macedonia. Someone shot film of it. When my daughter was in Horham around 2009 she saw the film. We weren't wearing bathing suits!"

On August 12, the 95th flew the final leg of the shuttle mission and conducted a bombing raid at the Toulouse-Francazal Airdrome in France. Escorted by fifty-eight P-51s that had been with the 95th at a point during the Russia mission, the bombers also met up with forty-two VIII Fighter Command P-51s after the bomb run. The planes then flew to England and landed, and the crews were glad to be back after their adventures.

The 95th participated in a third Russia shuttle mission on September 18. Along with several groups of B-24s, seventy-six B-17s from the 95th and 390th Bomb Groups flew a mission to bring some relief to the beleaguered Polish resistance fighters who had risen up against their German occupiers in Warsaw, the capital city. Royal Air Force crews also joined this resupply mission. The bombers continued on from their target, a Focke-Wulf factory at Rahmel, and accompanied by sixty-four P-51s from the 335th Fighter Group, the bombers refueled and rearmed at Mirgorod air base.

Bombardier-navigator David Webber flew on this mission as part of pilot Halcott B. Thomas's crew. His unpublished diary entry for the mission mentions an underlying ill feeling between the Russians and their American allies. "Today we got a truck which was driven by a Russian driver and went into Poltava. The people needed clothing and shelter badly. We took several pictures and acted as sightseers in general. The Russians seemed to resent our snooping around and they were justified in their resentment as we had warm clothing, plenty of gas and were well supplied with cigarettes. We carried our .45's and knives to protect ourselves because, to the freezing, clothes are worth more than the life of the wearer."[12]

The next day, they bombed two Polish targets—a synthetic oil refinery at Trezebinia and a marshaling yard at Szolnok before flying back to England. The B-17 piloted by Group Commander Carl Truesdell was hit by flak just before the target, knocking bombardier John S. Bromberg onto the narrow catwalk. Bromberg crawled back to his bombsight, released his bombs, then bailed out of the damaged plane. Truesdell managed to fly it to Italy, minus four crewmen who jumped, including Bromberg, and were captured by the SS.

While riding a train to a prison camp, Bromberg and his two German guards were forced to rush to a shelter during an air raid. A bomb killed the guards. Knocked unconscious and with shrapnel in both legs, Bromberg was loaded onto a stretcher and carried out with the other casualties. When the bearers discovered he was an American, however, they dumped him off the stretcher and loaded him back on the train.

Near Eisenbach, Germany, American P-47s strafed and wrecked the train, killing another of Bromberg's guards. Finally, the Germans took him to a hospital, where he was treated for his many wounds and was captive until the Eleventh Armored Division liberated it in early April 1945.[13]

The September 18 mission was the last Russian shuttle mission. That same month, Stalin denied the Allied air forces future landing rights in the Soviet Union. The 95th Bomb Group veterans remember the shuttle missions to Russia as tragicomic affairs, beset by disasters, snafus, and outrageous cultural differences. None of the men who flew on one is likely to forget the experience.

25 Final Combat Missions

Summer ended and fall returned to Horham. The 95th geared up for its 200th Mission Bash. No less a celebrity than the great bandleader Glenn Miller would appear. Miller had joined the U.S. Army Air Forces in 1942 at the peak of his popularity. At thirty-eight years of age he had been too old to be drafted, but he persuaded the military to allow him to enlist and to modernize the army band. In the summer of 1944, Miller received permission to take the Glenn Miller Army Air Force Band on tour. Leaving behind his wife and two young children, Miller and his fifty-piece band played seventy-one live concerts in England before a live audience totaling almost a quarter of a million.[1] The Miller concerts were so popular with USAAC personnel that Lt. Gen. Jimmy Doolittle claimed that next to a letter from home, Miller's band was the greatest morale builder in the European theater of operations.[2]

On September 9 and 10, 1944, Miller and his band played at the 95th Bomb Group's 200th Mission Bash. According to pilot Eugene Fletcher: "On the evening of the ninth I was ordered to report to Group Operations, with a skeleton crew, at 6:30 Sunday morning. We were told that we were flying up to Birmingham to pick up some VIPs who would participate in our big party."

Fletcher flew up early the next morning, piloting Bill Lindley's *Zoot Suiter II*. The VIPs turned out to be members of Glenn Miller's band.[3]

Contrails II reports: "The 200th mission, an event of magnitude to a slightly weary outfit, was celebrated in style. No flights were scheduled for the brief spell. The hangar was cleared and decorated for dancing, and free beer flowed to hundreds. There was a fancy outlay of food and a great deal of mutual admiration. It was just as well the celebrators didn't know they were going to go through 121 more missions before bringing down the curtain on the aerial show."[4] Photographs from the bash show a hangar—its stage backed by a gigantic American flag—packed with airmen, their dates, and local children enjoying the concert.

On December 14, Miller was preparing to leave England and fly to Paris, where he would give a concert for Allied troops at the Olympia Theater. He met Lt. Col. Norman Baessell at an Officers' Mess at Milton East not far from Northampton. Baessell mentioned that he was flying to Paris the next day from an RAF field at Twinwood Farm and offered Miller a seat, which he accepted.

On December 15, weather conditions were poor. A concerned Miller looked into the plane and remarked that he didn't see any parachutes. Lieutenant Colonel Baessell replied: "What's the matter with you, Miller? Do you want to live forever?"

The plane took off but never arrived in Paris. The official report was that the Norseman crashed into the English Channel owing to either iced-over wings or engine failure. Another theory is that Miller's aircraft flew slightly off course and under a group of RAF Lancaster bombers that were jettisoning bombs in a no-fly zone known as the South Jettison Area, a ten-mile circle located fifty miles south of Beachy Head over the English Channel. The planes were returning from an aborted bombing raid on Siegen in Germany. Major Miller's name is on the Wall of the Missing at the American Cemetery at Madingley near Cambridge, England.

December 1944 was a cold, damp month in East Anglia, and the mood at the 95th Bomb Group was low. A constant fog hung over the base, accompanied by a perpetual drizzle. In addition to the weather, many crewmen were suffering from stress and battle fatigue.

Christmas 1944 would be another one spent away from family and loved ones back in the States. However, the men still attempted to add a little Christmas cheer to the holidays. Shortly before Christmas, pilot John Walter was sent with a skeleton crew to pick up one of the group's airplanes at Woodbridge, Suffolk. Woodbridge was one of the Eighth Air Force's main emergency airfields where pilots could land badly damaged aircraft that they had nursed home across the English Channel. Since it was basically a square mile of blacktop, a plane in distress could land from any compass heading. Woodbridge was equipped with a fog, intense dispersal of (FIDO), system so that planes could land safely. One part of the blacktop was lined as a runway with a ditch on either side. These ditches could be filled with gasoline and ignited. Later, pipelines with burners ran down either side of the runway. The heat from the flames burned off the fog near the runway, and the flames themselves served as a beacon.

Upon arriving at the airfield, Walter remembers

the field had been cut out of a pine forest. As we climbed out of the airplane, one of the crew . . . asked if we could take back a Christmas tree. I said neither "yes" or "no." However, I *did* mention that I would enter and exit the airplane through the front hatch. Thus, if some strange cargo, such as a Christmas tree *or two*, found its way into the back of the airplane, I, more than likely, would be completely unaware of it. Further, I suggested that if he did leave the airplane, it probably would be a good idea to take the fire axe with him as some unprincipled person might steal it.

So, for Christmas 1944 one Enlisted Men's hut and one Officers' hut were decorated with live (recently cut) trees. What could be used to trim the tree? Popcorn and chaff, strips of aluminum foil used to confuse enemy radar, were excellent.

Later, we were told that we had committed a serious crime in that all of the trees at Woodbridge belonged to the King and there were severe penalties for cutting and/or stealing them. We were never caught, in spite of the fact that Base Public Relations took a photo of the trimmed tree in the enlisted crew quarters and sent copies to their hometown newspapers.

The photo shows five contented-looking enlisted men puffing on their pipes around a festive little tree, with the corrugated Nissen walls visible in the background.[5]

The end of 1944 also saw a change in leadership for the 95th Bomb Group. John Walter writes: "When we came to the 95th, the Group C.O.

was a likeable fellow by the name of Colonel Carl Truesdell, Jr. He was a ci-gar smoking West Pointer and the son of a General. He believed in running a somewhat easy-going but extremely proficient unit." However, Truesdell was promoted, and his replacement was "a white-haired Colonel by the name of Jack Shuck. He, too, was a West Pointer; but unlike Truesdell, he acted it. That is, 'All things military are serious. No time, space or place for deviations from the code exists.'"

The colonel instituted Saturday morning inspections. This decree and other changes that the men considered "chickenshit" rankled them. Care-ful reading of the *Officer's Guide* informed the men that only enlisted per-sonnel were required to stand at attention when a senior officer entered the room. Armed with this knowledge, the men in Walter's Nissen hut were ready for the CO's first inspection.

On the first Saturday morning set aside for the inspection, the Ad-jutant popped in the hut door and yelled "Attention!" The group stayed put. Those in the sack stayed there and the card players kept their seats but they did pause and look up to see what would hap-pen next. The Adjutant's face had a slightly perplexed look. The Colonel asked why the beds had not yet been made and the place straightened up. The reply was, "The orderly hasn't been around yet this morning, Sir." The Colonel and the Adjutant did some har-rumphing, commented on the general pigpen nature of the place and departed the scene. The Adjutant tried to save the day by say-ing, "As you were, men," as he went out the door. We heard later that while inspecting another hut, the Adjutant had attempted to exit through the nailed-shut rear door with the result that he crashed into it and the Colonel, in turn, crashed into him. The inspection routine was tried once more before the Colonel recognized this was going to be more of a loser than a winner.

Some time later, Walter and a crewmate named Olsen were enjoying a few drinks in the Officers' Club when a mission alert came in. They quickly rushed to the bar and bought half a case of beer and took it to the lounge area.

We had been there a short time when who shows up but the good Colonel. He eyed the case of beer and said, "My, what a windfall of beer! I think I'll join you." The other two fellows, as they departed, said they had to fly tomorrow and were going to hit the sack. This left Olsen, the Colonel and me. The Colonel asked if either of us were flying the next day. We didn't know, but said we were not. We found out later we were.

Our conversation was wide-ranging and more philosophical than anything else. In due course, age became the center topic. After some time, Olsen decided to issue his summation. It was, "I think all people over the age of 45 should be shot. That way we would avoid the Hitlers and Mussolinis of the world." I don't know how old the colonel was, but from his reaction, I expect he was over 45.[6]

Pilot Eugene Fletcher also remembers Shuck's arrival. As Fletcher's crew approached its thirty-five-mission mark, the men eagerly looked forward to the awards ceremony when they would be presented with the Distinguished Flying Cross. The crew had attended many DFC ceremonies for other crews and felt it was a real morale builder for the group. The new colonel, however, issued a directive discontinuing the ceremony. Writes Fletcher:

Flying missions against the enemy would be just a job. Apparently the art of preparing the citations had now become a far too difficult task.

Previously when a crew finished their last mission, they would pour on the coal and reach base ahead of the formation, and fly down the runway at 200 feet firing flares in a victory celebration. There would be cause for joy both in the airplane and among the crews observing on the ground. This was tangible evidence that a crew could live to finish a tour and it was also a real morale-booster. This practice was also ordered to cease.

Another honor accorded a crew completing thirty-five missions was the "Lucky Bastard Club" dinner. Eugene Fletcher writes that the honored crew "would dress in Class A uniform and come to the Combat Officers Mess Hall, where they were seated at a table of honor with a white tablecloth and given a steak dinner with a bottle of wine. During their dinner they would be given a standing ovation from the combat crew officers in the mess hall. It was the only time a combat officer and crew would receive steak at the 95th."[7]

Shuck canceled the Lucky Bastard Club dinner as well.

The early months of 1945 saw continued poor weather over the continent, so Pathfinder crews had to lead many missions while crews dropped bombs through clouds. The men were aware of what they were hitting. John Walter remembers writing on a bomb tag the purpose of a mission to Frankfurt on February 17, 1945: "To put rubble in the streets." A bomb tag for the February 25 mission to Munich lists the target as "arms, legs and old ladies."[8] The Pathfinders allowed the bombing of Germany to continue unabated, and 80 percent of the bombs hit their assigned targets.

Although Walter considers the January 2 mission a milk run, as well as the mission to Fulda on January 3, his next mission was unusual. On January 5, Colonel Shuck was flying in command of the group as lead copilot. His insistence that the group formation look perfect before it joined the bomber stream resulted in the 95th passing the departure point a few minutes late. The 95th had to pour on the coal to catch up, burning precious fuel.

Walter's plane soon developed major engine problems, and he was forced to make an emergency landing in Allied-controlled France. "When we returned to the base," writes Walter, "we learned the full extent of the Colonel's folly. Eight of the 36 group aircraft turned back early because of either equipment failure or fuel shortage. Nine aircraft, including us, were forced to land on the Continent. Then, guess what happened? The good colonel was awarded the Distinguished Flying Cross for 'outstanding' leadership under adverse conditions. The final insult was that we had to stand formation while the award was made. Nowhere in the citation was it mentioned that the adverse conditions were the Colonel's own making!"[9]

The year 1945 also brought snow to Horham. The base had enough equipment to keep the runways clear, but the taxiways and hardstands became a problem. The situation provided the fun-loving John Walter with a new thrill, taxiing a sixty-thousand-pound Fortress on an icy surface.

Walter remembers returning from another mission in early 1945 and seeing a huge billow of smoke and fire at a nearby base. The crew decided to go take a look. "When we got near and saw what it was, we sure got the hell out of there real quick. One of the 100th Bomb Group's Fortresses had crashed into their bomb dump. It was very, very spectacular. It could only happen to the 100th."[10]

On February 15, 450 B-17s from the Third Division flew a bombing raid to the railroad marshaling yards at Cottbus, deep in eastern Germany and not far from the Polish border. The 335th Squadron crew led by pilot Fred Volz Jr. was on only its second mission.

"At the early morning briefing, the Intelligence Officer warned us not to land in Russian territory if we got into trouble," remembers copilot Edward Pachnik. However, Volz's plane was badly crippled, and he was forced to make an emergency landing at a former Luftwaffe field ten miles north of Deblin. After the crew spent the first night trying to establish contact with the Russian Army by radio, a Russian colonel showed up and arranged for the men to stay at a bomb-damaged hotel in Deblin and put them under twenty-four-hour guard. "We were also visited and interviewed by a young Russian officer and his equally young female assistant. These two, we later discovered, were members of the NKVD [the People's Commissariat for Internal Affairs], the dreaded Russian secret police."

The crew was well treated and free to explore although still under Russian guard for eight days. Finally, on February 25, a Russian general from Poltava sent his personal aircraft to transport the crew, along with their secret police escort, to Lublin, Poland, and from there to Moscow.

After a farewell dinner of roast goose, Pachnik records, "The Russians escorted us to the American Embassy. U.S. Ambassador Averell Harriman was there to greet us at the Embassy door. The next day we met Robert 'Rosie' Rosenthal of the 'Bloody Hundredth' Bomb Group. His right arm was in a sling due to being fractured during his bail-out over Russian lines while flying his last mission. Rosie had flown over fifty missions with the 100th by this time."

The following day the Russians put the Volz crew, along with Lieutenant Rosenthal, on a train to Poltava, where they relaxed for a week before being flown to Iran in a C-46 transport plane. From Iran, they flew to Egypt, Athens, Naples, and then Rome. In Rome, they were transferred to Winston Churchill's converted B-24 Liberator for the flight back to Land's End, where a U.S. Navy DC-3 flew them back to Bovingdon.

"We were stranded until we found an abandoned B-17G parked out of sight back in the woods," writes Pachnik. "We flew this airplane back to the 95th Bomb Group at Horham two days later."[11]

Another 95th crew also ended up in Russia on the same mission. The C. D. Schaad crew became, in effect, Russian POWs but survived the war, according to Pachnik.

Sometime in February, radio operator/gunner William "Dubb" Vandegriff and his crewmates arrived at Horham to begin their tour. Vandegriff considers himself fortunate to have missed the major air battles earlier in the war: "When you send out three bombers and only one comes back, that takes some of the glamour out of the Air Corps advertisements." Vandegriff and his crew flew eighteen missions over the next few months, up until the end of the war.

On February 24, the group flew to Bremen to take out a railroad bridge. For the first time, Walter remembers carrying bombs heavier than a thousand pounds. He carried two bombs weighing two thousand pounds and another two that were a thousand pounds on the mission.

The Luftwaffe, meanwhile, had not remained idle. A major development in the German air arsenal, the Messerschmitt Me-262, had entered the fray in small numbers in 1943. This beautiful and highly advanced fighter was one of the first true jet airplanes. The Me-262 was powered by two Junkers Jumo 004B-1 turbojets and could fly at a maximum speed of 541 miles per hour—or 125 miles per hour faster than any other fighter in the world—with a range of 652 miles. Adolf Hitler misjudged when he insisted on using the Me-262 as a ground-attack fighter rather than as an interceptor.

By the time the 262 was rolling off the assembly lines in any kind of numbers, the Germans had lost both air superiority over the continent and so many fighter pilots that there was a severe shortage of skilled pilots to fly the new plane.[12] In the end, only 1,294 Me-262s were built. In contrast, more than 20,000 FW-190s and over 30,000 Me-109s rolled off the assembly lines.[13] The 95th BG's crewmen began seeing the Me-262 jets in the skies over Europe in the summer of 1944. George Hood's crewmates had no idea what they were looking at when they first encountered the Me-262. "The Bombardier poked me and said, 'What the heck is that?' It was a German plane like we had never seen before and it didn't seem to have a pro-peller! At a debriefing we were told it was an ME262, which meant nothing to us. That was our first knowledge of a 'Jet.'"[14]

Bill Connor of the 334th Squadron remembers seeing an Me-262 dur-ing the second Russia shuttle mission in August 1944. And 334th ball turret gunner Robert Fay saw 262s twice during his tour in late 1944 and early 1945. "Two of them flew right through our formation and by the time I got a burst they were gone! We knew they were there but we never knew when we'd run into them!" In December 1944 Tony Molino of the 335th Squad-ron and his crew sighted an Me-262 over Hamburg and took hits, but they managed to drop into a large cloud and lose the pursuer.[15]

Another revolutionary German aircraft the 95th crews spotted later in the war was the Me-163 Komet. Nicknamed the Flea by the Germans, this tiny aircraft was little more than a rocket engine with wings. The Flea took off similar to a conventional aircraft but was equipped with a detachable, reusable two-wheeled undercarriage. Once in the air, climbing at about 420 miles per hour, it would jettison its undercarriage, pull into a seventy-degree climb, and reach altitudes of up to forty thousand feet in only three minutes. It could attack in level flight at speeds of 550 miles per hour. A typical tactic of the Me-163 pilot involved making two quick passes through the Allied bomber stream at bombing altitude, after which time the 163 was out of fuel. Then the Komet became a glider and returned to earth.

Despite being easy to fly, the Flea had many drawbacks. First, it was so fast that only a pilot who was a superb gunner could hit anything with its weapons. Second, it landed on a belly skid and slid to a stop, often a liter-ally backbreaking experience for its pilots. Third, it was filled with volatile rocket fuel; a direct hit instantly turned it into a glowing fireball. Fourth, it had a very limited range of only twenty-five miles. Allied fighter pilots learned to wait until the Komet was out of fuel and gliding before jump-ing it. Another tactic was to follow the Komet back to base and then strafe it after it landed. Messerschmitt delivered ninety-one little Komets by the end of 1944. Their impact on the war was minimal, however; they shot down sixteen four-engine bombers while twelve Komets were lost. As with the Me-262, the Germans' chronic lack of fuel by late 1944 hampered the Komet's operations.

The Americans and British were hard at work on a jet fighter aircraft of their own. The P-59 Airacomet first flew in 1942, but USAAF leaders and test pilots were not impressed with the aircraft, which they found underpowered, prone to engine overheating, and with a long takeoff roll. Of the eighty ordered, only thirty were delivered before the program was canceled. However, at least one ended up in England, traded to the RAF for a Gloster Meteor F.1, Britain's early jet aircraft.

Robert Brown remembers seeing a demonstration of a jet aircraft at a replacement depot in England during the war. He writes: "About every three weeks we would fly to a replacement depot to get new planes for the Group. I saw my first American jet there, which they demonstrated for us. It immediately crashed and the pilot was killed."[16] This plane may actually have been a British Gloster Meteor that crashed on July 30, 1943, after an aileron failure. The P-59 Airacomet program was not a waste in the long run. The blueprints and lessons learned formed the basis for a highly successful postwar jet, the P-80 Shooting Star.

In the final analysis, it is also interesting to wonder what could have been if the German's top secret jet aircraft, the Horten Ho 229, had entered the war effort. That aircraft, whose flying-wing design strongly resembled the modern American B-2 Stealth bomber, was built and tested in March 1944 in response to a challenge from Luftwaffe chief Hermann Göring to build a "1,000, 1,000, 1,000" aircraft, or one that could carry 1,000 kilograms over 1,000 kilometers flying at 1,000 kilometers per hour. The central pod of the aircraft was a welded steel tube, with the rest made of wood. Not only did it have two Junkers Jumo 004 B-2 turbojet engines, but it also possessed an early version of stealth technology. The plane was coated with a mixture of charcoal dust and wood glue to absorb radar waves, making its detection by enemy radar difficult.[17]

The plane would have a 142-foot wingspan and be able to fly from Berlin to New York and back without refueling. Because of its speed, it could have been over London only eight minutes after being detected by British radar. The Germans only built three prototypes, and none of them ever flew.[18]

The role of jet aircraft in World War II was minimal, as the technology was in its infancy. As noted, by the time the Me-262 was available in large numbers, American and English bombing raids had reduced the Germans' oil production capacity, severely limiting the amount of aviation fuel available, and the Luftwaffe fighter corps had few top-notch pilots to fly the planes. Perhaps most telling of all about the sad state of affairs for the German Luftwaffe are accounts of state-of-the-art Me-262s being towed, often by horses, out to the runways to save fuel.

American fighter pilots also figured out ways to overcome the slower speeds of piston fighters. For example, P-51 Mustang pilots found that the 262 lost maneuverability in turns, rendering it vulnerable to attack. Fighters also began patrolling above the bomber streams, using their altitude to build airspeed in diving attacks on the German jets. Pilots also attacked the jets as they took off and landed, and began bombing the long concrete runways that the 262 required.

The discoveries made during the war years would reap huge benefits in the postwar years. Researchers and manufacturers made great strides in jet aircraft designs that would render traditional piston-powered, propeller-driven aircraft virtually obsolete by the end of the 1960s.

After the February 15 mission to Cottbus, Germany—and after the two 95th crews ended up in the Soviet Union—the 95th lost some aircraft to salvage after they crash-landed on the continent, but the group did not lose another crew until March 3. Much of the continent by this time was in Allied hands, and whereas a year previously these crews would have probably ended up as POWs, now they simply returned to base.

On March 9, the 95th flew to Frankfurt on its 291st combat mission. The W. E. Ourant crew was shot down and became POWs. The next 95th Fort lost wasn't until March 23, when the Dunwody crew went down after a midair collision returning from a mission to Unma, Germany. Most of the crew was killed.

On March 10, John Walter's crew flew its final mission, to Dortmund, Germany. "We'd been there three days before. We almost felt like commuters." Upon their return, the crew decided to celebrate and buzzed the field and shot some flares. As Walter began his descent, he radioed the crew to stop shooting flares, as they were now close to the ground. Each pass ended with "an appropriate chandelle," remembers Walter. "Some people thought that the B-17 was a stodgy old bomber, but it can put on a pretty impressive show at low altitude."[19]

When they climbed out of the plane, they were informed that one of tail gunner Charles Dye's flares had landed in the base fuel dump! He had not received the cease-fire order. Fortunately, someone in the dump threw a sandbag over the flare, or the 95th's dump would have gone up just as the 100th's had only a few months earlier.

After a hard night of partying, the unrepentant Dye stole the colonel's Jeep and crashed it into a ditch. He then retreated to a nearby hangar, where he either passed out or went to sleep. Dye was court-martialed, busted to buck private, and heavily fined. He ended up staying at Horham until the group was deactivated.

By March 1945, remembers General Doolittle: "Enemy opposition to our raids seemed to be dwindling, [but] the numbers of Luftwaffe jets began to increase, especially on our missions to Berlin. Now getting desperate, the Luftwaffe put out a call for volunteers for 'special and dangerous' operations. It became the German equivalent of the Japanese kamikaze squadrons. Flying Me109s, they were instructed to attack a bomber from extreme range and keep on firing until they rammed it, preferably in the fuselage aft of the wing."[20] This technique proved unsuccessful, destroying only eight Eighth Air Force Fortresses.

Another sad occurrence in March 1945 was the death of the 95th's own Sator "Smilin' Sandy" Sanchez, who would become the only enlisted man to have a B-17 named after him. Sanchez was born Satero Sierra in 1921 on the rough side of the tracks in Joliet, Illinois. His mother died in 1922 of tuberculosis, and his father was shot to death outside a bar in 1929, allegedly over a gambling debt. Satero and his older sister Magdelena then lived with their stepmother, Joquina Sanchez, who took excellent care of them until she passed away in 1934. The thirteen-year-old Satero and his sister then moved in with Joquina's parents, Fidencio and Belen Sanchez. The step-grandparents adopted the two teenagers, and the thirteen-year-old Satero changed his name to Sator Sanchez.

Young Sanchez became interested in the airplanes he saw flying out of a nearby airport, and he would walk or ride his bicycle five miles to the airport to watch the planes take off and land. While in high school, Sator joined Junior Reserve Officers' Training Corps. During summers in the late thirties, he worked for the Forest Service, and after graduating from high school, he joined the Civilian Conservation Corps, where he learned surveying and mechanics while working in Wisconsin and Montana.

In December 1939, Sanchez joined the U.S. Army and first trained as an infantryman before transferring into the air corps in May 1941. Posted to Moffett Field, California, as an airplane mechanic, Sanchez served in the 539th School Squadron, servicing the BT-13s used to train cadet pilots. The talented and hardworking Sanchez quickly advanced through the ranks, becoming a sergeant in mid-1942.

In August 1943, Sanchez arrived in England and was assigned to the 95th Bomb Group, 334th Squadron. Within a short time, he was flying missions as an aerial gunner. After completing his first combat tour, Sanchez decided to keep flying. After he flew his forty-fourth mission in the summer of 1944, a record for missions flown in the ETO, the group honored Sanchez by naming a new B-17 Fortress after him. Photos of Sanchez at the ceremony show him sitting on the nose of the plane above a cartoon version of himself and the number 44 denoting his mission count.

In the summer of 1944, Sanchez was sent Stateside to rest and to train others as a gunnery instructor. However, he soon got bored and volunteered for a third combat tour. Sent to the Fifteenth Air Force, 301st Bomb Group, stationed in Italy, he again began flying combat.

Eventually, even Sanchez admitted it was time to step down. However, he volunteered to fly one more mission, his sixty-sixth. On March 15, 1945, the 301st bombed Ruhland, Germany. Sanchez's airplane was hit by flak, and the crew bailed out. For some reason, Sanchez was unable to do so, and his body was found in the plane's wreckage. Six weeks later, the war in Europe was over, but it was six weeks too late for Smilin' Sandy Sanchez.

After the fall of the Berlin Wall, travel to the former East Germany became easier, and family members began trying to track down Sanchez's remains. In 1993, the navigator on Sanchez's final flight, along with a member of Sanchez's family, traveled to the crash site. They found a German farmer was using the left side of the vertical tail section from Sanchez's B-17G (42-97683) as a wall in his storage shed. The artifact was recovered and sent to the National Museum of the Air Force in Dayton, Ohio, where it is on display to this day. But Sanchez's body was never recovered, and it is likely he is still buried near the crash site.

In September 1994, a local Joliet veterans group had a city park named after Smilin' Sandy Sanchez. A Hispanic spokesman at the park's dedication remarked: "Here in Joliet we don't even have a street with a Hispanic surname, let alone a public facility. We need our kids to identify with something other than a lot of negative stuff that people identify the Hispanic kids with." Fittingly, fifty years after Smilin' Sandy's crash, the young man from Joliet who had faced so much tragedy and kept smiling continued to touch and inspire others.[21]

On April 4, a 95th Fort piloted by J. J. Tuss lost two engines over the target at Kiel and managed to stagger into neutral Sweden and internment. His was the last Fort to go down in the war that was not salvaged after landing in Allied-controlled areas on the continent.

"By the end of April, we were running out of targets," remembers General Doolittle. "Victory was in the air as the armies of the Allies moved rapidly and pushed back the German defenders." Still, on April 10 a force of fifty Me-262 jets managed to shoot down ten Eighth Air Force bombers, the largest loss of bombers to jets in the war.[22]

By mid-April, the German war industry had been almost completely crippled. "There were no more oil refineries," writes Doolittle. "The submarine pens were no longer a menace to the Allied navies. Only tactical bombings remained. We were now ready to call a halt to the strategic air war. On April 16, 1945, 'Tooey' Spaatz sent out messages announcing that the strategic air war was over and that we would henceforth operate with our tactical air forces in close cooperation with the ground forces."

Doolittle's statisticians estimated the Eighth Air Force dropped 701,300 tons of bombs in three years, including 531,771 tons on Germany. It had destroyed 18,512 enemy aircraft while losing 43,742 bomber crewmen killed or missing and 4,456 bombers.

On April 30, Hitler and his wife, Eva Braun, committed suicide in their Berlin bunker as Russian troops closed in. The bombers and their crews began flying much more pleasant missions as the war wound down, dropping food to the starving Dutch people in Holland on the Manna-Chowhound missions. The war in Europe ended May 8, 1945. Flight surgeon Dr. Jack McKittrick, who had flown several combat missions during the war, recalled where he was on V-E night:

I went to a little theater on Leicester Square [London]. I heard all this commotion and went outside. The streets were so packed with people it took me two hours to get to Piccadilly Circus. British "Tommys" and GIs were packed together in and on taxis, buses, and fire trucks. That night I couldn't buy a drink in London. Everything was free. I was at the Dorchester Hotel and we all listened to Winston Churchill's speech; it was the most exciting night I've ever seen. They lighted all the lights for the first time in six years; big department stores, Piccadilly Circus, Oxford Street, the Houses of Parliament were all shining brightly.

One thing I will always remember was the quietly spoken Englishman who said to me on that joyous night: "Thanks, Yank, we couldn't have done it without you."[23]

For the 95th Bomb Group, the war was over. But the story was just beginning.

26   POWs, Part II

As their comrades continued flying missions over Europe in 1944 and into 1945, the POWs from the 95th Bomb Group continued to fight a different war—one against hunger, boredom, and a general feeling of hopelessness.

"Days passed and became weeks and then another month. Christmas came and went and then another Christmas, and the war was still on," remembers pilot John Chaffin. The captives followed the progression of the Allied armies as helpless but hopeful spectators. "The Russian armies were moving," remembers Chaffin. "D-Day came and we rejoiced in thinking that the end was now in sight, and we were saddened by the knowledge that thousands of young men were dying to make that a reality."

Leonard Hanson remembers that the war's progress became a favorite topic behind the wire:

> Everyone was quite certain that the Allies would win, but there was always the "what if" syndrome. *What if* Hitler really had a secret weapon as he claimed? One of my roommates was a physics major, and he explained to us how all the great powers had scientific teams at work all attempting to split the atom. He went on to explain that if they could split the atom and the various particles went crazily searching for each other to reunite, there could be one hell of an explosion. In fact, they couldn't be sure it could be controlled and possibly it could destroy all living matter on earth.[1]

Gunner Edward Cunliffe of the 95th remembers, "We had a little radio, a crystal set somewhere in the camp. We'd get BBC news, and then messengers would report the news to the different barracks." While the messenger stood on a table and made his report, several POWs would guard each end of the barracks to make sure the Germans didn't show up.[2]

Mail call always brought momentary happiness and a few laughs. John Chaffin remembers that an American girl knitted a sweater for the Red Cross, which sent the sweater to a prisoner at Stalag Luft I. The prisoner wrote the girl a thank you letter and received an angry response: "I am sorry to hear that a prisoner is wearing the sweater I knitted for a fighting man." Another elderly relative wrote: "I am enclosing a calendar. I thought might come in handy because it has several years ahead on it." A sister wrote to one hungry POW: "I'm really worried about our cat. I took her to the vet and he said her diet was insufficient."

Warren Thomas, a radio operator on Eldon Broman's *Fritz Blitz* who spent nearly two years as a POW, recalls the bites of hungry fleas and lice. The little creatures were constant companions in the many hours of boredom. "Hours crept by like days," he remembers. "Card games, compound walks, reading, and picking fleas from clothing seams were the usual activities."[3]

Thomas's pilot, Eldon Broman, imprisoned at Stalag Luft I at Barth, remembers one pastime for a few POWs was planning their escape. He told me that he was pretty sure the Germans knew what was going on but figured it kept the POWs busy and occupied. "I didn't get too involved because I didn't want another brush with the Gestapo, but I helped get rid of the dirt from the tunnels. Each man took one Red Cross parcel full of dirt and dumped it on the parade ground. The Germans knew something was up when they saw us running all over the camp with parcels full of dirt."

On July 20, 1944, dissidents within the German hierarchy launched an unsuccessful assassination attempt against Hitler. It created a heightened level of paranoia and resulted in a crackdown against anyone whom the fanatical Nazis in Hitler's inner circle deemed lax. Luftwaffe officers who had resisted using the one-armed fascist salute now did so, and their treatment of POWs worsened. To make matters worse, as Russia advanced from the east and the other Allies from the west, the German-controlled area began to constrict, creating a problem for those who administered stalag lufts and worried about being overrun by Allied forces. Germany held 95,000 American prisoners, including 38,000 airmen. Allied High Command expressed fears that "Hitler may use as a last card a threat to murder all POWs in his hands unless the Allies come to terms," read one top-level memo.[4]

The SS began to develop a supervisory presence in many stalag lufts. Luftwaffe personnel, once openly contemptible of the SS, now appeared cowed by their presence. Fraternization between prisoners and guards declined.

Near the end of 1944, with the Russian advance less than sixty miles away, German officials at Stalag Luft III, a Luftwaffe-run camp for Allied prisoners near the eastern German town of Sagan, drew up plans to evacuate the camp. By January 25, 1945, with the Russian Army only forty-eight miles away, the POWs marched out of the camp.

John Chaffin wrote with a pencil stub in his battered logbook: "On January 27 we began what I term *'The Worst of Days'*. From this date until our liberation April 29 we were no longer confident about our future. We were cold, hungry, sick and downright miserable for 83 long days. It was during that time that Adolph [*sic*] Hitler ordered the execution of all American and British airmen in retaliation for the destruction of Dresden. Fortunately his officer corps refused to obey these orders."

Prisoners were given less than two hours to prepare to march. Chaffin rolled his earthly possessions into a pack he made out of a blanket. "I had a shirt, underwear, three pairs of socks, toilet articles, my log book, one towel, ten packs of cigarettes, two cans of meat, three-fourths of a loaf of bread and a box of crackers." He stuffed his pockets with cigarettes, pipe tobacco, food, and playing cards and wore layers of clothing to keep warm on the march.

Six inches of snow covered the ground, and the temperature hovered between zero and twenty degrees Fahrenheit. The road was jammed with prisoners, refugees, and retreating German soldiers. The POWs occasionally traveled in railroad boxcars and spent most nights in barns, but from time to time they were put up in other prison camps. Of the twenty-three hundred kriegies who started the grueling fifty-five-kilometer march at Sagan, only five hundred to six hundred POWs arrived at Muskau. Among the march's many dangers was being strafed by American fighter planes. POWs laid out an air corps symbol and the strafing ceased.

Eventually, the column ended up at Stalag Luft VII-A at Moosberg, packed with men from other overrun stalag lufts. On April 29, 1945, the men saw advancing GIs.

As John Chaffin recalls: "Within two hours a Red Cross unit with coffee and doughnuts came into the camp and a little later, General Patton himself. We were told to remain in camp until arrangements were made to take us out. The German guards were replaced with GIs who made no effort to keep us behind barbed wire. Some fellows did leave for a few hours and went into Moosburg where they committed acts that I'm sure were regretted later. This included taking personal property from civilians—an action called 'liberating.' So many months of deliberately holding back emotion conditioned me to hold my excitement in check, perhaps a subconscious fear of disappointment. It is an attitude of 'Well, hell, let's see what happens next.'"[5]

Top turret gunner James A. Kelley Jr. marched from Stalag Luft IV from February 4 until May 2, 1945. During this time his group marched 525 miles, averaging about 6 miles a day, and usually slept in the open. "I remember one day we marched 35 kilometers in the rain and snow," writes Kelley. "The ground was covered with slush and about dusk the guards told us we would have to sleep in the forest. We were soaking wet, it was snowing, we were given no food and we could not build any fires because of the wet conditions. I traded my high school class ring for half a loaf of bread and a chunk of cheese with some forced laborers. My mother had given me a wristwatch shortly before I entered the Army, for which she had paid over $100. I traded it for two-and-a-half loaves of bread, a small piece of sausage and a medium sized piece of cheese."

When the Germans had it, they supplied what food they could, mostly raw potatoes, kohlrabi, rutabagas, and sugar beets. On one occasion a horse had been strafed, and the men butchered it. They ate horse steak that night. Meanwhile, most of the men had dysentery. "You can imagine when someone in the barn had to go to the toilet in a hurry with no lights, crawling and stumbling across those between him and the door," remembers Kelley. "Tempers flared, especially if he did not get there in time."

"It wasn't until early April that I removed my long john underwear for the first time and took a bath. I don't understand now how we could stand each other or ourselves. We spent many hours picking lice and nits from our bodies. While we were marching and our body was not too warm the lice were very quiet, but when we lay down and became a little warm they would start parading and we would become miserable.

"On the morning of May 1, 1945 we got up there were no German guards to be found anywhere." A British sergeant in an armored truck liberated them later that day. They stripped naked and threw all their clothes into a pile to be burned, then were sprayed with dichlorodiphenyltrichoroethane (DDT) to kill the lice. Each man was then issued a complete British uniform.[6]

Radioman George Sulick also ended up at Stalag Luft IV. He remembers being packed into a boxcar and the men only being allowed out once a day to relieve themselves. "I don't know how many cars made up the train, but I do know that at least 1300 to 1400 men were relieving their bowels at the same time." While the men did so, a sleigh full of German teenagers came by. "This was the longest 'mooning line' in history."[7]

Ball turret gunner Frank Baca remembered that "we got very hungry on our march. One day, this little brown chicken was hanging around. We killed the chicken, went upstairs in a barn, gutted it out, and stuck it in a can of boiling water. Then the aroma got around. The Germans said, 'If the man who stole the chicken doesn't come forward, we'll kill eight Americans.' Nobody did. That's America for you." The Germans' threat, though, had been a bluff.

He continued, "One day, we had soup with shredded horse meat and maggots. We ate the maggots . . . they were goooood."

Pilot Eldon Broman was liberated by the Russian Army at Barth's Stalag Luft I. "The German civilians were so afraid of the Russians that the women would bring their toddler children to the camp, begging for us to let them in. Of course, we couldn't let them in. Some of the mothers killed their children right outside the gates of the camp and then committed suicide."

The newly liberated POWs from all over Europe were now squeezed into a few camps that were bursting at the seams. It was imperative to evacuate them before disease set in. Many were already in poor health from malnutrition and their long forced marches. Some men had lost more than a hundred pounds. The sickest were flown out first by C-46 hospital planes. Combat B-17s were stripped and equipped to carry the fitter POWs to temporary holding camps. Gaunt, smiling men lined up in orderly rows to board the B-17s for repatriation.

The 95th Bomb Group's Fortresses assisted in the repatriation of Allied POWs and civilians liberated from concentration camps. The group flew its first so-called revival mission on May 16, 1945. Twenty crews participated, and on May 19, eleven more aircraft were dispatched to the continent to pick up additional released POWs. Pilot Marion Turner recounted: "Our crew consisted of two pilots, the navigator, radio operator and flight engineer. Our aircraft had 4-by-8 sheets of plywood placed across the bottom of the bomb bay for seating space, and we loaded about forty former concentration camp survivors and flew them to their home country. We picked up our load near Paris and flew them to Czechoslovakia."

Three repatriated POW transit camps were hastily established. Named after popular brands of American cigarettes—Camp Lucky Strike, Camp Old Gold, and Camp Chesterfield—they were were appropriately called the Cigarette Camps. The freed airmen were classified as Salvage or Repatriated American Military Personnel (RAMPS).

George Sulick remembered waiting at Camp Lucky Strike for a ride back to England. "On arrival, we were stripped, deloused, showered, issued new uniforms and fed. I don't know how it was possible to keep track of the thousands of G.I.s that poured into the camp. We were immediately allowed to send a telegram to our folks telling them we were headed home. One health tip given to us was to be sure to drink a lot of eggnog. For this, an area was set up to dispense eggnogs all day and well into the evening. . . . Actually it was a social event, watching the endless line of G.I.s going for their tonic."[8] Within weeks, most of the kriegies had boarded ships and gone home to the United States.

Bomb navigator Willard Brown had been the 95th's group navigator before being shot down on the Kiel mission on June 13, 1943. "During the long months of captivity at Sagan, I made three escape attempts, all of which proved unsuccessful," he remembers. "After my second escape attempt, the Escape Committee in the British compound invited me to become the 'Mr. X' in the American compound. 'Mr. X' was the person who was responsible for all escape plans and intelligence communications. A very good friend of mine, Roger Bushell, was the 'Mr. X' in the British compound."

Bushell, a South African–born auxiliary air force pilot, became famous as the planner of the daring "Great Escape" that took place in March 1944. The Gestapo caught and executed him. No Americans were involved in the Great Escape.

Brown's next brush with destiny came in February 1945, when he accompanied a delegation of Stalag Luft III leaders including Brig. Gen. Arthur Vanaman and Col. Delmar Spivey to Berlin as part of a failed effort to negotiate an end to the war. "As it happened," writes Brown, "the day we were scheduled to meet Hitler at his chancellery headquarters in Berlin, 14 February, the Eighth Air Force bombed Dresden. Hitler gave a direct order to [the] Commander of the Waffen S.S., Lieutenant General Gottlob Berger to kill American POWs in retaliation. Fortunately, General Berger did not carry out Hitler's order. Instead, he proposed to send the group directly to Washington with a message for President Roosevelt and General Marshall.

"Berger promised, among other things, to eliminate Hitler and Gestapo Chief [Heinrich] Himmler, and asked that the U.S. and Britain join Germany in holding the line at the German border against the advancing Russians. Berger also promised the safety of POWs, and did all he could to make sure they were not evacuated to Hitler's 'Final Redoubt.'"[9]

Brigadier General Vanaman and Colonel Spivey were smuggled into Switzerland, and from there they went to France and Washington. Vanaman made a full report of the meeting to the War Department, but it was ignored. Vanaman insisted as late as 1967 that if the United States had negotiated with Berger, it would have prevented much of the subsequent Cold War.[10]

Some 95th Bomb Group members spent months and others spent years as Axis POWs. The first crewmen of the 95th to become POWs were members of the D. C. Schnebly crew, which went down on the group's sixth combat mission on May 21, 1943. The last POWs of the war were members of the W. E. Ourant crew, lost March 9, 1945, on a mission to Frankfurt.

27 Manna/Chowhound Missions

In addition to flying missions to pick up former POWs and displaced persons (DPs), the 95th Bomb Group was involved in one other final operation that provided relief to the beleaguered Dutch people at the end of the war. These humanitarian missions, known as Operation Manna/Chowhound, were for many men the most satisfying of the war.

The Dutch people had suffered greatly since the German invasion of May 10, 1940. At first, the Germans ruled with as much benevolence as can be expected from fascists; however, as time passed and it became apparent that the Dutch people were not going to not knuckle under, their treatment became worse.

The Dutch established a government in exile in London, under the symbolic leadership of Queen Wilhelmina. When the Germans announced their discriminatory policies against Holland's Jews, the Dutch called a general strike. In September 1944, during the Allied airborne forces' Operation Market Garden, the Dutch tried to tie up the German rail lines by again calling a general strike. Furious, the Germans retaliated, cutting off food shipments to western Holland. By the winter of 1944–45, the situation had become grave. Severe shortages of food, coal, and other necessary supplies plagued an area with as many as 3.5 million people.

Queen Wilhelmina appealed to Prime Minister Churchill and President Roosevelt in January 1945: "Conditions at present have become so desperate that it is abundantly clear that if a major catastrophe, the like of which has not been seen in Europe since the Middle Ages, is to be avoided in Holland something drastic has to be done now, before and not after the liberation of the rest of the country!"[1]

By March 1945, a Red Cross official warned that some inhabitants in the western provinces were eating flower bulbs. People cut down trees in gardens and carried them away during the night for fuel. Passers-by instantly butchered horses that had been killed in bombardments. A person's average calorie intake in western Holland dropped to five hundred calories a day and finally to four hundred, far below the recommended two thousand calories needed to sustain health. The official Supreme Headquarters Allied Expeditionary Forces' report compared the residents' diet to that of victims of concentration camps. Adults and children suffered equally. Half of the women examined had stopped menstruating entirely by April. By the spring of 1945 more than 12,000 Dutch had died of starvation and 4.5 million more were malnourished.[2]

On March 28, Allied officials met in the liberated part of Holland to figure out a way to get food to the people in the west. An estimated 1.9 million pounds of food was stockpiled in England and would require large bomber-type aircraft to make the food drops. The first bomb group committed to making the drops belonged to the Royal Air Force, and it promised all of its two hundred Halifaxes and Stirlings, each with a carrying capacity of 2.5 tons.[3]

On April 25, Winston Churchill opened direct negotiations with German occupation commanders. The same day, listeners to the Allied Radio Luxemburg heard an announcement about the food drop plan:

> German authority is restricted to only a few pockets of resistance in Germany. To alleviate the suffering of the Dutch people during the final phase of the fighting the Allied Supreme Commander decrees that the Dutch civilian population is to be supplied with food dropped by parachutes. A great number of aircraft of all types will be employed by day and night to carry these foodstuffs. These aircraft are not being used for purposes of war but serve to bring aid to a destitute population.[4]

The message also warned the German occupiers that interference with the drops would be considered a war crime.

Tests were run to find out the ideal method for dropping heavy loads of food. Results showed that if the bomber pilots lowered their flaps and landing gear, burlap sacks of food could be dropped, without a parachute, from two hundred to three hundred feet above the ground without significant damage to the parcel. The 95th Bomb Group, along with Fortresses from the 100th and the 390th—120 bombers in all—were slated to participate in the food drops. Crews set to work modifying the Forts for the mission. On April 25, 95th crews conducted a practice drop on the airfield at Horham. Photographs show white, burlap-looking sacks scattered across the grassy field.

The following directive was dropped on western Holland in the ensuing days:

Supreme Headquarters Allied Expeditionary Forces Announcement
To the Population of Occupied Holland

1. The enemy, who is responsible for your food supplies, has ignored the need for sufficient supplies during the period when the connections with Germany were still open. Now that he is isolated through our military advance and has taken the criminal decision to go on fighting until the last moment, he will not be able to prevent starvation of your people.

2. Since your food supplies are exhausted now, the Supreme Allied Commander has given orders that immediately food has to be dropped by aircraft over occupied Holland. . . .

4. The food supplies will be dropped by aircraft of various types, principally by heavy bombers. The aircraft will fly low and drop their loads on locations where collecting by you is easy. We will not be able to announce time when and where the food will be dropped and therefore you must observe the following instructions:

   a. Expect food drops by day or night.

   b. Create groups under the command of responsible persons to look out for our aircraft and to collect food parcels.

   c. As soon as you hear our aircraft approaching, you have to take cover if you are in places where food will be dropped. The parcels will not be dropped by parachutes and are heavy, so if they hit you they may injure or even kill you.

   d. Place guards as soon as our aircraft are approaching in order to observe where the parcels are dropped.

   e. Distribute the food as honestly as possible.

   f. When the enemy tries to steal away your food or if he tried to fire at our aircraft, then take notes of all possible details and in particular the names of those who do so. Report these details. The members of the enemy forces who are guilty will be considered to be war criminals and will be treated as such.

6. Don't forget, we are your friends and will continue to do everything possible to help you.[5]

On April 30, four German delegates met with Allied representatives in Achterveld. The four were led blindfolded from a Canadian staff car into the meeting, as they were now in Allied territory. At the meeting, the Germans pledged to honor the mercy flights and not fire on the low-flying bombers. The mercy missions were officially on.

The food drop zones had been carefully selected. They had to be large, flat areas that had not been flooded when the Germans breached the dikes. They had to be fairly easy to cordon off and manage, and they had to be free of civilians. German soldiers, Dutch police, and even Dutch Boy Scouts were recruited to police the drops and the distribution of food. If food landed outside the drop zone, people were instructed to take it to the nearest distribution point. Hoarding or stealing anything that fell would be dealt with harshly.

At Horham, the 95th's planes were reequipped and crews chosen to fly. Carl Voss remembered: "We were ordered to construct and strengthen the huge bomb bay doors in order that each bomber could carry 4,500 pounds of canned C rations in 50-pound cases. They were to be dropped in a free fall from an altitude of 300 feet." The crews could not release the parcels in the exact manner as they had dropped their bombs. Instead, two wooden panels were attached to each other in the bomb bay. The outside of the panel was hinged to the bomb rack while the other side was attached to a cable. A loop in the cable was attached to the bomb-release mechanism.

When the bombardier pressed the activator switch, the panel would drop down and the payload would fall out.[6]

Meanwhile, crew talk in the Officers' Club and Red Feather Club centered on fears that German acquiescence to such a large-scale, low-altitude mission, one flown without the protection of guns, was some kind of trick. Nonetheless, on April 29, 242 RAF Lancasters and their Mosquito escorts roared into the skies, their bomb bays crammed with foodstuffs. The first day, their crews delivered 526.5 tons.[7]

"We had become," writes 100th Group navigator Harry Crosby, who flew some of the missions side by side with the 95th, "another kind of air force, not strategic or tactical but humanitarian, part of a mission the British called Operation Manna, the Americans, less reverentially, Operation Chowhound. By agreement with the Germans, only skeleton crews without gunners were authorized to fly, but that order was universally disregarded. Everybody wanted to fly." Some men saw it as their chance to atone for the suffering they had caused to Europe's civilians on their bombing missions. Ground personnel seized the opportunity to fly along on the humanitarian mission.[8]

The first 95th Bomb Group's drop was scheduled for May 1. The target was Valkenburg. One hundred and twenty Forts from the 95th, 100th, and 390th Bomb Groups were scheduled to fly. As the B-17s approached the European coast at several hundred feet, the aircrews saw massive rolls of barbed wire strung for miles along the beaches. Uniformed German soldiers patrolled but only glanced up at the planes overhead. Antiaircraft guns tracked the heavies as they crossed the Dutch coast but did not fire. Chowhound crewman Voss said: "We were below steeple level; I think they said it was something like 250 feet, coming in. I could look *up* and see steeples. All of a sudden the intercoms were alive with laughter and joy. When we dropped the food, you could see the people picking up the food, putting it in wheelbarrows. I was glad I was an American."

Waist gunner Maynard Stewart of the 95th remembered: "The missions weren't dangerous; it was mostly entertaining. We flew practically tree top level. Holland was all flooded. The Germans had broken the dikes." Some parcels fell in the water in low areas. "I recall seeing German troops coming out of their barracks and raising their rifles, and firing at us. But we never got any holes in our airplane from that. I'm not sure all of them got the message."[9]

The Dutch people were overjoyed. A. J. Bus was a thirteen-year-old girl in Heemstede, Holland, at the time. She remembers the terrible, desperate winter, which she calls the Hunger Winter. Her mother was pregnant, and her father and eldest brother were covered with ulcers from malnutrition. They shared what little food they had. One day, "we heard heavy aircraft engines. Suddenly we saw great American bombers. They flew very low from the west to the east." She watched as items began to fall from the bombers. At first, she thought they were bombs and then paratroopers, but suddenly she realized, "They are dropping food! The Americans are bringing food!" She walked to the nearest distribution point, "a tall, skinny and pale-looking child in an old overcoat," shod in wooden shoes and with a pillowcase under her arm. "I will not forget the food drops as long as I live. These men saved my life. I am still grateful to these young men who saved us at the last moment."[10]

Despite the best efforts of the airmen and personnel on the ground, the heavy parcels still hit people on the ground. Near Terbregge, bags of food began raining down on a group of onlookers. Bus remembers:

> Within seconds people were lying on the ground, groaning in pain. I was one of the first to be hit. I fell down, and although I tried desperately, I could not get up anymore. I was completely paralyzed.
>
> Then other aircraft, possibly confused by the first one, began dropping their food. German soldiers rushed towards us to chase us away. A very young German soldier stayed with me and when the drops started again he covered me with his own body. At that instant he was terribly hit himself. I too received a tremendous blow against my right shoulder and fell unconscious. When I came to, the poor German was laying over me dead. I was taken away by ambulance and the German was laid down on the grass.

Ten days later, Bus regained full use of her extremities. "I asked everywhere about the German soldier. I would have liked to inform his relatives what he did for me, but I never have been able to find them. Later they told me that ten other people had been killed."[11]

Togglier Marvin Markus remembers that lead planes would drop bags of flour. "The burst flour bags were on purpose as this made a good target for sight from above. Most fun on these trips was each plane was armed with chocolate candy and we were allowed to drop those by hand after the main food was dropped. We would make one last pass down the main part of town and drop candy bars and you could see kids like little ants running every direction to pick up the candy."[12]

Everywhere, people were looking up, waving, laughing. As crews flew across the flat Dutch landscape, they noticed a tremendous field of tulips in full bloom. In one section of the field, where the tulips had been removed, the empty space spelled out the words "Thanks, Yanks."

Many a bomber pilot had yearned to fly fighter planes at low altitudes. Now, the "bus drivers" of the air war had their chance. They buzzed German troops until their superiors issued an order to desist immediately. Planes returned to base trailing telephone lines and tree branches. Pilot Harold "Pappy" Dulle remembers that on May 1, after his crew had completed their food drop, "the intercom burst into life with the voice of one of the crew, 'Lieutenant, you missed the chimney to starboard by three feet and the ball turret gunner wants to know what to do about the mud on his windshield!'"[13]

On May 7, 1945, the German army officially surrendered at Reims. On May 8, the German army surrendered in Berlin as 145 RAF Lancasters dropped the last 344.5 tons of food on Holland. Operation Manna and the war were over. But one 95th crew would have the sad distinction of being the last American bomber downed in Europe in World War II.

On May 8, pilot Lionel N. Sceurman, flying unnamed Fort 44-8640, took off along with thirty-nine other 95th Forts and headed toward a food drop at Utrecht, Holland. It was a short mission, only 322 nautical miles round-trip and two and a half hours' total flying time. The crew was upbeat as the plane droned toward Holland. In addition to Sceurman, a veteran of fourteen combat missions, those listed as being on the plane that day were 2nd Lt. James R. Schwartz, copilot; Staff Sgt. David Condon, togglier; First Lt. Russell H. Cook Jr. navigator; Staff Sgt. Gano H. McPherson, radio operator; Staff Sgt. Norbert I. Kuper, armorer/gunner; Staff Sgt. John R. Keller, ball turret gunner; and Staff Sgt. William R. Lankford, tail gunner.

Also on board the plane that day were members of the base's photo section: Staff Sgt. Edward H. Bubolz, Technical Sgt. Robert W. Korber; Staff Sgt. Gerald Lane, Sgt. Joseph R. Repiscack, and PFC George L. Waltari.

After an uneventful flight to Holland, the 95th dropped its food and then decided to do a little sightseeing. "We proceeded across other areas of Holland, the tulip fields, the dikes, canals and windmills, the rusting hulls of half-sunken ships in Rotterdam Harbor," remembers copilot Tony Braidic, flying in a different aircraft. "We also saw crowds of people looking up and waving to us from the town square in Amsterdam."[14] After they'd had a chance to enjoy the scenery, navigator Cook set a course for Horham. The Sceurman crew was in excellent spirits, singing and clapping to the tune "Deep in the Heart of Texas."

As Sceurman flew over the Dutch coast, he unwittingly flew directly over a flak battery at Ymuiden. In violation of the truce, the German battery opened up, and a 20mm shell hit the number 2 engine, setting it on fire. Lieutenant Sceurman put the plane into a steep dive, trying to extinguish the fire. When this maneuver failed, and at only five hundred feet, he gave the order to bail out.

According to an unpublished account by navigator Russell Cook's relative William Cook: "Navigator Cook, Gunner Cooper, and passenger Korber all bailed out of the forward escape hatch. Co-pilot Schwarz and Togglier Condon went out the left side of the bomb bay. Sceurman escaped through the left sliding window but drowned before he could be rescued. Cook was picked up alive by a British Air Sea Rescue Walrus but died before the plane reached base. Condon was picked up by an American PBY Catalina after swimming in the cold water for thirty minutes. Korber and Kuper's bodies were also recovered, and Keller's body washed ashore later. The additional men on board the plane—McPherson, Langford and the four men from the Photographic section—were never found and are presumed to still be in the wreckage of the ship at the bottom of the North Sea about four miles from the English coast."[15]

In *B-17s Over Berlin*, Tony Braidic writes:

As we walked from the flight line to the 334th Squadron area we were told by some of the other crews that Lt. Sceurman's B-17 had gone down on the return flight. That night at the Base Hospital we were overjoyed to discover that two crewmen had survived. But in another area of the hospital were the four bodies which had been recovered from the sea, "Spider" Sceurman, Russ Cook, Norbert Kuper, and one of the five passengers from the Photographic Section who had gone along for the ride. Another body was recovered later but the other five were never found. I attended the funeral services and burial of my former crewmembers at the American Military Cemetery near Cambridge as did other members of the 95th Group, including several representatives from the photo section.

B-17G 48640, 334th Squadron, 95th Bomb Group, was the last 8th Air Force B-17 to go down during the war in Europe.[16]

Between April 29 and May 8, American and British forces dropped more than 11,000 tons of food to the starving people of western Holland. The RAF dropped 7,029.9 tons from 3,181 RAF aircraft—mostly Lancaster heavy bombers—and the Americans dropped 4,155.8 tons from 2,210 American planes, which were mostly B-17s. The total number of aircrew involved was 5,391 personnel, of which 2,210 were Americans. The 95th Bomb Group alone dropped roughly 400 tons.

In all, the 95th Bomb Group flew six Manna/Chowhound missions between May 1 and May 7, the final day of the war in Europe. The missions were successful and uneventful, with no accidents or casualties until 44-8640 went down on the final mission.

In 1985, forty years after Operation Manna/Chowhound, 95th navigator Ellis Scripture returned to Holland. "The Dutch people remembered so vividly after forty years!" he enthused. "Many hours were graciously bestowed upon the representatives of the six nations representing the R.A.F. and the Eighth Air Force that flew the food-drop missions. That visit to Holland will be a highlight in the lives of all the veterans and their wives for all time. None of us privileged to be present had ever seen such a display of genuine emotion and great national pride as we witnessed during that memorable week."[17]

Scripture and Grif Mumford flew their final mission of the war on the May 4 Chowhound mission. They were the only two men left of the original flying cadre who had arrived at Alconbury in the spring of 1943. "For both of us, it was the most rewarding and satisfying way in which to end a WWII flying career that spanned almost two years of combat," remembered Scripture. "It was certainly a wonderful feeling to do something constructive instead of destructive. It was doubly rewarding, forty years later, to personally witness the emotional thanksgiving of an entire nation."[18]

After the Chowhound missions were over, the 95th Bomb Group continued to fly various peaceful missions. Navigator Delmar Jonas recalls: "After the war ended we still had a lot of aviation gasoline coming in and we had to use it up. So we flew some Cook's Tour flights."[19] These flights, named for the famous British travel agency, were intended to allow some of the ground personnel who had kept the heavy bombers flying for the past two years a chance to see what their flying comrades had been doing over the continent and, in particular, in the Ruhr Valley region. Also referred to as Trolley Runs, Roger Freeman wrote, "10,000 men enjoyed these sightseeing tours. The ruins of factories, bridges and marshaling yards evoked amazement amongst men who had led a hectic but safe war at English airfields."[20] The first Cook's Tour mission was flown May 10, 1945, and involved forty-two B-17s from the 95th BG. Another forty-two planes made the tour the next day.

The flights of May 16, 19, and 25 were perhaps some of the most satisfying for the 95th aircrews. On these revival missions they flew to various stops in Europe and took repatriated POWs and DPs from Austria to France. Twenty aircraft participated in the first run, eleven on the second, and thirty-two on the last mission. According to Freeman, "Each B-17, with a five-man crew, had up to forty passengers crammed in on each flight, twenty of them often traveling on timber platforms stretched across the bomb bay. There were no complaints—the 8,000 US and 1,500 British POWs were only too pleased to find such a quick means of leaving their final domicile."[21]

The Forts roared in for landings at one-minute intervals, and the POWs packed into each plane while the propellers continued to spin. Navigator Jonas flew on one of these missions. He recalled, "We went to Linz, Austria, to pick up displaced persons from a concentration camp. We made two trips to pick up prisoners. On the first trip, our plane held thirty extra people and had to keep below ten thousand feet due to oxygen. We flew from Austria to France, zig-zagging through the mountains all the way. On the second trip, we flew to Merville with thirty men, five women and three newborns."[22]

As the freed POWs flew at low altitude over destroyed German cities, one of them, Oscar Richard, turned to the man next to him and motioned at the runs below. "That could be us. That could be America. Nobody said we had to win this war."[23]

28   Coming Home

More than six hundred men who flew with the 95th Bomb Group did not live to see a joyous homecoming. While a small number of their now elderly crewmates are still alive, these six hundred men will always be young and smiling, their eyes forever gazing expectantly toward the future and the life they wanted "after the war" that was snatched from them.

In the winter of 1944, a young 388th Bomb Group tail gunner named Eugene Carson walked the crescent rows of lonely graves at the American Cemetery in Cambridge. Carson was preparing to return to the States, but first he wanted to visit his buddy, bombardier Michael J. Chaklos, killed on a mission in January 1944. "As I walked among the markers I silently cried my heart out," he remembers.[1]

Armorer/gunner Marvin Casaday of the 95th recalls laying the American Historical Wreath at Madingley on Memorial Day 1999. Even after more than fifty years, Casaday admitted, "I could not fulfill an interview afterwards. I was absolutely sobbing." The bond of an aircrew was tight. Many surviving crewmen made it a point to visit the families of their dead comrades after the war. Those who survived would be haunted ever after by the ghosts of their brothers who hadn't been so fortunate.

For the survivors, with the war in Europe over, the main question on most airmen's minds in 1945 was redeployment. Three Eighth Air Force Mustang fighter groups and nine Fortress bomb groups would become part of the occupation forces in Germany or be retained in Europe for other duties. The rest were destined for combat in the Pacific after training in the States.[2]

In a seven-week period beginning the third week in May 1945, 2,118 heavy bombers made return flights from England to the United States while carrying 41,500 non-crewmen, or approximately 20 per aircraft. While Lionel Sceurman's Fort was the last one lost at the end of the war, three Fortresses returning crews to the States crashed after V-E Day, killing an additional 49 men. By July 16 the U.S. Eighth Air Force had a new headquarters on the Japanese island of Okinawa.

Many flight crews had already returned to the States, beginning in early 1943. The high losses of early bomber crews meant that those men who had completed tours represented a mere trickle compared to those sent to Europe. Owing to the high loss rate in 1943 and early 1944, many of the early cadre were either dead or POWs. In all, the group had lost 554 men killed in action, 162 wounded in action, 20 killed in service, 64 interned in neutral countries, and 805 prisoners of war.[3] Leonard Herman, of the original cadre, once figured the number of original flight crewmen who completed twenty-five missions to be under twenty-five.[4]

Immediately after their return, flight crewmen who had not completed their enlistments were put to work on other jobs. Johnny Johnson's surviving *Brass Rail* crew was no exception. Pilot Kit Carson became a flight instructor, Randall Cowan became a gunnery instructor, and tail gunner Don Crossley, the Eighth Air Force's top aerial gunner, toured as a war hero, as did bombardier Leonard Herman. After a short stint training bombardiers in Galveston, Texas, Herman returned to Europe and flew a second tour with the Ninth Air Force, flying in A-26s and B-26s until the final days of the war.

Pilot John Walter finished his tour in March 1945 after flying thirty-five combat missions. As with Herman's original crew, not all of Walter's made it back to the States. Over Merseburg on their first combat mission, a close burst of flak flung jagged shrapnel through the cockpit. One piece severed the carotid artery of Walter's good friend, copilot Tom Sevald. By the time Walter landed the plane back in Horham, Sevald had bled to death.[5] On November 30, 1944, Walter lost his navigator, Nelson Kurz, when Kurz's oxygen hose came loose without his knowledge at thirty thousand feet over

Merseburg. After Walter poured on the coals and returned to base, the crew discovered Nelson was dead. Walter and his mates examined Nelson's log. "It was apparent that for some distance before the I.P., his handwriting began to deteriorate . . . until it trailed off into just a wavy line and then stopped," remembers Walter. Kurz had been so busy plotting the course and looking for fighters that he had neglected to check the oxygen regulator during oxygen checks, and "for the second time in a little over two months, we made the very sad journey to the American Military Cemetery at Cambridge."[6]

Once a crew had completed its missions, the men found that there was very little to do but sit around, go to London, and wonder when they would be going home. Walter remembers hoping his return would be on a luxury liner, but he was sadly disappointed when assigned to a troop ship, crammed three high in hammocks, and rationed to only two meals a day.

The troop ship was part of a convoy with destroyer escorts. "The seas had not yet been cleared of all enemy submarines. We had numerous discussions during the days about how really shitty it would be for us to have survived the Luftwaffe pilots and the German Army antiaircraft gunners 35 times, only to 'buy the farm' at the hands of the German Navy," says Walter.

While en route, the ship's captain informed passengers that President Roosevelt had passed away and Harry Truman was now president. Before docking in New York, Walter remembers that the passengers were warned not to try to smuggle war zone contraband into the United States. The men dutifully had turned over their hard-earned booty only to find that there was no inspection. "If it would have fit in our bags, we could have brought back a B-17 with nary a question or comment," says Walter. Walter later trained as a C-54 pilot, but then he decided to get out of the service and went to college on the GI Bill.[7]

Some 95th airmen were sent home after suffering serious war injuries. One of these men was bombardier Maurice Rockett. On April 29, 1944, Rockett had filled in as bombardier on "an untrained, undisciplined crew who engaged in too much intercom chatter . . . when fighters were in the vicinity, and who shot at bandits when out of range, wasting ammunition. It was a long bomb run over Berlin," he remembers. Sixty-three bombers and thirteen fighters were shot down in the fifth heaviest loss that the Eighth had suffered. One blast shot red-hot flak through the Plexiglas window. "A metal fragment grazed my right eye, spraying glass fragments into my face and both eyes. The percussion turned me halfway around, and the impact felt like a baseball bat had hit my head." He lay down on the floor, grasping his parachute in case he had to bail out, while the navigator wrapped bandages over his eyes.

Rockett's eye injuries were too serious to be treated at the base hospital. He was sent to a field hospital staffed with doctors and nurses from Duke University. "They cut a flap from the upper section of my right eyeball," he told me, "bringing it down over the center and stitched it in place. I recall the excess sutures hitting my face during the operation. Awake all of the time, I was asked to make eye movements requested by the surgeon. I was put in bed with my head between two towel-covered cinder blocks. This was my position for the next several days. Nobody told me anything. There was a possibility that I was blind. When they finally took the bandages off, I could see light out of my left eye. My spirits soared. Oh happy day!

"Life in the ward was no picnic. Many patients moaned, screamed, or cried during the night. I had only one visitor from the 95th, my friendly navigator. Also, they did not want me back on the base as one of the walking wounded. This would not go over well with combatants who already had enough on their minds. I understood their thinking.

"My hospital received many infantrymen wounded in the Normandy invasion. Most of them had on their combat clothing, salt-water wet, and partially sand covered from the beach areas.

"I flew home from Prestwick, Scotland, on July 3, routing to Iceland, Newfoundland, and finally landing at Mitchell Field [on] July 4. I was the only ambulatory passenger. Most were stretcher cases from Normandy. After a short stay in a New York hospital, it was off to Valley Forge Hospital in Phoenixville, PA. Here they specialized in eye cases, plastic surgery, and had a small psychiatric ward.

"Most of the serious cases did not like to be seen out in public," remembers Rockett. "They only wanted to be around vets who understood their problem. Among the patients was every conceivable type of wound. Both airmen and tank crews suffered terrible burns. Others had no ears, nose, arms, legs, or combinations thereof. The really bad cases were housed in separate rooms out of sight. Conceivably, many became whole again and, if they did, it was a long, tortuous road to recovery.

"My next move, in December, was to the Biltmore Resort in Coral Gables, Florida. I drove down to Florida with an infantry officer from Iowa. His car was a regular fortress, with a bazooka gun, rifle, and pistol. He delighted in firing at passing mailboxes. We were ready for anything, including World War Three."

In Florida, Rockett was retired for physical disability. "I was sworn in as an Aviation Cadet on April 29, 1942, ending my career April 29, 1944, with five months of combat, nineteen months of training, and twelve months of recovery." Rockett lost an eye and obliged the author's children by taking out the prosthetic eyeball when he visited some years ago.

Ground officer Richard Frank Knox went home shortly after V-E Day. Because he was a technical officer with specific skills, Knox and others who had been communications officers, engineering officers, and armament officers were sent to the States posthaste in order to be retrained to go to the Pacific. Upon their arrival in the States, they were put on a train headed west, and within three days they arrived at Fort Lewis in western Washington.

From there, Knox was sent to Santa Ana Army Air Base in California. It was summer 1945. He recalled, "We didn't have anything to do except go to Bing Crosby's race track or take a bus tour to see the movie stars' homes in Hollywood. It was getting monotonous. Finally I got orders to report to Colorado Springs, Colorado, Second Air Force Headquarters. I shipped out of Los Angeles one evening, and the next morning the train pulled into Albuquerque, New Mexico. It was quite evident that there [was] a big party going on, and . . . we learned that the war with Japan was over. I think the train crews didn't want to let us know, or their train would have been in shambles."[8]

Some ground personnel stayed in Horham to the very end. Adam Hinojos of the 457th Sub Depot was one of the last to leave England. "On April 15, 1945, our title changed to the 859th Engineering Squadron, to prepare us for more duties in the Pacific," he remembers. "On July 15, 1945, the 95th Bomb Group and its units were ordered to return to the United States. Everyone received a thirty-day leave, and at the end of thirty days, they were to return to their base station for duties over in the Pacific. But the war ended before thirty days' leave was up."

Hinojos transferred to the 100th Bomb Group in order to extend his stay in England. Assigned to the Quartermaster Squadron, his job was to travel around and close up all the American bases, disposing of all the equipment and supplies so that the bases could turned back over to England. His extended stay in England gave Hinojos time to marry his Scottish girlfriend, Annie, on September 18, 1945.[9]

Much of the food that was left at the bases was trucked to neighboring villages and dispensed to the locals. By the time the Americans had pulled out completely, the bases were mere shells. So they would remain for many years.

29   The Legacy Lives On

It must have seemed eerily quiet in Horham in the weeks after the Americans left. The base was a ghost town. Doors banged open and shut on hinges already beginning to rust in the East Anglian rain. Farmers moved tractors and other farm equipment into the abandoned air corps buildings. Lush green grass sprung up through cracks in the three mighty runways. Poppies danced on a cool breeze beside the hardstands where aircrews had waited for mission calls.

The 95th Bomb Group's beautiful B-17 Flying Fortresses—so lovingly named, so painstakingly decorated with nose art, and so good at bringing their crews home despite heavy damage—had all been flown home to the States and ended up with 150,000 other aircraft in storage facilities run by the Reconstruction Finance Corporation. By early 1946, Uncle Sam had sold 34,000 flyable aircraft as surplus and scrapped 29,000 more. At least a hundred brand-new B-32 bombers, which cost $800,000 to build, were flown directly from the assembly line to the boneyard at Kingman, Arizona. Today's warbird enthusiasts would have a field day if only they could go back to the immediate postwar years. A P-38 Lightning sold for a mere $1,250. A P-51 Mustang would set you back $3,500. The B-17, which had cost $238,000 to build, could be purchased for $13,750, though a Boy Scout troop bought one for $350. A community wishing to have one for a war memorial could often obtain one for free.[1]

American airmen tried to pick up their lives where they'd left them. They flooded onto college campuses, taking advantage of the GI Bill. They found wives and jobs and chased the American dream, which in the late 1940s seemed for the first time to be within the average American's reach. They moved their young families into starter homes, bought a family car, and perhaps splurged on a television set. World War II veterans were so common in the immediate postwar years that other than asking the cursory questions about which branch one served in and where, the topic of the war didn't come up often.

Ball turret gunner Frank Coleman told the author in 2002: "We had to go fight a terrible war, and then we came home and went back to school, and turned out, for the most part, to be pretty reasonable and success- ful people."[2] Crews that had bonded like brothers now relied on chance meetings and Christmas cards. With the postwar mobility of the American population, it was easy to lose touch.

Most had a copy of the group yearbook, *Contrails*, stashed in a bookshelf or box. *Contrails* had been the brainchild of Special Services officer Capt. Charles Brickley. Brickley had assembled a staff of photographers, artists, and writers in England to write the book, but the project was not complete when the men packed up and moved out of Horham in August 1945. Capt. David Henderson of the group's Photographic Section had been involved with the project in England. After his discharge in early 1946, he retrieved the boxes and finished the project with the support and cooperation of the Indianapolis Engraving Company and the A. H. Pugh Printing Company of Cincinnati. Eventually, he had printed three thousand copies.

Henderson tried to track down all living members of the 95th, a diffi- cult task given incomplete and outdated records. Family members of those 95th crewmen who had been killed in the war received a complimentary copy, and in cases where he could not track down a family with certainty, he donated a copy to the nearest public library.

Time passed, filled with jobs, mortgages, families, Little League base- ball games. The copies of *Contrails* came down off the shelf more and more rarely. For many men, remembering was painful. Like a fresh wound, it was better to let the memories scab over and heal for a while. It wasn't until years later that the veterans—many retired, their children grown, and their finances secure—began trickling back to Horham and seeking each other out again, compelled by an inner voice they themselves didn't completely understand.

Englishman Alan Johnson remembers attending a 95th Bomb Group reunion in the United States years ago. "There was a very small, quiet man who was always sitting off by himself," he remembers. "He didn't talk to the other people there. So I went up and sat down with him and asked him about his experience at Horham. He had a book, and he opened it. It turned automatically to a certain page. The page was scuffed and dirty, as if he'd looked at it every day for years. The rest of the pages in the book looked unread.

"'What's the picture of?' I asked him.

"'It's a photo of my plane,' the man said. 'I was a pilot in the 95th.'

"I looked at the photo. Half the tail plane had been shot off and the rest of the plane was heavily damaged.

"'Have you been back to Horham?' I asked.

"'I did go back a few years ago,' the man said. 'I took the train into Diss, and then I walked to Horham. By the time I got there, it was raining hard and no one was in the streets. I didn't know anyone and I couldn't remember how to get to the base, so I just walked back to Diss, got on the train, and went home.'"

Another 95th "Bomber Boy" who made an early return to Horham was group navigator Willard Brown. On a return trip to Europe in 1947 with his wife, he visited the old base at Horham. Then Brown traveled to Germany, rented a car, and found the farmhouse where he had hidden after being shot down. The same German farmer who had helped Brown during the war was working in the field nearby when Brown rolled up in his Pontiac. It was a memorable reunion.

Radio operator Ken Hutcherson returned to the ruins of his old base on August 23, 1972. "Everyone seemed to be on summer holiday and the train from London was packed," he recalled. "We finally managed to get seats in a compartment not unlike the ones all of us remember vaguely, with the webbing overhead for packages and luggage. It was a nice ride to Diss. The train traveled at a much greater speed than in 1943 and 1944 when it seemed to gasp for breath sometimes.

"We arrived at Diss at 10:30 a.m. under a beautiful summer sun. I asked a taxi about taking us to the old American air base at Horham. The driver did not know exactly where the base was and stopped at several farms to ask directions. After traveling the 8 miles to Horham, we pulled onto a hardstand at the edge of a wheat field. It was hard for me to comprehend because I was unable to get my bearings at first. There was a farmer across the road on a combine harvesting his wheat. He stopped it and came over to assist us and everything started to fall into place.

"One of the headquarters buildings was still there and the farmer took us through the briars and underbrush to get inside. You would find it hard to believe but there were still pin-up pictures pasted on the wall from *Yank* magazine and also a 'Sad Sack' cartoon stenciled on one wall. Over one doorway was stenciled 'Through These Doors Pass the Best Damn Flyers in the World.' Our barracks from the 335th was a crumbled mass of corrugated rusty steel. We couldn't get back there because of the crops and no roads but I took a picture of it from a distance. The control tower crumbled last year but the main runway is still there. We drove down the runway, which is still used for crop dusting planes. We took pictures there and also at the crossroads with the signs—Horham, Diss, Ipswich, Norwich, and Eye.

"We arrived back at the train station in Diss two hours later. The taxi driver had stayed with us all that time and did not want to accept a tip. It was a great experience that I will never forget."

Navigator Ellis Scripture writes: "It was not until 1974, at an early meeting of the Eighth Air Force Historical Society, that men of the 95th met to organize the 95th Bomb Group (H) Association. Since that date, veterans have met regularly in reunion; a relatively few copies of *Contrails* again surfaced from attics and other storage places and became cherished reminders of our time together in a great and worthy endeavor."[3]

In 1990, a new edition of *Contrails* was planned called the *Contrails II* Project. The group of men produced a new book containing all the content of the original yearbook, plus new sections. A panel of forty oversaw *Contrails II*'s production. The association's president at the time, William M. "Dub" Vandegriff, ushered the project through to completion. In 2003, the new, limited edition was published.

Other efforts to preserve the 95th BG's history began in the 1980s with the initiation of a new book project aimed at collecting and printing an oral history of the group. Coordinated by 95th members Leonard Herman and Ellis Scripture, it had a simple mission: "To tell the story of a collection of young American civilians who were suddenly thrown together amidst the maelstrom of a global war that took place nearly fifty years ago; how they rapidly adjusted to service life, how they lived, how they fought, how they died."

Herman acted as a clearinghouse for veterans' stories; his secretary transcribed hundreds of veterans' audiotapes and written accounts. The 95th's William "Ed" Charles contributed his massive collection of photographs. Scripture and Dave McKnight were heavily involved in the project. A young English historian named Ian Hawkins edited and compiled the final work, which was released in 1987 under the title *Courage, Honor, Victory* by a small publisher in Winston-Salem, North Carolina. The book was such a critical success that the major publisher Brassey's (now Potomac Books) purchased the rights and republished it in 1990 as *B-17s Over Berlin: Personal Stories from the 95th Bomb Group (H)* in 1990.

Meanwhile, on September 19, 1981, 95th Bomb Group veterans assembled in Horham and attended services at the Church of St. Mary. Afterward, the white-haired contingent crossed the narrow main street to a plot on the village green. After a short introductory speech a colonel from the nearby American air base at Bentwaters and another speech by an attaché from the American Embassy, a marble memorial in the distinctive swooping shape of a B-17 Flying Fortress's tail was unveiled. The tail rests on a marble plinth and its bronze plaque reads:

In memory of the men of the
95th Bombardment Group who
served at Horham Airfield
and to those who gave their
lives in the cause of freedom,
1943–1945
* * *
334th, 335th, 336th and 412th Bomb
Squadrons and Supporting Units.
Headquarters, 13th Combat Bomb
Wing, United States 8th Air Force
* * *
Dedicated 19th Sept. 1981.

At the ceremony, 95th Bomb Group (H) Association president Art Frankel praised the locals at Horham who supported the project. He acknowledged, "Without the seeds sown several years ago by our English friends, this truly beautiful memorial to our men would not be here today."[4]

British historian Roger Freeman then gave a speech:

> It wasn't long [after the group's arrival] before the people of Horham, Denham, Stradbroke, and the surrounding district began . . . to refer to the young Americans as "our boys." To all those men, however short a time they spent here, this little spot in England will always mean something. And for the locals? They have realized now that when this airfield was built in their village, it was the most momentous thing that ever happened to this ancient village and probably ever will happen to it. They realize that it is a part of their history just as it is part of the history of the men who flew from Horham Airfield years and years ago.[5]

After the dedication, the parish priest Reverend David Streeter gave the vets—including Dave McKnight, Art Frankel, Ed Charles, Al Brown, Roland "Lefty" Nairn, and others—a tour of the church. Lefty Nairn, in particular, was struck by the centuries-old history of the village, going all the way back to Saxon times; the church itself is mentioned in the 1086 Domesday Book. Streeter showed the veterans the ring of eight bells in St. Mary's tower. They were the oldest ring of eight bells in the world and had been cast between 1568 and 1673. A bell-ringing society at Horham had existed in the eighteenth century, and ancient graffiti on the tower arch reminds ringers to reward the sexton, who maintained the ropes. When Nairn asked if the bells still ring, the reverend told him, "No, unfortunately. The bells are in poor repair and have not rung since before World War One." Then, Streeter remembers, "the next minute he had pledged they would be rung again and that he would make sure the money was raised."

Nairn and Ellis Scripture started a drive the following year, sending out a letter to all living members of the 95th Bomb Group. Ellis Scripture wrote in the original appeal:

When we flew from Horham from 1943 to 1945, we were all too busy to think much about the history of the church tower we saw in the distance. But see it we did. For each crewman it was there to send us on the mission with the best wishes of each person in Horham. And it was there as our first sight of the Horham landscape when we returned. The Parish Church of St. Mary was always in sight as the many ground crewmen and support personnel worked diligently to attend the many important duties necessary for successful flight operations. Little did we realize that brave people have been worshipping on this site at least 803 years! Now that we're older and can reflect upon our earlier years, we realize how close are our ties to the good people of Horham. We also realize that we must seize this present opportunity to leave a lasting memorial to all who served in the 95th Bomb Group, one that may be heard for several hundred more years as future generations listen to the Bells of St. Mary's, Horham, and remember those who served and lived to become a part of the history of Horham.

The 95th Veteran Members who attended the 1988 reunion at Ohio unanimously and enthusiastically accepted the proposal to help rebuild and retune the eight bells. The total cost was estimated at $34,000. The 95th committed to raising $20,000 of that amount.[6]

Reverend Streeter added his appeal: "Since the war it has become our hope and prayer that a miracle could happen, that money could be made available to let the Bells of St. Mary's ring again. Your willingness to undertake a fund-raising campaign—combined with our own continuing efforts—most certainly make this dream a closer reality. The completion of this project will be another long-lasting statement of the friendship between our two nations."[7]

On May 15, 1992, the *Diss Express* reported: "Ex-US servicemen from the 95th Bomb Group, stationed at Horham in World War Two, have repaid villagers' friendship with nearly £20,000 to restore their church bells which last rung in 1911. Seventy-four veterans and their families returned last week for a special dedication service at St. Mary's Church to hear the oldest set of eight bells in the world ring again due to their generosity."[8]

When Lefty Nairn passed away, he was mourned not only by family and friends in the States but also by the residents of East Anglia. A long article in the *East Anglian Daily Times* reported: "A special peal is to be rung on the bells of the village church following the death of a former U.S. airman who spearheaded fundraising for their restoration."[9]

British friends in Suffolk also undertook similar efforts to rebuild the old base's buildings. The Red Feather Club was lovingly restored and is the main stop for returning 95th airmen. Each year, though, the number of veterans returning to Horham dwindles. In 2008, Brad Petrella, who as a young enlisted man had served as a bartender in the Red Feather Club, returned to find it restored and renamed Brad's Bar in his honor. He poured a few beers, his eyes sparkling as he was taken back over sixty years. Petrella passed away less than a year after his visit.

Supporters of the 95th are not limited to the United States and Great Britain, either. Veterans and their families have been in touch with people whose paths crossed those of the 95th vets in one way or another during or after the war. They have tracked down those who rescued them after they were shot down or those who witnessed the final moments of a loved one.

Rick Mangan's uncle, Danny Mangan, was killed in Belgium on June 24, 1944. The twenty-year-old pilot died parachuting from a crippled Fortress over the village of Haaltert.[10]

On June 22, 2004, sixty years after his uncle's death, Rick Mangan made the same jump in memory of his uncle. The local Belgians turned out to watch, "dressed in uniforms from a bygone age, a time never forgotten in this village," writes Mangan. "I discovered that I only had one piece of a giant puzzle . . . I learned that the Underground had been instrumental in the safety of four of the crew members, and the stories of their bravery still makes the hair stand up on the back of my neck. . . . I met a man named Albert Rapaille, who . . . as a young teenager was taken from his village for resistance involvement, along with thirteen others. He was the only one to return. He told me: 'Thank the American people for liberating my country. . . . Thank them and tell them we remember.'"[11]

In 2007, the 95th Bomb Group Foundation approached this author with the daunting task of writing a comprehensive unit history that covered every aspect of the 95th Bomb Group's life, from early in the war through the present day. Thanks to the farsightedness of the group's officers, this history will be published at a time when the answers to most questions are only a phone call or an e-mail away. Veterans are still with us.

Each year, a dwindling number of 95th Bomb Group veterans show up at the annual reunion somewhere in the United States. Some are stooped, others in wheelchairs, but all are full of excitement and joy at seeing their comrades one more time. And at the end of each reunion, the names of those who have passed away since the previous year are read aloud. The missing man flag is presented and placed in a seat of honor. This flag represents all the men of the 95th who have left formation in the previous year.

The stories become more poignant at each reunion. In 2008 a small cardboard box containing a trumpet mouthpiece and other personal effects was discovered at a Horham home; it was turned over to James Mutton, who traced its contents to former 95th BG member DeWayne Willis Long, who had played trumpet while in England during the war with a local dance band named the Guyford Dance Band. Mutton found that Mr. Long was alive and living near the 2008 reunion site in Tucson. It was the first time Long had been in touch with the 95th since the war. Emaciated, weak, and in poor health, he was wheeled into the general assembly room at the reunion to a standing ovation, and was deeply touched when Mutton gave him back his old trumpet mouthpiece. For one hour, DeWayne Willis Long was a young man in the 95th again. Two weeks later, he passed away.

Also each year, a small group of veterans makes the long journey to Horham on the 95th Museum's Open Day and watch one of the few flying B-17s left in the world conduct a flyover. They know that there will always be welcoming British friends to give them a bed, drive them around, albeit on the "wrong side of the road," and listen to their stories. If they visit the Church of St. Mary on a day when the bells are not ringing, they can still look across the street at the swoop-tailed monument on the village green and read the welcome of Horham in the quotation by Charles Dickens on a plaque on the church door: "If I know anything of my countrymen . . . the English heart is stirred by the fluttering of the Stars and Stripes as it is stirred by no other flag except its own."

In a few short years there will be no veterans left. However, the 95th had made the transition from a veteran's group into a legacy group, composed primarily of descendants and friends. The reunions often ring with the laughter of grandchildren and great-grandchildren. The future looks bright for the Big Square B. The 95th Bomb Group will continue to fly for a long, long time.

Glossary

A-2. A standard issue leather jacket worn by air corps personnel.

abort. A prisoner of war's nickname for the communal latrine.

AIS. An early experimental radar system that could successfully "read" terrain through clouds by bouncing radio waves off the ground.

anoxia. Oxygen deprivation. At altitudes above ten thousand feet, air crewmen breathed supplemental oxygen.

Aphrodite. A secret program to fly unmanned drone aircraft into rocket sites on the French coast. The program was a failure and is best known for having claimed the life of Joseph P. Kennedy Jr. on August 12, 1944.

appel. Roll call.

astrodome. A small Plexiglas bubble in the top of the plane's nose through which the navigator could shoot fixes of the stars.

B-17C. An early version of the B-17, discontinued because of its limited range and bomb load.

B-17E. An early version of the B-17, with a longer range and heavier bomb load than the B-17C. American aircrews first flew it in combat in August 1942.

B-17F. Engineered to reflect the needs of crews in combat, this model carried more fuel and had other improvements.

B-17G. A later model B-17 introduced during the war and most recognizable because of its added Bendix chin turret.

ball turret gunner. A noncommissioned officer who was in charge of defending the underside of the aircraft and was suspended in a Sperry ball turret underneath the aircraft's belly.

belly tank. An additional gas tank that increased the aircraft's range.

Big Week. An attempt by U.S. Eighth and Fifteenth Air Forces to destroy the German aircraft industry in attacks that lasted six days, beginning February 20, 1944.

Black Thursday. Nickname for October 14, 1943, when sixty heavy bombers were destroyed during the Allied raid on Schweinfurt, Germany.

Black Week. The week of October 8–14, 1943, so called because of the heavy losses on missions to Bremen, Munster, Marienburg, and Schweinfurt.

bomb bay. The section of the airplane where the bombs are hung and from which the bombs are dropped.

bomb group. A functional unit of an air force, made up of four squadrons, each with twelve aircraft. The group was the largest functional unit that could operate out of one base, according to air corps leadership, and included all flying and support personnel. During the war, the 95th Bomb Group had more than eight thousand men serving in it, though not all at one time.

bombardier. Officer in charge of dropping the bombs on the target.

Bovingdon. The Replacement Depot for crews arriving in England for assignment.

chaff. Strips of aluminum foil dropped from airplanes to confuse enemy radar.

charge of quarters. Individual in charge of getting men from their quarters to their assignments.

chin turret. Another name for the Bendix turret on the B-17G that protected the front of the aircraft from attack.

Chowhound. American name for the food drop missions over Holland at the end of the war. *See* Manna.

Cigarette Camps. Three camps named after famous brands of cigarettes from the forties—Lucky Strike, Old Gold, and Chesterfield—that were set up for processing repatriated American prisoners of war.

combat box. A close formation flown by American bombers over Europe with aircraft in staggered high, medium, and low positions to maximize defensive firepower against enemy fighters.

combine. A group of POWs, usually roommates in a barrack, who joined together to share food and cooking and washing duties.

Comet Line. The twelve-hundred-mile Underground escape route in occupied Europe from Brussels to Gibraltar.

command pilot. The highest rating a pilot could attain, above pilot and senior pilot.

contrail. Short for condensation trails, contrails were formed by condensed vapor from aircraft engines at high altitude.

copilot. An officer trained as a pilot but flying as subordinate to the command pilot. Many copilots eventually became command pilots.

daylight precision bombing. American policy for bombing Europe that focused on attacking specific targets by day to minimize collateral damage.

Distinguished Flying Cross (DFC). Award for "heroism or extraordinary achievement while participating in aerial flight."

eighty-eights. The 88mm antiaircraft shells used by German defenses to fire flak at high-flying aircraft.

electric flight suits. Basically long underwear with wires running through it that heated up when the suit was plugged into a power source. Sometimes called bunny suits.

enlisted man. A member of the military below the level of officer. The flight engineer, radio operator, waist gunners, tail gunner, and ball turret gunner were all enlisted men. Because they were also noncommissioned officers, their rank prevented them from being used as labor if they became POWs. Most ground personnel on base were also enlisted men.

European theater of operations (ETO). The European theater was only one front in World War II. Other troops were sent to Southeast Asia, the Pacific, Alaska, and elsewhere.

evadee/evader. An airman who was able to escape from enemy territory.

ferret. A German guard in a prison camp whose job was to sneak around under the barracks and listen to conversations. Also called moles.

forty-and-eights. Standard-size European rail car, so named because it was designed to carry forty men or eight horses. They were often used to transport prisoners of war.

.50-caliber. Standard large-caliber shell used in most of the B-17s' defensive armaments.

fifty-mission cap. Also called a crusher, this hat was the standard-issue officer's cap. Most men took out the wire support in the top of the hat so that they could crush the wool cap down under their headphones while in flight. It was called a 50-mission cap or crusher because of its well-worn, battered, combat-proven look.

flak. Jagged shards of metal shot up at the airplanes, usually with 88mm guns.

flak helmet. A GI helmet with metal earflaps to cover the headset. Flight crews wore them in combat situations.

flak house. A home where men could go to rest if it was deemed the crew was under great stress. Also called flak farms or rest homes.

"flakked up." An expression that flight crews used to mean "suffering from combat fatigue and stress."

flight engineer. A noncommissioned officer with technical and mechanical training who took care of the airplane in the air. Most flight engineers also manned the top turret gun.

Flying Fortress. The nickname for the Boeing B-17, so named because of its heavy armament.

457th Sub Depot. The ground support group that both kept the 95th Bomb Group's planes and equipment repaired and flying and took care of other important jobs on the base at Horham.

Gee. First-generation radio navigation system developed by the British.

Geneva Convention. International rules for the care and treatment of prisoners of war.

goon. An unflattering Allied nickname for German guards in prisoner of war camps.

(H). When used after the Bomb Group number, the *H* denotes "heavy bomber." The heavy bombers were the B-17, B-24, and B-29.

H2S. First-generation air-to-ground radar system developed by the British.

H2X. U.S. version of the British H2S radar system. The H2X was code-named Mickey Mouse and later shortened to Mickey.

hangar queen. A bomber that has been so heavily damaged that it can only be used for parts.

hardstand. A concrete parking area for an aircraft.

initial point (IP). The beginning of the bomb run.

internee. An airman who landed in neutral Switzerland or Sweden and was kept there for the rest of the war. Internees were not considered prisoners of war and, in most cases, were treated well by their hosts.

interphone. The in-plane communications system.

KLIM. "Milk" spelled backward, a brand name of a powdered milk given to prisoners of war in their Red Cross parcels. Resourceful POWs used KLIM cans to make many items.

KP (kitchen patrol). GI slang for kitchen duty.

kriegie. Nickname that Allied prisoners of war gave themselves and was an abbreviated form of the German word *Kriegsgefangener* (prisoner of war).

lager. Another nickname for a prison camp.

Lucky Bastard. A crewman who survived his mission tour, which ranged from twenty-five missions early in the war to thirty-five by the war's end.

Lucky Bastard Club. Any Lucky Bastard was a member, and many bases had a special table in the mess for club members.

luftgangster. A derogatory German name for Allied pilots, translated as "sky gangster."

Mae West. Nickname for the life jacket, usually yellow, that flight crews used in case of ditching over water. So called because of the buxom Hollywood movie star of the 1920s.

Manna. Code name for the British mission to supply food and other necessities by air to the starving Dutch people at the end of the war. *See* Chowhound.

mess. Cafeteria.

Mickey or Mickey Mouse. *See* H2X.

missing in action (MIA). Refers to crewmen who were lost in action and not recovered.

milk run. Airman slang for an easy mission.

MP. Military Police.

Mustang. The P-51 escort fighter, which protected the bomber stream all the way to distant targets and helped to win the air war.

navigator. Officer with the duty of keeping the aircraft on the correct course.

Nissen hut. A corrugated steel structure for living quarters.

Noball. Missions flown to the known German rocket-launching sites.

noncommissioned officer (NCO). Military personnel with a rank of sergeant. All flying crews were noncommissioned officers and officers to ensure better treatment under the Geneva Convention if captured.

Norden bombsight. A device that allowed the bombardier to bomb a target accurately from high altitude.

Oboe. Second-generation radio navigation system developed by the British.

officer. A member of the military with a commission. Officers began as second lieutenants. The pilot, copilot, navigator, and bombardier were all officers, as was the leadership on the ground.

oxygen mask. Worn by flight personnel at high altitudes over their nose and mouth.

Pathfinder. A specially equipped aircraft with radar that allowed the crew to "see" through cloud cover to ensure accurate bombing.

Piccadilly commando. Nickname for the prostitutes who worked the Piccadilly Circus area in London.

plan position indicator (PPI). Mechanism used on aircraft radar systems to "read" terrain.

Plexiglas. A type of hardened glass used for windows on the aircraft.

Purple Heart. Medal awarded to men who are wounded or killed in combat.

Purple Heart Corner. Nickname for the most vulnerable position in the combat box, often assigned to new crews.

radio operator. Noncommissioned officer in charge of all incoming and outgoing radio transmissions from an aircraft.

Red Cross parcel. A box supplied to prisoners of war that contained food, cigarettes, and essential items.

S2H. British radar system that was also known as Stinky.

salvage. Term for when an aircraft is so badly damaged that it will never fly again and is usually reserved for spare parts.

SPAM. Tinned meat eaten by GIs because it could be kept indefinitely.

Splasher beacon. A British navigational device that allowed planes to assemble in overcast skies with less chance of collision.

squadron. A subgroup of a heavy bomb group comprising twelve aircraft, their crews, and support personnel. Each bomb group had four squadrons.

stalag. A German prisoner of war camp.

stalag luft. A German prisoner of war camp for Allied airmen. *Luft* is German for "air."

supercharger. A device that forces oxygen into an engine and increases performance.

sweating out the mission. A slang term that ground personnel used for the long hours of waiting for the group's aircraft to return. Also used by flight crews to talk about mentally preparing for a mission.

Tail End Charlie. The last aircraft in a combat formation, often the most vulnerable to attack from German fighters.

tail gunner. Noncommissioned officer in charge of defending the aircraft from attacks from the rear. The tail gunner sat facing aft in the back of the plane.

terrorflieger. A derogatory name Germans used for Allied airmen, translated as "terror flier."

throat mike. The device used to communicate on a B-17. To use it, the wearer pressed the receiver against his throat.

Thunderbolt. The nickname of the American escort P-47 fighter. The Thunderbolt was also sometimes called the Jug because it looked like a milk jug.

togglier. Member of the B-17 crew, usually not a trained bombardier, who worked the bomb release controls after bombing was initiated from a lead bombardier rather than from each individual aircraft later in the war.

Tokyo tanks. Large fuel tanks added to the bellies of bombers for long-range missions.

Underground. The secret organization set up in enemy territory to help downed airmen escape.

V-1. The V-1 flying bomb (V-1 stood for *vergeltungswaffe*, or "vengeance weapon") that the Germans launched from coastal batteries in France at England during the war. Also known as a buzz bomb, the jet-powered V-1 killed many English civilians and destroyed property. The first V-1 landed and exploded in London on June 13, 1944.

V-2. The world's first ballistic missile, the V-2 rocket was fired at England, killing or injuring more than nine thousand British.

waist gunner. A noncommissioned officer in charge of defending the sides of the aircraft. One waist gunner stood on either side of the waist section of the plane, aft of the wings.

walk-around bottle. A portable oxygen canister that a crewman could carry with him at high altitudes. Otherwise, flight crews attached their oxygen systems directly to the aircraft.

Notes

Chapter 1. The Creation of an Air Force

1. Geoffrey Perrett, *Winged Victory: The Army Air Forces in World War II* (New York: Random House, 1993), 98.

2. "Overview: Early Years," Air Force History, http://www.airforcehistory. af.mil/overview/index.asp, accessed April 7, 2012.

3. Donald L. Miller, *Masters of the Air: America's Bomber Boys Who Fought the Air War Against Nazi Germany* (New York: Simon & Schuster, 2006), 159.

4. Ibid., 156.

5. "History of 95th Bombardment Group (BG)" (unpublished manuscript, 1945), 3.

6. Harry M. Conley, *No Foxholes in the Sky* (Trumbull, CT: FNP Press, 2002), 41.

7. Ibid.

8. Ian L. Hawkins, ed., *B-17s Over Berlin: Personal Stories of the 95th Bomb Group (H)* (Washington, DC: Potomac Books, 2006), 5.

9. John Walter, *My War: The True Experiences of a U.S. Army Air Force Pilot in World War Two* (Bloomington, IN: AuthorHouse, 2004), 153–57.

10. Robin Neillands, *The Bomber War: The Allied Air Offensive Against Nazi Germany* (London: Overlook TP, 2003), 94–95.

11. Rob Morris, *Untold Valor: Forgotten Stories of American Bomber Crews over Europe in World War II* (Washington, DC: Potomac Books, 2006), 146.

12. Ibid.; interview with Robert Capen, 153.

13. Adam Hinojos, "The History of the 457th Sub Depot" (unpublished manuscript, no date).

Chapter 2. Across Oceans and Continents

1. Leonard Herman, *Combat Bombardier: Memoirs of Two Combat Tours in the Skies over Europe in World War Two*, with Rob Morris (Philadelphia: Xlibris, 2007), 16.
2. Hawkins, *B-17s Over Berlin*, 7.
3. Ibid., 11.
4. Ibid., 8.
5. Ibid.
6. Ibid., 9.
7. Herman, *Combat Bombardier*, 27.
8. Hawkins, *B-17s Over Berlin*, 9.
9. Herman, *Combat Bombardier*, 29.
10. Hawkins, *B-17s Over Berlin*, 11–12.
11. Ibid., 9.
12. Ibid., 29.
13. Ibid., 7.
14. Ibid., 29.
15. "History of 95th," 5.
16. Hawkins, *B-17s Over Berlin*, 29.

Chapter 3. Alconbury and Early Missions

1. William "Ed" Charles, "History of the 95th Bomb Group," slideshow presented at reunion of 95th Bomb Group (H), Cleveland, Ohio, 1999.
2. Eric Hammel, *The Road to Big Week: The Struggle for Daylight Air Supremacy over Western Europe, July 1942–February 1944* (Pacifica, CA: Pacifica Military History, 2009), 155–56.
3. John Chaffin, "Memories of WWII: John H. Chaffin, Flight Officer, 95th Bomb Group, 335th Squadron" (unpublished manuscript, 1997), 94–95.
4. Conley, *No Foxholes*, 77.
5. Roger Freeman, *The Mighty Eighth: A History of the Units, Men, and Machines of the US 8th Air Force* (New York: Cassell, 2000), 47.
6. Cajus Bekker, *The Luftwaffe War Diaries*, trans. and ed. Frank Ziegler (New York, Ballantine, 1972), 56.
7. Herman, *Combat Bombardier*, 34.
8. Alan E. Snyder, *The 95th B-17 Bomb Group (H) Flight Crews, WWII, May 13, 1943–May 25, 1945* (privately published, no date), 1.
9. Freeman, *Mighty Eighth*, 47.

10. Herman, *Combat Bombardier*, 35.
11. Snyder, *95th B-17 Bomb Group*, 4–5.
12. Hawkins, *B-17s Over Berlin*, 14.
13. Herman, *Combat Bombardier*, 32.
14. Conley, *No Foxholes*, 163–64.
15. Hawkins, *B-17s Over Berlin*, 15.

Chapter 4. Mission Day
1. Engineering Report, 95th BG, June 15, 1943. 95th BG Archives, accessed June 2010.
2. *Contrails II: A Pictorial History of the 95th Bomb Group (H), 8th United States Army Air Force, Horham, England, 1943–1945* (Marceline, MO: Walsworth Publishing, 95th Bomb Group [H] Association, 2003). *Note*: This volume does not have page numbers.
3. Sgt. Walter Peters, "Night Before a Mission," *Yank Army Weekly*, January 30, 1944, 6–7.
4. A young gunner, Staff Sgt. Vincent Barbella, was killed in action on February 10, 1944. A Veterans of Foreign Wars post, #8501, in Brooklyn is named after him.
5. Peters, "Night Before a Mission," 6–7.
6. Walter, *My War*, 138–39.
7. David Webber, unpublished diary, no date.
8. Walter, *My War*, 141–42.
9. Chaffin, "Memories."
10. *Contrails II.*
11. Walters, *My War*, 146.
12. *Contrails II.*
13. Walter, *My War*, 134.
14. Hawkins, *B-17s Over Berlin*, 211–12.
15. Walter, *My War*, 134.
16. Ibid., 146–47.
17. Chaffin, "Memories."
18. *Contrails II.*
19. Walter, *My War*, 203.
20. Chaffin, "Memories."
21. Bekker, *Luftwaffe War Diaries*, 192.
22. Chaffin, "Memories."

23. Bob Brown, letter to author, September 9, 1996.
24. Morris, *Untold Valor*, 153.
25. Willis Frazier (former operations officer, 601st Squadron, 398th Bomb Group), "The B-17's Automatic Flight Control Equipment," 398th Bomb Group Memorial Association, http://www.398th.org/Research/B17_AFCE.html, accessed December 12, 2010.
26. *Contrails II*.

Chapter 5. Then Came Kiel

1. Hawkins, *B-17s Over Berlin*, 15.
2. Ibid., 30.
3. Ibid., 196.
4. Herman, *Combat Bombardier*, 39.
5. Bob Woods, interview with Willard W. Brown, Cleveland, Ohio, March 7, 1977. Transcript from 95th BG Archives, accessed July 2010.
6. Hawkins, *B-17s Over Berlin*, 17–18.
7. Ibid., 19.
8. 95th post-mission report.
9. Woods, interview with Brown.
10. Robert Cozens, Int Ops Interrogation, Mission Reports. 95th BG Archives, accessed July 2010.
11. Herman, *Combat Bombardier*, 40.
12. Hawkins, *B-17s Over Berlin*, 21–22.
13. Report of the Office of Armament Officer, 95th Bomb Group, June 14, 1943. 95th BG Archives, accessed July 2010.
14. Cozens, Int Ops Interrogation.
15. Hawkins, *B-17s Over Berlin*, 29.
16. William Irving, "The Yankee Queen" (unpublished manuscript, no date), 61–63.
17. Miller, *Masters of the Air*, 139.
18. Hawkins, *B-17s Over Berlin*, 24–25.
19. Ibid., 24.

Chapter 6. The British

1. "Britain's Secret Army," Museum of the British Resistance Organisation, Parham Airfield, Framlingham, Suffolk, http://www.parhamair fieldmuseum.co.uk/brohome.html, accessed December 12, 2010.

2. "B-17 Crash," Redlingfield Local History of the Second World War, http://redlingfield.onesuffolk.net/home/local-history/the-second -world-war-2/b-17-crash-view-from-the-village/, accessed April 7, 2012.

3. Hawkins, *B-17s Over Berlin*, 222.

4. Ibid., 191.

5. Ibid., 191–92.

6. Morris, *Untold Valor*, xii–xiii.

Chapter 7. Cold Sky

1. Freeman, *Mighty Eighth*, 51.

2. *Contrails II.*

3. Hawkins, *B-17s Over Berlin*, 31.

4. Irving, "Yankee Queen," 55.

5. Freeman, *Mighty Eighth*, 51.

6. *Contrails II.*

7. Hawkins, *B-17s Over Berlin*, 52.

8. Ibid., 32.

9. Ibid., 36–37.

10. Ibid., 38.

Chapter 8. DNIF: Duties Not Involving Flying

1. Hawkins, *B-17s Over Berlin*, 285.

2. See 95th Bomb Group (H) Memorials Foundation website, http://95thbg .org/joomla/.

3. *Contrails II.*

4. Ibid.

5. Hawkins, *B-17s Over Berlin*, 262.

6. Ted Lucey, "View from the Ground Up" (unpublished memoir, 1983).

7. Hawkins, *B-17s Over Berlin*, 250.

8. George Betts, "Recollections of Life in 95th BG Aero Repair" (unpub- lished memoir, 2006).

Chapter 9. From Kiel to the Eve of Regensburg

1. Freeman, *Mighty Eighth*, 63.

2. "Campaign Summaries of World War 2: Norway, 1940–1945," Naval -History.Net, http://www.naval-history.net/WW2CampaignsNorway.htm.

3. Herman, *Combat Bombardier*; and interviews with Herman.
4. Irving, "Yankee Queen," 73.

Chapter 10. Replacement Crews

1. Irving, "Yankee Queen," 53.
2   Walter, *My War*, 112.
3   Irving, "Yankee Queen," 53.
4. Bob Sullivan, "Bob Sullivan's WWII Memoirs" (unpublished manuscript, no date), 6–9.
5. John Black, "Colonel Noel T. Cumbaa," *Delta Democrat Times Magazine* (Summer 2009): 14–18; and author telephone interview with Noel T. Cumbaa, 2009.
6. George R. Herman, "A Bad Day at Douglas Army Air Field," *Journal of Arizona History* 36, no. 4 (1995): 379.
7. Irving, "Yankee Queen," 55.
8. James B. Gregory, "Es War Einmal" (unpublished manuscript, 2004), 6.
9. *Contrails II*; and Stewart McConnell, interview with author, 2009.
10. Morris, *Untold Valor*, 218.

Chapter 11. Wives and Mothers

1. Herman, *Combat Bombardier*, 44.
2. Cassie Messner, "V-Mail Service," Smithsonian National Postal Museum, March 7, 2008, http://postalmuseum.si.edu/VictoryMail/operating/, accessed on December 19, 2010.
3. Poem courtesy of Charles Shaughnessy's daughter, Judi Park.
4. Interview with Geri Marshall in 2009. Hers was the most intense interview I conducted for this book. It was painful for her to recount, and her words give a voice to many who lost a loved one in the war.

Chapter 12. Sudden Death

1. Robert J. Brodersen, unpublished memoir (no date).
2. Edwin A. LeCorchick, "Combat Diary of Edwin A. LeCorchick, written while Stationed at Horham Airfield (Station 119), Suffolk County, England, 95th BG, 334th BS" (unpublished memoir, no date).
3. Lucey, "View from the Ground Up."
4. William H. Greene, unpublished war diary (no date).

5. Robert J. Evans, "95th Bomb Group, Vergene Ford Crew" (unpublished memoir, no date).

6. Conley, *No Foxholes*, 150–51.

7. Hawkins, *B-17s Over Berlin*, 98–99.

8. Ibid., 97.

Chapter 13. Entertainment and London

1. Eugene Fletcher, *The Lucky Bastard Club: A B-17 Pilot in Training and in Combat, 1943–1945* (Seattle: University of Washington Press, 1992).

2. Herman, *Combat Bombardier*; and interview with author.

3. *Contrails II.*

4. Ibid.

5. Brodersen, unpublished memoir.

6. Earle Bogacki, unpublished memoir (no date), 95th Bomb Group Archives.

7. William Gifford, unpublished memoir (no date), 95th Bomb Group Archives.

8. Walter, *My War*, 164.

9. Gifford, unpublished memoir.

10. Lucey, "View from the Ground Up."

11. Daniel L. Kinney, "World War II Memories" (unpublished memoir, 2005).

12. Miller, *Masters of the Air*, 210.

13. James T. Hammond, *Tom's War: Flying with the U.S. Eighth Army Air Force in Europe, 1944* (New York: iUniverse, 2007), 78.

14. Lucey, "View from the Ground Up."

15. Gifford, unpublished memoir.

16. Greene, unpublished war diary.

17. Harrison Salisbury, *A Journey for Our Times: A Memoir* (New York: Carroll and Graf, 1984).

18. Patrick Bishop, *Fighter Boys: The Battle of Britain, 1940* (London: Penguin, 2003), 196.

19. Bogacki, unpublished memoir.

Chapter 14. Regensburg Shuttle Mission

1. Irving, "Yankee Queen," 75.

2. Freeman, *Mighty Eighth*, 67.

3. Hawkins, *B-17s Over Berlin*, 49.

4. Mission report, August 14, 1943, 95th BG Archives.

5. Freeman, *Mighty Eighth*, 67.
6. Conley, *No Foxholes*, 57.
7. Irving, "Yankee Queen," 79.
8. Mission report, August 13, 1943, 95th BG Archives.
9. Ibid.
10. Irving, "Yankee Queen," 79.
11. Mission report, August 13, 1943.
12. Freeman, *Mighty Eighth*, 68.
13. Hawkins, *B-17s Over Berlin*, 50.
14. Ibid., 51.
15. Morris, *Untold Valor*, 126.
16. Irving, "Yankee Queen," 80.
17. Freeman, *Mighty Eighth*, 69.
18. Conley, *No Foxholes*, 123–24.
19. Chaffin, "Memories."
20. Ibid., 119–20.
21. Conley, *No Foxholes*, 125.
22. Chaffin, "Memories."
23. Irving, "Yankee Queen."
24. Conley, *No Foxholes*, 126.
25. Hawkins, *B-17s Over Berlin*, 51.
26. Perrett, *Winged Victory*, 310.
27. Bekker, *Luftwaffe War Diaries*, 177.
28. Ibid., 181.

Chapter 15. Black Week

1. Maurice Rockett, e-mail interview, April 8, 2012.
2. Dan Culler, e-mail interview, April 8, 2012.
3. C. Peter Chen, "Ira Eaker," World War II Database, http://ww2db.com /person_bio.php?person_id=647, accessed April 8, 2012.
4. Ian L. Hawkins, *The Munster Raid: Before and After* (Trumbull, CT: FNP Military Division, 1999), 89.
5. Ibid., 89–90.
6. Hawkins, *B-17s Over Berlin*, 67.
7. Chaffin, "Memories," 162–63.
8. Conley, *No Foxholes*.
9. Hawkins, *Munster Raid*, 93.

10. Chaffin, "Memories," 64.
11. Ibid., 65.
12. Mission report, October 10, 1943.
13. Kring, *Rhapsody in Flak.*
14. Hawkins, *B-17s Over Berlin,* 72.
15. Ibid., 69.
16. Mission report.
17. Hawkins, *B-17s Over Berlin,* 72.
18. Chaffin, "Memories," 172.
19. Hawkins, *B-17s Over Berlin,* 75.
20. Hawkins, *Munster Raid,* 236.
21. Ibid., 225.
22. Mission report.
23. Frank D. Murphy, *Luck of the Draw: Reflections on the Air War in Europe* (Trumbull, CT: FNP Military Division, 2001), 78.
24. Martin Caidin, *Black Thursday* (New York: Bantam, 1981), 17.
25. Ibid., 18.
26. Albert Speer, *Inside the Third Reich,* trans. Richard and Clara Winston (New York: Avon, 1971), 365.
27. Ibid., 304.
28. John T. Correll, "The Cost of Schweinfurt," *Air Force Magazine* 93, no. 2 (February 2010): 60–63.
29. Hawkins, *B-17s Over Berlin,* 91.
30. Freeman, *Mighty Eighth,* 79.
31. Speer, *Inside the Third Reich,* 372–73.
32. Ibid., 373.
33. Ibid., 363.
34. Caidin, *Black Thursday,* xi.
35. Bekker, *Luftwaffe War Diaries,* 212.
36. Miller, *Masters of the Air,* 213.

Chapter 16. POWs, Part I

1. Sullivan, "Memoirs," 12.
2. Ibid., 13–14.
3. Chaffin, "Memories," 175–77.
4. Miller, *Masters of the Air,* 383.
5. Gregory, "Es War Einmal," 12.

6. Ibid.
7. George Sulick, interview, 95th Bomb Group (H) Memorials Foundation, http://95thbg.org/95th_joomla/index.php?option=com_content&view =article&id=236&Itemid=347, accessed April 8, 2012.
8. Fred Kennie, speech at the Reunion POW Breakfast, Tucson, 2008.
9. U.S. Air Force Academy, "Stalag Luft 3," official website of the 392nd Bomb Group, http://www.b24.net/pow/stalag3.htm.
10. Chaffin, "Memories."
11. Miller, *Masters of the Air*, 399–410; and POW interviews with John Chaffin and Irv Rothman.
12. Chaffin, "Memories."
13. Sulick interview.

Chapter 17. Internment in Switzerland and Sweden
1. "Aircraft Listing by Order of Arrival in Switzerland," Swiss Internees Association website, http://swissinternees.tripod.com/aircraft.html, retrieved April 8, 2012. Also personal correspondence with Norris King, president of Swiss Internees Association, in 2000–2001.
2. Bob Long, interview, 2000. Long was president of the Swiss Internees Association. See as well the original report to General Spaatz dated November 7, 1944, in the Swiss Internees Association Archives.
3. Stephen Tanner, *Refuge from the Reich: American Airmen and Switzerland during World War II* (Rockville Centre, NY: Sarpedon, 2000), 209.
4. Cathryn J. Prince, *Shot from the Sky: American POWs in Switzerland* (Annapolis, MD: Naval Institute Press, 2003), 70–71.
5. Tanner, *Refuge from the Reich*, 183–84.
6. Robert Long, statistics from the Swiss Internees Association Archives; and Miller, *Masters of the Air*, 334–35, 346.
7. Sam Mastrogiacomo, telephone interview, June 1, 2001.

Chapter 18. Escape and Evasion
1. Miller, *Masters of the Air*, 98.
2. Ibid.
3. Ibid., 100.
4. Hawkins, *B-17s Over Berlin*, 44–46.
5. Ibid., 41.
6. Ibid., 42.

7. Jennings Beck, "1/29/44" (unpublished memoir, 2007), 22.
8. Ibid., 38.
9. Ibid., 43.
10. Hawkins, *B-17s Over Berlin*, 109.

Chapter 19. MIA
1. Michael I. Darter, *Fateful Flight of the Lonesome Polecat II* (New York: iUniverse, 2004).
2. Ibid., 60.
3. Ibid., 65.
4. Individual Deceased Personnel File of Harold Coffman, MIA, U.S. Department of the Army, Washington, DC.

Chapter 20. Pathfinders and Aphrodites
1. Marshall J. Thixton, George E. Moffat, and John J. O'Neil, *Bombs Away by Pathfinders of the Eighth Air Force* (Trumbull, CT: FNP Military Division, 1998).
2. "H2S Radar," http://www.fact-archive.com/encyclopedia/H2S_radar, accessed July 2010.
3. Thixton, Moffat, and O'Neil, *Pathfinders*, 65.
4. Ibid., 68.
5. Ibid., 69.
6. Ibid.
7. Adolf Galland, *The First and Last: The Rise and Fall of the German Fighters Forces, 1938–1945,* trans. Mervyn Savill (New York: Holt, 1954), 187.
8. Jack Olsen, *Aphrodite: Desperate Mission* (New York: G. P. Putnam's Sons, 1970), 20.
9. Ibid., 17–18.
10. Ibid., 27–30.
11. Miller, *Masters of the Air*, 301.
12. Ibid., 303.
13. Roger Freeman, *Mighty Eighth War Manual* (London: Cassell, 2001), 105.

Chapter 21. Big Week
1. Gen. James H. Doolittle, *I Could Never Be So Lucky Again: An Autobiography,* with Carroll V. Glines (New York: Bantam, 1992), 352.
2. Ibid., 352.

3. Ibid., 353.
4. Ibid., 347.
5. Ibid., 355.
6. Ibid., 360.
7. Miller, *Masters of the Air*, 254.
8. Bekker, *Luftwaffe War Diaries*, 226.
9. Charles, "History."
10. Glenn B. Infield, *Big Week!* (New York: Pinnacle Books, 1979).
11. Ibid.
12. Hammel, *Road to Big Week*, 250–51.
13. Ibid., 252.
14. Ibid., 253.
15. Freeman, *Mighty Eighth*, 112.
16. Doolittle, *So Lucky Again*, 357.
17. Wilbur H. Morrison, *Fortress Without a Roof: The Allied Bombing of the Third Reich* (New York: St. Martin's, 1982), 259.
18. Speer, *Inside the Third Reich*, 427.
19. Ibid., 428.
20. Morrison, *Fortress*, 259.

Chapter 22. "Big B"

1. "First Over Berlin," *Life* (March 27, 1944): 34–35.
2. A. C. Grayling, *Among the Dead Cities: The History and Moral Legacy of the WWII Bombing of Civilians in Germany and Japan* (New York: Bloomsbury, 2006), 332.
3. Freeman, *Mighty Eighth*, 113.
4. Hawkins, *B-17s Over Berlin*, 142.
5. Mission report, March 4, 1944, National Archives, Washington, DC. Retrieved July 2010.
6. Thixton, Moffat, and O'Neil, *Pathfinders*, 115.
7. Hawkins, *B-17s Over Berlin*, 144.
8. Ibid., 147.
9. Thixton, Moffat, and O'Neil, *Pathfinders*, 115.
10. William Owen, interview with author, August 16, 2009; and Thixton, Moffat, and O'Neil, *Pathfinders*, 117.
11. Freeman, *Mighty Eighth*, 113.
12. Thixton, Moffat, and O'Neil, *Pathfinders*, 117.

13. Ibid., 119. In my interview with Bill Owen, he figured they were eighteen miles off course.

14. Hawkins, *B-17s Over Berlin*, 147.

15. Thixton, Moffat, and O'Neil, *Pathfinders*, 120.

16. Ibid., 120.

17. William Gifford, unpublished memoir (no date).

18. Hawkins, *B-17s Over Berlin*, 145–46.

19. Conley, *No Foxholes*, 230–31.

20. Thixton, Moffat, and O'Neil, *Pathfinders*, 121.

21. Doolittle, *So Lucky Again*, 368–69.

22. Hawkins, *B-17s Over Berlin*, 152.

23. "First Over Berlin," 34–35.

24. Eric Hammel, *Air War Europa: America's Air War Against Germany in Europe and North Africa, 1942–1945: Chronology* (Pacifica, CA: Pacifica Press, 1994), 258–59.

25. Doolittle, *So Lucky Again*, 369.

Chapter 23. D-Day

1. Bert Stiles, *Serenade to the Big Bird* (New York: Bantam, 1983), 91–93.

2. Morrison, *Fortress*, 299.

3. Ibid., 152.

4. Freeman, *Mighty Eighth*, 152.

5. Speer, *Inside the Third Reich*, 445.

6. Miller, *Masters of the Air*, 291.

7. Morrison, *Fortress*, 297–98.

8. Hawkins, *B-17s Over Berlin*, 202.

9. Official Eighth Air Force Headquarters Report, June 6, 1944, National Archives, Washington, D.C. Retrieved July 2010.

10. Ibid.

11. Hawkins, *B-17s Over Berlin*, 202.

12. Ibid., 203.

13. Miller, *Masters of the Air*, 291–92.

14. Ibid., 293–94.

Chapter 24. The Russia Shuttle Missions

1. Marshall B. Shore, *War Stories* (Spokane, WA: private printing, 2000), 55.

2. Wolfgang Saxon, "Joseph Moller, 93, a Decorated World War II Pilot," *New York Times*, October 13, 1993.
3. Hawkins, *B-17s Over Berlin*, 192.
4. Shore, *War Stories*, 56.
5. Freeman, *Mighty Eighth*, 158.
6. Shore, *War Stories*, 57.
7. Ibid., 57–58.
8. Freeman, *Mighty Eighth*, 158.
9. Shore, *War Stories*, 75–80.
10. "Nude Welcome to Russia Shocks Pilots," *New York Daily News*, July 19, 1944.
11. Hammel, *Europa*, 354.
12. Webber, unpublished memoir.
13. Hawkins, *B-17s Over Berlin*, 245–46.

Chapter 25. Final Combat Missions
1. George Thomas Simon, *Glenn Miller and His Orchestra* (New York: De Capo Press, 1974), 369.
2. "History of the Airmen of Note," Airmen of Note, United States Air Force Band, http://www.airmenofnote.com/history/Introduction.htm.
3. Fletcher, *Lucky Bastard*, 386–87.
4. *Contrails II.*
5. Walter, *My War*, 186–88.
6. Ibid., 197–98.
7. Fletcher, *Lucky Bastard*, 389.
8. Walter, *My War*, 246.
9. Ibid., 201.
10. Ibid.
11. Hawkins, *B-17s Over Berlin*, 257–59.
12. Bekker, *Luftwaffe War Diaries.*
13. Ibid., 238–39.
14. George Hood, oral interview, 95th Bomb Group (H) Memorials Foundation, http://www.95thbg.org/95th_joomla/index.php?option=com_content&view=category&id=66%3Astoriesinterviews&layout=default&Itemid=1, accessed April 8, 2012.
15. Robert Fay, interview; and Tony Molino, oral interview, 95th Bomb Group (H) Memorials Foundation, http://95thbg.org/95th_joomla

/index.php?option=com_content&view=article&id=117&Itemid=246, accessed April 8, 2012.

16. Robert Brown, unpublished untitled manuscript, 95th BG Archives.
17. "Horten H IX V3," Smithsonian National Air and Space Museum, http://www.nasm.si.edu/collections/artifact.cfm?id=A19600324000, accessed December 28, 2010. See also "Germany's Stealth Bomber," http://sf260w.com/N/.
18. Marcus Dunk, "Hitler's Stealth Bomber: How the Nazis Were First to Design a Plane to Beat Radar," *London Daily Mail,* July 8, 2009, http://www.dailymail.co.uk/news/worldnews/article-1198112, accessed December 27, 2010.
19. Walter, *My War. 232.*
20. Doolittle, *So Lucky Again*, 404.
21. Photo available at National Museum of the U.S. Air Force, http://www.nationalmuseum.af.mil/shared/media/photodb/photos/051019-F-1234P-048.jpg.
22. Doolittle, *So Lucky Again*, 404.
23. Hawkins, *B-17s Over Berlin,* 262.

Chapter 26. POWs, Part II
1. Hawkins, *B-17s Over Berlin,* 226–27.
2. Edward Cunliffe, oral interview, 2007, Savannah, GA, at 95th Bomb Group (H) Memorials Foundation, http://95thbg.org/95th_joomla/index.php?option=com_content&view=article&id=210:edward-cunliffe&catid=66:storiesi-interviews&Itermid=331, accessed April 8, 2012.
3. Hawkins, *B-17s Over Berlin,* 274.
4. John Nichol and Tony Rennell, *The Last Escape: The Untold Story of Allied Prisoners of War in Europe, 1944–45* (New York: Viking, 2002), 56.
5. Chaffin, "Memories."
6. James A. Kelley Jr., "Wartime Memoirs" (1994). Kelley was with the Donald Severson crew, 336th Squadron, 95th BG.
7. Sulick, interview.
8. Ibid.
9. Woods interview with Brown.
10. Miller, *Masters of the Air,* 499–500.

Chapter 27. Manna/Chowhound Missions

1. Hans Onderwater, *Operation Manna-Chowhound: The Allied Food Droppings April/May 1945* (Utrecht, Holland: Roman Luchtvaart, 1985), 19–20.
2. Ibid., 90.
3. Ibid., 22.
4. Ibid., 23.
5. Directive quoted in ibid., 23.
6. Ibid., 80.
7. Ibid., 131.
8. Harry H. Crosby, *A Wing and a Prayer: The "Bloody 100th" Bomb Group of the U.S. Eighth Air Force in Action over Europe in World War II* (New York: HarperCollins, 1993).
9. Maynard Stewart, oral interview, 95th Bomb Group (H) Memorials Foundation Archives. http://95th bg.org/95th_ joomla/index/index .php?option=-com_content&view=article&id=117&Itemid=246, accessed April 8, 2012.
10. Onderwater, *Manna-Chowhound*, 94–95.
11. Ibid., 93.
12. Marvin Markus, private letter, no date, 95th Bomb Group (H) Memorials Foundation Archives.
13. Onderwater, *Manna-Chowhound*, 83.
14. Hawkins, *B-17s Over Berlin*, 303.
15. William R. Cook, "Final Flight of B-17 44-8640: The Last 95th BG Plane Down in the War" (unpublished manuscript, 1984).
16. Hawkins, *B-17s Over Berlin*, 303–4.
17. Ibid., 277–78.
18. Ibid.
19. Delmar Jonas, letter to author, July 8, 2010.
20. Freeman, *Mighty Eighth*, 230.
21. Ibid.
22. Delmar Jonas, interview with author, October 5, 2008.
23. Miller, *Masters of the Air*, 515.

Chapter 28. Coming Home

1. Eugene Carson, *Wing Ding: Memories of a Tailgunner* (Bloomington, IN: Xlibris, 2000), 191.
2. Freeman, *Mighty Eighth*, 232.

3. Casualties and POWs, 95th Bomb Group (H) Memorials Foundation website, http://95thbg.org/95th_joomla/index.php?option=com_content&view=article&id=44&Itemid=164, accessed April 8, 2012.

4. Leonard Herman, phone interview, September 2006.

5. Walter, *My War*, 151.

6. Ibid., 184.

7. Ibid., 225–27.

8. Knox, oral interview. September 12, 2004, Tysons Corner, VA, 95th Bomb Group (H) Memorials Foundation website, http://95thbg.org/95th_joomla/index.php?option=com_content&view=article&id=179:frank-knox&catid=66:stories-interviews&Itemid=305, accessed April 8, 2012.

9. Hinojos, "History," 3.

Chapter 29. The Legacy Lives On

1. "Kingman Airport, Arizona: World War II Aircraft Disposal," *Wikipedia*, http://en.wikipedia.org/wiki/Kingman_Airport_(Arizona), accessed December 28, 2010.

2. Morris, *Untold Valor*, 158.

3. Ellis Scripture, as quoted in the introduction of *Contrails II*.

4. Hawkins, *B-17s Over Berlin*, 301.

5. Ibid., 303.

6. Ellis Scripture, Ring of Eight fundraising letter, 1989, 95th Bomb Group Archives.

7. David Streeter, letter of appeal to the 95th Bomb Group Association, 1989, 95th Bomb Group Archives.

8. "Bells Again Ring at St. Mary's," *Diss (UK) Express*, May 15, 1992.

9. David Green, "Bells to Ring out in Memory of 'Lefty,'" *East Anglian Daily Times*.

10. Rick Mangan, "Mourning Glory" (unpublished article, 2009).

11. Ibid.

Selected Bibliography

Books and Unpublished Manuscripts

390th Bomb Group Anthology, Volume I. Tucson, AZ: 390th Memorial Museum Foundation, 1983.

Astor, Gerald. *The Greatest War: Americans in Combat, 1941–1945.* Novato, CA: Presidio Press, 1999.

———. *The Mighty Eighth: The Air War in Europe as Told by the Men Who Fought It.* New York: Dell, 1997.

Beck, Jennings B. "1/29/44." Unpublished memoir, 2007.

Bekker, Cajus. *The Luftwaffe War Diaries.* Translated and edited by Frank Ziegler. New York: Ballantine, 1972.

Betts, George. "Recollections of Life in 95th BG Aero Repair." Unpublished memoir, 2006.

Binnebose, William H. "The Memories Remain." Unpublished memoir (95th BG gunner/POW), 1987.

Bishop, Patrick. *Fighter Boys: The Battle of Britain, 1940.* London: Penguin Books, 2003.

Bogacki, Earl. Unpublished memoir. 95th Bomb Group Archives, no date.

Borrett, Albert. Unpublished memoir (Horham, Suffolk, stationmaster), no date.

Bowman, Martin. *Castles in the Air: The Story of the B-17 Flying Fortress Crews of the U.S. Eighth Air Force.* Wellingborough, UK: Patrick Stephens, 1984.

———. *Wild Blue Yonder: Glory Days of the US Eighth Air Force in England.* London: Cassell, 2003.

Boyne, Walter. *Clash of Wings: World War II in the Air*. New York: Touchstone, 1997.

Brodersen, Robert J. Unpublished memoir, no date.

Brown, Robert. Unpublished untitled manuscript. 95th BG Archives.

Bucklin, Walter. "Poltava Shuttle Mission." Unpublished manuscript, 1955.

Caidin, Martin. *Black Thursday*. New York: Bantam, 1981.

Carson, Eugene. *Wing Ding: Memories of a Tailgunner*. Bloomington, IN: Xlibris, 2000.

Chaffin, John. "Memories of WWII: John H. Chaffin, Flight Officer, 95th Bomb Group, 335th Squadron." Unpublished manuscript, 1997.

———. "The 'Other Side's' Views by Stalag Luft III Inmate #1032." Unpublished manuscript, no date. Author's collection.

Conley, Harry M. *No Foxholes in the Sky*. Trumbull, CT: FNP Press, 2002.

Contrails II: A Pictorial History of the 95th Bomb Group (H), 8th United States Army Air Force, Horham, England, 1943–1945. Marceline, MO: Walsworth Publishing, 95th Bomb Group (H) Association, 2003.

Cook, William R. "Final Flight of B-17 44-8640: The Last 95th BG Plane Down in the War." Unpublished manuscript, 1984.

Crosby, Harry H. *A Wing and a Prayer: The "Bloody 100th" Bomb Group of the U.S. Eighth Air Force in Action over Europe in World War II*. New York: HarperCollins, 1993.

Darter, Michael I. *Fateful Flight of the Lonesome Polecat II*. New York: iUniverse, 2004.

Doolittle, Gen. James H. *I Could Never Be So Lucky Again: An Autobiography*. With Carroll V. Glines. New York: Bantam, 1992.

Durand, Arthur A. *Stalag Luft III: The Secret Story*. Baton Rouge: Louisiana State University Press, 1988.

Edgar, Jesse B. "Bombs Away! Thirty Was Enough: A Bombardier's Diary Account of Combat as a Member of a B-17 Crew with the Eighth Air Force." Unpublished manuscript, no date.

Ethell, Jeffrey, and Alfred Price. *Target Berlin: Mission 250: 6 March 1944*. London: Greenhill, 2002.

Evans, Robert J. "95th Bomb Group, Vergene Ford Crew." Unpublished memoir, no date.

FitzGibbon, Constantine. *London's Burning*. New York: Ballantine. 1970.

Fletcher, Eugene. *The Lucky Bastard Club: A B-17 Pilot in Training and in Combat, 1943–1945*. Seattle: University of Washington Press. 1992.

Freeman, Roger. *B-17 Fortress at War.* New York: Charles Scribner's Sons. 1977.

———. *The Mighty Eighth: A History of the Units, Men, and Machines of the US 8th Air Force.* New York: Cassell, 2000.

———. *The Mighty Eighth War Manual.* London: Cassell, 2001.

Galland, Adolf. *The First and the Last: The Rise and Fall of the German Fighters Forces, 1938–1945.* Translated by Mervyn Savill. New York: Holt, 1954.

Gifford, William. Unpublished untitled memoir, no date.

Grayling, A. C. *Among the Dead Cities: The History and Moral Legacy of the WWII Bombing of Civilians in Germany and Japan.* New York: Bloomsbury, 2006.

Greene, William H. Unpublished war diary, no date.

Greening, C. Ross, and Angelo M. Spinelli. *The Yankee Kriegies.* New York: National Council of Young Men's Christian Associations, 1945.

Gregory, James B. "Es War Einmal." Unpublished manuscript, 2004.

Grove, Gerald W. "Story of the Max Wilson Crew, 95th BG, 335th Bomb Squadron." Unpublished manuscript, 1990.

Hammel, Eric. *Air War Europa: America's Air War Against Germany in Europe and North Africa, 1942–1945: Chronology.* Pacifica, CA: Pacifica Press, 1994.

———. *The Road to Big Week: The Struggle for Daylight Air Supremacy over Western Europe, July 1942–February 1944.* Pacifica, CA: Pacifica Military History, 2009.

Hammond, James T. *Tom's War: Flying with the U.S. Eighth Army Air Force in Europe, 1944.* New York: iUniverse, 2007.

Hawkins, Ian L., ed. *B-17s Over Berlin: Personal Stories of the 95th Bomb Group (H).* Washington, DC: Potomac Books, 2006.

———. *The Munster Raid: Before and After.* Trumbull, CT: FNP Military Division, 1999.

Herman, Leonard. *Combat Bombardier: Memoirs of Two Combat Tours in the Skies over Europe in World War Two.* With Rob Morris. Philadelphia, PA: Xlibris, 2007.

Hinojos, Adam. "The History of the 457th Sub Depot." Unpublished manuscript, no date.

"History of the 95th Bomb Group." Unpublished, 1945.

Infield, Glenn B. *Big Week!* New York: Pinnacle Books, 1979.

———. *The Poltava Affair: A Russian Warning: An American Tragedy.* New York: Macmillan, 1973.

Irving, David. *The Destruction of Dresden.* New York: Ballantine, 1973.

Irving, William. "The Yankee Queen." Unpublished manuscript, no date.

Jablonski, Edward. *Airwar: An Illustrated History of Air Power in the Second World War.* Garden City, NY: Doubleday, 1971.

———. *Flying Fortress: The Illustrated Biography of the B-17s and the Men Who Flew Them.* Garden City, NY: Doubleday, 1965.

Jonas, Delmer A. Unpublished memoir (334th navigator), no date.

Kelley, James A., Jr. Unpublished memoir, 1994.

Kinney, Daniel L. "World War II Memories." Unpublished memoir, 2005.

Kring, Leslie. *Rhapsody in Flak.* Unpublished memoir, no date.

LeCorchick, Edwin A. "Combat Diary of Edwin A. LeCorchick, Written while Stationed at Horham Airfield (Station 119), Suffolk County, England, 95th BG, 334th BS." Unpublished memoir, no date.

Levine, Alan J. *Captivity, Flight and Survival in World War Two.* Westport, CT: Praeger/Greenwood, 2000.

Lucey, Ted. "View from the Ground Up." Unpublished memoir, 1983.

Matheny, Ray. *Rite of Passage: A Teenager's Chronicle of Combat and Captivity in Nazi Germany.* Clearfield, UT: American Legacy Media, 2009.

McManus, John C. *Deadly Sky: The American Combat Airman in World War II.* Novato, CA: Presidio, 2002.

Mets, David R. *Master of Air Power: General Carl A. Spaatz.* Novato, CA: Presidio, 1988.

Miller, Donald L. *Masters of the Air: America's Bomber Boys Who Fought the Air War Against Nazi Germany.* New York: Simon & Schuster, 2006.

Morris, Rob. *Untold Valor: Forgotten Stories of American Bomber Crews over Europe in World War II.* Washington, DC: Potomac Books, 2006.

Morrison, Wilbur H. *Fortress Without a Roof: The Allied Bombing of the Third Reich.* New York: St. Martin's, 1982.

Murphy, Frank D. *Luck of the Draw: Reflections on the Air War in Europe.* Trumbull, CT: FNP Military Division, 2001.

Murray, Williamson. *Luftwaffe: Strategy for Defeat.* Baltimore: The Nautical and Aviation Publishing Company of America, 1985.

Mutton, James. *The Story of the Sam Gyford Band and Its American Member, DeWayne Long.* Privately published, 2008.

Neillands, Robin. *The Bomber War: The Allied Air Offensive Against Nazi Germany* (London: Overlook TP, 2003), 94–95.

Nichol, John, and Tony Rennell. *The Last Escape: The Untold Story of Allied Prisoners of War in Europe, 1944–45.* New York: Viking, 2002.

———. *Tail-End Charlies: The Last Battles of the Bomber War, 1944–45.* New York: Thomas Dunne Books, 2006.

Olsen, Jack. *Aphrodite: Desperate Mission.* New York: G. P. Putnam's Sons, 1970.

Onderwater, Hans. *Operation Manna/Chowhound: The Allied Food Droppings April/May 1945.* Utrecht, Holland: Roman Luchtvaart, Unieboek, 1985.

Overy, Richard. *Goering.* New York: Barnes & Noble, 2003.

Perrett, Geoffrey. *Winged Victory: The Army Air Forces in World War II.* New York: Random House, 1993.

Prince, Cathryn J. *Shot from the Sky: American POWs in Switzerland.* Annapolis, MD: Naval Institute Press, 2003.

Rockett, Maurice. Unpublished memoir, no date.

Salisbury, Harrison. *A Journey for Our Times: A Memoir.* New York: Carroll and Graf, 1984.

Shore, Marshall B. *War Stories.* Spokane, WA: Private printing, 2000.

Simon, George Thomas. *Glenn Miller and His Orchestra.* New York: De Capo Press, 1974.

Snyder, Alan E. *The 95th B-17 Bomb Group (H) Flight Crews, WWII, May 13, 1943–May 25, 1945.* Privately published by the author, no date.

Speer, Albert. *Inside the Third Reich.* Translated by Richard and Clara Winston. New York: Avon, 1971.

Stewart, Maynard D., and H. Griffin Mumford. *Memorials of the 95th Bomb Group (H).* Marceline, MO: Walsworth Publishing Co., 1987.

Sullivan, Bob. "Bob Sullivan's WWII Memoirs." Unpublished manuscript, no date.

Swenson, Curtis G. "26 Missions over Germany and France." Unpublished mission diary, no date.

Tanner, Stephen. *Refuge from the Reich: American Airmen and Switzerland during World War II.* Rockville Centre, NY: Sarpedon, 2000.

Thixton, Marshall J., George E. Moffat, and John J. O'Neil. *Bombs Away by Pathfinders of the Eighth Air Force.* Trumbull, CT: FNP Military Division, 1998.

Titus, Jim. Unpublished memoir, 1997.

Tricker, Roy. *The Parish Church of St. Mary.* Horham, UK: Tanside Press, 1986.

United States Air Force Association. *Air Force 50.* Arlington, VA: Turner Publishing, 1998.

Varian, Horace L., ed. *The Bloody Hundredth: Missions and Memories of a World War II Bomb Group.* Thorpe-Abbotts, UK: 100th Bomb Group Committee, 1979.

Walter, John. *My War: The True Experiences of a U.S. Army Air Force Pilot in World War Two.* Bloomington, IN: AuthorHouse, 2004.

Waters, Donald Arthur. *Hitler's Secret Ally, Switzerland.* La Mesa, CA: Pertinent Publications, 1992.

Webber, David. Unpublished memoir, no date.

Weir, Adrian. *The Last Flight of the Luftwaffe: The Fate of Schulungslehrgang Elbe, 7 April 1945.* London: Arms & Armour Press, 1997.

Williams, Geoffrey. *Flying Through Fire: Fido—the Fogbuster of World War Two: Freeing the RAF's Airfields from the Fog Menace.* London: Grange Books, 1996.

Wright, Richard. Unpublished manuscript, no date.

Yeager, Chuck, and Leo Janos. *Yeager: An Autobiography.* New York: Bantam, 1985.

Ziegler, Jean. *The Swiss, the Gold, and the Dead: How Swiss Bankers Helped Finance the Nazi War Machine.* Translated by John Brownjohn. New York: Penguin, 1999.

Articles, Websites, and Other Sources

95th BG Heritage Association, http://www.95thbg-horham.com/.

95th Bomb Group Memorials Foundation, http://95thbg.org/joomla/.

100th Bomb Group (Heavy): The Bloody Hundredth. http://www.100thbg.com/.

482nd Bomb Group Website (P), http://www.482nd.org/.

American Battle Monuments Commission. "The Cambridge American Cemetery and Memorial." http://www.abmc.gov/cemeteries/cemeteries/ca.php, accessed December 19, 2010.

Black, John. "Colonel Noel T. Cumbaa." *Delta Democrat Times Magazine*, Summer 2009, 14–18.

Blanc, Nicole. "War Ace Looks Back at WWII." *Wellsburg (WV) Herald Star*, circa 1985.

Blankenstein, Kimberly. "Little Joe Noyes: The Story of a Second World War B-17 Pilot from Seattle." http://littlejoenoyes.com.

Chambers, Sarah. "Flying Revisit for Veterans." *East Anglian Daily Times*, May 24, 2004.

Charles, William "Ed." "History of the 95th Bomb Group." Slideshow presented at reunion of 95th Bomb Group (H), 1999. Cleveland, OH.

Chen, C. Peter. *Ira Eaker.* World War II Database. http://ww2db.com/person _bio.php?person_id=647, accessed April 8, 2012.

Comins, Londa. "Best Tail Gunner from Wellsburg." *Wellsburg (WV) News-Register,* circa 1985.

"Consolidated B-32 Dominator: 1942," Aviastar Virtual Aircraft Museum. http://www.aviastar.org/air/usa/cons_dominator.php, accessed December 29, 2010.

Correll, John T. "The Cost of Schweinfurt." *Air Force Magazine* 93, no. 2 (February 2010).

Green, David. "Bells to Ring Out in Memory of 'Lefty.'" *East Anglian Daily Times* (date unknown).

———. "Grant Will Save Historic Wall Murals." *East Anglian Daily Times* (date unknown).

Herman, George R. "A Bad Day at Douglas Army Air Field." *Journal of Arizona History* 36, no. 4 (1995): 379.

Leader, Bill. "English Preserve Memories of Mighty Eighth." *DFW (Dallas, TX) People: The Airport Newspaper,* June 17, 2004.

Life. "First Over Berlin." March 27, 1944.

Mangan, Rick. "Mourning Glory." Unpublished article, 2009.

Messner, Cassie. "V-Mail Service." Smithsonian National Postal Museum, March 7, 2008. http//postalmuseum.si.edu/VictoryMail/operating, accessed December 19, 2010.

Miccio, Ralph. "My Army Career in the USA and Now England" (World War II diary), March 7, 2008.

Mighty Eighth Air Force Message Board, December 2010. http://m8mb .preller.us/viewtopic.php?f=3&t=15.

Museum of the British Resistance Organisation, Parham Airfield, Framlingham, Suffolk. http://www.parhamairfieldmuseum.co.uk/brohome .html, accessed December 12, 2010.

National Museum of the Air Force. "Duty Above All: Tech. Sgt. Sator 'Sandy' Sanchez." August 28, 2009. http://www.nationalmuseum.af.mil/fact sheets/factsheet.asp?fsID=1666.

Parker, Sam. "Red Letter Day for Red Feather Club." *Diss (UK) Express,* May 28, 2004.

Peters, Walter. "Night Before a Mission." *Yank Army Weekly,* January 30, 1944.

Spink, Master Sgt. Barry L. "Sator S. 'Sandy' Sanchez." U.S. Air University, http://www.au.af.mil/au/.

Sulick, George. Interview at 95th BG Memorial Foundation Webpage, undated. http://95thbg.org/95th_joomla/index.php?option=com_content&view=article&id=236&Itemid=347, accessed April 8, 2012.

Woods, Bob. Interview with Willard W. Brown. Cleveland, Ohio, March 7, 1977.

Other Documents

Coffman, Harold. Individual Deceased Personnel File of, MIA. U.S. Department of the Army, Washington, DC.

"Duties and Responsibilities of the Airplane Commander," *B-17 Pilot Training Manual* (1943). Army extract reproduced on Hell's Angels, 303rd Bomb Group (H) website. http://www.303rdbg.com/crew-duties.html.

Eighth Air Force Headquarters documents. National Archives, Washington, DC.

Majer, Theodore. Notes taken during World War Two. Private collection.

Miller, Maj. Glenn. Documents relating to the death of, declassified. National Archives, Washington, DC.

Missing Aircraft Reports. National Archives, Washington, DC.

95th Bomb Group mission documents, National Archives, Washington, DC.

War Crimes Trail Record, Deputy Judge Advocate's Office, 7708 War Crimes Group, European Command. *United States vs. Albert Ningelgen.* April 15, 1947. U.S. Army Records, National Archives, Washington, DC.

Newspapers used frequently

Diss (England) Express
East Anglian Daily Times
Philadelphia Inquirer

Author's Interviews and Correspondence

THE AIRMEN

Alf, Herbert. Pilot, POW, 100th Bomb Group. 2002–2005.

Baca, Frank. Ball turret gunner, POW, 95th Bomb Group/336th Squadron. April 2008.

Bertram, Jack. Pilot, 95th BG/412th Squadron. October 2009.

Besser, Charles A. Pilot, 95th BG/335th and 336th Squadrons. October 2010.

Brainard, Russell. Ball turret gunner, 95th BG/335th Squadron, 2009.

Broman, Eldon. Pilot, POW, 95th BG/335th Squadron. April 2008 and August 7, 2009.

Buchholz, Lawrence "Larry." Right gunner, 95th BG/336th Squadron. April 2008.

Capen, Robert. Ball turret gunner, 95th BG/335th and 336th Squadrons. 2001–2010.

Casaday, Marvin R. Armorer/gunner, 95th BG/335th Squadron. July 2009.

Cassidy, Charles. Bombardier, 303rd BG. Swiss internee. 2000.

Chaffin, John. Copilot, POW, 95th BG/335th Squadron. 2000–2003.

Charles, William "Ed." Navigator, 95th BG/336th Squadron. 2000–2002.

Coleman, Franklyn. Ball turret gunner, 95th BG. 2001–2004.

Conley, Harry. Pilot, original 95th BG. 2002.

Connelley, Neal F, Jr. 95th Ground Detachment.

Cozens, Robert. Pilot, original 95th BG/335th Squadron. 2001–2011.

Crosby, Harry. Navigator, original 100th BG. 2002.

Cross, Arl. Top turret/engineer, 95th BG. October 2009.

Cumbaa, Noel T. HQ/pilot, 95th BG. June 2009.

Davidson, Ed. Pilot, 96th BG. 2008.

Dillon, Richmond "Red." Ball turret gunner, POW, 95th BG. October 2009– October 2010.

Ennis, Richard "Dick." Radio operator, POW, 95th BG. 2008.

Fay, Robert. Ball turret gunner, 95th BG/334th Squadron. October 2009.

Forrester, Albert. Navigator, 95th BG/412th Squadron. April 2008 and June 2009.

Fournier, James. Bombardier, Sweden internee, 95th BG/334th Squadron. April 2008.

Gallagher, Charles. Top turret gunner/flight engineer, 95th BG/336th Squadron. April 2008 and October 2009.

Geary, James. Pilot, POW, 390th BG. 2001.

Gilmore, Clyde. Radio operator, 95th BG. October 2009.

Greene, Guy. Gunner, 95th BG/336th Squadron. October 2009.

Grove, Ronald. Tail gunner, internee/escapee, 95th BG/335th Squadron. June 21, 2009.

Hawk, Frank. Bombardier, 95th BG/335th and 336th Squadrons. October 2009.

Herman, Leonard. Bombardier, original 95th BG/412th Squadron. 2000– 2008.

Hinojos, Adam. Ground crewman, 95th BG/457th Squadron. April 2008 and October 2010.

House, Gale. Pilot, original 95th BG/336th Squadron. 2008–2009.

Hull, Harry. Bombardier, 95th BG/412th Squadron. August 2010.

Hutcherson, Ken. Radio operator, 95th BG/335th Squadron. June 2009.

Inman, Robert "Bob." Navigator, 95th BG. October 2009.

Jacobson, Ed. Pilot, 95th BG/336th Squadron. October 2009 and October 2010.

Jonas, Delmar. Navigator, 95th BG/334th Squadron. Summer 2008.

Joswick, Earl. POW, 95th BG/334th Squadron. October 2009.

Kennie, Fred. Copilot, POW, 95th BG/334th Squadron. April 2008 and October 2009.

Kidd, John. Commanding officer, original 100th BG. 2002.

Knox, Richard Frank. Communications officer, 95th Headquarters. 2011.

Kring, Leslie. Pilot, 95th BG/412th Squadron.

Larson, Owen. Navigator, 100th BG. 2001–2003.

Long, DeWayne Willis. Ground echelon, 95th BG. April 2008.

Long, Robert. Pilot, Swiss internee, 303rd Bomb Group. 2000–2001.

Mastrogiacomo, Samuel. Tail gunner, Swedish internee, 445th BG. June 1, 2001.

McConnell, Stewart. Togglier, 95th BG/335th Squadron. June 2009.

McGinty, Elmer. Waist gunner, 95th BG/335th Squadron. April 2008.

McReynolds, Leonard. Pilot, 95th BG. October 2009.

Mencow, Nathaniel. Navigator, original 390th BG. 2000–2006.

Meyer, Julian A. Bombardier, 95th BG. July 2009.

Morrison, Edward. Ball turret gunner, 95th BG/336th Squadron. June 2009.

Mumford, Harry "Grif." Squadron commanding officer, pilot, original 95th BG/412th Squadron. 2001–2005.

Murphy, Frank. Navigator, POW, original 100th BG. 2000–2004.

Murray, Keith. Bombardier, Pyrenees Mountains evader, original 95th BG/335th Squadron. October 2009 and August 2010.

Owen, William. Pilot, 95th BG, and pilot, 482nd Pathfinder. August 15, 2009.

Petrella, Bradley, Sr. Ground support, 95th BG. April 2008.

Rockett, Maurice. Bombardier, 95th BG/335th Squadron. 2000–2010.

Rothman, Irving. Engineer/top turret gunner, POW, 95th BG. October 2009 and August 2010.

Rosenthal, Robert. Pilot, 100th BG. 2002–2003.

Roujansky, Ben. Waist gunner, 95th BG/336th Squadron. April 2008.

Russell, Jack. 95th BG. October 2009.

Schulz, Delmar. Pilot, 95th BG/334th Squadron. June 2009.

Scott, Lew. Bombardier, 95th BG/334th and 335th Squadrons. April 2008.

Scripture, Ellis. Group navigator, 95th BG. 2003.

Shore, Marshall. Group navigator, 390th BG. 2001–2004.

Smith, Richard M. Pilot, evader, 95th BG. August 2009.

Spencer, Melvin. Navigator, POW, 95th BG. October 2009.

Spinnenweber, Robert. Bombardier, 95th BG/334th Squadron, August 2010.

Stitt, Walter. HQ, 95th BG. June and August, 2009.

Thomas, Halcott. Pilot, 95th BG/336th Squadron. October 2010.

Turner, Marion. Pilot, 95th BG/335th Squadron. June 2009 and February 2010.

Vandegriff, William M. Radio operator, 95th BG/412th Squadron. July–August 2009.

Voss, Carl. 95th BG/859th Engineering Squadron. October 2008 and August 2010.

Walter, John. Pilot, 95th BG/412th Squadron. 2008–2010.

Watson, Art. Bombsight technician, 95th BG/335th Squadron. 2008 and July 24, 2009.

Wilkov, Herbert. Navigator, 95th BG/336th Squadron. April 2008.

Wright, Kenneth. Copilot, 95th BG/334th Squadron. October 2009 and August 2010.

THE WIVES

Capen, Bettylou. Wife of ball turret gunner Robert Capen. 2001–2009.

Cozens, Patsy Ann. Wife of pilot Robert Cozens. 2008 and 2009.

Marshall, Geri. Widow of pilot Fred Delbern, Jr. October 2009.

Scripture, Peggy. Wife of group navigator Ellis Scripture. September 11, 1999.

OTHER RELATIVES

Darter, Michael. Brother of MIA Eugene Darter. 2001–present.

Dillon, Paul. Son of Richmond 'Red' Dillon. 2008–present.

Endris, Linda Charles. Daughter of William "Ed" Charles. 2008–present.

Grove, Gerald. Son of Ronald Grove. 2008–present.

THE BRITISH

Albrow, Tony. Horham resident. Owner of the 95th Bomb Group Hospital Museum. June 2008.

Anthony, Clifford. RAF communications leader for 95th BG. June 2008.

Blott, John. 95th BG historian and Horham resident. June 2008.

Cooper, Gerald. Horham resident. June 2008.

Feltwell, Norman. 95th BG current photographer and historian, Horham. June 2008.

Hawkins, Ian. 95th BG historian, Horham. 2001–2008.

Johnson, Alan. 95th BG historian and Horham resident. 2007–2009.

Johnson, David. 95th BG historian and Horham resident. June 2008.

Leader, Ann. 95th BG historian and Horham resident. June 2008.

Leader, Noel. 95th BG historian and Horham resident. June 2008.

Mutton, James. 95th BG historian and current director of Red Feather Club Museum, Horham. June 2008–October 2011.

Sherman, Frank. 95th BG historian and Horham resident. June 2008.

Ward, Marjorie. Horham resident. June 2008.

Wheeler, Enid. Horham resident. June 2008.

Index

About the Authors

Rob Morris is a teacher and writer who lives near Idaho Falls, Idaho. He is the author of *Untold Valor: Forgotten Stories of American Bomber Crews over Europe in World War II* and the editor of Leonard Herman's memoir *Combat Bombardier: Memoirs of Two Combat Tours in the Skies over Europe in World War II.*

Ian Hawkins first became interested in the history of the Eighth Air Force as a young boy growing up in England surrounded by the airfields from which the aircrews flew. He is the author or editor of three books, including *B-17s Over Berlin: Personal Stories from the 95th Bomb Group.* He lives in Bacton, Suffolk.